Sport Psychology

Concepts and Applications

Second Edition

Sport Psychology
Concepts and Applications
Second Edition

Richard H. Cox
Ball State University

 Wm. C. Brown Publishers

Book Team

Editor *Chris Rogers*
Developmental Editor *Cindy Kuhrasch*
Production Coordinator *Carla D. Arnold*

 Wm. C. Brown Publishers

President *G. Franklin Lewis*
Vice President, Editor-in-Chief *George Wm. Bergquist*
Vice President, Director of Production *Beverly Kolz*
Vice President, National Sales Manager *Bob McLaughlin*
Director of Marketing *Thomas E. Doran*
Marketing Communications Manager *Edward Bartell*
Marketing Manager *Kathy Law Laube*
Production Editorial Manager *Colleen A. Yonda*
Production Editorial Manager *Julie A. Kennedy*
Publishing Services Manager *Karen J. Slaght*
Manager of Visuals and Design *Faye M. Schilling*

Consulting Editor
Aileene Lockhart

Cover design by David Lansdon

Equations on pages 107 and 108 are reprinted by permission of
C. L. Hull.

Photo on p. 408, copyright, *The Muncie Evening Press*. Reprinted
with permission.

Library of Congress Catalog Card Number: 88–63536

ISBN 0–697–01340–5

Printed in the United States of America by Wm. C. Brown Publishers,
2460 Kerper Boulevard, Dubuque, IA 52001

10 9 8 7 6 5 4 3 2 1

Joseph Iacobellis

Contents

Preface

I have written this book specifically for the undergraduate student interested in sport psychology and/or the psychology of coaching. The great challenge in writing this text has been to bridge the gap between the "smocks" and the "jocks"—between the scholar interested in research and the coach and/or teacher interested in application. In writing the second edition of my text I have been especially sensitive to this challenge and trust that I have been successful.

A significant number of pedagogical aids have been included in the text for the benefit of students, teachers, and coaches. Most significantly, I have included many sports-related examples throughout each chapter. Concepts and applications have been inserted after major themes and topics in each chapter. The concept and application sections highlight and refocus the reader's attention to important concepts immediately after they are discussed. These concepts are derived from the pertinent scientific literature and are followed by a suggested application for the coach or teacher.

Other important pedagogical aids included in each chapter are key terms, a chapter summary, review questions, a glossary, and recommended readings. The key terms, which appear at the beginning of each chapter, draw the student's attention to important terms and concepts. The key terms also appear in the glossary and in bold print where they are introduced in the text.

Finally, to help maintain student interest I have included numerous visual aids. Each chapter contains clarifying figures and tables as well as motivating photographs. The photographs that appear in each chapter were carefully selected to highlight the particular topic under consideration.

In revising my text I have updated each chapter with references and discussion derived from the most recent research findings. In all cases the new material has been introduced in such a manner that it can be readily understood and used by students, coaches, teachers, and sport psychologists.

Acknowledgments

I am indebted to a host of people who have contributed to the completion of this work. First of all, to my wife, Linda, and my four children, Candice, Clayton, Ryan, and David for their patience and forbearance. Second, to the reviewers who went the extra mile to ensure that the work would be a success: Dr. Michael Bretting, Professor Alan Burton, Professor Kathleen Haywood, Professor Bill Kozar, Professor Lawrence A. Martin, Dr. Linda Petlichoff, Professor Dave Poehler, Professor Karen Ruder, Dr. Josie Sifft, Professor Robert Symons, and Professor Eric Vlahov. Third, to my colleagues who were always willing to share ideas and resources. Finally, I am most grateful to the reserve librarians at Kansas State and Ball State Universities who were more than happy to help me locate foreign and other references not in the respective libraries. The sources they found for me must have been in the hundreds.

INTRODUCTION

There is hardly a subject associated with sport that is more intriguing than the subject of sport psychology. Perhaps this is because it is a comfortable subject for so many people associated with sport. Few spectators care to offer a biomechanical explanation for why an athlete achieves a near superhuman feat, yet the same spectator is often more than willing to give a psychological explanation. In many ways this is good, but it is also the reason why many athletes and coaches don't feel the need for a professional sport psychologist on their team. As we look at some of the great basketball and football coaches of our time it is easy to see why. John Wooden, former coach of U.C.L.A., would have to fall into this category. Coach Wooden's athletes were always prepared mentally for competition. They may not always have had the best talent but they always seemed to be in control of the emotional and psychological aspects of the game. Can the sport psychologist learn something about performance enhancement from coach Wooden? Yes, I think so, but I also believe that great coaches such as John Wooden and Larry Brown could benefit a great deal from a qualified sport psychologist. Successful coaches and athletes are people who make it a point to study their sport and master the mental elements of the game. This process can be speeded up and refined through the correct application of the scientific principles of sport psychology. A Canadian research report revealed that elite athletes generally recognize the need for a professional sport psychologist. This perception was observed to increase as athletes came into actual contact with sport psychologists' services (Orlick & Partington, 1987).

This text offers the prospective coach and athlete the opportunity to learn correct principles and applications of sport psychology, even though sport psychology is not a perfect science. We have a great deal to learn about mental preparation for sport competition. We will always have a need for the scientist who is interested in discovering new knowledge. As you read this text I encourage you to keep an open mind and become interested in sport psychology as a science.

In the paragraphs that follow I will discuss a number of peripheral issues that provide background information for the study of sport psychology. Specifically,

I will provide a definition of sport psychology, sketch a brief history of the development of sport psychology as a discipline, discuss the various roles of the sport psychologist, and finally, I will mention the issue of ethics in sport psychology.

Sport Psychology Defined

Sport psychology is a science in which the principles of psychology are applied in a sport setting. These principles are often applied in order to enhance performance. The true sport psychologist is interested in much more than performance enhancement. The sport psychologist sees sport as a vehicle for human enrichment. A win-at-all-costs attitude is inconsistent with the goals and aspirations of the best sport psychologist. As a sport psychologist I am interested in helping every sport participant reach his or her potential as an athlete. If helping a young athlete develop self-control and confidence results in superior athletic performance, so be it. However, it is also possible that a quality sport experience can enhance an athlete's intrinsic motivation without necessarily winning. Taken as a whole, sport psychology is an exciting subject dedicated to the enhancement of both athletic performance and the social-psychological aspects of human enrichment.

History of Sport Psychology as a Discipline

Sport psychology as a field of study is extremely young and still evolving. In writing this brief sketch of the rise of sport psychology in North America I have relied a great deal on excellent reviews by David Wiggins (1984), an outstanding sport historian, and upon the writings of Jean Williams and Bill Straub (1986), both nationally active sport psychologists.

Historically, perhaps the first clear example of research being conducted in the area of sport psychology was reported by Norman Triplett (1897). Drawing upon field observations and secondary data, Triplett analyzed the performance of cyclists under conditions of social facilitation. He concluded from this "milestone" research that the presence of other competitors was capable of facilitating better cycling performance. While Triplett provided an example of one of the earliest recorded sport psychology investigations, he was not the first person to systematically carry out sport psychology research over an extended period of time. This distinction is generally attributed to Coleman Roberts Griffith, often referred to as the father of sport psychology in America (Kroll & Lewis, 1970). Griffith is credited with establishing the first sport psychology laboratory at the University of Illinois in 1925. Over an extended period of time, Griffith studied the nature of psychomotor skills, motor learning, and the relationship between personality variables and motor performance.

It was not until the 1960s that sport psychology began to emerge as separate and distinct from other areas of motor behavior research. It was only after the Second World War that American universities began to offer courses in the parent discipline of motor learning. Such notables as Franklin M. Henry at the University of California, John Lawther at Pennsylvania State University, and Arthur Slater-Hammel at Indiana University pioneered these courses.

Another significant event in the 1960s was the publication of *Problem Athletes and How to Handle Them* by Bruce Ogilvie and Thomas Tutko (1966). This book and the authors' personality inventory for athletes—the Athletic Motivation Inventory—caught on with coaches and athletes like a storm. However, Ogilvie and Tutko's work was not well received by the sport psychology scientific community; their contribution to sport psychology is much better received today than it was only a few short years ago. Dr. Ogilvie is referred to as the father of *applied* sport psychology (Williams & Straub, 1986).

A number of professional sport psychology organizations have evolved since the 1960s. In 1965 the International Society of Sport Psychology (ISSP), which sponsors worldwide meetings and publishes the *International Journal of Sport Psychology,* was organized in Rome. The purpose of the ISSP is to promote and disseminate information about the practice of sport psychology throughout the world.

In 1965, a small group of physical educators from Canada and the United States met in Dallas, Texas, to discuss the feasibility of forming a professional organization distinct from the American Association of Health, Physical Education, and Recreation (AAHPER). The efforts of this small group came to fruition in 1966 when it was recognized by the ISSP. The name of the new organization became the North American Society for the Psychology of Sport and Physical Activity (NASPSPA). The first annual meeting of NASPSPA was held prior to the 1967 AAHPER National Convention in Las Vegas. Since that time, NASPSPA has evolved into the world's most influential academic society focusing on sport psychology (Salmela, 1981).

NASPSPA's primary goal has been to advance the knowledge base of sport psychology through experimental research (Williams & Straub, 1986). This has been reflected in the kind of articles that have appeared in periodicals such as the *Journal of Sport and Exercise Psychology.*

Shortly after the emergence of NASPSPA in the United States, another significant professional organization came into existence in Canada in 1969. This organization was called the Canadian Society for Psychomotor Learning and Sport Psychology (CSPLSP). CSPLSP was originally organized under the auspices of the Canadian Association for Health, Physical Education, and Recreation, but in 1977 it became an independent society.

Diverging Sport Psychologies

In recent years two sport psychologies have emerged (Martens, 1987). The first is referred to as *academic sport psychology* and the second *applied sport psychology*. The former or traditional (academic) sport psychology continues to focus on the disciplinary or research-oriented aspects of the field. Conversely, applied sport psychology focuses on the professional or applied aspects of the field of sport psychology.

The division took place because many sport psychologists who were interested in application did not think NASPSPA was meeting their needs. Consequently, the Association for the Advancement of Applied Sport Psychology (AAASP) was formed in the fall of 1985. At the same time, sponsored by the ISSP, a new journal called *The Sport Psychologist* was introduced. Even though it appears that two competing organizations have emerged, in actuality I believe that these two organizations will work together to advance the discipline of sport psychology and facilitate application in the real world of sport. Many of the prominent sport psychologists who are actively involved in research are also members of the AAASP and conversely, many of the practicing sport psychologists are also active members of NASPSPA.

To make matters even more interesting, the American Psychological Association (APA) formed a new section within its structure in 1986 called Division 47, which is dedicated to issues dealing with exercise and sport psychology. In years to come, the future of applied sport psychology will be greatly influenced by the success and directions taken by this new organization.

What Does the Sport Psychologist Do?

In an effort to promote the virtues of sport psychology to coaches, athletes, and prospective students, many thoughtful professionals have suggested contributions that sport psychologists can make to sport. Robert N. Singer, current president of the ISSP, has been particularly helpful (Singer, 1984). He has outlined different roles and functions that the sport psychologist can play. Generally, these roles and functions fall into the categories of the sport psychologist as *researcher, educator,* and *clinician.*

The Research Sport Psychologist In order for sport psychology to be a recognized and respected social science, the knowledge base must continue to grow. It is the scientist and scholar who serves this important role. In order for the practicing sport psychologist to enjoy professional credibility, there must exist a credible scientific body of knowledge.

The Educational Sport Psychologist Most sport psychologists who received their academic training through departments of physical education consider themselves to be educational sport psychologists. These are individuals who have mastered the knowledge base of sport psychology and serve as practitioners. They use the medium of education to teach correct principles of sport psychology to athletes and coaches. In general, their mission and role is to help athletes develop psychological skills for performance enhancement. They also help athletes, young and old, to enjoy sport and to use sport as a vehicle for improving their quality of life.

The Clinical Sport Psychologist The clinical sport psychologist is generally a person trained in clinical psychology and is a licensed psychologist. Generally, the clinical sport psychologist also has a deep interest and understanding of the athletic experience. Training may also include course work and experience in sport psychology from programs in physical education. The clinical sport psychologists are individuals who are prepared to deal with emotional and personality disorder problems that affect some athletes. The athletic experience can be very stressful to some athletes, and can negatively affect their performance or their ability to function as healthy human beings. In these cases, a sport psychologist who is trained in counseling psychology and clinical psychology is needed.

Ethics in Sport Psychology

While the ethical application of sport psychology principles is discussed throughout the text, I feel it is important to emphasize the topic here. In recent years it has become clear that theories and techniques derived from the study of sport psychology can provide the winning edge for athletes and athletic teams. In this text, you will learn many of the psychological theories and techniques that can make you a more effective teacher and/or coach. This does not mean, however, that you will be qualified to provide psychological services to coaches and athletes. It takes much more than one course in sport psychology to become a sport psychologist. This is true despite the fact that at the present time there are limited licensing procedures in sport psychology; anyone can claim to be a sport psychologist. However, without certain minimal qualifications this would be unethical. When one considers the dangers involved in the inappropriate application of psychological theory, personality assessment, and intervention strategies, it is no wonder that many professionals are concerned (Harrison & Feltz, 1979; Nideffer, DuFresne, Nesvig & Selder, 1980).

The practice of sport psychology, whether by a coach or by a licensed psychologist, involves two diverse components. The first has to do with teaching, while the second is clinical in nature. For example, the sport psychologist uses teaching principles to help an athlete learn how to use imagery and/or relaxation techniques effectively. This is the kind of thing that a relatively well-trained and informed coach or teacher ought to be able to do. However, when the sport psychologist is called upon to provide clinical services such as crisis counseling, psychotherapy, or psychological testing, it is important that that person be specifically trained and licensed to do so. To do otherwise would be unethical and irresponsible.

To help the sport psychologist deal effectively with the ethical issues of the profession, the NASPSPA issued a set of "Ethical Standards for Provision of Services by NASPSPA Members" (NASPSPA, 1982). These standards are summarized by these nine principles:

1. *Responsibility* Sport psychologists accept responsibility for the consequences of their acts and make every effort to ensure that services are used appropriately.
2. *Competence* Sport psychologists provide services and use techniques for which they are qualified by training and experience.
3. *Moral and Legal Standards* Sport psychologists refuse to participate in practices that are inconsistent with legal, moral, and ethical standards.
4. *Public Statements* Sport psychologists accurately and objectively state their professional qualifications and affiliations.
5. *Confidentiality* Sport psychologists respect the confidentiality of information obtained from clients or subjects in the course of their work.
6. *Welfare of the Client* Sport psychologists respect the integrity and protect the welfare of the people and groups with whom they work.
7. *Professional Relationships* Sport psychologists are sensitive to the needs and concerns of colleagues in other sport-related fields.
8. *Assessment Techniques* In the development, publication, and utilization of assessment techniques, sport psychologists promote the best interests of their clients.
9. *Research with Human Participants* In conducting psychological research, sport psychologists are first of all concerned with the welfare of the participants according to federal, state, and professional standards.

Part One   **Personality**

This section on personality and sport is composed of a single chapter. Chapter 1, "Personality and the Athlete," deals with the athlete's personality as it relates to athletic performance. While only one chapter of this textbook is specifically devoted to the study of personality, it should be noted that nearly 25 percent of the book *could* be classified under this broad heading. Anxiety is discussed in chapter 4 and achievement motivation in chapter 6. Both of these psychological constructs fall under the broad heading of personality, since both can be considered personality traits. Additionally, in chapter 8 I discuss aggression in sport. Aggressiveness is considered by many psychologists to be a personality trait.

In this section on personality, the intent is to concentrate on those items most germane to sport and athletic performance. However, chapter 1 in no way represents a comprehensive review of personality theory. Literally hundreds of textbooks have been written on this subject. The chapter nevertheless does represent a complete treatment of personality literature as it relates to sport psychology.

The chapter on personality appears first in this text because the topic is of extreme interest to coaches, teachers, and sport psychologists. When two teams are evenly matched physically, it is always interesting to observe how athletes from both teams rise to the occasion. Is it possible that an athlete's basic personality would have something to do with this? ■

1 Personality and the Athlete

Key Terms

AMI
Cattell 16 PF
cause-and-effect
   relationship
correlational approach
CPI
credulous argument
EPI
factor analysis
first-order traits
iceberg profile
interaction model
mental health model
MMPI
multivariate approach
personality

POMS
projective procedures
psychological core
psychological profile
role-related behavior
Rorschach test
second-order traits
situational approach
skeptical argument
source traits
state
surface traits
Thematic Apperception
   Test
trait
typical responses

Consider the following scenario. You are among a group of fifty athletes competing for one of fifteen places on your country's Olympic volleyball team. On the first day of the tryouts you are taken into a room and asked to take a three-hour battery of pencil-and-paper tests. The test administrator tells you to answer all the questions as honestly as you can and that the results would help the selection committee determine your personality profile. You are not too concerned about the psychological testing because you know that you are one of the top setters and defensive players in your country. After four days of grueling workouts in which you perform very well, you are taken aside by the coach and informed that you are not going to be selected for the Olympic team. In tears you ask the coach how this could be, since you felt that you had had an excellent try out and that you performed as well or better than many of the other athletes. The coach tells you that he is sorry, but that your personality profile, as measured through the tests you took, indicate that you lack the mental toughness and aggressiveness necessary for world-class competition.

A scenario such as this actually happened (Ryan, 1976), and probably happens on a regular basis in other sports and other equally critical situations. If athletic performance can actually be predicted from psychological testing, then the use of personality tests to make team selections makes some sense. However, if it cannot be done with at least 90-percent accuracy, the process could be considered highly unethical.

In many ways, the study of personality as it relates to sports participation is one of the most intriguing and exciting areas of sport psychology. Ruffer (1975, 1976a, 1976b), for example, cites 572 sources of original research in a compilation of references on the relationship between personality and athletic performance. However, in recent years the interest seems to have waned somewhat. Fewer articles appear in journals such as the *Journal of Sport and Exercise Psychology,* the *International Journal of Sport Psychology,* and the *Journal of Sport Behavior.*

Based on the great interest in personality research, one might incorrectly conclude that the relationship between personality and athletic performance would by now be crystal clear. Unfortunately, this is not the case. In fact, a random sample of the references cited by Ruffer could easily reveal conflicting conclusions.

During the last ten years, the relationship between personality and performance has become significantly clearer, thanks to the critical eye of many sport psychologists. This is not to say that we now have all of the answers, but many of the problems plaguing scientific inquiry have been identified and rectified.

In this chapter, I will take a close look at many of the problems that have been identified and see what progress has been made. I will begin with a basic study of what personality is and how it can be measured. Next, I will turn to a discussion of the various issues that have led to a better interpretation of the research findings. Finally, the relationship between athletic performance and the personality of the performer will be discussed.

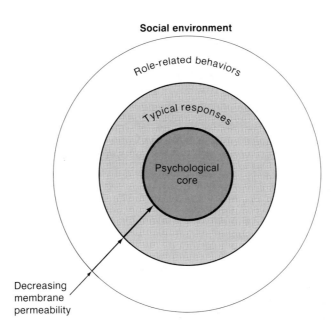

Figure 1.1 Hollander's notion of personality structure. From *Principles and Methods of Social Psychology,* by Edwin P. Hollander (fig. 10.2, p. 394). Copyright © 1971 by Oxford University Press, Inc. Reproduced by permission.

The Structure of Personality

The concept of personality is so broad that it is difficult to define precisely. Regardless of what definition is put forth, there will be those who argue that it is either too broad or too narrow. One definition that has withstood the test of time was put forth by Allport (1937). According to Allport, **personality** "is the dynamic organization within the individual of those psychophysical systems that determine his unique adjustments to his environment" (p. 48). Hollander (1971) gave a similar yet simpler definition when he wrote that personality was "the sum total of an individual's characteristics which make him unique" (p. 394). No matter what definition is selected, it is clear from both the Allport and Hollander definitions that the personality of each individual is unique.

Perhaps the best way to understand personality is to look at its structure. Such a structure has been outlined by Hollander (1971) and adapted to sport psychology by Martens (1975). A schematic view of personality structure is illustrated in figure 1.1. While the basic concepts for the structure of personality as shown in this figure are outlined by Hollander, the unique manner of presenting these concepts should be attributed to Martens.

As can be observed in figure 1.1, a personality can be divided into three separate but related levels. These are (1) the psychological core, (2) typical responses, and (3) role-related behaviors. The psychological core is further represented as being internal and consistent in nature, while typical responses and role-related behaviors are considered external and dynamic.

The relative effect of the social environment on the three levels of personality is reflected by the thickness or permeability of the lines that separate each level from the environment. Permeability is a word that conveys the degree to which a membrane or dividing structure can be penetrated. For example, a sieve used for straining vegetables is very permeable, while a concrete wall is relatively impermeable.

As can be observed in the figure, role-related behaviors are most susceptible to the influence of the environment, while the psychological core is somewhat insulated from the environment.

The **psychological core** of an individual holds that person's image of what he or she is really like. It includes the individual's self-concept. The psychological core represents the centerpiece of a person's personality; it includes basic attitudes, values, interests, and motives. In short, it's "the real you."

Typical responses represent the typical manner in which we respond to environmental situations. For example, a person may exhibit typical mannerisms in responding to such things as frustration, humor, and anxiety. Typical responses are learned modes of dealing with the environment. Unless a person is playacting or has an unstable personality, typical responses will be a valid indicator of a person's psychological core. For example, if a person consistently responds to all types of environmental situations with feelings of apprehension and tension, we may confidently conclude that this is an anxious person. However, if we were to conclude from a single observation that a person was aggressive because he or she displayed aggression on one occasion, we could be very wrong. The person may have exhibited aggressive behavior because of the situation (responding to a physical attack) or may have been playacting.

Role-related behavior represents the most superficial aspect of our personalities. We engage in role-related behavior to fit our perception of our environment. Consequently, as the environment or our perception of it changes, our behavior changes. These are not typical responses, and are certainly not valid indicators of the psychological core. Consider the example of the athlete who is being recruited to play football at a major university. The university representative asks the high school football coach about the athlete's personality. The coach responds that he is very quiet, hardworking, and untalkative. When this same question is asked of the athlete's girlfriend, she replies that he is actually very sociable, outgoing, and talkative. We would certainly be on dangerous ground if we tried to affix a particular personality trait to someone based upon role-related behavior.

A clear understanding of Hollander's personality structure should be of great value as we proceed with our discussion of personality. In measuring an athlete's personality, we want to get at the *real* person, or in Hollander's terms, the psychological core. Yet it should be clear from Hollander's personality structure that this can best be done at the level of typical responses. Psychologists have long attempted to measure personality directly through the use of projective tests such as the Thematic Apperception Test. However, as we shall learn, projective tests suffer a great deal from low reliability and validity. Consequently, the most common and objective manner of measuring personality is on the level of typical responses using some type of questionnaire. This should not be construed to mean, however, that questionnaires are devoid of problems.

1. **Principle** The personality of an individual may be represented by three distinct levels. The most superficial level is role-related behavior, while the deepest and most meaningful is the psychological core. The psychological core is best reflected in terms of the athlete's typical responses.

   Application To understand athletes, the coach must not be deceived by role-playing behavior. The athlete may play the role of a "hotshot," but in truth be rather insecure. Take the time to study your athletes and find out what they are really like, deep down.

Theories of Personality

In this section we will consider three of the major theoretical approaches to the study of personality. There are the psychodynamic theories, social learning theory, and the trait theory approach. Each will be briefly discussed.

Psychodynamic Theories

Perhaps the most influential proponent of psychodynamic theory was Sigmund Freud. However, in the years since Freud, a number of psychoanalytic theorists have proposed modifications in Freud's original theory. Among the neo-Freudians are Carl Jung, Erich Fromm, and Eric Erickson (Mischel, 1986). Most of the neo-Freudian positions evolved from the theorists' personal experiences with patients during psychotherapy.

Freud's psychodynamic theory and his method of treating personality disturbances were based primarily upon self-analysis and extensive clinical observation of neurotics. Two distinguishing characteristics of the psychodynamic approach to personality have been its emphasis upon in-depth examination of the *whole* person, and its emphasis upon unconscious motives.

In Freud's view, the id, ego, and superego form the tripartite structure of personality. The id represents the unconscious instinctual core of personality; in a sense, the id is the pleasure-seeking mechanism. In contrast, the ego represents the conscious, logical, reality-oriented aspect of the personality. The superego represents the conscience of the individual; it is the internalized moral standards of society impressed upon the person by parental control and the process of socialization. Freud proposed that the superego aids in the resolution of conflicts between the id and the ego. Essentially, Freud advocated a conflict theory of personality. In this respect, the three parts of psychic structure are always in conflict. The individual's personality is the sum total of the dynamic conflicts between the impulse to seek release and the inhibition against these impulses (Mischel, 1986).

The individual's unconscious sexual and aggressive instincts are major determinants of behavior, according to Freud. Athletic aggression represents a potential example of this approach. As we shall learn in chapter 8, instinct theory provides one explanation for the phenomenon of violence in sport.

Social Learning Theory

From the viewpoint of social learning theory, behavior is not simply a function of unconscious motives (psychoanalytic theory) or underlying predispositions. Rather, human behavior is a function of social learning and the strength of the situation. An individual behaves according to how he or she has learned to behave, consistent with environmental constraints. If the salience of the environmental situation is strong enough, the effect of personality traits or unconscious motives upon behavior should be minimal.

The story is told of the boy who brought his report card to his father and wanted to know if his poor performance was inherited or due to his social environment. This was certainly a no-win situation for the father. However, from a social learning theory perspective, the answer would clearly be his social environment. According to social learning theory, a child's performance and behavior is a function of the child's experiences and environment.

The origin of social learning theory can be traced to Clark Hull's 1943 theory of learning. Hull's stimulus-response theory of learning was based on laboratory experimentation with animals. According to stimulus-response theory, an individual's behavior in any given situation is a function of his or her learned experiences. Other researchers such as Miller and Dollard (Miller, 1941), Mischel

(1986), and Bandura (1977) extended the Hullian notions of complex human behavior. Miller and Dollard had early access to Hull's manuscript, which explains why Miller's article appeared prior to 1943 (Monte, 1977).

Two of the primary mechanisms through which individuals learn are modeling and social reinforcement. *Modeling,* or imitative behavior, refers to the phenomenon of learning through observation. Albert Bandura's social learning theory is based primarily upon this important concept. According to Bandura, behavior is best explained as a function of observational learning. *Social reinforcement* is based upon the notion that rewarded behaviors are likely to be repeated. Martens (1975) has defined social reinforcement as verbal and nonverbal communication passing between two individuals that can increase the strength of a response.

A youth league football player observes on television that professional athletes are often able to intimidate quarterbacks and wide receivers through aggressive hard-hitting tackles. Using the professional athlete as his model he tries the same tactics on his youth league team and is reinforced by the coach with a pat on the back. This example illustrates how young athletes develop questionable behaviors through modeling and social reinforcement.

Trait Theories

The basic position of trait or factor theory is that personality can be described in terms of **traits** possessed by individuals. These traits are considered synonymous with predispositions to act in a certain way. Traits are considered to be stable, enduring, and consistent across a variety of differing situations. Those who exhibit the trait or need to achieve success, for example, can be expected to have a predisposition toward competitiveness and assertiveness in many situations. A predisposition toward a certain trait does not mean that the individual will *always* respond in this manner, but that a certain likelihood exists.

Among the most ardent advocates of trait psychology are psychologists such as Gordon Allport, Raymond Cattell, and Hans Eysenck. Cattell (Cattel, Eber & Tatsuoka, 1980) claims to have successfully identified sixteen different and independent source traits that he believes describe a personality. Using a similar approach, British psychologists (Eysenck & Eysenck, 1968a) have concentrated on the dimensional traits of neuroticism-stability and introversion-extroversion.

Since the notion of an enduring, somewhat genetically-founded trait approach to personality offends the social-learning theorist, it is important to point out that Cattell has never ignored the importance of the environment. Cattell (1965) believed that typical responses are a function of both the situation (environment) and the personality disposition. This is evident from his formula, $R = f(S \cdot P)$, in which R = response, S = situation, and P = personality. This revelation may be somewhat startling to social-learning advocates who oppose trait theory on the grounds that it does not consider the environment.

The great strength of the trait theory of personality is that it allows for the easy and objective measurement of personality through the use of inventories. If it can be demonstrated that a collection of traits can accurately describe a person's psychological profile, then this certainly is superior to a psychoanalytic approach in which personality is inferred through less objective techniques. Conversely, the weakness of the trait approach is that it may fail to consider the whole person, since personality according to this approach is represented by a collection of specific traits.

The Interaction Model

The **interaction model** is not a theory of personality at all, but a concept introduced first by Bowers (1973) and later by Carron (1975) to suggest a **situational approach** to explaining the nature of the relationship between the personality and the environment.

An athlete brings his or her basic personality into a sporting event. However, the most powerful and salient part of this whole scenario may not be the athlete's personality, but the situation the athlete is placed in. For example, if you are asked to pinch hit in the bottom of the ninth inning with bases loaded, two outs, and score tied, you can bet that you are going to be anxious. *This will be true, regardless of whether you are high in trait anxiety or not or are characteristically an anxious person.* The degree to which your basic personality can and will influence performance is dependent upon the interaction between the person (personality) and the situation (environment).

In a sense, the interaction model of personality is an eclectic or composite model that takes into consideration the important components of psychodynamic, trait, and social learning theory. In this model, unconscious motives and underlying predispositions interact with the environment. Important research by Endler and Hunt (1966), Bowers (1973), and Fisher and Zwart (1982) have been very instrumental in clarifying the nature of the interaction model.

The relationship between the personality of the individual and the situation is illustrated in figure 1.2. In this figure, the total pie represents all of the factors that can contribute to athletic behavior or performance. Only a small part of the total pie is due to factors associated with the athlete's personality. Another small portion is due to factors directly related to the situation and independent or unrelated to the person. Next, a certain part of the pie is represented by the interaction between the personality and the situation. When factors associated with the athlete's personality, the environmental situation, and the interaction between these three are summed, approximately 30 to 50 percent of the athlete's behavior is accounted for. If we were to consider only the athlete's personality, then we could only explain about 10 to 15 percent of the athlete's performance or behavior.

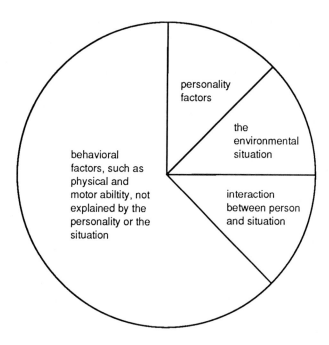

Figure 1.2 Illustration showing the contribution of personality and situation to total athlete behavior.

A close examination of figure 1.2 should make it very clear that personality alone accounts for only a small part of the total pie. When the environmental situation is taken into consideration, much more of the total pie is accounted for. However, even then, the largest part of the pie is dominated by unexplained factors. This should not be interpreted to mean that the contribution of personality to performance is trivial. It simply means that athletic performance is made up of many other factors, such as physical abilities, motor abilities, difficulty of the task (level of competition), and the particular situation. A case in point is a study by Silva, Shultz, Haslam, Martin, and Murray (1985), in which qualifiers for the United States Olympic Wrestling Team were accurately classified and identified 89 percent of the time when a combination model involving psychological as well as physiological variables was used. However, a model utilizing physiological variables alone accounted for only 61 percent accuracy, while a purely psychological model accurately categorized successful athletes 78 percent of the time. These results make it clear that psychological considerations have considerable merit and should be used along with other measures.

2. **Principle** There are three basic approaches or theories for understanding what personality is. These are the psychodynamic, trait, and social learning approaches. None of the three by itself can adequately explain the phenomenon of personality.

   Application In attempting to explain or predict athletic performance on the basis of personality, it is important that the teacher/coach adopt the interaction model. The interaction model requires that both the situation (e.g., baseball game) and the person (personality traits) be considered simultaneously, although in some cases the sheer power of the environment is so powerful that personality becomes a trivial factor. Being called upon to pinch hit in the bottom of the ninth inning with bases loaded might be such a situation.

The Measurement of Personality

This section will identify and briefly discuss various techniques used for assessing personality. It should be pointed out that the various methods of assessing personality correspond closely to the basic personality theories we have just discussed. For example, projective tests such as the Rorschach test are closely linked to the psychoanalytic theory of personality. Conversely, the various paper-and-pencil inventories are linked to the trait theory. In this brief overview of personality measurement techniques, the reader should be aware that many issues regarding personality assessment remain unresolved. The methods outlined here are not perfect, nor do psychologists agree on the meaning of the results of any particular test.

Cofer and Johnson (1960) identified three basic classes of measurement techniques. These are (1) rating scales, (2) unstructured projective tests, and (3) questionnaires. Each of these three categories will now be discussed, with particular emphasis upon the questionnaire method. The questionnaire method is highlighted because of its demonstrated objectivity, validity, and reliability (Whiting, Hardman, Hendry & Jones, 1973). Additionally, it is the measurement technique most commonly used by sport psychologists today.

Rating Scales

Characteristically, *rating scales* involve the use of a judge or judges who are asked to observe an individual in some situation. The judges employ the use of a checklist or scale that has been predesigned for maximum objectivity. Usually, if the checklist is used properly and the judges are well trained, the results can be fairly reliable and objective.

Typically, two types of situations are involved in personality assessment using rating scales. These are the *interview* and the *observation of performance.* In the interview, the judge asks the subject numerous open-ended and specific questions designed to ascertain personality traits and general impressions. Generally, several interviews are necessary to gain impressions about underlying motives (the core of personality). If the interview is conducted properly, carefully, and systematically, the results can be reliable and valid. However, much depends upon the skill and sensitivity of the person conducting the interview.

Observation of a subject during some type of performance situation is the second kind of rating system used for ascertaining personality. As with the interview, observations can be effective if the checklist being used is well designed and planned, and if the observer is highly trained. Typically, for personality assessment, the checklist would contain specific traits and behaviors that the observer would look for. These traits, as they are observed, would then be rated in terms of strength and clarity.

Unstructured Projective Procedures

The foregoing rating methods are generally used for ascertaining data on traits of personality, although in many instances inferences may be made concerning underlying motives. **Projective procedures** may also be used to identify traits, but they are commonly used to determine information about underlying motives. Projective techniques allow subjects to reveal their inner feelings and motives through unstructured tasks. These unstructured techniques are used primarily in clinical psychology and are somewhat synonymous with the psychoanalytic approaches to explaining personality. The underlying assumption in the unstructured test situation is that if subjects perceive that there are no right or wrong responses, they will likely be open and honest in their responses.

Several kinds of unstructured tests have been developed. Among them are the Rorschach Test (Sarason, 1954), the Thematic Apperception Test (Tompkins, 1947), the Sentence Completion Test (Holsopple & Miale, 1954), and the House-Tree-Person Test (Buck, 1948). For our purposes, only the Rorschach (also known as the "inkblot") and Thematic Apperception Tests (TAT) will be discussed. The inkblot and the TAT are by far the most commonly used projective tests.

The Rorschach Test

Herman Rorschach, a Swiss psychiatrist, was the first to apply the inkblot to the study of personality (Fredenburgh, 1971). The **Rorschach test** was introduced in 1921, and remains the most famous of all the projective testing devices. The test material consists of ten cards. Each card has an inkblot on it, which is symmetrical and intricate. Some of the cards are entirely in black and white, while others have a splash of color or are nearly all in color. The cards are presented to the subject one at a time and in a prescribed order. As the cards are presented, the subject is encouraged to tell what he or she sees. The tester keeps a verbatim record of the subject's responses to each, and notes any spontaneous remarks, emotional reactions, or other incidental behaviors. After all the cards have been viewed, the examiner questions the subject in a systematic manner regarding associations made with each card.

In general, the Rorschach test is not recommended for use on athletes. Sixty years of clinical use has revealed that the test is not a reliable, objective, and valid measure of personality (Ryan, 1981). Furthermore, it relies much too heavily on the intuitions and expertise of the tester.

The Thematic Apperception Test

The **Thematic Apperception Test** was developed by Henry Murray and his associates in 1943 at the Harvard University Psychological Clinic. The TAT has been nearly as widely used as the Rorschach test. The TAT is composed of nineteen cards containing pictures depicting vague situations and one blank card. The subject is encouraged to make up a story about each picture. In contrast to the vague blots in the Rorschach test, pictures in the TAT are rather clear and vivid. For example, the sex of the characters in the picture and their facial expressions are generally identifiable. It is believed that subjects reveal or project important aspects of their personalities as they weave the characters and objects in the pictures into either an oral or a written story.

Like the Rorschach test, the TAT has been subjected to scientific inquiry. It too has not fared very well. The TAT seems to be very sensitive to temporary conditions that may influence a subject during test administration. It has also failed to demonstrate acceptable objectivity, reliability, or validity (Ryan, 1981).

Structured Questionnaires

The structured questionnaire is a paper-and-pencil test in which the subject answers specific true-false or Likert scale–type statements.

A typical Likert scale–type statement is illustrated in the following example:

In athletic situations I find myself getting very uptight and anxious as the contest progresses.

Definitely	1	2	3	4	5	6	7	8	9	10	Definitely
False											True

Three categories of questions are often employed in the questionnaire-type personality test. The first category of questions is generally biographical in nature. Rather specific questions are asked about a person's background. The second category has to do with symptoms. For example, the subject may be asked to answer questions about perceptions of fatigue, unpleasant feelings, nightmares, or positive feelings of health and well-being. The third category consists of questions about how subjects typically respond in a given situation. For example, they may be asked whether or not they enjoy meeting new people at a social affair.

There are many different kinds of questionnaire-type personality inventories. Some of them have been designed for use with abnormal patients, while others are for normal patients. Generally speaking, certain specific personality characteristics or traits are believed to be identified through the administration of these questionnaires. The specific questionnaires that have been selected for our discussion have been used extensively in sport psychology literature. While they are believed to be superior to projective and rating tests in terms of reliability and validity, they are still far from perfect.

Minnesota Multiphasic Personality Inventory (MMPI)

The **Minnesota Multiphasic Personality Inventory (MMPI)** appeared in the early 1940s as a new kind of psychometric tool for the assessment of personality. It was designed to provide objective assessment of some of the major personality characteristics that affect personal and social adjustment in persons of disabling psychological abnormality. Nine scales were originally developed for clinical use and were named for the abnormal conditions on which their construction was based. The twelve scales now in the test include the following: hypochondriasis (Hs), depression (D), hysteria (Hy), psychopathic deviate (Pd), masculinity-femininity (Mf), paranoia (Pa), psychasthenia (Pt), schizophrenia (Sc), hypomania (Ma), lie (L), validity (F), and correction (K). The test is designed for subjects sixteen years of age or older who have had at least six years of successful schooling. While the test was designed for abnormal patients, it can be and has been used with normal patients (Dahlstrom & Walsh, 1960; Hathaway & McKinley, 1967).

California Psychological Inventory

The **California Psychological Inventory (CPI)** evolved directly from the MMPI. In fact, the CPI has been described as the "sane man's MMPI," and about half of its 480 true-false items have come directly from the MMPI (Fredenburgh, 1971). The test items are designed to measure eighteen different scales or facets of interpersonal behavior, and are grouped into four main categories. A summary

Table 1.1 Scales and Categories in the California Psychological Inventory. Reproduced by special permission of the publisher, Consulting Psychologists Press, Inc., Palo Alto, CA 94306, from the *Manual for the California Psychological Inventory* by Harrison Gough, Ph.D., Copyright 1957, 1975.

Categories	Scales
Class I. Measures of poise, ascendancy, self-assurance, and interpersonal adequacy	Dominance (Do) Capacity for status (Cs) Sociability (Sy) Social presence (Sp) Self-acceptance (Sa) Sense of well-being (Wb)
Class II. Measures of socialization, maturity, responsibility, and intrapersonal structuring of values	Responsibility (Re) Socialization (So) Self-control (Sc) Tolerance (To) Good impression (Gi) Community (Cm)
Class III. Measures of achievement potential and intellectual efficiency	Achievement via conformance (Ac) Achievement via independence (Ai) Intellectual efficiency (Ie)
Class IV. Measures of intellectual and interest modes	Psychological-mindedness (Py) Flexibility (Fx) Femininity (Fe)

of the eighteen scales and four categories are shown in table 1.1. The inventory has been given to subjects as young as twelve years of age, but generally requires a reading comprehension level equal to about the tenth grade (Gough, 1975; Lake, Mites & Earle, 1973).

Meyers-Briggs Type Indicator

The Myers-Briggs type indicator (MBTI) is a personality inventory that yields four dichotomous scores that indicate an individual's preferences for different kinds of activities (Myers & McCaulley, 1985). The MBTI was designed to make it possible to test C. G. Jung's (1921, 1971) theory of psychological types, and to put the results to practical use. The MBTI is based on Jung's ideas about perception and judgment, and the way that individuals interact with their environment.

The four basic dichotomous indices identified by the MBTI are (1) extroversion/introversion, (2) sensing/intuitive, (3) thinking/feeling, and (4) judgment/perception. Preferences on the four basic indices yield sixteen different personality types. For example, an individual scoring high in extroversion, sensing, thinking, and judging would be categorized as type ESTJ. This type of individual is practical, organized, and cerebral.

The MBTI is published in three forms. Form G is composed of 126 items, Form F has 166 items, and the abbreviated form (AV) is composed of 50 items. Form G is recommended because the items critical for identifying personality type appear early in the test. The test is a forced-choice, untimed inventory appropriate for adults and high-school–age students. (Myers & McCaulley, 1985).

Cattell Sixteen Personality Factor Questionnaire

Perhaps the most sophisticated paper-and-pencil test of personality is the **Personality Factor Questionnaire (16 PF)** designed and tested by Cattell (1973). Cattell employed the methods of **factor analysis** in his study of personality and firmly believed that his test measured the sixteen **source traits** of personality. Factor analysis procedures allow the researcher to identify major factors or clusters associated with a particular test. Cattell and his associates have conducted extensive research over the last forty years to find support and verification for these source traits (Cattell, Eber & Tatsuoka, 1980).

Additionally, Cattell believed that the sixteen source traits can be reduced to four secondary or **surface traits.** The surface traits of introversion-extraversion, anxiety, tough-mindedness, and independence represent a superficial cluster of several source traits and relate to learned behavior (Fredenburgh, 1971). Thus we may infer that second-order factors are learned, while the primary factors (source traits) are fundamental structures of personality. The sixteen source traits are shown in table 1.2. Each trait has a high- and a low-score description. Sten scores of three or less represent low scores, while Sten scores of eight or more are considered high. Sten scores are used by Cattell to standardize each person's raw score compared to other people who have taken the test. Scores above four and less than seven are considered average.

The 16 PF stands as the most sophisticated and scientifically sound approach to the measurement of personality yet devised. It is, of course, not without its critics, but most personologists point to the 16 PF as being the single best tool for measuring personality traits. The 16 PF has great significance for our purposes, since most researchers have adopted the 16 PF for personality assessment.

Table 1.2 Cattell's 16 PF Source Traits. From *Administrator's Manual for the 16 Personality Factor Questionnaire.* Copyright © 1972, 1979, 1986 by the Institute for Personality and Ability Testing, Inc. All rights reserved. Reproduced by permission.

Factor	Low Sten Score Description (1–3)	High Sten Score Description (8–10)
A	Reserved (Sizothymia)	Warmhearted (Affectothymia)
B	Less intelligent (Lower scholastic mental capacity)	More intelligent (Higher scholastic mental capacity)
C	Affected by feelings (Lower ego strength)	Emotionally stable (Higher ego strength)
E	Humble (Submissiveness)	Assertive (Dominance)
F	Sober (Desurgency)	Happy-go-lucky (Surgency)
G	Expedient (Weaker superego strength)	Conscientious (Stronger superego strength)
H	Shy (Threctia)	Venturesome (Parmia)
I	Tough-minded (Harria)	Tender-minded (Premsia)
L	Trusting (Alaxia)	Suspicious (Protension)
M	Practical (Praxernia)	Imaginative (Autia)
N	Forthright (Artlessness)	Shrewd (Shrewdness)
O	Unperturbed (Untroubled adequacy)	Apprehensive (Guilt proneness)
Q_1	Conservative (Conservatism of temperament)	Experimenting (Radicalism)
Q_2	Group-oriented (Group adherence)	Self-sufficient (Self-sufficiency)
Q_3	Undisciplined self-conflict (Low integration)	Controlled (High self-concept control)
Q_4	Relaxed (Low ergic tension)	Tense (High ergic tension)

The Eysenck Personality Inventory

Eysenck's work in personality theory parallels Cattell's in both scope and general direction. Eysenck, a British psychologist, and Cattell, an American psychologist, both relied a great deal upon factor analytic procedures and upon the trait theory approach. However, whereas Cattell's theory rests heavily upon specific source traits, Eysenck preferred to concentrate upon the higher-order secondary or surface traits (Eysenck, 1972, 1976, p. 1).

Eysenck believed that personality can best be studied by two basic dimensions or traits. These two are extroversion-introversion and neuroticism-stability. Eysenck and Eysenck (1968b) also proposed a third dimension, psychoticism. These three dimensions (especially the first two) are considered to be independent of each other.

Compared to Cattell's 16 PF, the **Eysenck Personality Inventory (EPI)** has been of small consequence in American personality research (Janis, Mahl, Kagen & Holt, 1969). However, thanks to the work of Morgan (1980b) and associates, the EPI has become very important in sport psychology literature. In fact, in Morgan's recent work the higher-order traits of extroversion and neuroticism are the only personality traits measured (with the exception of Spielberger's A-trait). The rest of the psychological factors that Morgan typically measures have been "state" measures as opposed to trait measures. Much of Morgan's research will be reviewed later in this chapter.

The Athletic Motivation Inventory

The **Athletic Motivation Inventory (AMI)** was developed by Thomas Tutko, Bruce Ogilvie, and Leland Lyon at the Institute for the Study of Athletic Motivation at San Jose State College (Tutko & Richards, 1971, 1972). According to its authors, the AMI measures a number of personality traits related to high athletic achievement. These traits are: drive, aggression, determination, responsibility, leadership, self-confidence, emotional control, mental toughness, coachability, conscience development, and trust.

The reliability and validity of the instrument has been seriously questioned by Corbin (1977) and Martens (1975). However, Tutko and Richards (1972) do say that thousands of athletes have been tested and that the AMI was originally based upon the 16 PF and the Jackson Personality Research Form (Ogilvie, Johnsgard & Tutko, 1971). Due to the apparent lack of research evidence to support its claims, the AMI has been poorly received by the scientific community. In this regard, Rushall (1973) has written:

> . . . a peculiar situation has risen with this institute. For all its findings and developed tests, no data, data analysis or experimental verifications have been presented. This means that one must be extremely wary of the work produced by

that organization. Professional sport psychologists are beginning to publicly scorn the products of that organization. This writer adopts the approach of completely ignoring the work of that institute because it is not substantiated and therefore not valid (pp. 285–86).

Perhaps the real concern of sport psychologists is not that the test is more or less reliable than other personality inventories, but that the developers make grandiose claims about its ability to predict athletic success. No other organization, researcher, or promoter has made similar claims about any of the other more distinguished personality inventories. This would indeed seem strange. Rushall's 1973 statement would seem to merit serious consideration by coaches and teachers interested in athlete personality assessment.

The Profile of Mood States

The **Profile of Mood States (POMS)** differs from the other inventories described here in that it measures affective **states** as opposed to relatively stable personality traits. Traits suggest a predisposition to behave in a certain way regardless of the sitaution; states reflect a specific psychological state or mood that is situation specific and somewhat transitory in nature. For example, the predisposition to be anxious in a wide variety of situations is a personality trait, whereas the actual manifestations of anxiety is situation specific and is called state anxiety.

The POMS is mentioned here because of its popularity as a research tool among sport psychologists interested in the personality of athletes (Morgan, 1974). The POMS measures six identifiable mood or affective states: tension, depression, anger, vigor, fatigue, and confusion. It was originally designed for use on psychiatric patients, but has been found to be effective in measuring mood states of normal patients as well (McNair, Lorr & Droppleman, 1971).

Eight State Questionnaire

In recent years, a number of sport psychologists have started to use a mood state inventory called the Eight State Questionnaire (8SQ). The 8SQ is similar to the POMS in that mood states are being measured instead of personality traits. It is composed of eight important psychological states that are related to the athletic experience. The test is composed of ninety-six items and takes approximately thirty minutes to complete (IPAT, 1979).

Perhaps due to dissatisfaction with the POMS, Silva and associates have used the 8SQ successfully in measuring psychological states of elite world-class marathoners and runners (Silva, Shultz, Haslam, Martin & Murray, 1985; Silva & Hardy, 1986).

3. **Principle** Many personality inventories are available for measuring the personality traits of athletes. Each of these inventories or tests was designed for a specific purpose and with a particular subject in mind. Tests should be selected with care.

Application In terms of reliability and validity, there is little doubt that the Cattell 16 PF is the best test to be used for measuring the personality of athletes. When using this test, consult your team sport psychologist, school counselor, or other trained professionals regarding the correct administration of the test and interpretation of results.

The Credulous versus Skeptical Argument

Several years ago, Morgan (1980a) published an article entitled, "Sport Personology: The Credulous-Skeptical Argument in Perspective." In this article, Morgan explained that many sport psychologists are polarized by the credibility of personality research. On one side are a few researchers who seem to believe that

positive and accurate predictions can be made about sport performance from personality profiles based on measured traits. Proponents of this position are considered **credulous** in nature and are generally willing to use results of personality testing in predicting athletic success. Researchers such as Ogilvie and Tutko (1966) seem to fall into this position. On the other side are sport psychologists who tend to be **skeptical,** who minimize the value of personality assessment in predicting athletic success. Among the members of this camp are such distinguished sport psychologists as Rushall (1973), Kroll (1970), and Martens (1976). Morgan (1980b) and Kane (1980), however, take a position between these two extremes and declare that if the research is conducted properly, a modest but significant relationship can be observed between personality traits and athletic performance.

Where does this argument leave the practitioner? The exchange between members of these camps (skeptical, credulous, and in-between) is interesting. Rushall stated in 1973 (in support of the skeptical position) that he had reviewed all available athlete-personality research conducted between 1960 and 1967, and found them all to be flawed in terms of research design and/or method. His point was that research supporting the credulous position could not be believed. Morgan (1980a) countered that if Rushall's own research on the subject of personality and the athlete had not been flawed, it would have supported the credulous position!

4. **Principle** The credulous versus skeptical argument suggests that there is some debate about how useful personality testing is for predicting athletic performance. This should serve as a warning to the practitioner, to be wary of grandiose claims made by some authors about the usefulness of personality tests in predicting athletic performance, and to be wary of making clinical corrections based upon the results of a personality test.

   Application A coach or teacher should never make a decision to cut or bench an athlete based solely on personality testing. With the best research available and sophisticated testing procedures, only 70 to 80 percent of elite athletes can be correctly categorized using psychological testing procedures. This is not good enough. It would be unethical to act contrary to this recommendation.

Methodological Concerns in Sport Personality Research

The key to resolving the credulous versus skeptical argument lies in conducting and interpreting research that has not been fraught with experimental and design errors.

What are some of the design errors that have drawn the criticism of so many sport psychologists (Carron, 1980; Martens, 1975, 1976; Morgan 1972b, 1980a, 1980b)? Briefly, a few of the most serious problems are:

1. *Theoretical versus atheoretical personality research.* A large percentage of the sport personality research has been conducted *atheoretically.* That is, the researchers had no particular theoretical reason for conducting the research in the first place. They just arbitrarily selected a personality inventory, tested a group of athletes, and proceeded to "snoop" through the data for "significant" findings. Unfortunately, far too many of these atheoretical studies have been published and believed by interested coaches and teachers.

2. *Poorly defined independent variables.* When you have over six hundred published articles on sport personology, each of them using different and sometimes inadequate terms to define the variables, you have a real problem. The results of past research on personality have been consistently inconsistent. Part of the problem can be directly traced to the *independent variable.* This is the variable that is used by the researcher to predict the value of the *dependent variable.* For example, the question might be asked whether being an athlete (independent variable) is predictive of a certain personality trait (dependent variable). Rushall (1972) classified football players according to skill level based upon first-, second-, or third-string designations. This procedure presents a problem, since it tends to lump all categories of football players together, regardless of the position they play. How can you compare the performance of a second-string quarterback, for example, with the performance of a first-string lineman?

Other examples of poorly defined independent variables have to do with the multiple-sport performer and what constitutes an athlete. Some studies compare type of sport in terms of personality and fail to recognize that many athletes play more than one sport. Other studies compare athletes to nonathletes, failing to consider how the term is used by other researchers. Lack of standardization of terms is a very serious problem in athlete personality research.

3. *Poorly defined dependent variables.* As we learned from the section on personality measurement, there are many ways of measuring personality. It would be folly to compare research results whose dependent variable was assessed by a projective test with results obtained by a structured questionnaire. Even more common is the difficulty encountered when researchers attempt to compare the results of a questionnaire designed for normal subjects (16 PF) with one designed for abnormal subjects (MMPI). The point is that researchers must be very careful in selecting tests for measuring personality, since the results could vary considerably depending upon the subjects tested, the situation, and the nature of the dependent variable.

4. *Poor sampling procedures.* Perhaps the main problem here is in comparing personality profiles of one subgroup with that of another. Researchers have typically determined the average personality profile of a group of athletes from one school, team, or sport and wondered why it differs so much from the profile of another group in another school or area of the country. This is a little bit like sampling an elephant from his ears, tusks, and trunk and concluding that an elephant is three different things. If subjects were randomly selected from three different athletic teams, then inferences can only apply to the three teams sampled. When researchers measure the psychological profiles of an intact group of twenty elite wrestlers, then generalizations can only be made to those twenty wrestlers. The danger occurs when researchers or those interpreting the research conclude that the profile applies to all elite wrestlers.

5. *Failure to use an interaction model.* Fifty years of research with personality should have taught us one thing: failure to consider both the situation (environment) and the person (traits) leads to invalid results. The only exceptions to this rule would be either the case in which the situation is so strong that personality variables are insignificant, or one in which a particular personality trait is so powerful that the situation is insignificant. Since neither of these events is very likely to occur, it is best to adopt an interaction model in personality research and application.

6. *Failure to adopt a multivariate approach to data analysis.* Sport personality research has typically involved the measurement of personality through the use of an inventory designed to measure a number of traits (e.g., the sixteen personality factors involved in Cattell's 16 PF). In many cases, researchers have analyzed the multiple traits using a univariate approach. That is, a simple F- or T-test is made between categories of an independent variable (e.g., athlete vs. nonathlete) for each of the sixteen or so traits

measured. This approach defies all logic, since it treats each trait as an independent entity, when in fact each trait is only one aspect of the total personality. It is much more appropriate to deal with the multiple measures of personality using a **multivariate approach.** This approach considers all of the personality traits together at one time and as a unit. The statistical analysis involved in a multivariate analysis is beyond the scope of this text, but the interested student is referred to Kroll and Peterson (1965) for a classic discussion of this issue.

7. *Cause-and-effect relationships.* Related to the statistical analysis problems discussed previously is the problem of improperly interpreting data that are analyzed using a **correlational approach.** Specifically, this means ascribing a **cause-and-effect relationship** to a significant correlation between a personality trait and athletic performance. For example, if it can be observed that a significant correlation exists between the length of basketball players' sweatpants and their field-goal shooting percentages, one might conclude that length of sweatpants *causes* field-goal accuracy. This, of course, is nonsense, since it is more likely that the height of the players was the more important factor. The point is that cause-and-effect relationships deduced from correlational data are highly suspect. In sport personality research, this problem has surfaced when researchers have observed a significant correlation between a personality trait and athletic performance, and have concluded that the trait caused the superior performance. This logic is flawed, since many other factors could have caused the effect.

5. **Principle** A significant statistical correlation between a personality trait (e.g., dominance, intelligence, aggressiveness) and an athletic ability does not necessarily imply a cause-and-effect relationship. Statistical correlations simply mean that two variables are associated with each other, not that they cause one another.

 Application You will read in this text and in the sport psychology literature generally of instances in which certain personality traits are known to be related to athletic ability. For example, numerous studies have shown that athletes are more extroverted than nonathletes. One cannot assume from this that athletics caused the extroversion.

A correlational analysis between two variables yields a number called a correlation coefficient (*r*). The size of the correlation coefficient tells the researcher how closely related two variables are to each other. Correlation coefficients range from zero to 1.00. The closer the *r* is to 1.00, the stronger the relationship. Correlations can be positive or negative, suggesting that an increase in one variable can be associated with either an increase (positive *r*) or a decrease (negative *r*) in a second variable. To state that a correlation is significant merely indicates that the relationship between two variables probably did not occur by chance.

8. *Failure to account for response distortion.* Failure to control or adjust for response distortion by subjects has been identified by Morgan (1980b) as a major problem in Rushall's (1972) research with football players using Form A of the 16 PF. While this may have been a major problem in the past, for those researchers adopting the popular 16 PF (Forms A and B), it should not be a problem any longer. This is because of the addition of the faking good, faking bad scales to Forms A and B of the 16 PF (Krug, 1978). The inclusion of the distortion scales makes it possible for the researcher to adjust the scores of subjects purposely faking good or bad responses. However when major distortion efforts are discovered, it would seem prudent to remove those subjects from the study rather than attempt an adjustment. Many of the other psychological inventories such as the MMPI have lie scales built into them. The bottom line is that distortion scales should be used, and when they are not, the research should be considered suspect.

9. *Failure to use second-order surface traits.* It is Morgan's (1980a, 1980b) position, and to some degree Kane's (1976), that researchers would be well advised to work at the level of second-order factors and to ignore the first-order traits. Recall that **first-order traits** (source traits) are considered to be fundamental structures of personality, while the **second-order traits** (surface traits) are learned. Morgan (1980a) points out that if Rushall (1972) had worked with the second-order rather than first-order personality traits, he would have gotten the same positive results as did Kane (1970). Both Kane and Rushall conducted similar kinds of personality research with athletes, but came up with completely different results and conclusions. Morgan feels that this was partly due to Rushall's failure to work with the higher-order factors. This is not to say, however, that the source traits should be ignored, only that the surface traits should also be considered.

In retrospect, it would appear that the relationship between athletic performance and personality variables would be much clearer if all of these methodological and conceptual problems had been minimized in the published research.

	Team	Individual
Direct	Basketball Football Soccer	Wrestling

Parallel	Volleyball
	Baseball
		Long
		  Golf, tennis, cross country
		Short
		  Track, swimming,
		  gymnastics

Figure 1.3 Sport classification model used by Schurr et.al. (1977). From K. T. Schurr, M. A. Ashley, and K. L. Joy, Multivariate analysis of variance of male athlete personality characteristics: Sport types and success. *Multivariate Experimental Clinical Research, 3* (2), 1977, 53–68. Reprinted by permission of the publisher.

A study published by Schurr, Ashley, and Joy (1977) seems to have avoided most of the pitfalls evident in the previous research. Because of the importance of this study to the purposes of this section specifically, and to the chapter generally, I will review it in some detail.

Schurr, Ashley, and Joy Research

The research by Schurr, Ashley, and Joy (1977) was conducted by a moderately large midwestern university. The study involved 1,596 male college students who completed the Cattell 16 PF questionnaire as entering freshmen during a five-year period. Eight hundred and sixty-five of these subjects were categorized as athletes, based on participation in the university's intercollegiate athletic program. The remainder of the subjects were classified as nonathletes, and were randomly selected from a larger pool of nonathletes.

The four grouping (independent) variables in the study were:

1. *Athletes versus nonathletes.* Based on participation in the university intercollegiate athletic program.
2. *A years factor.* Compared entering freshmen during years one, two, and three with the entering freshmen during years four and five.
3. *Skill level of athletes.* Consisted of letter winners versus nonletter winners. A letter winner/nonletter winner dichotomy permitted constant definition of success over all sports.
4. *Sports classification.* Athletes who participated in more than one sport were classified in the sport in which they won the most awards. Four different methods of classifying subjects by sport were used, as illustrated in figure 1.3.

The data were analyzed using a multivariate analysis of variance (MANOVA), with the second-order factors of the 16 PF serving as the multiple dependent variables. Recall that a multivariate approach considers the surface traits simultaneously rather than individually. Four main effects yielded significant results. These were (1) athletes versus nonathletes, (2) the years factor, (3) individual versus team sports, and (4) direct versus parallel sports. Noticeably, the skill level (letter versus nonletter) main effect was not significant. Also of importance (in terms of replication) was the fact that the results were reasonably consistent for the two sets of entering freshmen (years 1, 2, and 3 versus years 4 and 5).

Given the generally dismal picture portrayed by the literature regarding studies of relationships between personality and athletic performance, the results of this study conform fairly well with the following general hypotheses. First, individual-sport athletes are less anxious, less dependent, and more self-sufficient than team-sport athletes (Cratty, 1983; Vanek & Cratty, 1970). Second, direct-sport participants are high in mental toughness, dominance, and endurance, while parallel-sport participants tend to be high in tactical ability and ability to delay aggression (Berger, 1970; Vanek & Cratty, 1970). Third, athletes tend to differ from nonathletes on such factors as extroversion, anxiety, independence, and abstract reasoning (Hardman, 1973). While athletes tend toward extroversion, the marathon runner tends to be an introvert (Silva & Hardy, 1986).

Personality and Sport Performance

Since 1960, several comprehensive reviews of the literature have attempted to clarify the relationship between personality and sport performance. Most of them have concluded that there is a positive relationship between personality and some aspect of athletic performance. In most cases, the authors have pointed out that these relationships are correlational and do not prove a cause-and-effect relationship. That is, while statistically a relationship may be observed to exist between athletic ability and, say, extroversion (Kane, 1980), one should not conclude from this that a particular personality trait caused a particular event.

Since these reviews may be of considerable interest to the student of sport psychology, a brief summary of each of them will be included here. Proceeding chronologically, Cofer and Johnson (1960) reviewed a number of studies of personality and various athletic groups, but refused to generalize any specific characteristics of athletes. Ogilvie (1968, 1976), on the other hand, reviewed numerous studies and concluded that eight personality traits were closely linked to athletic performance. These traits were: emotional stablity, tough-mindedness, conscientiousness, self-discipline, self-assurance, low tension, trust, and extroversion.

Ogilvie arranged his review according to the personality inventory used in the various investigations. Cooper (1969) reviewed research conducted from 1937 to 1967 and concluded that athletes were clearly achievement oriented. He also suggested that athletes tended to exhibit the traits of extroversion, dominance, self-confidence, competitiveness, low anxiety, low compulsiveness, and tolerance for pain.

In 1973, Hardman reviewed twenty-seven studies conducted from 1952 to 1968, involving forty-two samples of athletes, in which the Cattell 16 PF was used. Hardman concluded that participation in sport was associated with high intelligence, instability, assertiveness, enthusiasm, low superego strength, shyness, suspiciousness, and tension. Perhaps more importantly, in terms of second-order factors, Hardman concluded that participation in sport was associated with low anxiety and independence. The relationship between sport and extroversion revealed great intersport variability. A close analysis of Hardman's conclusions reveals that only the first-order trait factor of high intelligence showed a consistent and high association with sport participation. The Sten scores for this factor were average or above average for all forty-two samples. Table 1.2 is an overview of the personality traits measured by the 16 PF.

Finally, it appears that Morgan (1980b) provided the most comprehensive and significant review to date of the relationship between motor performance and personality. Morgan noted that at the Second International Congress of Sport Psychology held in 1968, Kane (1970) presented data in support of the view that personality traits can account for 20 percent of the variance in sports participation among men and women. At the same Congress, Rushall (1970a) stated that personality was not a significant factor in sport performance. Morgan's position in his 1980 article was essentially a repudiation of Rushall's position and a general endorsement of Kane's. Morgan does not say that a credulous view about trait psychology should be accepted to the extent that it is a precise predictor of motor behavior. Rather, he simply says that, taken in conjunction with other indicators such as physiological and environmental factors, it is useful. He readily admits that 50 to 75 percent of the variance relative to motor performance is unexplained by personality traits. However, he points out that this means that 25 to 50 percent is. Morgan concludes his signal review with the following statement:

> The research reviewed in this section reveals that athletes differ from nonathletes on a variety of psychological states and traits, and these differences become most noticeable when the elite performer is considered. There is less agreement concerning differences in the psychological characteristics of athletes differing in ability level. Again, however, psychological differences are consistently demonstrated where response distortion is considered, and the data are analyzed by means of multivariate as opposed to univariate procedures. This research, however, consistently leaves 50–75 percent of the variance in performance or group discrimination unexplained. It would not be appropriate, therefore, to rely on a state, trait, or state-trait model (narrow or broad) alone in attempting to predict behavior. It is quite obvious that numerous physiological variables, for example, play a profound role in sport performance (p. 66).

Our discussion of this issue will close with some generalizations. While it is good to remember that the relationship between sport performance and personality is still far from crystal clear, it seems equally true that certain general conclusions can be made. These relationships are, of course, statistical in nature, and do not necessarily mean that a cause-and-effect relationship exists. Research that supports these general conclusions will also be cited for the benefit of the reader.

Athletes versus Nonathletes

Athletes differ from nonathletes on many personality traits (Geron, Furst & Rotstein, 1986). It is often a matter of conjecture whether these differences favor the athletes or the nonathletes. Schurr, Ashley, and Joy (1977) clearly showed that athletes who participate in team and individual sports are more independent, objective, and less anxious than nonathletes. From Hardman's (1973) review it also seems rather clear that the athlete is often more intelligent than the average. Additionally, Cooper (1969) describes the athlete as being more self-confident, competitive, and socially outgoing than the nonathlete. This would seem to agree with Morgan's (1980b) and Kane's (1976) conclusions, that the athlete is basically an extrovert and low in anxiety.

In several recent investigations, a number of comparisons have been made between an athlete's score on various personality and psychological inventories and scores associated with norm groups. For example, compared to published normative data, professional cowboys tend to be alert, enthusiastic, forthright, self-sufficient, reality based, and practical (McGill, Hall, Ratliff & Moss, 1986). Compared to norm groups, elite rock climbers exhibit low anxiety, emotional detachment, low superegos, and high levels of sensation seeking (Magni, Rupolo, Simini, DeLeo & Rampazzo, 1985; Robinson, 1985).

While the evidence favors the conclusion that the athlete differs from the nonathlete in many personality traits, the problem arises in the definition of what constitutes an athlete. In the Schurr et al. (1977) research, an athlete was defined as a person who participated in the university intercollegiate athletic program. This would seem to be a viable criterion. However, this classification system has not been universally adopted by researchers. Some studies, for example, have classified intramural and club sports participants as athletes. Other studies have required that participants earn an award, such as a letter, in order to be considered athletes. Until some unifying system is adopted, it will always be difficult to compare results from one study with those from another.

---

6. **Principle** Generally speaking, athletes differ from nonathletes in many personality traits. For example, it can be demonstrated that athletes are more independent, more objective, and less anxious than nonathletes.

   Application As a coach, expect your athletes to be generally higher in such traits as independence, extroversion, and self-confidence and lower in anxiety than nonathletes. One cannot, however, rank athletes on the basis of these traits or make team roster decisions based on them. A statistical relationship (often low) does not suggest a cause-and-effect relationship.

Developmental Effects of Athletic Participation upon Personality

Given that athletes and nonathletes differ on the personality dimensions of extroversion and stability (anxiety), is this due to the athletic experience (learning), or is it due to a natural selection process in which individuals possessing certain personality traits gravitate toward athletics? Perhaps the final answer to this question will never be known; however, the evidence typically supports the genetic or *gravitational hypothesis* (Morgan, 1974). Individuals who possess stable, extroverted personalities tend to gravitate toward the athletic experience. Additionally, as the competitive process weeds out all but the keenest of competitors, those who remain are those having the greatest levels of extroversion and stability. This could be described as sort of an athletic Darwinism (survival of the fittest). Some of the studies that support the gravitational model are those by Yanada and Hirata (1970), Kane (1970), and Rushall (1970a).

The viability of the gravitational model, however, does not preclude the possibility that sport participation can enhance personality development. In this respect, Tattersfield (1971) has provided longitudinal evidence that athletic participation before maturity has a developmental effect upon personality. Specifically, Tattersfield monitored the personality profiles of boys participating in an age group swimming program across a five-year training period. Significant changes were observed in the boys during this period toward greater extroversion, stability, and dependence. From an educational perspective, all but the factor of dependence would be considered positive in nature.

Similarly, in recent years the medical profession has recognized the possibility that such psychological traits as anxiety, confidence, and a feeling of well-being can be enhanced through regular aerobic exercise. This welcome acceptance of the mental health benefits of exercise and sport participation has been facilitated by the numerous scientific investigations on the subject (Bahrke, 1979; Balog, 1983; Dulberg & Bennett, 1980; Mehrabian & Bekken, 1986; Morgan, 1979a; Morgan, 1981). Dulberg and Bennett (1980), for example, demonstrated that a six-week jogging program enhanced the psychological well-being of both normal and emotionally disturbed adolescent males.

---

7. **Principle** Athletes tend to be more extroverted, independent, and self-confident than nonathletes because of a process of "natural selection," and not due to learning. Individuals who exhibit certain personality traits tend to gravitate toward athletics. An important exception to this principle occurs in the formative years before the young athlete reaches maturity. During the early maturing years, the youth sport experience is critical in forming positive personality traits such as self-confidence and independence.

   Application Coaches and teachers who work with young boys and girls must be very careful that the athletic experience is a positive one in the lives of young people. Athletic programs designed for youth should place a premium on the development of feelings of self-worth, confidence, and independence, and relegate winning to a position of secondary importance. At least it must not be more important than the needs of the boys and girls.

Personality Sport Type

Can personality profiles of athletes in one sport be reliably differentiated from those in another sport? Perhaps the first real attempts to answer this question were made with bodybuilders. Research by Henry (1941), Thune (1949), and Harlow (1951), for example, suggested that bodybuilders suffer from masculine inadequacy, and are overly concerned with health, body build, and manliness. A recent study by Thirer and Greer (1981), however, would tend to cast doubt on these earlier stereotypes. In what appears to be a well-conceived and controlled study, the authors concluded that intermediate and competitive bodybuilders were high in achievement motivation and resistance to change, but relatively normal in all other traits measured. They found no support for the previous generalities and negative stereotyping sometimes attributed to bodybuilders.

Kroll and Crenshaw (1970) reported a study in which highly skilled football, wrestling, gymnastic, and karate athletes were compared on the basis of Cattell's 16 PF. The results showed that when the football players and wrestlers were contrasted with the gymnasts and karate participants, significantly different personality profiles emerged. The wrestlers and football players had similar profiles, while the gymnasts and karate athletes differed from each other as well as from the wrestlers and football players.

Similarly, Singer (1969) observed that collegiate baseball players (a team sport) differed significantly from tennis players (an individual sport) in several personality variables. Specifically, the tennis players scored higher than the baseball players on achievement, autonomy, intraception, dominance, and aggression, but lower on abasement.

Finally, Schurr, Ashley, and Joy (1977), in their signal research, clearly demonstrated that personality profile differences exist between team and individual sports, and between direct and parallel sports. Team sport athletes were observed to be more anxious, dependent, extroverted, and alert-objective; but less sensitive-imaginative than individual sport athletes. Direct sport athletes (basketball, football, soccer, etc.), were observed to be more independent and to have less ego strength than parallel sport athletes (volleyball, baseball, etc.).

The literature shows that athletes in one sport often differ in personality type and profile from athletes in other sports. It seems reasonable, for example, to expect the football player to be more aggressive, anxious, and to have a greater pain tolerance than a golfer or a tennis player. However, the point still needs to be made that the state of the art (or science) is still not so refined that one could feel justified in arbitrarily categorizing young athletes based on their personality profiles.

8. **Principle** Generally speaking, it can be demonstrated that a difference exists among the personalities of athletes who engage in different types of sports. Perhaps the clearest distinction occurs between athletes involved in team sports and those involved in individual sports. For example, team sport athletes are more extroverted, dependent, and anxious than individual sport athletes. Certainly, one might expect some differences to emerge between football players and tennis players in terms of personality traits.

   Application Personality profiles may be used by trained sport psychologists to help an athlete decide which sport to devote his or her energies toward, but they should never be used to coerce the athlete into making such a decision. If a young athlete with a tennis player's personality wants to be a golfer, so be it. Occasionally, an athlete reaches a junction in his or her athletic career when he or she must decide between two sports in order to devote adequate time to academic work. Perhaps consideration of an athlete's personality profile would be useful at this point.

Player Position and Personality Profile

In the previous section I discussed the notion of personality types among athletes of differing sports. It was concluded that in many circumstances, clear differences exist between the personality profiles of athletes from different sports. The same concept can be raised about whether athletes of a single sport exhibit different personality profiles based on player position.

In recent years we have experienced an age of superspecialization in team sports. In baseball, outfielders are inserted based on whether they hit left- or right-handed. In football, you have an offense and defense who rarely come in contact with each other. Offensive linesman are supposed to be very organized and neat, while defensive players are reportedly just the opposite. In volleyball, hitters and setters have specialized roles that dictate the sorts of defensive and offensive assignments they fulfill. Similar kinds of specializations can be observed with most other team sports.

While this area of research would seem to be of interest to coaches and athletes, in actuality very little has been reported. In my study (Cox, 1987a), I asked the following question relative to the sport of volleyball: do center blockers, strong-side hitters, and setters display different psychological profiles due to their different assignments? The subjects were 157 female volleyball players who participated in an invitational volleyball tournament. The results indicated that the three groups of athletes were very similar in terms of their psychological profiles with the exception of certain attentional focus variables. Compared to middle blockers and strong-side hitters, setters were observed to have a broad internal focus and be able to think about several things at one time. The setter on a volleyball team is like a point guard on a baseball team or the quarterback on a football team. She must be cognizant at all times of what plays to call, strengths and weaknesses of front-line attackers, as well as the strengths and weaknesses of the opposing team's blockers and defensive alignment.

In a similar study reported by Schurr, Ruble, Nisbet, and Wallace (1984), a comparison was made between player position in football and personality traits. Using the Myers-Briggs type inventory (MBTI), the authors concluded that linesmen differed significantly from backfield players in terms of the traits of judging and perceiving. Linesmen tend toward being more organized and practical while defensive and offensive backs are more flexible and adaptable. Interestingly, no reliable differences were noted between offensive and defensive linesmen, while offensive backs tend to be more extroverted and defensive backs more introverted.

Personality Profiles of Athletes Differing in Skill Level

There does seem to be sufficient evidence to suggest that elite, high-level performers can be distinguished from lower-level performers when psychological state *and* trait profiles of the athletes are considered. This point has been well documented by Morgan and his associates (Morgan & Costill, 1972; Morgan & Johnson, 1977, 1978; Morgan & Pollock, 1977; Nagle, Morgan, Hellickson, Serfass & Alexander, 1975) using elite distance runners, wrestlers, and oarsmen.

Nevertheless, the ability to distinguish between successful and unsuccessful athletes in any particular sport using personality traits *only* has never been particularly successful (Morgan, 1980b). For example, Kroll (1967), using collegiate wrestlers, and Kroll and Carlson (1967), using karate participants, could not successfully distinguish between the successful and unsuccessful performers. Rushall (1972), using football players, and Singer (1969), using tennis and baseball players, likewise could not distinguish between the successful and unsuccessful players. In addition, Craighead, Privette, and Byrkit (1986) were unable to distinguish between starters and nonstarters in high school boys' basketball.

Added to this lack of relationship between personality traits and skill level are the results of the Schurr et al. (1977) research. As the reader may recall, successful and unsuccessful sport participation in this study was based on whether or not the athlete earned a letter or award. The results of this comparison using the second-order factors of the 16 PF failed to show a significant relationship between performance and personality. It does not seem reasonable to expect that a group of first-string athletes could be separated from a group of second-string athletes based solely on personality traits. Both of these groups consist of highly skilled athletes in the first place, or they would not be on the team. Additionally, the task of differentiating between two groups of relatively successful performers on the basis of skill itself is a very tenuous and arbitrary task. Why then, should a coach expect to be able to do the same thing based on personality traits? A study by Williams and Parkin (1980) seems to provide credence to this line of reasoning. Specifically, they compared the personality profiles (Cattell's 16 PF) of eighteen international-level male hockey players with those of thirty-four national-level and thirty-three club players. Their results showed that the international players had significantly different profiles from the club players, but that the national-level players could not be distinguished from either of the other two groups.

Finally, it is perhaps important to point out that the research evidence as outlined here is consistent with practices of many professional sports leagues. If athletic performance could be accurately predicted through the use of personality inventories, there is no question that they would be used by professional scouts. Professional scouts are brokers of athletic talent, and would welcome the use of a simple personality test that would accurately predict the best performers. However, their use is shunned by players' unions, who are aware of the serious limitations of personality testing for purposes of predicting athletic performance.

The Female Athlete

The conclusions and generalizations that have been drawn from the previous comparison areas have been done primarily through research conducted on male rather than female subjects. This is due mainly to the fact that until recently very little personality research had been done with female athletes as subjects. This is not to say that the conclusions would have been any different if female subjects had been used. Indeed, we should expect the results to be essentially the same. However, after a thorough review of the available literature, Morgan (1980a) concluded that: "Comparisons of college athletes and nonathletes, or athletes from different sport groups, did not appear to be consistent in the literature dealing with females" (p. 60). Morgan blames methodological and design problems for the inconsistent results. He points out that this inconsistency seems to disappear when the successful or elite female athlete is compared with the "normative" female.

After reviewing much of the available literature on the female athlete and personality, Williams (1980) cautiously concluded that the "normative" female differs in personality profile from the successful female athlete. Specifically, the female athlete is found to exhibit personality traits much like the normative male and the male athlete (i.e., assertive, achievement-oriented, dominant, self-sufficient, independent, aggressive, intelligent, and reserved). For example, in comparison with available norms, female bodybuilders were observed to be more extroverted, vigorous, less anxious, less neurotic, less depressed, less angry, and less confused (Freedson, Mihevic, Loucks & Girandola, 1983). On the other hand, the normative female tends toward passiveness, submissiveness, dependence, emotionality, sociability, low aggression, and low need achievement.

Additionally, Williams (1980) cites numerous studies that show low personality variation within sport groups such as fencing, ice hockey, track, and lacrosse. This observation would suggest the existence of specific personality types or profiles for different sports.

Thus, it would appear that like her male counterpart, the female athlete differs from the nonathlete in terms of personality. As with the male athlete, female athletes from one sport are likely to differ to some degree from female athletes in another sport in terms of their personality profiles. Differentiation between athletes of varying skill levels on the basis of personality factors is only feasible on the level of the elite performer.

---

9. **Principle** While it is true that most personality research has involved male rather than female subjects, there is ample evidence that the principles apply equally to athletes of both sexes.

   Application In this respect the coach should not consider the female athlete to be any different than the male athlete. However, all athletes must be treated as individuals, and it must be recognized that gifted athletes of either sex can exhibit psychological profiles that differ from the norm.

Psychological Profile of the Elite Athlete

By definition, an elite athlete is one who has achieved world-class or true professional status as in the case of Olympic qualifiers and professional sport players. Without a doubt, the most significant contribution to our understanding of the **psychological profile** associated with elite athletes comes to us from the work of William P. Morgan and his associates. The notion of a psychological profile is that successful world-class athletes have a distinctive set of scores relative to personality and psychological inventories. Sporting types that have been studied include elite wrestlers (Gould, Weiss & Weinberg, 1981; Highlen & Bennett, 1979; Morgan & Johnson, 1977; Silva, Shultz, Haslam & Murray, 1981; Silva, Shultz, Haslam, Martin & Murray, 1985), elite long-distance runners (Morgan & Costill, 1972; Morgan & Pollock, 1977; Silva & Hardy, 1986), elite oarsmen (Morgan & Johnson, 1978), and elite cyclists (Hayberg, Mullin, Bahrke & Limberg, 1979).

The research that has been done with elite athletes in the 1970s and early 1980s represents both a psychosphysiological and a trait-state approach. That is, in attempting to improve on the prediction model, sport psychologists have measured physiological as well as psychological variables, and have measured both personality traits and situation-specific states. Thus, rather than entitling this section, "Personality Profiles of Elite Athletes," it has been entitled, "Psychological Profiles of Elite Athletes." This is an important distinction, because it represents a significant departure from the earlier trait approach of studying personality and its effect upon skilled performance.

Several important concepts have emerged from Morgan's research with elite athletes. The first is a mental health model for discriminating between successful and unsuccessful performers. While Morgan has never recommended the use of the model for selecting athletes for berths on international teams, his post hoc results (both clinical and statistical) have allowed him to correctly classify approximately 70 percent of the cases (Morgan, 1979b). Using essentially the same measurement techniques, Silva, Shultz, Haslam, and Murray (1981) reported being able to accurately classify 80 percent of a group of elite wrestlers using a psychological model, and 93 percent using a psychophysiological model.

The **mental health model** proposes that successful world-class athletes enjoy greater positive mental health than do unsuccessful performers. Each of the trait and state measures that Morgan typically administers to the elite athletes could be considered a clinical measure of mental health. The one notable exception to this would be Eysenck's measure of extroversion. While the psychological tests typically employed by this group of researchers have varied to some degree, three have remained consistent throughout. The first is Spielberger's state-trait inventory; the second is Eysenck's test of extroversion-introversion and neuroticism-stability; and the third is McNair, Lorr, and Droppleman's (1971) Profile of Mood States. In total, these three inventories sample ten different personality traits and/or psychological states. These ten psychological factors are illustrated in figure 1.4. Associated with these ten factors are two hypothetical profiles. The negative mental health profile would suggest an unsuccessful athlete, while the positive would suggest a successful one. From a clinical standpoint, athletes having a clear-cut successful profile would be expected to emerge as the most likely to win a berth on an international team, while those with the negative profile would not. Of course, not all athletes fall into one category or the other. Many elite athletes fall in a moderate category. Nevertheless, the research evidence is very convincing that the successful athlete is likely to enjoy positive mental health (Morgan, 1979a; Morgan & Johnson, 1977, 1978).

Psychological factors	Negative mental health profile			Positive mental health profile		
	Low	Moderate	High	Low	Moderate	High
State anxiety						
Trait anxiety*						
Tension						
Depression						
Anger						
Vigor						
Fatigue						
Confusion						
Extroversion*						
Neuroticism*						

*Indicates traits

Figure 1.4 Psychological profiles of unsuccessful (negative profile) and successful (positive profile) elite athletes. From Prediction of performance in athletics by W. P. Morgan. In *Coach, athlete, and the sport psychologist* by P. Klavora and J. V. Daniel (eds.), 1979. School of Physical and Health Education, Publications Division, University of Toronto. Reproduced by permission of Publisher.

A second important concept that has emerged from Morgan's research is that of an **iceberg profile** to represent the successful world-class athlete. In essence, the iceberg profile is simply one aspect of the mental health model. However, the very concept of an iceberg profile serves to represent some important relationships between psychological factors and successful athletic performance. On the Profile of Mood States (POMS), the successful world-class athlete is typically well below the population mean on all mood states except for vigor. In the case of vigor, the successful athlete clearly emerges well above the mean of the population. As can be observed in figure 1.5, the profile of the successful world-class athlete looks very much like an iceberg, while in contrast, the less successful athlete has a rather flat profile.

In general, the successful world-class athlete is low in the trait measures of anxiety and neuroticism, and high in extroversion. In terms of psychological mood states, the world-class athlete is low in anxiety, tension, depression, anger, fatigue, and confusion, but high in vigor. In total, the psychological profile of the successful world-class athlete is consistent with positive mental health.

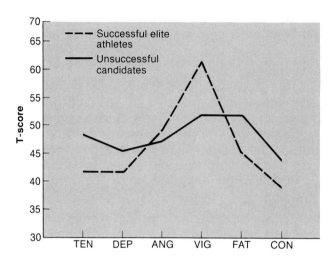

Figure 1.5 The iceberg profile and the elite athlete. From Prediction of performance in athletics by W. P. Morgan. In *Coach, athlete, and the sport psychologist* by P. Klavora and J. V. Daniel (eds.), 1979. School of Physical and Health Education, Publications Division, University of Toronto. Reproduced by permission of Publisher.

10. **Principle** The psychological profiles of elite world-class athletes can be accurately distinguished from less gifted athletes between 70 and 80 percent of the time. Personality profiles that do not include situational measures of psychological states are not nearly so accurate. Additionally, when one gets below the level of the elite performer, even psychological profiles that include trait and state measures are suspect in terms of predicting performance.

    Application On the level of the elite performer, the coach is justified in using psychological profiles for the purpose of *assisting* in the selection of athletes, but never for the purpose of discriminating on this basis alone. Decisions of this type should never be made on the basis of personality traits alone. Situation-specific state measures should also be included. For example, one certainly would not decide to cut a player on the basis of scores on the AMI or any other personality inventory.

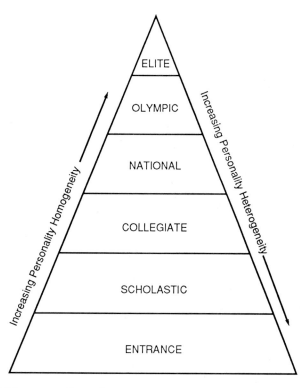

Figure 1.6 The personality-performance athletic pyramid. From Personality and sport performance: Controversy and challenge by John M. Silva, III. In *Psychological foundations of sport* by Silva, J. M., III and R. S. Weinberg (eds.), 1984 Human Kinetics Publishers, Inc. Reproduced by permission of publisher.

Finally, it seems paradoxical that in an earlier section it was observed that personality testing could not be used to discriminate between athletes of differing skill levels, yet in this section it has been observed that the elite athlete has a psychological and personality profile that often differs from lesser-skilled athletes. How can this paradox be explained?

Silva (1984) has provided a plausible explanation. As illustrated in figure 1.6, as the prospective elite athlete moves up the athletic pyramid, athletic participants become more alike in their personality and psychological traits. At the base or entrance level of sport, athletes are very heterogeneous or have different personalities. However, through a process of "natural selection," certain personality traits will enhance an athlete's likelihood of advancing to a higher level, while other traits will detract. At each higher level of the athletic pyramid, the athletes become more alike or more homogeneous in their personality traits. When we try to differentiate between athletes of varying skill levels in the middle and lower parts of the pyramid we meet with failure. Elite athletes, however, will exhibit similar profiles and will differ as a group from lesser-skilled groups.

Summary

Personality is defined as the dynamic organization within the individual of those psychophysical systems that determine his or her unique adjustments to the environment. The structure of personality is described on three levels: the psychological core, typical responses, and role-related behaviors. Three theories or approaches to studying personality were reviewed. These were (1) the psychodynamic approach, (2) social learning theory, and (3) the trait theory approach. A number of different approaches to measuring personality were also discussed. Basically, these included rating scales, projective procedures, and pencil-and-paper inventories. A number of different personality inventories were described, including the Cattell 16 PF, which is considered to be the single best written test of personality traits.

In discussing the credulous versus skeptical argument in sport personality research, a number of methodological problems were identified that have led to differences in research results and conclusions. Among these methodological shortcomings are poorly defined independent and dependent variables, incorrect sampling procedures, failure to use an interaction model, and failure to use second-order surface traits in research.

Several factors were considered concerning the question of whether or not a relationship exists between motor performance and an athlete's personality. Generally, the following conclusions were drawn: (1) athletes differ from nonathletes on many personality traits; (2) athletes in one sport often differ in personality, type, and profile from athletes in other sports; (3) with the use of trait and state psychological inventories, elite world-class performers can be discriminated from less-gifted athletes 70 percent of the time; and (4) female athletes are very similar to male athletes in the general conclusions we have drawn.

Review Questions

1. Define personality and describe its structure. How does an understanding of the various levels of personality help you to understand the nature of personality generally?

2. What are the key features of the three basic theories of personality? In your judgment, what is the best approach? Why?
3. Describe the situational and interactional approaches to the study of personality. How does the situational approach relate to the notion of personality disposition?
4. Name and describe four different personality inventories. Which one is best for testing athletes? Why?
5. Discuss the credulous versus skeptical argument and explain why you feel one view is stronger than the other. Can you substantiate your answers?
6. Is it possible to predict athletic success based on personality testing? Qualify your answer.
7. If it can be shown that a significant correlation of .70 exists between a personality trait and motor performance, does this mean that one causes the other? Explain your answer.
8. Based upon the research discussed in this chapter, what are some of the relationships that exist between athletic performance and personality traits?
9. Discuss the notion of homogeneity in terms of the personality of the athlete, and explain its impact upon the relationship between personality and athletic performance.

Glossary

AMI The Athletic Motivation Inventory developed by Tutko, Ogilvie, and Lyon for measuring personality traits.

Cattell 16 PF Personality inventory developed by Cattell that measures the sixteen source traits of personality.

cause-and-effect relationship A condition in which one variable (independent) causes another to behave in a certain manner (dependent). Concluding that such a relationship exists is an especially risky assumption when a correlational approach is used.

correlational approach Attempt to show a statistical relationship between two variables using a correlation coefficient (r).

CPI The California Psychological Inventory. Designed for normal subjects, it is a questionnaire-type test for measuring facets of interpersonal behavior.

credulous argument The argument that athletic performance can be predicted from personality traits.

EPI The Eysenck Personality Inventory. It emphasizes second-order surface traits as opposed to source traits.

factor analysis A complex statistical procedure wherein test items are grouped into factors representing personality traits.

first-order traits Synonymous with Cattell's notion of innate source traits of personality.

iceberg profile Profile of the elite athlete on the six factors measured by the POMS.

interaction model Based on the notion that both personality traits and situational states should be used in any prediction equation.

mental health model Developed by Morgan, the mental health model proposes that the elite athlete is a mentally healthy individual.

MMPI Minnesota Multiphasic Personality Inventory; a twelve-scale test designed for abnormal subjects.

multivariate approach A statistical analysis procedure in which several dependent variables (traits) are considered simultaneously.

personality The dynamic organization of psychological systems that determines an individual's uniqueness.

POMS Profile of Mood States designed to measure a person's affective states.

projective procedures Psychological tests in which responses are unstructured and open-ended.

psychological core A person's true self.

psychological profile Based upon a number of inventories, the profile is a distinct pattern of responses that a particular group of subjects, such as elite athletes, displays.

role-related behavior The most superficial aspect of a personality. It is the behavior we engage in to fit our perception of the environment.

Rorschach test A projective test in which the subjects describe an inkblot.

second-order traits Synonymous with Cattell's notion of surface or learned traits.

situational approach Recognition that an environmental situation is often more salient and powerful than a personality disposition.

skeptical argument The argument that athletic performance cannot be predicted from personality traits.

source traits See **first-order traits.**

state A transitory emotional condition.

surface traits See **second-order traits.**

Thematic Apperception Test Personality test in which the personality is projected through storytelling.

trait Relatively stable personality predisposition.

typical responses Manner in which a person typically responds to environmental situations.

Recommended Readings

Anshel, M. H. (1987). Psychological inventories used in sport psychology research. *The Sport Psychologist, 1*, 331–349.

Bowers, K. S. (1973). Situationalism in psychology: An analysis and a critique. *Psychological Review, 80*, 307–336.

Carron, A. V. (1975). Personality and athletics: A review. In B. S. Rushall (ed.), *The status of psychomotor learning and sport psychology research*. Dartmouth, Nova Scotia: Sports Science Associates.

Carron, A. V. (1980). *Social psychology of sport*. Ithaca, NY: Mouvement Publications.

Cattell, R. B. (1973, July). Personality pinned down. *Psychology Today, 7*, 40–46.

Fisher, A. C., Borowicz, S. K., & Morris, H. H. (1978). Behavioral rigidity across sports situations. In D. M. Landers & R. W. Christina (eds.), *Psychology of motor behavior and sport, 1977*, Champaign, IL: Human Kinetics Publishers.

Horsfall, J. S., Fisher, A. C., & Morris, H. H. (1975). Sport personality assessment: A methodological re-examination. In D. M. Landers (ed.), *Psychology of sport and motor behavior II*. University Park: Pennsylvania State University Press.

Kane, J. E. (1980). Personality research: The current controversy and implications for sport studies. In W. F. Straub (ed.), *Sport psychology: An analysis of athlete behavior* (2d ed.). Ithaca, NY: Mouvement Publications.

Kroll, W. (1970). Current strategies and problems in personality assessment of athletes. In L. E. Smith (ed.), *Psychology of motor learning*. Chicago: The Athletic Institute.

Martens, R. (1975). *Social psychology and physical activity*. New York: Harper & Row Publishers.

Martens, R. (1982). *Sport competition anxiety test*. Champaign, IL: Human Kinetics Publishers.

Mischel, W. (1986). *Introduction to personality*. New York: Holt, Rinehart, and Winston.

Morgan, W. P. (1979b). Prediction of performance in athletics. In P. Klavora & J. V. Daniel (eds.), *Coach, athlete, and the sport psychologist*. Champaign, IL: Human Kinetics Publishers.

Morgan, W. P. (1980a). Sport personology: The credulous-skeptical argument in perspective. In W. F. Straub (ed.), *Sport psychology: An analysis of athlete behavior* (2d ed.). Ithaca, NY: Mouvement Publications.

Morgan, W. P. (1980b). The trait psychology controversy. *Research Quarterly for Exercise and Sport, 51*, 59–76.

Ogilvie, B. C. (1976). Psychological consistencies within the personality of high-level competitors. In A. C. Fisher (ed.), *Psychology of sport*. Palo Alto, CA: Mayfield Publishing Company.

Rushall, B. S. (1970a). An evaluation of the relationship between personality and physical performance categories. In G. S. Kenyon (ed.), *Contemporary psychology of sport: Second International Congress of Sports Psychology*. Chicago: The Athletic Institute.

Rushall, B. S. (1973). The status of personality research and application in sports and physical education. *Journal of Sports Medicine and Physical Fitness, 13,* 281–290.

Schurr, K. T., Ashley, M. A., & Joy, K. L. (1977). A multivariate analysis of male athlete characteristics: Sport type and success. *Multivariate Experimental Clinical Research, 3,* 53–68.

Silva, J. M., III, Schultz, B. B., Haslam, R. W., Martin, T. P., & Murray, D. F. (1985). Discriminating characteristics of contestants at the United States Olympic Wrestling Trials. *International Journal of Sport Psychology, 16,* 79–102.

Part Two   Attention and Arousal

According to William James (1890), attention is "the taking possession by the mind, in clear and vivid form, of one out of what seem several simultaneously possible objects or trains of thought. . . . It implies withdrawal from some things in order to deal effectively with others" (pp. 403–4). In sport, there can be nothing more important than paying attention to the object at hand. On the surface, the idea of paying attention seems simple enough, but psychologists have long recognized that the attention process can be very complex.

Posner and Boies (1971) suggest that attention can be categorized into three major divisions: (1) the ability to selectively attend to one source of information at the expense of another, (2) the notion that humans have a limited capacity in terms of the amount of information they can attend to at one time, and (3) the process of maintaining alertness or arousal. We will consider each of these aspects in our discussion of attention as it relates to sport psychology.

In this section I have devoted two chapters to the study of attention. Chapter 2, "Attention in Sport," will deal with the notions of selective attention, limited information processing capacity, and an important discussion on the measurement and control of attention in sport. In chapter 3, "Arousal in Sport," I will discuss the notions of arousal and activation as they affect sport and athletic performance. Several theories of physiological arousal will be discussed. ■

2   Attention in Sport

Key Terms

associaters
attentional focus
attentional narrowing
attentional style
attenuation
bit
bottleneck
Broadbent model
B-TAIS
capacity model
centering procedure
cocktail party
  phenomenon
cue utilization theory
dissociaters
gate out
information conveyed
information processing
  model

LTM
memory storage
pertinence model
predictive validity
processing capacity
RAQ
refocusing
response delay
retrieval
RT probe
selective attention
selective filter
sensory register
shadowing
STM
TAIS
thought stopping
T-TAIS
Triesman model

Few topics in sport psychology are as important to athletic performance as attention or concentration. Consider the following illustration: In the 1985 baseball World Series a situation occurred that highlights the critical nature of concentration in athletic competition (Fimrite, 1985). It was the bottom half of the ninth inning in game 6 between the Kansas City Royals and the St. Louis Cardinals. The Cardinals held a 3 to 2 game lead in the series and had a 1 to 0 lead in the game. It looked like the Cardinals were going to win the game and the series. Through a series of miscues on the part of the Cardinal defense and a questionable call at first base, the Royals had the bases loaded and one out with a pinch hitter at the plate. Dane Iorg, a left-handed pinch hitter, was inserted into the line-up to face right-handed relief pitcher Todd Worrell. Iorg had been used by the Royals all year as a pinch hitter with only moderate success. As Dane stepped into the batter's box the tension began to mount. What was going through this young athlete's mind? Here he was, in the World Series, bases loaded, ninth inning, and the game on the line. As the TV cameras zeroed in on the batter, you could just see the total concentration and attention that he was giving to the pitcher. Dane let the first pitch, a fast ball, go by and then stroked the next pitch into right field for a game-winning single. He was a hero! As history has recorded, the Kansas City Royals went on to win the seventh game and the World Series.

This story highlights the critical importance of selective attention to sport and to successful performance. If Dane Iorg had become too focused or had allowed the historical significance of the event to overwhelm him, he could have been just an easy out and his name would not appear in this book. In this chapter I will address the topic of attention in such a manner as to explain and clarify why it is so important in human performance generally, and athletic performance specifically. First, I will discuss the nature of information processing as it relates to attention, human memory, and to the measurement of information. I will then discuss two critical factors that operate to limit and control attention. Finally, I will conclude with a discussion of attentional focus, how it is measured, and how it can be controlled.

Information Processing

In the pages to follow I will discuss the meaning and importance of information processing to athletic performance. However, before I do this I would like to provide you with an example of information processing *overload*. This should help you understand the nature of information processing before I discuss it in psychological terms.

Perhaps the most critical difference between the modern games of basketball, volleyball, and football and these same games twenty years ago is in the complexities of their offenses. Twenty years ago, volleyball was a relatively predictable game in which the spiker attacked from one of two positions on the court. These two positions were the left and right sides of the court near the sidelines. The ball was always set high and there was never any deviation from this pattern. This changed in the late 1960s and early 1970s when the Japanese revolutionized the game with their version of the multiple offense. In this remarkable offense, attackers spiked the ball from numerous positions at the net. In so doing, the spikers often switched attack positions and called for sets of variable height and speed. The result was predictable. Defensive net players were jumping at the wrong time, responding to the wrong attackers, crashing into their own players, and generally falling all over themselves. From an information processing point of view, they were simply overwhelmed. Up to this point the blockers had only been required to attend to one or two spikers at a time. But now they had to deal with three or four times as much information. Later on, when opposing teams were able to study the multiple offense, defensive players were taught to ignore irrelevant movement and fakes and to concentrate on the important elements of the attack.

In a very general way, there are two basic approaches to explaining behavior. The first and probably better understood is the behavioral or stimulus-response approach. In this way of looking at things, the world is explained through a series of stimulus-response or S-R connections. In fact, psychologists such as B. F. Skinner (1938) would have us believe that all behavior can be reduced to a mathematical model in which specific stimuli go in and predicted responses come out. With animals, this approach has been extremely successful. However, for human beings this approach seems too simplistic. There seems to be more to human behavior than the simple act of strengthening the bond between a stimulus and a response. Certainly, a great deal goes on in the brain between the time that a stimulus is given and the time that a response is initiated. This notion is well accepted by cognitive psychologists, and is illustrated in figure 2.1. It is referred to as the **information processing model** of behavior. The information processing model contains a stimulus and a response, but a large number of mental operations occur between the two. The three general stages of information processing also appear in figure 2.1.

In its most elemental form, information processing involves the storage of information in memory, the retrieval of information from memory, and the execution of a movement in response to information (Keele, 1973). For a person to experience a stimulus and respond to it at a later time, there must be a **memory storage** capability. That is, we must have a memory or place to save important information. Once the information has been saved, we must be able to reactivate

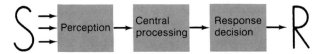

Figure 2.1 The general information processing model. From Magill, Richard A., *Motor learning: Concepts and applications.* © 1980 Wm. C. Brown Publishers, Dubuque, Iowa. All rights reserved. Reprinted by permission.

or retrieve it. **Retrieval** enables us to use the information to make decisions about forthcoming responses. A football quarterback stores thousands of pieces of information about offenses and defenses. As he approaches the line of scrimmage after calling one play in the huddle, he may observe the defensive alignment and change the play prior to the snap (this is termed "calling an audible"). What has happened here? The answer is simple. Previously stored information about the opposing team was retrieved from memory and used to initiate a different but appropriate response. This is information processing in action, and it takes place constantly on the athletic field or court. The concept is based on the notion of a storage or memory system, which we will discuss next.

Memory Systems

One basic question we may ask about memory is whether there is one memory system or several. While many researchers have tried to show that the different types of memory are clearly distinct from each other, the current thinking is that the distinction among memory systems is for convenience and should not be taken to mean that these systems reside in different parts of the brain (Ellis, Goggin, & Parenté, 1979). With this in mind, let us describe the three basic memory systems.

Sensory Information Store

The first stage in the human memory system is the sensory information store, sometimes called the **sensory register.** This storage system is capable of holding large amounts of sensory information in store for a very brief amount of time before most of it is lost (Sperling, 1960). Information is thought to remain in the sensory register for up to one-half second before it is either lost or transferred to a more permanent storage system. The images in the sensory store may be iconic (visual) or echoic (auditory), or they may come from any of the other senses, such as touch or taste. The limitations of the sensory register are illustrated in a volleyball-officiating situation. Events often occur so rapidly in a play at the net that it is hard for the referee to make an immediate decision. However, if the decision is not immediate, the referee will discover that the iconic image is no longer available. The same thing occurs in basketball officiating when the ball is knocked out-of-bounds by one of two opposing players. The information in the sensory register decays very rapidly and may be effectively scanned for only about one-half second. That portion of the information that we can effectively attend to is passed on to a short-term memory system for further processing.

Short-Term Memory (STM)

The **short-term memory (STM)** is the center of activity in the information processing system. It is the crossroad of activity. Information comes into STM from both the sensory store and from permanent memory for rehearsal. Information that comes into STM from the sensory store is often new or original information. If we do not rehearse and memorize it quickly, we will likely forget it. For example, when a telephone operator gives us a new telephone number for a friend, we will repeat it several times while dialing it. If we did not do this, we would forget the number before we could dial it. This is an example of rehearsing new information in STM. Conversely, a quarterback uses STM to rehearse information already permanently stored in memory. For example, just before a game, the quarterback will retrieve from memory the plays that he has learned and will rehearse them to make sure he knows them well. This process tends not only to refresh his memory of the plays, but also to strengthen their representation in memory. Generally, if a person can rehearse information for twenty to thirty seconds in STM, it will be sufficiently learned to be passed on to long-term memory for permanent storage.

Long-Term Memory (LTM)

Whereas information in short-term memory is present for only a brief period of time, information in **long-term memory (LTM)** is relatively permanent. The purpose of the memory system is to store information in LTM. Once information is stored in LTM, it is theoretically permanent. This may seem difficult to understand, since we all have occasionally had trouble remembering things we thought were permanently learned. Nevertheless, under psychoanalysis or hypnosis, people have remembered bits of information from early childhood that they could not have remembered under normal conditions. In conjunction with STM, information in long-term memory can be continually updated, reorganized, and strengthened. New information can also be added to LTM. The relationship between the three basic memory systems is illustrated in figure 2.2.

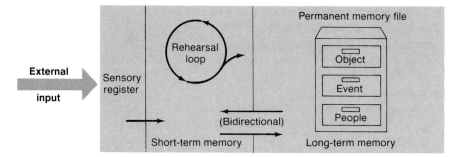

Figure 2.2 The three stages of memory. From *Foundations of contemporary psychology* by Merle E. Meyer. Copyright © 1979 by Oxford University Press, Inc. Reproduced by permission.

Measuring Information

Our consideration of information processing as it relates to attention would not be complete without some discussion of the procedures sport psychologists use to measure information.

The difficulty of any athletic event can be calculated in terms of the amount of information conveyed, responded to, and transmitted. The more information an event conveys, the more difficult the perceptual-motor event. For example, an athlete would react more quickly to a single light source than to one of several lights that might flash, because several lights convey more information (Keele, 1973). Placed in the context of a sport situation, a basketball center who always dribbles once before shooting is less difficult to guard (conveys less information) than a center who may do one of several things before shooting.

The amount of **information conveyed** by an event is equivalent to the number of questions that would have to be asked to accurately predict the event's occurrence. If one question needs to be asked, we say that the event conveys one bit of information. The word **bit** is short for *binary digit;* the number of bits corresponds to the number of questions that must be asked to accurately predict an event's occurrence. Thus, a five-bit perceptual-motor problem would convey more information and would be considerably more difficult than a one-bit problem.

---

1. **Principle** The difficulty of an athletic response can be represented in terms of information conveyed.

   Application The quantification of an athlete's ability to perform can provide the coach or teacher with the information needed to either increase or decrease the athlete's effectiveness.

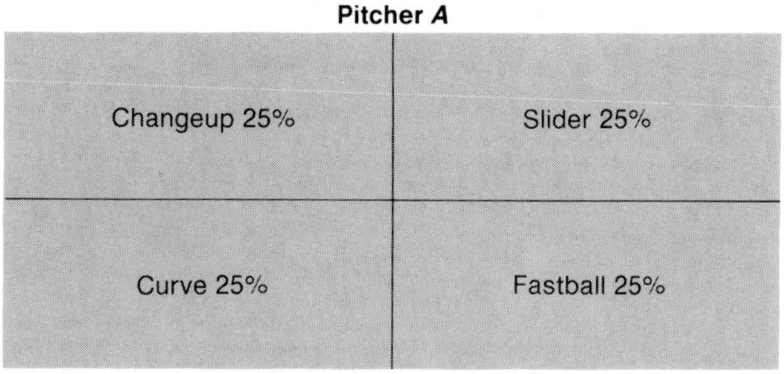

Pitcher A

Changeup 25%	Slider 25%
Curve 25%	Fastball 25%

Figure 2.3 Pitcher A has four pitches at his command. The probability of his throwing any one of the pitches is 25 percent. What is the average amount of information conveyed?

Consider the situation in which a baseball pitcher has complete control of four basic pitches. If each pitch has an equal probability of being thrown, then the probability of any one pitch being thrown will be 25 percent. On the average, how many bits of information does this problem convey? There are two ways to solve this problem. The first is simply to determine how many questions are needed to select the appropriate pitch, and the second is to calculate information conveyed using a simple mathematical formula.

First, how many questions are needed to solve this problem? Consider the problem as displayed in figure 2.3. My first question would be, "Is he going to throw one of the pitches in the top row?" If the answer is no, my second question would be, "Is he going to throw a fastball?" If the answer is no, I don't need to ask a third question, since I know there is only one possibility left, a curve. Therefore, the average amount of information conveyed by this problem is two bits. If a pitcher only has two pitches that he throws with equal likelihood, the information conveyed would be one bit. Suppose a pitcher only had one pitch? Say it's a fastball. How much information would this convey? Since you don't have to ask which pitch is coming, the event carries no information and should present a good batter with little difficulty.

It is also possible to calculate information conveyed using a mathematical formula. However, since the mathematical approach is rather tedious and complex it is beyond the scope of this text. Students interested in pursuing the mathematical derivation of information conveyed may do so by consulting the writings of Fitts and Posner (1967) and Keele (1973).

Estimating information conveyed is relatively easy when events are equally likely to occur. For example, estimating the amount of information conveyed in figure 2.3 was relatively easy. However, if the probability of one of several events occurring is unequal, then the calculation of information conveyed is complex

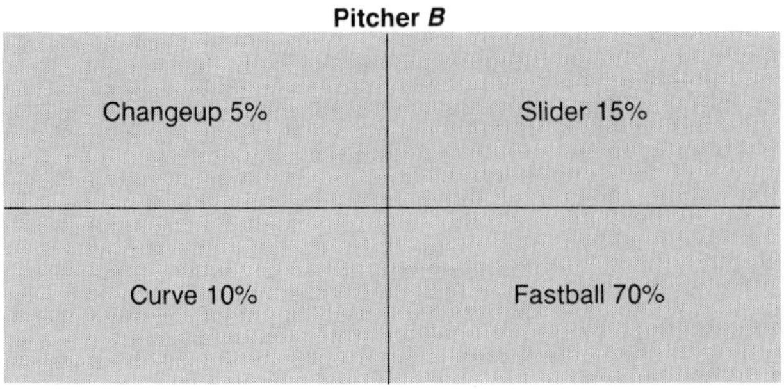

Pitcher B

Changeup 5%	Slider 15%
Curve 10%	Fastball 70%

Figure 2.4 Pitcher B has four pitches at his command. However, the probabilities are not equal. What is the average amount of information conveyed?

requiring a mathematical approach to solve. Consider the baseball example displayed in figure 2.4. In this case the pitcher (pitcher B) has four pitches at his command, but he does not throw them each with equal regularity; rather, he tends to throw his fastball 70 percent of the time. Would this situation convey more or less information than the equal probability case displayed in figure 2.3? The answer is that it would convey less information (1.25 bits) than the equal probability case (2.00 bits) and therefore present less of a challenge to the hitter. It is harder to outguess a pitcher who throws four pitches with equal probability than to outguess a pitcher who throws the same four pitches with unequal probability. Why is this so? Because you would be right 70 percent of the time if you "sat" on or looked for the pitcher's fastball.

The practical implication of all this is enormous. Since bits of information represent difficulty or complexity, athletes should increase the amount of information that their movements convey to the opposition. At the same time, they must learn to reduce the amount of information that is being presented to them. How can they do this?

First of all, let's consider how information conveyed can be increased. For one thing, you can learn to make each of your responses equally likely. If you are a basketball center, don't always dribble the ball before shooting. Develop several alternatives, and use them with equal probability. If you are a spiker in volleyball, master all the different shots and use them with equal probability. You also need to disguise your responses so that you don't "telegraph" your intentions. What good does it do to have four pitches at your command if you tip the batter off by some idiosyncrasy? Finally, and perhaps most importantly, master as many offensive moves as you can. A tennis player capable of making eight different shots conveys more information than a player who can make only four. The difference between eight shots and four shots, if they are all equally likely, is one bit of information, which is a great deal.

2. **Principle** An athletic response can be made more difficult to interpret in terms of information conveyed.

   Application Let's use the baseball pitching example. Your pitcher's difficulty in terms of information conveyed can be increased in three ways. First, the pitcher must master as many different pitches as possible. Second, the pitcher must throw each pitch with equal probability. Finally, the delivery should provide no cues to the batter as to which pitch is coming. A combination of these three factors maximizes the amount of information conveyed.

Finally, let's consider how to reduce the information a person conveys. One way is to study the other person. Take the baseball pitching example. Say you are a major league player. Find out from your scouts how many different pitches the opposing pitcher has at his command. If he has several, find out which one he throws most often and with what regularity. Does he have a pitch he likes to throw in critical situations? If so, what pitch is it? How about mannerisms? Does he telegraph pitches? Even in the major leagues, some pitchers are quite predictable, although the best are not. Another approach to minimizing information is through positioning and strategy. Basketball players, boxers, and volleyball players do this. If you are guarding a basketball player who loves to fake right and drive left, then overplay that person on the left so that he or she cannot drive left. This will leave the right side open, and since that player does not prefer this, the information is effectively reduced.

Let us consider one final example in the game of volleyball. While on defense, the back row player who is playing directly behind the block has responsibility for covering hard down-the-line spikes and short tips or "dinks" just over the block. This assignment is very difficult and conveys a relatively large amount of information. If the player starts approximately 20 feet from the net and with the outside foot on the right sideline, then the player has to look for a dink, a hard spike to the left, the right, and one directly at him or her. If each event is equally likely, this problem conveys two bits of information. The information in this problem can be reduced to less than two bits in several ways. The first and most obvious way is to become familiar with the opposing spiker's capabilities and the likelihood of spiking or dinking in a given situation. A second approach to minimizing the information conveyed would be to straddle the sideline instead of placing the outside foot on it. This would increase the danger of having an out-of-bounds ball hit the player's leg, but it would reduce the possible responses to

three instead of four (1.5 bits of information). A third way to reduce the information conveyed would be to teach the player how to "read" the block. Specifically, if the set ball "disappears" behind the block, then the defensive line player should predict dink, since a ball spiked down the line should be blocked. There is some danger in having a spike go over the block and down the line, but with the middle back defense, this ball should be covered by the middle back player anyway (Cox, 1980, p. 63). With some imagination, this same procedure of estimating information conveyed and then reducing it can be applied to literally hundreds of sport-specific situations.

3. **Principle** Through careful analysis and study, the amount of difficulty conveyed by an athletic situation can be reduced.
   Application A case in point is the reduction in information conveyed by the "wish bone" offense in football. By teaching defensive players to key in on specific offensive players, coaches have learned to defeat or at least contain this high-powered offense. In this case, the important thing is for athletes to focus their attention on their assignment and to ignore other distracting movements.

In most dynamic sporting events the critical and decisive difference between success or failure is delay in responding, or in **response delay**. Response delay is literally a function of the amount of information conveyed. For example, in basketball the offensive player with the ball can usually defeat a quicker defensive opponent if the offensive player can cause a delay in responding. If the offensive player is both an inside and outside threat, a feint toward the basket will allow the offensive player the split second necessary to get an outside jump shot off. The feint increases the information conveyed and in turn increases the response time of the defensive player to try to stop the jump shot. A nearly identical situation develops in the game of badminton when the attacking player feints a smash or deep clear but hits a drop shot instead.

Selective Attention

Humans' ability to **gate out** or ignore irrelevant sensory information, and to pay **selective attention** to relevant information is of incalculable value. Perhaps the best way to dramatize this point is to consider the schizophrenic patient who may suffer an impaired capacity to sustain attention. At one extreme, the patient may attend to some internal thought to such an extent that he or she becomes catatonic. At the other extreme, the patient may be incapable of selectively attending to anything. Although young schizophrenic patients describe their difficulties in different ways, the following extract is considered typical (McGhie & Chapman, 1961):

> I can't concentrate. It's diversion of attention that troubles me . . . the sounds are coming through to me but I feel my mind cannot cope with everything. It is difficult to concentrate on any one sound . . . it's like trying to do two or three different things at one time. . . . Everything seems to grip my attention although I am not particularly interested in anything. I'm speaking to you just now but I can hear noises going on next door and in the corridor (p. 104).

Each of us has experienced the feeling of overstimulation that can result in an inability to concentrate, but can you imagine experiencing this problem every waking hour? If it were not for our ability to concentrate on one or two relevant items at a time, we simply could not function. While you are reading this page, you are selectively attending to one thing at the expense of several others.

The ability to selectively attend to the appropriate stimuli is critical in most athletic situations. In basketball, the athlete must concentrate on the basket while shooting a free throw rather than being distracted by the noise from the crowd. In volleyball, the athlete must selectively attend to the server instead of being distracted by thoughts of a previous play. In baseball, the base runner must attend to the pitcher, and not to the jabbering of the second baseman. In football, the quarterback must selectively attend to his receivers, while gating out the sights and sounds of the huge defensive linesmen who are lunging at him. Of course, some athletes are better than others at selectively attending to important cues. This is one of the differences between the good athlete and the outstanding athlete.

As we watch sport on television and in person, many times athletes can be observed engaging in various psychological ploys to gain an advantage. Usually these ploys are manifested in some sort of verbal dialogue, such as commenting on things unrelated to the contest. Base runners, in baseball, have been picked off first or second base while engaging in innocent chatting with an infielder. When and if these ploys (intentional or otherwise) are successful, it is usually related to inappropriate selective attention. The athlete simply is not attending to the appropriate stimuli. This, as well as information overload, will cause a delay in responding.

---

4. **Principle** Selective attention is perhaps the single most important cognitive characteristic of the successful athlete.

   Application All sporting events contain critical "keys" or cues that must be selectively attended to. In volleyball, blocking may be the most decisive offensive weapon in scoring points, because a team is generally blocking when it is serving, and points can only be scored off the serve. To take advantage of this situation, the blockers must selectively attend to the assigned attacker, and must not be distracted by actions of the setter, fakes by other spikers, or even by the ball.

Our discussion of selective attention would not be complete without a brief review of some of the research on this important topic. The basic question that researchers have asked is "How can we selectively attend in the first place?" While they have been unable to answer this question completely, they have provided some guidelines. If you refer back to figure 2.1, the information processing model, you will see that initially the individual receives numerous stimuli, perhaps hundreds. Somehow these stimuli are either **attenuated** (reduced) or gated out so that the individual can concentrate on the most important stimuli.

E. Colin Cherry, an English psychologist, was perhaps the first to experimentally study selective attention. Cherry (1953) addressed himself to the problem of the **cocktail party phenomenon.** He observed that, at a cocktail party, one stands in a crowded room talking with one group of people while at the same time trying to listen to all sorts of interesting conversations going on nearby. Cherry asked two questions about this situation. First, how is it that we can selectively attend to one conversation when others are occurring all around us? Second, how much do we retain of the conversations we are not listening to, but are nevertheless hearing?

Cherry, of course, could not find the answers to these questions at a cocktail party, so he proceeded to study them in a laboratory. The basic experimental design of his studies has become a model for much of the later research. Specifically, Cherry introduced the concept of **shadowing.** In his research, the subjects were exposed to two different spoken messages at the same time. Through headphones, one message was presented to the left ear, while the other was presented to the right ear. Subjects were then asked to repeat out loud (shadow) the message to the right ear without making any errors. Afterwards, the subjects were asked to repeat anything that they heard in the left ear. Subjects reported that they could tell if a man or woman was speaking, and whether the left ear signal was human or not, but that was about all. They could not correctly report detailed aspects such as language spoken, individual words, or semantic content.

From this early work by Cherry, several models of selective attention have emerged that purport to explain the cocktail party phenomenon. All of these models have one thing in common: They all hypothesize that somewhere in the model a **bottleneck** or **selective filter** occurs that restricts the amount of information that can be selectively attended to at one time. While the various models all hold that a bottleneck does exist, they tend to differ on where in the model it occurs. One category of model holds that the bottleneck occurs during the stimulus categorization phase of information processing. This sort of theory proposes that only selected stimuli receive detailed analysis by the brain, and that most information from the senses is gated out and is never analyzed. Broadbent (1957, 1958) proposed such a model, which is known as the **Broadbent model.**

Another model, called the **pertinence model** (Norman, 1968), holds that the bottleneck occurs when the person is required to select a response. This model proposes that all stimuli automatically activate their representations in memory and are analyzed. However, it is important to understand that this analysis does not require attention. In fact, it is not until the person tries to select a response to a stimulus that the bottleneck occurs, or attention is required.

A third category of model, called the **Triesman model** (Triesman, 1965), is basically a combination of the Broadbent and Norman models. While Tiesman's model is very complex, it effectively addresses the strengths and weaknesses of the other two models. Selective attention is a process by which the brain attenuates irrelevant information, while at the same time saving a large amount of information for analysis. The information that reaches memory is analyzed but not attended to unless it is determined to be important or critical. Once the athlete's attention is captured by a certain event, he or she cannot be distracted until something more pertinent contacts memory.

For highly trained and skilled athletes, the process of selective attention is very efficient. When skilled basketball players step up to the foul line, they refuse to allow anyone or anything beside the task at hand to capture their attention. Coaches refer to this process as "concentration." However, some athletes never do learn how to cope with distraction. Every little event distracts them, or they concentrate on the wrong things (e.g., dribbling), and relevant cues are missed.

---

5. **Principle** Selective attention is a skill that can be learned.
   Application There is no doubt that some athletes are better at selective attention than others. However, there is no reason to believe that this skill cannot be learned. The secret is for the coach to identify the important cues and then to provide drills that require the athlete to selectively attend to them. A good example might be shooting free throws in basketball. The key, of course, is to concentrate on the basket. However, few athletes learn to do this during practice, since there are rarely any distractions to cause their attention to wander. A game-like situation with fans and opponents would help the athlete to learn selective attention.

Limited Information Processing Capacity

An alternative approach to studying attention is to view it in terms of information **processing capacity** or *space*. In the previous section we discussed attention in terms of our ability to selectively gate out irrelevant information. In this section, we are concerned with the capacity to attend to more than one thing at a time. In view of our discussion of selective attention, this may seem paradoxical. However, we can readily see that human beings seem to be able to attend to more than one thing at a time. For example, a skilled basketball player can dribble a basketball, hold up one hand and signal a play, and respond to a teammate who is cutting to the basket. A person driving a car can carry on a conversation with a passenger, steer the car, and shift gears all at the same time. How can this be? Didn't we just conclude that the human mind can attend to only one piece of information at a time? Not necessarily; we only concluded that the human mind is capable of selectively attending to one thing at the expense of others.

According to Kahneman (1973), a person's limited ability to do several things at the same time seems to indicate that the total amount of attention that can be deployed at one time is limited. Different tasks impose demands on this limited

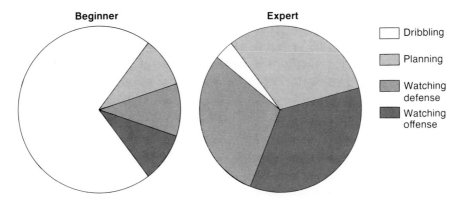

Figure 2.5 Relative amounts of available information processing space for a beginning basketball player and a skilled player.

capacity. When the supply of attention does not meet the demands of the tasks, performance suffers. This view is consistent with Keele's (1973) observation that information processing capacity is synonymous with the concept of available space. If some motor task cannot be performed simultaneously with another verbal or motor task, then one or both tasks are said to take space. Conversely, if several tasks can be performed at the same time, then apparently some or all of them require no space. Thus, in this **capacity model** of attention, when two tasks cannot be performed simultaneously without a decrement in performance, we do not ask where the bottleneck is, but rather how much information processing space does each task demand? This important concept is illustrated in figure 2.5.

In the capacity model of attention, more than one input can be attended to at one time and more than one response can be made at one time, if the demands on available space are not too severe. If any particular task requires all available space, then only that task will be attended to, and all others will suffer a performance decrement.

6. **Principle** Each athlete's information processing capacity or space is limited.

   Application If, as a coach, you require athletes to attend to more information than they have processing space to handle, you are inviting failure. The notion of processing space is not the same as intelligence.

The concepts of selective attention and limited information processing capacity are germane to the sport psychologist, coach, or teacher who is interested in improving athletic performance. Wrisberg and Shea (1978) demonstrated through the use of the **reaction time probe technique (RT probe)** that the attentional demands of a motor act decrease as learning increases. In other words, as a motor act becomes automatic or learned, the demands on the limited information processing capacity of the athlete decrease, and the athlete can attend to other cues. In the RT probe procedure, the subject must perform a simple reaction time task while at the same time performing a primary motor task. If reaction time is slower than normal, then the primary task is judged to require attention and hence, information processing space. The significant difference between a beginning basketball player and a skilled one appears in the demands placed on information processing space. In a game, dribbling requires nearly all of the available processing space of the beginner. He or she cannot hear the coach, see the basket, see other players, or do anything except attend to the task of dribbling. On the other hand, the skilled player has reduced the attentional demands of dribbling to such a degree that he or she can see and hear all kinds of relevant cues while dribbling.

In critical game situations, a highly disciplined tennis player can benefit from this even if the opponent is equally skilled. For example, in a close game of professional tennis, one can expect close calls by line judges to significantly distract each player. The professional who is able to gate out the adverse decisions and attend to the game should have a decisive advantage. This is true because playing flawless tennis and fretting over a bad call both demand information processing space. To try to attend to both will result in a decrement in performance.

---

7. **Principle** The information content of various skills and processes can be reduced so that available information processing space seems to increase.

   Application For a beginning soccer player, the mere act of dribbling the ball will require so much information processing space that there is room for nothing else. The athlete will not be able to pass to the open player, see plays develop, or even avoid an opponent. However, once the skill of dribbling is mastered, the player will be able to do all of this and more. It is not that information processing space has increased, but the information content of dribbling has been reduced to near zero.

Attentional Narrowing

An athlete's ability to attend to appropriate stimuli during competition has been termed **attentional focus.** The concept of attentional focus includes the ability of an athlete both to narrow and to broaden his or her attention when necessary. For example, in basketball the guard who initiates a fast break must be able to broaden his or her attentional focus in order to see teammates on either side as they break toward the basket. This same player must be able to narrow attentional focus while shooting free throws in order to gate out distractions from the crowd.

The notion of **attentional narrowing** is best understood in terms of **cue utilization.** As explained by Easterbrook (1959), attentional narrowing is a function of available cues. Environmental cues provide the athlete with needed information for a skilled performance. In any sport task, many cues are available to the

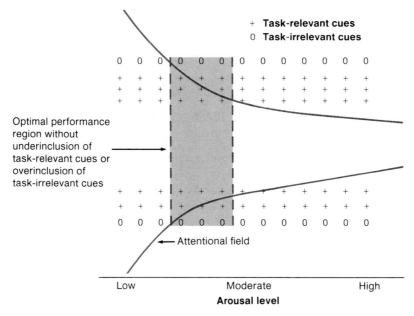

Figure 2.6 Cue utilization and the arousal-performance relationship. From Daniel M. Landers, the arousal-performance relationship revisited. *Research Quarterly for Exercise and Sport,* 1980, *51,* 77–90. Reprinted by permission of the publisher, the American Alliance for Health, Physical Education Recreation and Dance, 1900 Association Dr., Reston, VA 22091.

athlete. Some of these are relevant and necessary for quality performance; others are irrelevant and can damage performance. Under conditions of low arousal, the athlete picks up both relevant and irrelevant cues. The presence of irrelevant cues should result in a decrement in performance. As arousal increases, the athlete's attention begins to narrow (Landers, Qi & Courtet, 1985). At some optimal point, attentional narrowing gates out all of the irrelevant cues and allows the relevant cues to remain. At this point performance should be at its best. If arousal increases still further, attention continues to narrow and relevant cues will be gated out, causing a deterioration in performance. The phenomenon of attentional narrowing is illustrated in figure 2.6.

When a quarterback drops back for a pass, he needs a relatively wide band of attentional focus in order to pick up his receivers. However, if the band is too wide, he will pick up such irrelevant cues as the noisy crowd and the cheerleaders. This will cause a decrement in performance (arousal level is too low). As arousal level increases, attention narrows and irrelevant cues are eliminated. However, in a very intense game situation, arousal may be very high. Consequently, further narrowing of attention may cause the quarterback to gate out such relevant cues as the secondary receivers, position of defensive backs, or the possible outlet pass.

8. **Principle** Attentional narrowing has the effect of reducing cue utilization.

   Application Broad attentional focus allows the athlete to attend to important cues, but the distraction of irrelevant cues can hurt performance. Narrow attentional focus allows the athlete to attend to only the most critical cues, but can also hurt performance because many relevant cues could be eliminated. Successful athletes are often required to adjust their attentional focus so that it is appropriately narrow in one situation, yet broad in another. A point guard in basketball must have broad attentional focus to be able to pass to the open player on offense, but must have a narrow band of attention on the foul line.

Measuring Attentional Focus

Landers (1988) has identified three primary ways in which attention may be measured by sport psychologists. In method one, a *behavioral* assessment of attention is made using the reaction time probe technique. In this procedure, attention demands of a primary task are estimated based on a subject's performance on a secondary reaction time task.

The second method used by sport psychologists for assessing attention is through *physiological indicators*. As illustrated in figure 2.6, physiological arousal and attentional focus are closely related. As the level of arousal increases, an individual's attentional focus tends to narrow.

The third method identified by Landers for assessing attention is through the use of the *self-report*. While behavioral and physiological indicators of attention tend to measure attentional abilities at a specific point in time, the self-report method has tended to be more of an indicator of attentional focus as a personality trait or disposition. The primary originator of the self-report method for assessing attentional focus is Robert Nideffer (1976a, 1976b, 1980a, 1980b). Nideffer called his self-report inventory the **Test of Attentional and Interpersonal Style (TAIS).** Basing his research on reviews by Silverman (1964) and Wachtel (1967), Nideffer reasoned that an athlete's attentional processes could be represented as a function of two independent dimensions. The first he called width and the second he called direction. As illustrated in figure 2.7, the width dimension of the athlete's attentional focus ranges from broad to narrow, while the direction dimension varies from internal to external. Figure 2.7 also gives examples of athletic situations that fall at certain points on the two-dimensional scale. Some situations require the athlete both to broaden and to narrow attentional focus at the same

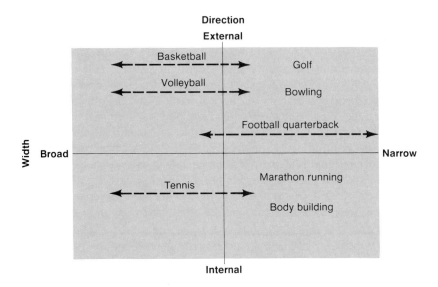

Figure 2.7 Attentional styles of various types of athletes. Dotted lines suggest flexibie styles that can accommodate varying situations. From R. M. Nideffer, Test of attentional and interpersonal style. *Journal of Personality and Social Psychology*, 1976, *34*, 394–404. Copyright 1976 by the American Psychological Association. Adapted by permission of Robert M. Nideffer, Ph.D., Enhanced Performance Associates, San Diego, CA.

time. For example, the quarterback in American football needs to narrow his focus of charging linemen, but broaden it of the three or four receivers he has on the field.

The vertical axis in figure 2.7 identifies the attentional focus dimension of direction. Some athletes seem to be internally directed, while others seem externally directed. Bowlers must attend to certain external cues such as the arrows on the lane and the spots on the floor. However, one might expect marathon runners to be inner directed and to attend to internal cues that will help them, whereas a linebacker in football might be categorized as ideally having a broad-external attentional style. However, it is important to point out that the superior linebacker should also be able to narrow his focus while tackling and to internalize while contemplating the next defensive play. Thus, the effective athlete should have an attentional focus that is appropriately flexible. The manner in which an athlete directs his or her attention is referred to as **attentional style.**

Table 2.1 Attentional Subscale Definitions. From R. M. Nideffer, *The inner athlete: Mind plus muscle for winning,* 1976. Reproduced with permission of Robert M. Nideffer, Ph.D., Enhanced Performance Associates, San Diego, CA.

BET (Broad-External)
The higher the score, the more the individual's answers indicate that he deals effectively with a large number of external stimuli. He has a broad-external focus that is effective.

OET (External Overload)
The higher the score, the more the individual's answers indicate that he makes mistakes because he is overloaded and distracted by external stimuli. He has difficulty narrowing attention when he needs to.

BIT (Broad-Internal)
The higher the score, the more the individual indicates that he is able to think about several things at once when it is appropriate to do so. He has a broad-internal focus.

OIT (Internal Overload)
The higher the score, the more the individual indicates that he makes mistakes because he thinks about too many things at once. He is interfered with by his own thoughts and feelings.

NAR (Narrow Effective Focus)
High scorers indicate that they are able to narrow attention effectively when the situation calls for it.

RED (Errors of Underinclusion)
High scorers have chronically narrowed attention. They make mistakes because they cannot broaden attention when they need to.

Development and Use of the TAIS

Nideffer (1976b) developed the TAIS using college students as subjects. On the basis of theoretical formulations, he identified seventeen different aspects of attentional and interpersonal behavior. Of the seventeen TAIS variables, six reflect attentional processes, two reflect behavioral and cognitive control, and nine describe interpersonal style. Test development procedures identified 144 items (questions) belonging to the seventeen variables or subscales. The six subscales that reflect attentional processes are broad external attentional focus (BET), overloaded by external stimuli (OET), broad internal attentional focus (BIT), overloaded by internal stimuli (OIT), narrow attentional focus (NAR), and reduced attentional focus (RED). Each of these six attentional style subscales is defined in table 2.1.

High scores on three of the six attentional subscales reflect positive attentional traits (BET, BIT, and NAR), while high scores on the remaining scales reflect negative attentional traits (OET, OIT, and RED). As you will recall from our discussion in chapter 1 on personality, a trait is considered to be a relatively stable personality disposition.

9. **Principle** A person's general attentional style can be measured through the use of Nideffer's Test of Attentional and Interpersonal Style (TAIS).

    Application For a modest fee, the TAIS can be purchased from the Behavioral Research Applications Group. Like any other personality test, correlations between actual athletic performance and scores on the test will be low. If used properly, the test results can help athletes and coaches recognize areas of attentional strengths and weaknesses.

Table 2.2 Attentional Assessment Using TAIS Short Form. From R. M. Nideffer, *The inner athlete: Mind plus muscle for winning,* 1976. Reproduced with permission of Robert M. Nideffer, Ph.D., Enhanced Performance Associates, San Diego, CA.

BET (Broad-External)
1. I am good at quickly analyzing a complex situation, such as how a play is developing in football or which of four or five kids started a fight.
2. In a room filled with children or on a playing field I know what everyone is doing.

OET (External Overload)
1. When people talk to me, I find myself distracted by the sights and sounds around me.
2. I get confused trying to watch activities such as a football game or circus where many things are happening at the same time.

BIT (Broad-Internal)
1. All I need is a little information and I can come up with a large number of ideas.
2. It is easy for me to bring together ideas from a number of different areas.

OIT (Internal Overload)
1. When people talk to me, I find myself distracted by my own thoughts and ideas.
2. I have so many things on my mind that I become confused and forgetful.

NAR (Narrow Effective Focus)
1. It is easy for me to keep thoughts from interfering with something I am watching or listening to.
2. It is easy for me to keep sights and sounds from interfering with my thoughts.

RED (Errors of Underinclusion)
1. I have difficulty clearing my mind of a single thought or idea.
2. In games I make mistakes because I am watching what one person does and I forget about the others.

Since use of the entire TAIS is somewhat impractical for the coach or teacher, Nideffer recommends a shortened version for use by the athlete. This shortened version is a selection of two questions each from the six attentional process subscales (Nideffer, 1976a, 1976b). These twelve questions are selected from the fifty-two designed to measure attentional processes. Since this self-assessment version of the TAIS is so short, it would not be as reliable as the entire test, and is not recommended for research purposes.

Questions for the short self-assessment version of the test are reproduced in table 2.2. The athlete merely responds to each question on the following Likert-style scale: 0, never; 1, rarely; 2, sometimes; 3, frequently; and 4, all the time.

Using procedures explained by Nideffer, the athlete then adds his or her scores for each of the subscales and plots them on a graph as illustrated in figure 2.8.

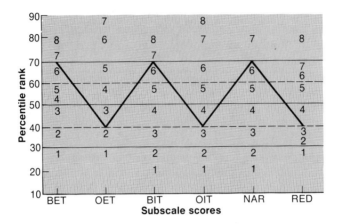

Figure 2.8 Profile of an effective attentional style. From R. M. Nideffer, *The inner athlete: Mind plus muscle for winning,* 1976. Reproduced with permission of Robert M. Nideffer, Ph.D., Enhanced Performance Associates, San Diego, CA.

The profile shown in this figure is that of an athlete who theoretically has an effective attentional profile.

A helpful adaptation of the self-assessment test might be to reverse the Likert scale during scoring for the OET, OIT, and RED subscales. This would eliminate the confusing zigzag line on figure 2.8, and would result in a relatively straight line that would be either high (effective attentional profile) or low (ineffective profile). This would also make it possible to sum the scores on the subscales and come up with a total composite score that would be representative of the attentional focusing ability of each athlete.

Validity of the TAIS

While Nideffer has demonstrated that the TAIS is a reliable test, no persuasive evidence has been presented to demonstrate that it is a valid test, or that it measures what it claims to measure—in other words, that it has **predictive validity.** In sport research, Nideffer (1976b) reported that compared to skilled swimmers, less-skilled swimmers were overloaded with external (OET) and internal (OIT) stimuli. However, differences on other attentional subscales were not apparent. Among rifle marksmen, Landers and Courtet (1979) and Landers, Furst, and Daniels (1981) did not observe a reliable relationship between shooting ability and attentional processes. They did observe, however, that the BIT subscale correlated significantly with the shooting performance of highly experienced marksmen, and that better shooters were less likely to be overloaded with external stimuli or to make mistakes due to exclusion of important cues. Additionally, Van Schoyck and Grasha (1981) demonstrated that the TAIS could not effectively discriminate among three skill levels of tennis players. Finally, Landers (1982) summarized the research on the TAIS and concluded that the strength of the questionnaire lies in its ability to detect breadth of attention. However, its weakness lies in its inability to predict the direction of attention (internal-external).

Critics of the TAIS seem to feel that the test is not valid because of low correlations with athletic performance. However, since the TAIS is essentially a personality inventory, this sort of argument would render all personality tests invalid! Personality characteristics account for a small part of the total picture in terms of predicting athletic success. Yet, these factors do play a consistent and decidedly important role in the long view.

In answering his critics, Nideffer (1987) developed a very compelling argument in favor of using the TAIS as a diagnostic rather than a predictive tool. Using data from fifteen elite springboard and tower divers, he demonstrated that the predictive validity of a test could be increased simply by altering an athletes response set when taking the test. Yet, this same procedure renders the test ineffective as a diagnostic tool. Nideffer altered the athletes' response set by asking them to respond to each item in a diving context and to compare themselves with the average elite diver as they selected their response.

Sport-Specific Tests of Attentional and Interpersonal Style

Perhaps the reason that the Nideffer test has not demonstrated a high degree of predictive validity is that it is not a sport-specific or situation-specific test. As you may recall from the chapter on personality of the athlete, researchers and practitioners were cautioned to adopt an interaction or situation-specific model when dealing with athletes and their personalities. The development of situation-specific personality inventories is one way to conform to the need for an interactional model. Since Nideffer's test is a general test of the personality traits associated with attentional style, then the development of situation-specific tests should prove useful.

At least three serious attempts have been made to develop situation-specific attentional style tests from the TAIS. Etzel (1979) conducted the first study with rifle shooters. Hypothesizing that attention consists of five subcategories, Etzel developed the **riflery attention questionnaire (RAQ)**. The RAQ is a sport-specific test with questions related to the following subcategories of attention: capacity, duration, flexibility, intensity, and selectivity.

Van Schoyck and Grasha (1981) developed a sport-specific test for tennis (**T-TAIS**) and compared it with the Nideffer parent test (TAIS) for internal consistency, test-retest reliability, and predictive validity. For the T-TAIS, Van Schoyck and Grasha rewrote each item of the Nideffer test for the dimensions of BET, OET, BIT, OIT, NAR, and RED. Both the TAIS and T-TAIS (for the six specified dimensions) were administered to ninety tennis players (forty-five men and forty-five women) who were ranked according to tennis-playing ability. Results of the analysis revealed that the internal consistency and test-retest reliability of the tennis-specific test were superior to Nideffer's parent test. The T-TAIS was also a better predictor of tennis-playing ability than the TAIS. Van Schoyck and Grasha's results challenge Nideffer's basic contention that attentional style is a function of both width and direction of focus. Rather, they observed that attentional style is best represented by the width dimension. It appears that the dominant and multidimensional nature of band width tends to minimize the importance of direction. In summary, the authors concluded that a situation-specific test of attentional style is more reliable and valid than the general test.

Finally, Albrecht and Feltz (1987) developed the baseball/softball batting test of attentional and interpersonal style (**B-TAIS**). Like the situation-specific test of batting attentional style, the B-TAIS demonstrates higher levels of reliability and internal consistency than the parent test. In terms of predictive validity (correlations with season batting averages) the B-TAIS was again superior to the TAIS. The B-TAIS demonstrated positive correlations between effective attention subscales and performance, whereas the TAIS did not. In the case of ineffective subscales, both the TAIS and the B-TAIS correlated negatively with performance. From these results it would appear that the ineffective subscales (OET, OIT, and RED) for both tests correlate appropriately with batting performance. However, only the effective subscales (BET, BIT, and NAR) for the B-TAIS correlate appropriately with performance. As with most situation-specific personality tests, the predictive validity of the test is enhanced when an interaction model between the person and the situation is used.

In terms of practical application, coaches and teachers could develop situation-specific versions of the shortened TAIS (table 2.2). For example, table 2.3 is a situation-specific adaptation of Nideffer's short form. The twelve general questions in table 2.2 were rewritten for table 2.3 to fit the volleyball situation.

---

10. **Principle** Situation-specific tests of attentional style that increase the predictive validity of Nideffer's TAIS have been developed.
    Application Tests of attentional style have been developed for tennis (T-TAIS), riflery (RAQ) and baseball/softball (B-TAIS). Situation-specific shortened versions of the TAIS can be easily developed by the teacher or coach. For example, a shortened version of the TAIS for measuring volleyball attentional focus appears in table 2.3.

Table 2.3 Attentional Assessment Using V-TAIS Short Form. From R. M. Nideffer, *The inner athlete: Mind plus muscle for winning,* 1976. Reproduced with permission of Robert M. Nideffer, Ph.D., Enhanced Performance Associates, San Diego, CA.

BET (Broad-External)
1. I am good at quickly analyzing a complex situation, such as how a play is developing in the three-attack multiple offense.
2. During a long rally in a volleyball match, I am totally aware of what every other player is doing.

OET (External Overload)
1. During time-outs, when the coach is talking to me, I find myself distracted by the sights and sounds around me.
2. I get confused trying to keep track of my responsibilities on the volleyball court when there is so much switching going on by both teams.

BIT (Broad-Internal)
1. All I need is a little information about my teammates, and I can come up with some good volleyball plays for the team.
2. In the game of volleyball, it is easy for me to bring together all kinds of situations and ideas that could help our team perform better.

OIT (Internal Overload)
1. When I am trying to concentrate on the service reception, I am distracted by thoughts about previous plays in the game.
2. When I am trying to concentrate on the court, I have so many things on my mind that I become confused and forgetful.

NAR (Narrow Effective Focus)
1. When I am preparing to receive a serve or dig a spike, it is easy for me to keep irrelevant thoughts and noises from distracting my concentration.
2. When I am thinking about a particular response to a play in volleyball, it is easy for me to keep sights and sounds from distracting me.

RED (Errors of Underinclusion)
1. I have difficulty clearing my mind of the memory of an unforced error.
2. I make mistakes because I am watching the setter, or one particular player, and I forget about the others.

Associative versus Dissociative Attentional Strategies

As defined by Morgan (1978) and Morgan and Pollock (1977), **associaters** are marathon runners who internalize the direction dimension of attentional focus and attend to the body's feedback signals. **Dissociaters** are defined as marathon runners who externalize the direction dimension of attentional focus and gate or block out feedback from the body. Morgan believed that elite marathon runners tend to be associaters, while less proficient runners tend toward being dissociaters. Morgan's basic theory has generated a great deal of interest on the part of sport psychologists and serious runners in recent years.

The evidence indicates that using an associative strategy is not necessarily the most effective in terms of resultant work, nor do elite marathoners use an internal attentional style to a greater degree than elite runners. Gill and Strom (1985) demonstrated that athletes trained on a leg-extension machine were able to do more repetitions if they used a dissociative strategy than if they used an associative strategy. Furthermore, the athletes reported that they preferred the external attentional style to the internal. Schomer (1986) monitored the attentional behavior of a group of marathoners and demonstrated that superior runners tend to use a wide range of mental strategies ranging from very little to a great deal of internal focusing.

Another interesting research finding (Schomer, 1986) is that a clear linear relationship exists between associative thought processes and increased intensity of the workout. As the level of perceived exertion increases, marathon runners tend to internalize their attentional focus. This principle is illustrated in figure 2.9. Schomer (1987) also concluded that, from the standpoint of safety, the marathon runner is better off using an internal attentional focus. This strategy allows the athlete to be aware of danger signals that might warn him or her of potential injuries.

---

11. **Principle** Using an internal focus during marathon running is not necessarily the most effective and enjoyable strategy, but it is the safest.

    Application Athletes can be taught to use an internal attentional style through training (Schomer, 1987). The coach should provide ongoing positive reinforcement to athletes as they practice associative strategies during long-distance training runs.

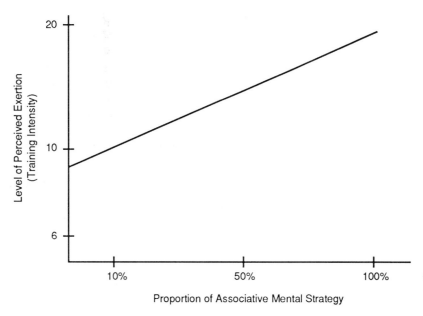

Figure 2.9 Mental strategies and perception of effort of marathon runners. From H. H. Schomer, Mental strategies and perception of effort of marathon runners. *International Journal of Sport Psychology,* 1986, *17,* 41–59. Adapted with permission of the Publisher.

Attentional Focus Training

In this section I will discuss ways in which athletes can use principles of attention for enhanced performance. High level of performance in any human activity requires a certain amount of concentration and attention. If you are a pretty good athlete in any particular sport, then you have mastered some aspects of attention control already. The student who has learned to read a book while others are watching television has developed a high degree of attentional focus. To maximize athletic performance, the athlete must develop a highly refined and developed ability to focus and refocus. As you studied the section of this chapter on cue utilization, you learned that the *width* of your attentional focus narrows as you become more alert and aroused. Thus, it should be apparent to you that attention is tied very closely to the degree of mental and physical activation. As one attends precisely to an event, there is an associated increase in certain internal arousal mechanisms (Fitts & Posner, 1967). In the following chapter on arousal, I will discuss these mechanisms in greater detail.

Types of Attentional Focus

As outlined by Nideffer (1978, 1986), four different types of attentional focus can be attained. These four types of attention have already been illustrated in figure 2.7 as a function of width and direction of attention. An athlete's attentional focus may be categorized as being broad-internal, broad-external, narrow-internal or narrow-external. Different types of attentional focus are required for different athletic situations and events (Nideffer, 1985).

Whether or not attention will be directed internally or externally is primarily a function of required cognition or thought. For example, in order to mentally rehearse a skill or mentally plan a strategy, we must focus internally. Internal attentional focusing can be accomplished with the eyes open or closed. Conversely, external attention requires the athlete to focus on people, events, or objects in the external environment.

Whether or not attention should be broad or narrow is primarily a function of arousal and the number of environmental elements that must be scanned. In order for an athlete to be able to take into account several different game situations and objects, he or she must employ a broad attentional focus. In order to have a broad external focus, the athlete must be able to reduce the level of arousal activation in his or her body. That is why a young quarterback who is in danger of being sacked may fail to see the open receiver. Due to increased arousal, the athlete narrows attention too much and fails to see the big picture. Experienced quarterbacks are often able to find the open receiver, even when a full-scale rush is on. Conversely, the baseball or softball player must focus on a single element when trying to hit a moving ball with a bat. This situation requires an acute or sudden burst of narrowed attention as the ball is released and approaches the plate. Prior to the vital pitch, the batter must display a fairly broad external focus in order to remain relaxed, see the coach's signs, and avoid becoming tense.

Because of the complex nature of attentional focus, it is easy to see why an athlete might adopt an inappropriate pattern of attention for a specific situation. Figure 2.10 illustrates the fluctuation in attentional style that might be necessary for a quarterback in football. Attentional control training requires the athlete to be aware of the various types of attentional focus and to learn to apply each at the appropriate time. Once the athlete understands which type of focus is necessary for specific athletic situations, attentional control can be self-taught and practiced. Harris and Harris (1984) has identified a number of strategies that can be used to improve general concentration. However, for best results, the athlete must practice attentional focus skills in gamelike situations.

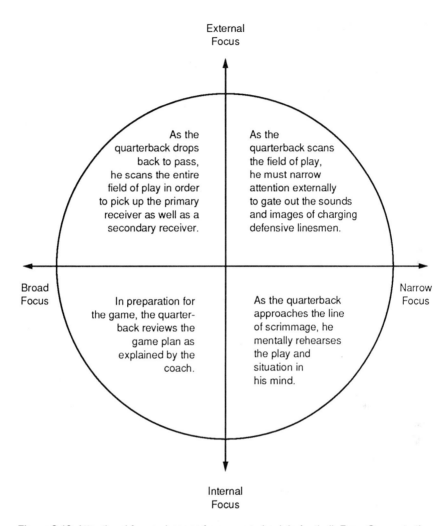

External
Focus

As the quarterback drops back to pass, he scans the entire field of play in order to pick up the primary receiver as well as a secondary receiver.

As the quarterback scans the field of play, he must narrow attention externally to gate out the sounds and images of charging defensive linesmen.

Broad
Focus

Narrow
Focus

In preparation for the game, the quarterback reviews the game plan as explained by the coach.

As the quarterback approaches the line of scrimmage, he mentally rehearses the play and situation in his mind.

Internal
Focus

Figure 2.10 Attentional focus changes for a quarterback in football. From Concentration and attention control training by Robert M. Nideffer. In *Applied sport psychology* by Jean M. Williams, editor, by permission of Mayfield Publishing Company. Copyright © 1986 by Mayfield Publishing Company.

Along with learning various attentional styles, it is critically important that the athlete learn to use attention to stop negative thoughts and to focus on positive thoughts. This is a problem that confronts athletes daily. To overcome feelings of self-doubt, it is necessary to apply the principles of selective attention as discussed in this chapter. In other words, the athlete must develop a high degree of attention control.

Nideffer (1981) defined attention control as a technique designed to keep the athlete from slipping into the cycle of anxiety and self-doubt. Ziegler (1980) refers to the process as **thought stopping.** When athletes feel they are losing control or are attending to irrelevant cues, they must center attention on the most relevant cues. Nideffer calls this the **centering procedure.**

Athletes must learn to recognize the signals that warn them that they are losing control. Let's take a specific example. Say you are standing at the foul line and are about to shoot a game-winning (or -losing) foul shot. The thought goes through your mind, "I'm going to miss, I can feel it. The basket is too small, it's a mile away, and I'm scared!" You are losing control. To successfully use the centering procedure, you must immediately stop the negative suggestion with a positive thought and follow this by attending to a relevant task-oriented suggestion. In this case you should say to yourself, "No, I'm an excellent shooter, and even if I do miss the target it may still bounce in." Now you should follow the positive thought with the task-oriented suggestion, "follow through, and put a little backspin on the ball." By using the centering procedure correctly and practicing it in many different situations, you will have an instant weapon to use against the anxiety spiral.

The following basic steps are used in thought stopping or centering (Nideffer, 1981). One must practice them a great deal before using them in a game.

1. Relax, take a deep breath, and exhale slowly.
2. Displace any negative thought that comes into your mind with a positive thought.
3. Focus or center your attention on an important cue that is relevant to success.
4. Concentrate on a task-oriented suggestion associated with proper form.
5. Use an internal attentional focusing strategy to form a mental image of success.

Learning the centering procedure takes practice. A number of important concepts that I will discuss in detail in the chapter on intervention are involved. These are the processes of relaxation and visual imagery. The critical thing to understand, at this point, is that negative thoughts can be displaced and that through the process of centering, the thoughts that capture our attention can be controlled.

The conscious process of centering will divert the athlete's attention from threatening thoughts and anxiety-producing stimuli. Selective attention will effectively gate out the unwanted thoughts if the correct thoughts are pertinent and meaningful to the athlete.

---

12. **Principle** Thought-stopping and centering skills help an athlete avoid errors caused by negative thoughts and diverted attention.
    Application Thought-stopping skills practiced and developed prior to competition can be used when they are needed. Specific positive thoughts, relevant cues, and task-oriented suggestions can be practiced and readied for competition.

Closely related to the notion of centering and focusing, is the important psychological skill of **refocusing.** In sporting events, it is easy for an athlete to allow his or her attention and concentration to be distracted after initially being very centered and focused. Often this occurs as a result of an error or an official's call. The athlete, rather than refocusing attention on appropriate cues, centers attention inwardly on the distraction. The failure to develop refocusing skills has been the downfall of many athletes. For example, Landers, Boutcher, and Wang (1986) observed a significant relationship between archery performance and focusing on past mistakes. The athlete who focuses on errors and distractions, instead of refocusing on the task, will generally suffer a performance decrement.

From a human performance point of view, there is ample evidence to support the position that attention is an important ingredient for improving athletic performance (Magill, 1985; Schmidt, 1987). In the specific case of thought stopping and centering, Nideffer (1981) presented several case histories involving athletes who reportedly benefited from the procedure. In a study Weinberg, Gould, and Jackson (1980) conducted to determine the effects various cognitive strategies had on the tennis serves of advanced and beginning tennis players, attentional focus (centering) was one of the strategies associated with improved performance. More recently, Boutcher and Crews (1987) demonstrated that the use of a preshot attentional routine can be used to facilitate the performance of female golfers (putting).

Summary

The information processing model of attention includes many variables and processes between a stimulus and a response. Memory plays an important role in information processing. The three types or stages of memory are the sensory register, short-term memory, and long-term memory. Information is measured in bits. The amount of information conveyed by a particular problem can be quantified in terms of questions asked or in terms of a mathematical formula.

People's ability to gate out irrelevant information and to attend to important information is called selective attention. A number of structural models of selective attention have been proposed. Three models reviewed in this chapter were the Broadbent model, Norman's pertinence model, and the Triesman model. Each model proposes that a bottleneck occurs somewhere in the process, resulting in selective attention.

The notion of limited information processing capacity helps explain the difference between skilled and unskilled athletes. If a particular task requires all of a person's information processing space, then none will be left over for attending to other tasks that also require attention.

Easterbrook's cue utilization theory deals with the phenomenon of attentional narrowing. As an athlete's arousal increases, his or her attentional focus narrows. The narrowing process tends to gate out irrelevant cues, and sometimes relevant ones as well.

An athlete's attentional style can be measured through the use of Nideffer's Test of Attentional and Interpersonal Style (TAIS). Situation-specific versions of the TAIS have been developed for riflery (RAQ), tennis (T-TAIS), and baseball/softball (B-TAIS). Coaches can use a shortened version of the TAIS to measure an athlete's attentional focus.

Marathon runners tend to both internalize (associate) and externalize (dissociate) in terms of attentional focus. Associative strategy is not necessarily the most effective in terms of performance enhancement, but it is the safest and is highly correlated with intensity of the running pace. As intensity increases, so does the degree of attentional associating.

Thought stopping and centering is an attentional focusing strategy designed to counter negative thoughts and feelings of self-doubt. Negative thoughts are displaced with positive thoughts and task-oriented suggestions.

Review Questions

1. What is information processing?
2. How much information is conveyed by a pitcher who has mastered four pitches that he throws with equal probability?

3. How could the amount of information conveyed by a pitcher who throws four pitches with unequal probability be increased?
4. Define selective attention. Describe the critical differences between the Broadbent and Norman models of selective attention.
5. How can selective attention help the quarterback in American football? The server·in tennis and volleyball? The shooter in basketball and the receiver in volleyball?
6. How does the concept of selective attention differ from that of processing capacity?
7. In terms of information processing space, explain the difference between the beginning and the advanced basketball player, both of whom are dribbling the ball.
8. What is the effect of arousal upon attentional focus?
9. Discuss some practical applications for the TAIS.
10. Which is better for the tennis player, the TAIS or the T-TAIS? Why?
11. Discuss the importance of attention to athletic performance.
12. In terms of attention and long-distance running, what is an associater? A dissociater?
13. Discuss the different attentional styles displayed by athletes and relate them to actual competitive situations.
14. What is thought stopping and centering? How are they related to attention and how can they improve athletic performance?

Glossary

associaters Long-distance runners who internalize or adopt an internal attentional focus.

attentional focus In sports, an athlete's ability to focus on relevant information during competition.

attentional narrowing The narrowing of an athlete's attentional focus due to an increase in arousal.

attentional style An athlete's particular style of attending to stimuli.

attenuation A weakening of the strength of stimuli.

bit A term that stands for binary digit, a unit of information measurement. The number of bits corresponds to the number of questions needed to accurately predict the occurrence of an event.

bottleneck A restriction in the amount of information that can pass at a certain point in structural models of attention.

Broadbent model A selective attention model devised by Broadbent, who suggested that irrelevant stimuli are eliminated before they reach memory.

B-TAIS Baseball/softball batting test of attentional and interpersonal style.

capacity model A model of attention based on limited information processing space.

centering procedure The process whereby an athlete's attention is brought to focus on an important task-oriented suggestion.

cocktail party phenomenon Cherry's term for the phenomenon that humans standing in a crowded room can selectively attend to one particular conversation to the apparent exclusion of all others.

cue utilization theory Theory proposed by Easterbrook that predicts attentional narrowing and gating out of environmental cues.

dissociaters Long-distance runners who externalize or adopt an external attentional focus.

gate out To exclude or ignore information.

information conveyed The amount of information, in bits, contained in a particular problem. For example, a reaction-time problem containing four lights conveys two bits of information if all four lights are equally likely to flash.

information processing model A model based on the theory that humans process information rather than merely respond to stimuli. Many cognitive processes are involved. For example, information must be stored, retrieved, and rehearsed.

LTM Long-term or permanent memory.

memory storage The notion that all information that reaches memory and can be recalled for later use must be stored.

pertinence model A model of selective attention that proposes that the most pertinent stimuli are attended to.

predictive validity The ability of a test to measure what it claims to measure.

processing capacity The notion that people have a limited amount of space available for the processing of information.

RAQ Riflery Attention Questionnaire, which is a situation-specific test of a person's attentional focus in a rifle-shooting situation.

refocusing The process of returning attention to a relevant stimuli after being distracted.

response delay Delay in reacting or responding to an environmental stimulus.

retrieval The mental process of retrieving information from LTM.

RT probe Used in attention research to determine if a certain primary task requires information processing space.

selective attention The notion that humans are capable of attending to one stimulus at the exclusion of others.

selective filter A filter that either eliminates or attenuates less important information; found in most models of selective attention.

sensory register A short-term sensory store that effectively retains information for about one-half second.

shadowing A research procedure in which a subject is exposed to two different spoken messages at the same time through earphones. This subject's task is to ignore one message and selectively attend to the other. Later, the subject is asked to recall information received in the nonattended ear.

STM Short-term memory, considered to be the center of activity in the information processing system. New information must remain in STM for a minimum of twenty to thirty seconds or it will be lost.

TAIS Nideffer's Test of Attentional and Interpersonal Style.

thought stopping In sport, the process of replacing a negative thought with a success-oriented positive thought.

T-TAIS A tennis-specific TAIS.

Triesman model A complex model of selective attention in which irrelevant cues are attenuated but reach memory for analysis.

Recommended Readings

Broadbent, D. E. (1957). Mechanical model for human attention and immediate memory. *Psychological Review, 64,* 205–215.

Fitts, P. M., & Posner, M. I. (1967). *Human performance.* Belmont, CA: Brooks/Cole.

Keele, S. W. (1973). *Attention and human performance.* Pacific Palisades, CA: Goodyear Publishing Company.

Landers, D. M. (1982). Arousal, attention, and skilled performance: Further considerations. *Quest, 33,* 271–283.

Nideffer, R. M. (1976a). *The inner athlete: Mind plus muscle for winning.* New York: Thomas Y. Crowell Company.

Nideffer, R. M. (1976b). Test of attentional and interpersonal style. *Journal of Personality and Social Psychology, 34,* 394–404.

Nideffer, R. M. (1980a). Attentional focus—self-assessment. In R. M. Suinn (ed.), *Psychology in sports: Methods and applications.* Minneapolis: Burgess Publishing Company.

Nideffer, R. M. (1987). Issues in the use of psychological tests in applied settings. *The Sport Psychologist, 1,* 18–28.

Norman, D. A. (1976). *Memory and attention: An introduction to human information processing* (2d ed.). New York: John Wiley and Sons.

Sperling, G. (1960). The information available in brief visual presentations. *Psychological Monographs, 74*(11), 1–29.

Triesman, A. M. (1965). Our limited attention. *The Advancement of Science, 22,* 600–611.

3   **Arousal in Sport**

Key Terms

arousal
arousal reaction
cerebral cortex
distractibility
drive
drive theory
electroencephalogram
hypothalamus
inverted-U theory
learning

noise
optimal arousal
parasympathetic
   nervous system
performance
reaction potential
reticular formation
signal detection theory
signal plus noise
sympathetic nervous
   system
Yerkes-Dodson law

The story is told of an African hunter who, after losing his weapon, was pursued by a lion. He was running along as fast as he could go with the lion in hot pursuit, when he spotted a tree limb about twelve feet off the ground. Without breaking stride, he leaped with all his might, hoping to jump higher than he ever imagined possible. As luck would have it, he missed the limb going up, but he caught it coming down! This tale illustrates an interesting fact about the phenomenon of arousal. When extremely aroused, we are often capable of astonishing feats. However, note that the man in the story *missed* the tree limb going up. Luckily for him he caught it on the way down, but what does this say about his accuracy?

In the introduction to part two, alertness, or what we shall call **arousal,** is described as one of the three important components of attention. Arousal is synonymous with the notion of alertness; the aroused individual is in a physiological state of readiness. This state of readiness can be represented on a continuum that goes from deep sleep to extreme excitement. The quality of an athlete's performance often depends on how aroused the athlete is.

In this chapter I will explain the neurophysiology of arousal and discuss the relationship between arousal and athletic performance. In chapter 5 of the text I will discuss various intervention strategies for controlling stress and high arousal. In order to really grasp the concepts to be developed in chapter 5, it is critical that the reader understand the neurophysiological causes and mechanisms involved in the outward manifestation of physiological arousal.

As this chapter unfolds, it is also important for you to recognize the relationship between attention and arousal or activation. The process of arousal is one of the important components of attention. As an athlete becomes more keenly aroused, he or she becomes more attentive and more focused. As you will learn later in this chapter, too much arousal can have a negative effect upon athletic performance. Conversely, however, not enough arousal can also have a negative impact on athletic performance.

Neurophysiology of Arousal

To understand arousal is to understand what basic changes take place in the body when the organism is activated. When we speak of arousal, we are talking about the degree of activation of the organs that are under the control of the autonomic nervous system. Much of our understanding of arousal comes to us from the writings of Duffy (1962) and Malmo (1959). These authors discuss arousal in terms of the degree of excitement of the organism. They represent arousal by a continuum ranging from deep sleep to extreme excitement. A term that is often used interchangeably with arousal is *motivation.*

Motivation has to do with the intensity and the direction of a response (Sage, 1984b). The intensity component of motivation is physiological arousal. An athlete may really be charged up to do something physical in a game situation, but without a specific purpose and goal, most of the activity will be wasted. In a later section of the text I will discuss motivation from a directional or goal-related perspective. For the time being, however, I will only consider the intensity dimension of motivation.

Autonomic Nervous System

The nervous system in humans contains two major divisions. These two divisions are the peripheral nervous system, the nerves in the skeletal muscles of the body, and the autonomic system, the nerves in the smooth muscles and glands of the body. That part of the nervous system directly related to activation and arousal is the autonomic nervous system (ANS). It is autonomic in the sense that we do not normally have voluntary control over the organs and glands innervated by it. This is not entirely true, of course, but it is true that normally we do not control such bodily functions as heart rate, blood pressure, skin conductivity, or respiration.

The autonomic nervous system is itself divided into two divisions. These two divisions are the **sympathetic** and **parasympathetic** divisions. The sympathetic division is primarily responsible for changes in bodily functions associated with arousal. For example, it is the sympathetic division that brings about sweating of the hands, increased heart rate, pupil dilation, increased respiration, release of glucose from the liver, and decreased kidney output. The sympathetic division releases catecholamines (adrenalin and noradrenalin) at the postganglionic innervation site of the gland or smooth muscle (with the exception of palmar sweat glands).

The sympathetic division tends to result in arousal of the organism, while the parasympathetic system selectively reduces the effects of the sympathetic division. Stimulation of the parasympathetic division results peripherally in pupil constriction, decrease in heart rate, decrease in respiration, and in general, a return to a homeostatic balance of bodily functions.

Brain Mechanisms

Fundamental to the concept of arousal is the notion that levels of activation come under control of progressively higher levels of the nervous system. Structures of the central nervous system (CNS) that are closely related to the phenomenon of arousal include the cortex of the brain, the hypothalamus, and the reticular formation or ascending reticular activating system (see figure 3.1).

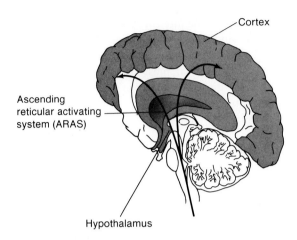

Figure 3.1 Three important brain structures associated with arousal. From Groves, Philip W., and Schlesinger, Kurt, *Introduction to biological psychology,* 2d ed. © 1979, 1982 Wm. C. Brown Publishers, Dubuque, Iowa. All rights reserved. Reprinted by permission.

The **cerebral cortex** is the area of the brain responsible for higher brain functions and conscious thought processes (Hole, 1981). The functional part of the cerebral cortex is comprised of a thin layer of neurons. The total cerebral cortex contains approximately 10 billion neurons (Guyton, 1976). The electrical activity of the cortex is measured with the electroencephalograph (EEG). The EEG can monitor frequency and amplitude of electrical potential changes in the brain. High states of arousal are associated with EEG waves that are desynchronized, fast, and of low amplitude. Low states of arousal are associated with a synchronous pattern of EEG waves (Guyton, 1976).

The **hypothalamus,** a part of the mid-brain, has been shown to be an important part of the arousal system. Lesions of the posterior aspect of the hypothalamus cause sleep and drowsiness (Ranson, 1939), while electrical stimulation of these same areas has been reported to cause alertness and excitement (Hess, 1957). Stimulation of the posterior hypothalamus also causes the secretion and release of catecholamines (neurotransmitting substances) by the adrenal medulla (Sage, 1984a).

The **reticular formation** is a complex set of neurons and nuclei that extends throughout the brain stem from the medulla to the posterior hypothalamus. This network of neurons sends diffuse fibers throughout the nervous system and cortex. It appears that the reticular formation organizes sensorimotor behavior through its interconnections with the cortex, hypothalamus, and nervous system. Along with the cortex and hypothalamus, the activity of the *ascending reticular activating system (ARAS)* is closely associated with the onset of arousal. The ascending axons of the ARAS facilitate the higher brain center neurons. Stimulation

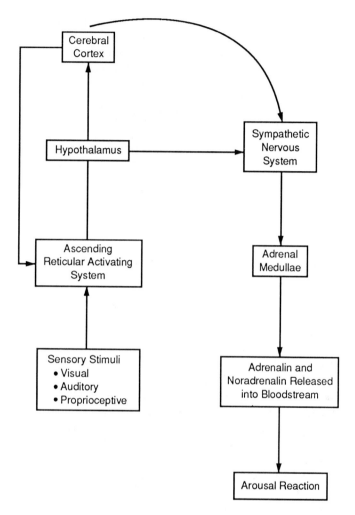

Figure 3.2 Simplified illustration of the anatomical and physiological basis of the arousal reaction.

of the ARAS of sleeping animals results in EEG waves resembling those they would have if awake (Milner, 1970). Lesions of the ARAS in cats result in somnolence (Lindsley, Schreiner, Knowles & Magoun, 1950). When an individual perceives a situation to be threatening or arousing, the reticular formation is activated, and this in turn governs the arousal sequence (Lykken, 1968).

An overview of the process by which the **arousal reaction** is initiated is illustrated in figure 3.2. Any type of sensory stimulus from the environment or from the cerebral cortex can initiate the arousal reaction at the level of the reticular formation (Guyton, 1976). The reticular activating system responds very quickly to bring about a general activation of other brain structures. Almost simultaneously, the sympathetic nervous system is activated by centers in the cortex, spinal cord, brain stem, and hypothalamus. Stimulation of sympathetic nerves to the adrenal medulla causes large quantities of adrenalin and noradrenalin to be released into the circulating blood stream. Until these drugs are reabsorbed into body tissues, the organism will remain in an aroused state.

---

1. **Principle** Stimuli from the environment that are interpreted by the brain as threatening to the individual will automatically initiate the arousal reaction.

   Application It is extremely important for the athlete and coach to understand the rudiments of the physiology of arousal.
   Intervention and stress-management strategies are based in a large degree on learning to reverse the arousal reaction. One must first understand what the arousal reaction is and what causes it.

Preferred State of Arousal

Arousal varies along a continuum from deep sleep to extreme excitement. Yet researchers have consistently observed that organisms seek to attain a level of arousal that is ideal for the task at hand; that is, a level of **optimal arousal.** Schultz (1965) called this internal drive for seeking a state of optimal arousal *sensoristasis.* Duffy (1957) observed that the optimal degree of activation appears to be moderate—not too much arousal and not too little. The curve representing the relationship between arousal and the quality of performance is quadratic, taking the form of an inverted U. Further discussion on this curve appears later in this chapter.

Electrophysiological Indicators of Arousal

There are many electrophysiological methods for measuring arousal level. Some of the more common methods will be outlined here. We should remember that no single measure of arousal can be considered completely accurate; correlations among the various measures of arousal are very low (Gershon, 1984). This means, for example, that someone exhibiting a fast heart rate might not exhibit a decrease in palmar skin resistance.

Electrocortical activity. As we saw earlier, the electrical activity of the brain can be measured by an electroencephalograph (EEG), which measures the amount of electrical activity put out between two scalp electrodes. An **electroencephalogram** (EEG) is the tracing of the brain waves made by an electroencephalograph. Three types of brain waves are associated with the arousal states of sleep (theta waves), awakeness (alpha waves), and excitement (beta waves). Depression of EEG alpha-wave activity is considered to be a strong indicator of heightened arousal (Landers, 1980b).

Biochemical indicators. The arousal or activation response in the brain triggers the release of catecholamines into the bloodstream by the adrenal medulla. Thus, one way to determine arousal levels is to directly measure the amount of adrenalin and noradrenalin in the bloodstream (Lykken, 1968). The accurate assessment of catecholamines requires immediate blood samples, since they readily diffuse into body tissues.

Heart rate. The heart rate of an aroused person is easily obtained with an electrocardiograph (EKG), a device for measuring the electrical activity of the heart. The heart rate can also be indirectly measured with a pulse monitor or by finger palpation. The heart rate is not considered to be a good single indicator of arousal. Its correlation with other more viable indicators is quite low (Lykken, 1968).

Muscle tension. The electrical potentials of muscles can be measured with an electromyograph (EMG), a device that measures electrical activity in a muscle. Woodworth and Schlosberg (1954) have shown that muscle tension levels are roughly equivalent to levels of arousal. Weinberg (1978) and Weinberg and Hunt (1976) have successfully used EMG recordings to indicate arousal levels in motor performance research.

Respiration rate. Rate of respiration is not entirely under the control of the autonomic nervous system, but it is still a fairly reliable indicator of heightened arousal. With a spirometer, a person's respiratory rate, tidal volume, inspiratory reserve volume, expiratory reserve volume, inspiratory capacity, and vital capacity can be measured.

Blood pressure. Arterial blood pressure can be measured with a sphygmomanometer. Blood pressure is an indication of the relative dilation or constriction of the blood vessels associated with the autonomic nervous system. Since blood pressure is generally monitored through repeated application of the pressure cuff and stethoscope, only intermittent recordings can be obtained. For this reason, blood pressure is not considered to be a very good measure of arousal (Martens, 1974).

Palmar sweating. In a threatening situation the increased levels of activation are associated with an increase of sweat from sweat glands on the hands. According to Harrison and MacKinnon (1966), sweat glands of the human palm do not function in response to environmental changes but are activated by alerting stimuli. Techniques for counting palmar sweat glands are detailed by Sutarman and Thompson (1952), Johnson and Dabbs (1967), and Dabbs, Johnson, and Leventhal (1968).

Galvanic skin response. Associated with increased palmar sweating during periods of heightened arousal is a corresponding change in the resistance of the skin to the passage of an electrical current (ohms of resistance). Increased palmar sweating causes a decrease in skin resistance, or galvanic skin response (GSR). A decrease in skin resistance to the passage of electricity from one electrode to another is equal to an increase in skin conductivity. The galvanic skin response is mediated through the sympathetic cholinergic nerve supply to the skin and is attributed to changes in the number of active sweat glands (Montagu & Coles, 1966). Therefore, increased skin conductivity is directly related to an increase in the number of active palmar sweat glands.

The Performance-Arousal Relationship

We turn now to the most important part of this chapter. Nearly every coach or athlete is interested in the effects of arousal on performance. The coach wants to help the athlete reach a level of arousal that will result in the best possible performance. Intuitively, the coach knows that if the athlete is either overaroused or underaroused, that athlete will not produce a stellar performance. The athlete also is aware, from past experience, that a certain optimum level of arousal results in the best performance. However, what neither the coach nor the athlete knows for sure is exactly what level of arousal is ideal, and what can be done to reach this ideal state. It has fallen to the researcher and the sport psychologist to provide answers to these questions.

The rest of this chapter will be devoted to theories that explain the performance/arousal relationship. We will also examine the research support that each theory has received. At times, studies that deal with cognitive and verbal tasks will be reviewed, but our central thrust will be toward understanding the relationship between athletic performance and arousal.

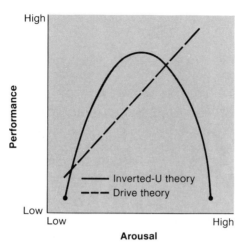

Figure 3.3 Relationship between drive and inverted-U theories.

There are only two basic theories of the performance/arousal relationship. The first is **inverted-U theory,** and the second is **drive theory.** Inverted-U theory includes many subtheories that explain why the relationship between arousal and performance takes the form of the quadratic curve while drive theory is a multidimensional theory of **performance** and **learning.** Drive theory basically proposes a linear relationship between arousal and performance. These two basic theories are illustrated in figure 3.3.

Inverted-U Theory

The inverted-U theory has been around for as long as the arousal/performance relationship has been studied. It simply states that the relationship between performance and arousal is quadratic as opposed to linear and takes the form of an inverted-U (figure 3.3). While it is described as a theory or hypothesis, researchers such as Duffy (1957) and Malmo (1959) consider it to be an observed fact.

One of the difficulties encountered in testing the inverted-U theory with humans is our inability to precisely measure arousal. For example, if in a particular study, researchers fail to demonstrate that heightened arousal causes a decrement in performance, this is not particularly damaging to the theory. The reason for this is that it can always be argued that for that particular task, arousal was not high enough. If it had been higher, we may argue, performance would have declined.

The problem is that there is a limit, from a human rights standpoint, to the amount of arousal that researchers can induce. For example, if arousal is induced through electrical shock, how high can the researcher elevate the shock without violating the subject's rights? Not very high.

The foundation for inverted-U theory is the classic work of Yerkes and Dodson (1908). Using dancing mice as subjects, Yerkes and Dodson set out to discover the relationship between arousal and task difficulty in their effect on performance. Performance was measured as the number of trials needed for the mice to select the brighter of two compartments. Arousal consisted of high, medium, and low intensities of electrical shock. Task difficulty was manipulated in terms of the differences in brightness between two compartments (high, medium, and low difficulty). Results showed that the amount of practice needed to learn the

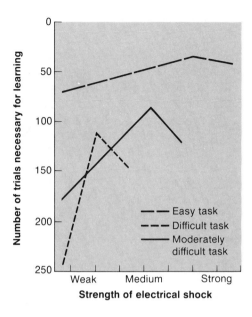

Figure 3.4 Results of the Yerkes-Dodson (1908) research showing the effect of arousal and task difficulty on performance. From R. M. Yerkes and J. D. Dodson, The relationship of strength of stimulus to rapidity of habit formation, *Journal of comparative neurology and psychology,* 1908, *18,* 459–482. Adapted with permission of Alan R. Liss, Inc., publisher and copyright holder.

discrimination task increased as the difference in brightness between two compartments diminished. These findings led to the so-called **Yerkes-Dodson law.** This law states that " . . . an easily acquired habit, that is, one which does not demand difficult sense discrimination or complex associations, may readily be formed under strong stimulation, whereas a difficult habit may be acquired readily only under relatively weak stimulation" pp. 481–482.

The results of the Yerkes-Dodson research are illustrated in figure 3.4. As can be observed in this figure, the optimal level of electrical shock (arousal) for a difficult task was much lower than for an easy task. Additionally, an optimal level of arousal (electrical shock) is indicated for each task. Before and after the optimal point, performance drops off. This is the inverted-U.

In terms of practical sport application, the Yerkes-Dodson law is illustrated in figure 3.5. This figure shows that as the complexity of a skill increases, the amount of arousal needed for optimal performance decreases.

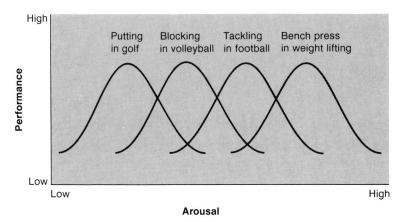

Figure 3.5 Application of the Yerkes-Dodson law in athletic events.

As can be observed in figure 3.5, a high level of arousal is necessary for the best performance in gross motor activities such as weightlifting. Conversely, a lower level of arousal is best for a fine motor task such as putting in golf. Each sport skill has its theoretical optimal level of arousal for best performance. Regardless of which type of skill is being performed, they all conform to the inverted-U principle. Specifically, performance is lowest when arousal is very high or low, and highest when arousal is moderate or optimum.

---

2. **Principle** The relationship between athletic performance and arousal takes the form of the inverted-U.
   Application Preparing the athlete for competition involves more than psyching up. It involves finding the optimal level of arousal for each athlete.

Another important consideration relating to the Yerkes-Dodson law is skill level. Just as putting in golf is a complex activity compared to weightlifting, learning to dribble a basketball is more difficult for a beginner than performing the same task as an expert. The optimal level of arousal for a beginner should be considerably lower than the optimal level for an expert performing the same task. As illustrated in figure 3.6, this concept explains why highly skilled athletes perform better in competitive situations than do novices (Oxendine, 1970).

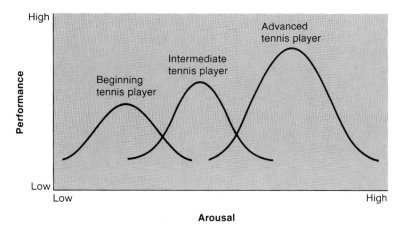

Figure 3.6 Application of the Yerkes-Dodson law to tennis players at varying levels of skill.

3. **Principle** The optimal level of arousal varies as a function of the complexity of the task and the skill level of the athlete.
   Application Highly skilled athletes and athletes performing simple tasks need a moderately high level of arousal for maximum performance. Less skilled athletes and athletes performing a complex task require a relatively low level of arousal for maximum performance.

The notion of an inverted-U relationship between motor performance and arousal is well documented in the literature for such tasks as reaction time (Lansing, Schwartz & Lindsley, 1956), auditory tracking (Stennet, 1957), and hand steadiness (Martens & Landers, 1970). More recently, evidence supporting the relationship in basketball has been reported (Klavora, 1977; Sonstroem & Bernardo, 1982).

Klavora (1977) hypothesized that precompetitive arousal/anxiety and basketball performance would have an inverted-U relationship as predicted by inverted-U theory. In the research, he obtained precompetition arousal/anxiety scores for 145 male high school basketball players throughout the second half of a competitive season. After each game, the coach assessed the performance of each player using a three-point scale (poor, average, outstanding). By plotting each boy's game performance against his arousal/anxiety score for that game, Klavora came up with a bell-shaped curve very close to the expected hypothetical

U-shaped curve. That is, the outstanding performances were associated with the moderate levels of arousal/anxiety, while average and poor performances were associated with the low and high arousal/anxiety scores.

Using a pencil-and-paper test of anxiety as a measure of arousal/anxiety, Sonstroem and Bernardo (1982) demonstrated that an inverted-U relationship exists between basketball performance and arousal/anxiety. In this research, subjects were female university varsity basketball players from eight teams who played at least three games in a preseason double elimination tournament. The performance score was a composite score that included performance on shooting as well as rebounds, assists, steals, fouls, and turnovers. For purposes of analysis, each subject's performance score was plotted against her arousal/anxiety score for that game. Arousal/anxiety scores were categorized as low, moderate, and high without regard for the order of games. Thus for one athlete, the highest level of arousal/anxiety may have occurred during the first game of the double elimination tournament, while for another it may have been the third or fourth. The order of games is not important, but the observation that a moderate level of arousal/anxiety is associated with a high level of performance is important.

Using the same intraindividual analysis procedures outlined by Sonstroem and Bernardo (1982), studies reported by Gould, Petlichkoff, Simons, and Vevera (1987) and Burton (1988) have also confirmed an inverted-U relationship between arousal/anxiety and performance. In the Gould et al. (1987) study, performance was measured as a function of pistol shooting, while in the Burton (1988) study, performance was measured as a function of swimming performance. In both of these studies, the inverted-U relationship was observed when arousal was measured as a function of somatic or bodily arousal/anxiety. When anxiety was purely cognitive in nature, an inverted-U relationship was not observed. I will talk more about the multifaceted nature of anxiety and its relationship to arousal in the following chapter on anxiety.

In yet another study, Beuter and Duda (1985) observed that heightened arousal has a detrimental effect on the motor performance of children. In this kinematic study, it was clearly demonstrated that under conditions of optimal arousal, children perform smooth and automatic movement patterns. However, under conditions of high arousal, movement patterns come under volitional control and are observed to be less smooth and efficient.

While it seems relatively clear that the nature of the relationship between athletic performance and arousal takes the form of the inverted U, it is not clear why this occurs. In the following subsections, three theories that predict an inverted-U theory will be briefly reviewed.

Easterbrook's Cue Utilization Theory

Easterbrook's (1959) notion of cue utilization theory was introduced in chapter 2 and illustrated in figure 2.6. The basic premise of cue utilization or attentional narrowing theory is that *as arousal increases, attention narrows*. The narrowing of attention results in some cues being gated out, first irrelevant cues and later relevant cues. From figure 2.6 it should be clear that attentional narrowing predicts an inverted-U relationship between arousal and performance. When arousal is low, the attentional band is wide and both irrelevant and relevant cues are available. The presence of the irrelevant cues is distracting and causes a decrement in performance. At a moderate or optimal level of arousal, only the irrelevant cues are eliminated, and therefore performance is high. Finally, when arousal is high, attentional focus is narrow and both relevant and irrelevant cues are gated out. This results in a decrement in performance as predicted by the inverted-U theory.

At the higher levels of arousal, it is also important to recognize the phenomenon of **distractibility** (Kahneman, 1970, 1973; Schmidt, 1987). When arousal levels become very high, cue utilization theory predicts that attention narrows. However, there is a point at which a person's attention begins to jump randomly from one cue to another. This process of sporadically directing attention to many different sources is referred to as distractibility. The athlete who experiences this will be confused by the many relevant and irrelevant cues that are momentarily attended to. Page 59 contains a quote from a young schizophrenic patient who suffered from symptoms of distractibility.

---

4. **Principle** Very high levels of arousal may result in distractibility, a phenomenon in which the athlete cannot concentrate on one specific cue.

   Application The phenomenon of distractibility will clearly indicate to the coach that arousal is extremely high. Procedures designed to lower the level of arousal should be immediately implemented (see chapter 5).

The phenomenon of attentional narrowing is easily applied to a sport setting. When a football quarterback drops back for a pass, an optimal level of attention will cause a gating out of irrelevant cues. However, if arousal becomes too high, the quarterback may either suffer from distractibility or gate out relevant cues as a result of his narrow band of attention.

Research supporting this concept of attentional narrowing is very strong, but it is primarily of the laboratory variety. Little if any sport-related research on this theory has been reported.

The basic paradigm used in most of the research was to monitor the performance of some peripheral task while performing a central task under conditions of increased arousal. Typically, as arousal increased, the performer attended to the central task at the expense of the peripheral task. While most of this research equates a peripheral task with an irrelevant task, this is somewhat misleading, since an irrelevant cue need not be a peripheral cue.

Bahrick, Fitts, and Rankin (1952) instructed subjects to perform a central motor tracking task while responding to either irrelevant peripheral light stimuli or the deflection of a needle. Subjects were also placed in either of two conditions of motivation. Results showed that as arousal increased, attention narrowed so that performance on the central task improved but performance on the peripheral tasks grew worse.

Bursill (1958) had subjects perform a central pursuitmeter task while at the same time requiring them to respond to random peripheral lights. Stress was applied in the form of hot and cold room temperatures. Results showed that as thermal temperature increased, subjects narrowed their attention to the central task, and peripheral task performance dropped off.

Weltman and Egstrom (1966) conducted underwater research in which the divers' central task was an addition or dial-watching task, while the peripheral task was to respond to signal lights. Arousal or stress was increased by varying the task environment from the surface to a diving tank to the ocean. Results showed that when subjects were submerged, their response time to the peripheral tasks increased while they maintained constant performance on the central task. Peripheral vigilance was not adversely affected while subjects were on the surface.

Weltman, Smith, and Egstrom (1971) tested the perceptual narrowing hypothesis during simulated pressure-chamber exposure. Subjects were asked to perform a central visual acuity task in an underwater environment while simultaneously performing a peripheral light detection task. Peripheral task performance fell off significantly between the subjects in the stress environment and a control group. The researchers concluded that perceptual narrowing had occurred as a result of psychological stress.

In a study by Bacon (1974), subjects simultaneously performed a pursuit-rotor tracking task and an auditory signal detection task. Results indicated that arousal effectively narrows the range of cues that subjects can process, systematically reducing responsiveness to those aspects of a situation that initially attract less attention.

Most recently, Landers, Qi, and Courtet (1985) reported a sports-related study in which Easterbrook's attentional narrowing theory was supported. In this field experiment, rifle shooters were required to respond to a peripheral auditory reaction time task while at the same time attending to a primary shooting task. Arousal was manipulated as a function of time between rounds fired. The results demonstrated that increased arousal caused a narrowing of attention for the primary task at the detriment of the secondary reaction-time task.

Taken as a whole, this brief review of the attentional narrowing research provides clear support for Easterbrook's cue utilization theory. Increased arousal causes attention to become narrower and more restricted. This can enhance performance up to a certain point, but thereafter it causes a performance decrement. Thus, attentional narrowing theory supports an inverted-U relationship between arousal and performance.

5. **Principle** Increased arousal has the effect of narrowing an athlete's attention.

 Application Athletes who participate in a sport that requires broad attentional awareness need low levels of arousal for best performance. The setter in volleyball must be particularly aware of all aspects of the game. Tunnel vision would seem to be particularly damaging to the setter's play selection.

6. **Principle** Decreased arousal has the effect of broadening an athlete's attentional focus.

 Application Athletes who participate in a sport that requires narrow attentional focus need appropriately increased levels of arousal for the best performance. An athlete attempting a single feat of power and force will need a narrowed focus of attention.

Signal Detection Theory

Another theory that predicts a quadratic relationship between arousal and performance is **signal detection theory** (SDT). Signal detection theory has not been field-tested for the inverted-U concept; however, from a theoretical point of view it should be of interest to the reader.

In its simplest form, signal detection theory holds that the intensity of **noise** (N) in the nervous system falls along a continuum ranging from low to high. The addition of a signal to the noise naturally increases the neural activity. It is the subject's task to discriminate between noise (N) alone and **signal plus noise** (SN). The signal is typically a sound.

Repeated random presentations of test intervals in which a signal may or may not be presented is theoretically represented by two bell-shaped curves. One curve represents the noise distribution, and the other represents the signal plus noise distribution (see figure 3.7). These two curves are believed to be normally distributed, with the greatest frequency of observations occurring at about the mean of each distribution.

The task of subjects in an SDT experiment is to respond by saying "yes" if they detect a signal and "no" if they do not. Obviously, the constant presence of neural noise makes the task potentially difficult. If the neural activity seems high, the subject will likely respond "yes." If the neural activity associated with a test interval seems low, he or she will be likely to respond "no." A subject's ability to

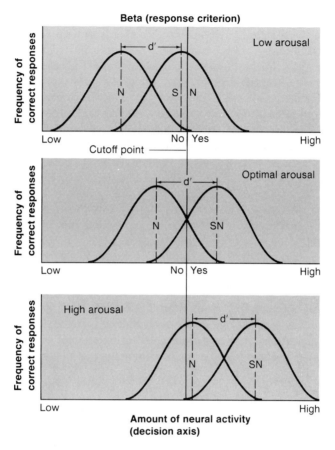

Figure 3.7 Relationship between level of arousal and signal detectability. From "Stress and performance" by A. T. Welford, 1973, *Ergonomics, 16*(5), 567–580. Copyright © 1973 by Taylor & Francis, Ltd. Adapted with permission of the publisher.

discriminate between the noise and the signal plus noise distributions is called the subject's "sensitivity." In figure 3.7, sensitivity is indicated by d'. It represents the distance between the means of the N and SN distributions.

One important factor that determines whether a subject will respond yes or no to a particular stimulus is the subject's response bias or *response criterion* (beta). Some people exhibit a very stringent criterion and refuse to respond yes unless they are positive they heard a signal. Others have a lenient criterion and will respond yes even if the signal appears weak. Subjects with a stringent criterion miss detecting many signals, while those with a lenient criterion often identify signals that do not in fact appear.

Welford (1973) has hypothesized that high or low levels of arousal have the effect of altering the position of a subject's response criterion. Figure 3.7 shows this. Increased arousal causes brain cells to become activated and more ready to fire. Increased activation of brain cells would increase the neural activity of any particular point along the decision axis in figure 3.7. As this occurs, both distributions would tend to shift to the right due to increased neural activity. Since the response criterion is relatively stationary, shifting the distributions to the right would cause the response criterion to shift to the left in relation to the two distributions. This process would be reversed during sleep or low arousal.

In the low-arousal situation, the errors tend to be a failure to detect a signal (error of omission). In the high-arousal situation, the errors tend to be false identification of signals (error of commission). In the optimal arousal situation, the errors are ideally balanced between false alarms and misses. This model is very appealing, because one would expect errors to increase with high and low levels of arousal, but the nature of the error is different due to the activation or deactivation of brain cells.

---

7. **Principle** Sports that require instant decisions require a moderate level of arousal to avoid errors of commission or omission.
   Application An overly aroused batter in baseball will tend to swing at bad pitches (error of commission), while the underaroused hitter will allow called strikes (error of omission). A moderate level of arousal will tend to balance out the two kinds of decision errors.

From this explanation, it should be clear that with extreme shifts in the response criterion from the left to the right, we have the inverted-U relationship between signal detectability and arousal. For example, consider what would happen in the high arousal situation if beta shifted clearly to the left of both distributions. This would result in a totally lenient response criterion by which subjects would respond yes every time they were asked if they detected a signal. Assuming a signal was presented 50 percent of the time, this would yield a 50 percent error rate. Conversely, if in the low-arousal situation, the criterion shifted completely to the right of both distributions, the subject would respond no to every test observation. Again, a 50 percent error rate would result. Thus, high and low levels of arousal yield a decrement in performance, while an optimum level of arousal yields the best performance.

In sport, the SDT model can be applied to officials, who must routinely make split-second decisions. Was the pitch a ball or a strike? Was the runner safe or out? The SDT model is easily applied to these situations by simply assigning the two curves to each of two possible decisions (Cox, 1987; Hutchinson, 1981). The theory can be used to determine an official's bias and sensitivity. As with athletes, when the official is underaroused or overaroused, he or she will make more errors than when optimally aroused.

Information Processing Theory

The basic predictions of information processing theory for the stress/performance relationship are identical to those of signal detection theory. Both theories predict the inverted-U relationship between performance and arousal, and both support the Yerkes-Dodson law. Welford (1962, 1965) gives a basic outline of the theory's predictions. However, the theory is presented without the support of research evidence in the motor domain.

According to Welford (1962), brain cells become active with increased levels of arousal and they begin to fire. As this happens, the information processing system becomes noisy and its channel capacity is reduced. At low levels of arousal the system is relatively inert, and performance is low. At high levels of arousal, a performance decrement occurs because of the reduced information processing capacity of the channels. At some optimal level of arousal, the information processing capacity of the system is at its maximum, and performance is at its best.

Drive Theory

Perhaps the great contribution of drive theory is that it helps to explain the relationship between learning and arousal, as well as between performance and arousal. Many young athletes are just beginning the process of becoming skilled performers. The effect of arousal upon a beginner may be different than upon a skilled performer. The basic relationship between arousal and an athlete's performance at any skill level is given in the following formula:

$$\text{Performance} = \text{Arousal} \times \text{Skill Level}$$

This formula represents a very simple summary of drive theory. Specifically, performance on a task is a function of the person's arousal multiplied by how well the task is learned.

Drive theory, as developed by Hull (1943, 1951) and Spence (1956), is a complex stimulus-response theory of motivation and learning. The complexity occurs as Hull and Spence attempt to link the stimulus conditions (S) with the overt response through a series of presuppositions. The basic formula as agreed on by the two researchers is reflected in the following equation:

$$S \longrightarrow \boxed{H \times D = RP} \longrightarrow R$$

The items in the box are intervening variables (theoretical constructs) that cannot be observed, but only inferred.

Drive (D) was originally conceived in terms of need reduction. That is, an organism responded because of an unsatisfied need, which was referred to as a drive. When the need (e.g., hunger, thirst, sex) was fulfilled, the drive was reduced or eliminated. The notion of drive later included learned drives. This adjustment allowed the concept of drive to be used in sports.

Habit (H) is a hypothetical construct that represents the true state of learning (Schmidt, 1972). For Hull and Spence, learning takes place as a result of the contiguity (proximity) of a stimulus and response under the condition of reinforcement. The strength of the habit, given contiguity of stimulus and response, is a function of the number of previous reinforcements. For our purposes, habit strength will be considered to be synonymous with degree of learning of a motor skill.

The effect of drive (arousal) upon a learned habit is to raise the **reaction potential** (RP) of the organism. Reaction potential represents the level of excitement of the organism. In any condition of competing responses, one correct and the other incorrect, the selected response is the one associated with the highest reaction potential. This concept is clearly represented in the following two equations:

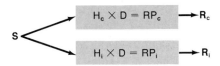

In any situation, there is generally more than one possible response as a result of one stimulus or set of stimuli. One of the possible responses would be the correct response (R_c), while the other or others would be an incorrect response (R_i). There can be many incorrect responses, but typically only one correct response. Increased arousal will elicit the dominant response among several competing responses, where the dominant response is the one associated with the strongest RP. The dominant response may or may not be the correct one (R_c), and we should expect the dominant response to be incorrect with a complex task or in the early stages of learning. Thus, increased drive or arousal would result in a decrement in performance. Conversely, in the late stages of learning or with a simple task, the dominant response should be the correct one, and increased arousal should facilitate performance. In summary, drive theory proposes that:

1. Increased arousal (drive) will elicit the dominant response.
2. The response associated with the strongest reaction potential is the dominant response.

3. Early in learning or for complex tasks, the dominant response is the incorrect response.
4. Late in learning or for simple tasks, the dominant response is the correct response.

From these drive theory tenets we can make several practical applications. First, heightened levels of arousal should benefit the skilled performer but hamper the beginner. The coach with a relatively young team should strive to create an atmosphere relatively low in anxiety and arousal. Low levels of arousal should increase the beginner's chances of a successful performance. In turn, the experience of success should strengthen self-confidence. Skilled athletes, on the other hand, will benefit from an increase in arousal. Similar applications can be made to the performance of simple and complex tasks. For example, a complex task, such as throwing a knuckleball in baseball, will always require a low level of arousal. Conversely, a very simple task, such as doing a push-up, would seem to benefit from arousal.

---

8. **Principle** The effect of increased arousal on an athlete performing a complex task or learning a novel task will be to elicit an incorrect response, which will be the dominant response.
   Application With beginners it is important that the environment be one of low arousal and stress. Young athletes tend to make more mistakes if they become excited and overly activated.

---

9. **Principle** The effect of increased arousal on an athlete performing a simple or well-learned task will be to elicit a correct response, which will be the dominant response.
   Application Highly skilled athletes will often benefit from increased arousal. The effect of psyching up a basketball star like Larry Bird could have grave consequences for the opposing team.

Since we previously observed that the relationship between performance and arousal is quadratic (inverted U), the linear prediction of drive theory is contradictory. At least, this is true for the well-learned or simple task. How can this be? Do we simply dismiss drive theory, as Martens suggests (1971a, 1974), or is there a plausible explanation? Actually, proponents of drive theory recognized this problem at an early date, and recommended adjustments in the model. Broen and Storms (1961) suggested that the problem could be handled within the drive theory framework by hypothesizing a maximum ceiling effect for the RP. Thus, when the ceiling is reached, higher levels of drive cannot raise the RP any higher, and at some point (as arousal increases) the reaction potential for the correct and incorrect responses will be equal. This will again cause competition between the correct and incorrect responses, and performance will deteriorate.

---

10. **Principle** Even though drive theory predicts a linear relationship between arousal (drive) and performance, at extremely high levels of activation, performance will be negatively affected.

   Application The coach and athlete must recognize that too much arousal is detrimental for any athletic task. As with inverted-U theory, an optimal level of arousal should be identified for each task and athlete combination.

Research support for drive theory is mixed, especially in terms of motor performance. The complexity of the theory makes it difficult to test. For example, how do researchers determine when a response shifts from being dominant to nondominant? And how do researchers determine if a subject is skilled or unskilled, or whether a task is simple or complex? Many ingenious studies have been designed by inventive researchers to solve these problems. Yet, if a study fails to support drive theory, does one conclude that drive theory is faulty, or that the experimental design failed to satisfy the complexities of the theory? There is no easy answer to this question. The theory is very appealing and has survived over thirty years of research. As Janet Spence (1971) wrote, "What can you say about a twenty-year-old theory that won't die?"

Research on the theory has taken two directions. First, researchers hypothesized that drive is synonymous with the personality trait of anxiety. If an individual scores high on a pencil-and-paper test of general anxiety, they are categorized into a high-drive condition. This approach failed miserably, as reviews by Martens (1971a) attested. One simply cannot reliably predict athletic performance based on a single personality variable such as anxiety. For example, Sonstroem and Bernardo (1982) with basketball players and Gould, Horn, and Spreeman (1983a) with wrestlers were unable to show a relationship between the two. The relationship is tenuous at best.

A second approach taken by researchers studying drive theory was to equate drive with a situation-specific measure of anxiety or arousal. This was accomplished through a physiological measure of arousal or a pencil-and-paper test of situation-specific anxiety (i.e., feelings of tension and apprehension). This approach has proven much more rewarding, if not less complex.

In the following review, this second approach was adopted by the investigators; specifically, the authors equate drive with the terms stress, anxiety, and arousal.

Castaneda and Lipsitt (1950) trained subjects to press a button in response to a stimulus light. Half of the subjects performed a dominant tendency correct (DTC) task in which stimulus lights and response buttons were congruent. The other half performed a dominant tendency incorrect (DTI) task in which the lights and response buttons were incongruent. Results supported drive theory, in that stress facilitated the performance of the DTC group, but inhibited performance of the DTI group.

Ryan (1961) had subjects practice on a stabilometer task for five days. Subjects received twelve thirty-second trials each day. They were treated identically during days one through four, but on day five, half of the subjects received an electrical shock during their twelve practice trials. Results showed no differences in performance between the stress and no-stress groups for day one or day five. Thus, stress did not facilitate performance of well-learned tasks as predicted by drive theory. The author, however, wondered if the correct response was learned well enough after the five days of practice to be considered a dominant response. In a follow-up study, Ryan (1962) again tested subjects on the stabilometer, but manipulated the degree of task difficulty. Subjects received twelve practice trials, and those under stress conditions received shock on seven of the twelve trials. Results provided support both for and against drive theory. Differences were not noted between the high- and low-stress conditions on the simple task. Under drive theory, the stressed group should have shown better performance. But the control group was superior to the group under shock conditions on the complex task, and this finding was consistent with drive theory, since stress should inhibit the performance of a complex task.

Finally, Griffiths, Steel, and Vaccaro (1979) observed that anxiety correlated significantly with performance of complex scuba diving tasks. Specifically, they asked sixty-two beginning scuba diving students to perform four increasingly difficult underwater tasks. Results revealed significant negative correlations of −.46 and −.32 between anxiety and performance on the most difficult tasks. Thus, subjects exhibiting the highest anxiety scores performed most poorly on the difficult tasks. The authors concluded that the results were in general agreement with drive theory, since high levels of drive should inhibit performance on unlearned or complex tasks.

While studies mentioned here generally support drive theory, it should be clear that the theory is difficult to test. For this reason, interest in drive theory has waned in recent years in favor of the inverted-U theories. But drive theory is attractive because it makes useful predictions about the relationship between learning and arousal. The other theories deal primarily with performance.

We can conclude that the relationship between arousal and athletic performance takes the form of an inverted U. And while drive theory does not specifically predict a quadratic relationship between performance and arousal, neither is it inconsistent with this hypothesis. As noted by Broen and Storms (1961), minor adjustments in the drive theory model can accommodate the inverted-U hypothesis.

Summary

Arousal, synonymous with activation and alertness, is one aspect of attention. The neurophysiology of arousal was discussed relative to the autonomic nervous system, specific brain mechanisms, and electrophysiological indicators of arousal and activation. The two divisions of the autonomic nervous system are the sympathetic and parasympathetic. The sympathetic division is responsible for heightened arousal while the parasympathetic division helps to maintain homeostasis. Three of the brain structures and mechanisms that are of significant importance in arousal are the ascending reticular activating system, the hypothalamus, and the cerebral cortex. Some of the electrophysiological indicators of arousal are electrocortical activity (EEG), heart rate, muscle tension (EMG), and the galvanic skin response (GSR).

The relationship between arousal and athletic performance is represented best by the inverted-U curve. The foundation of inverted-U theory is the classic work of Yerkes and Dodson (1908). Three theories that predict a quadratic relationship between performance and arousal are cue utilization theory, signal detection theory, and information processing theory. Cue utilization is based on the principle of relevant and irrelevant cues and attentional narrowing. Signal detection theory is based upon the notion of errors of commission and omission and on a subject's response criterion. Information processing theory is based upon channel capacity and neural activity. Each of the inverted-U theories hypothesize that an optimal level of arousal is necessary for best performance.

Drive theory was discussed in terms of the effects of arousal on learning and performance. In its simplest form, drive theory posits a linear relationship between athletic performance and arousal or drive. According to drive theory, increased arousal elicits the dominant response. For beginners, or when practicing a highly complex task, the dominant response is generally the incorrect response. For simple tasks, or for highly skilled performers, the dominant response is generally the correct response.

Review Questions

1. Explain the role that the autonomic nervous system has in arousal and activation. What are the divisions of the autonomic nervous system? What are the different functions of the two divisions of the autonomic nervous system?
2. Identify specific brain structures and mechanisms associated with the onset and control of arousal. How do these structures interact with each other and the environment to bring about general arousal?
3. What are some of the electrophysiological techniques for assessing arousal? Discuss advantages and disadvantages of each.
4. Discuss the research conducted by Yerkes and Dodson (1908) and explain how their findings relate to inverted-U theory.
5. As hypothesized by inverted-U theory, what is the nature of the relationship between arousal and athletic performance?
6. Discuss the concepts of distractibility and optimal arousal relative to inverted-U theory and athletic performance.
7. Explain how cue utilization theory proposes an inverted-U relationship between arousal and performance. How can the theory take into consideration such factors as skill level and complexity of the task?
8. Explain how signal detection theory proposes an inverted-U relationship between arousal and performance. What is a subject's response criterion? How is sensitivity of a subject determined?
9. Discuss the arousal/performance relationship in terms of drive theory.
10. According to drive theory, arousal enhances the elicitation of the dominant response. In terms of learning and performance, what does this mean?

Glossary

arousal Activation of the various organs of the body that are under the control of the autonomic nervous system.

arousal reaction Arousal of the individual through sudden activation of the reticular activating system.

cerebral cortex A layer of neurons, approximately 10 billion in number, on the surface of the brain.

distractibility A condition that occurs with high arousal, in which an athlete's attentional focus moves randomly from cue to cue, resulting in poor performance.

drive A notion similar to anxiety and arousal, originally conceived in terms of need reduction.

drive theory Complex theory of learning that predicts a linear relationship between drive (arousal) and learning.

electroencephalogram Measurement of the electrical activity of the brain.

hypothalamus A portion of the brain stem that is involved in the regulation of sleep, wakefulness, and bodily activation.

inverted-U theory Describes the observed relationship between arousal and performance. The term originates from the shape of the curve that results when the arousal/performance relationship is plotted on a graph.

learning A relatively permanent change in behavior.

noise In signal detection theory, noise represents random firing of the nervous system.

optimal arousal The notion that for every skill there exists an optimal level of arousal for maximum performance. Explicit to the understanding of the inverted-U relationship between arousal and performance.

parasympathetic nervous system A branch of the autonomic nervous system that operates to maintain bodily homeostasis.

performance Used to estimate learning, but susceptible to fluctuations caused by such factors as motivation, boredom, and fatigue.

reaction potential The level of potential excitement of the individual. A psychological construct associated with drive theory.

reticular formation A diffuse area of the core of the brain responsible for general alerting and activation of the brain.

signal detection theory Psychophysical method based on statistical decision theory for determining a person's response bias and sensitivity.

signal plus noise Signal presented against a noise background in signal detection.

sympathetic nervous system A branch of the autonomic nervous system that is responsible for preparing the individual for action.

Yerkes-Dodson law A result of the classic work by Yerkes and Dodson (1908), the law predicts an inverted-U relationship between arousal and performance. It also states that complex tasks require less arousal than do simple tasks for optimal performance.

Recommended Readings

Broen, W. F., Jr. & Storms, L. H. (1961). A reactive potential ceiling and response decrements in complex situations. *Psychological Review, 68,* 405–415.

Easterbrook, J. A. (1959). The effect of emotion on cue utilization and the organization of behavior. *Psychological Review, 66,* 183–201.

Gould, D., Horn, T., & Spreeman, J. (1983a). Competitive anxiety in junior elite wrestlers. *Journal of Sport Psychology, 5,* 58–71.

Guyton, A. C. (1976). *Structure and function of the nervous system.* Philadelphia: W. B. Saunders Company.

Hole, J. W., Jr. (1981). *Human anatomy and physiology.* Dubuque, IA: Wm. C. Brown Company Publishers.

Klavora, P. (1977). An attempt to derive inverted-U curves based on the relationship between anxiety and athletic performance. In D. M. Landers & R. W. Christina (eds.), *Psychology of motor behavior and sport.* Champaign, IL: Human Kinetics Publishers.

Landers, D. M. (1980b). The arousal-performance relationship revisited. *Research Quarterly for Exercise and Sport, 51,* 77–90.

Martens, R. (1971a). Anxiety and motor behavior: A review. *Journal of Motor Behavior, 3,* 151–179.

Martens, R. (1974). Arousal and motor performance. *Exercise and Sport Sciences Reviews, 2,* 155–188.

Sage, G. H. (1984). *Motor learning and control: a neuropsychological approach.* Dubuque, IA: Wm. C. Brown Company Publishers.

Sonstroem, R. J., & Bernardo, P. (1982). Intraindividual pregame state anxiety and basketball performance: A re-examination of the inverted-U curve. *Journal of Sport Psychology, 4,* 235–245.

Spence, J. T. (1971). What can you say about a twenty-year-old theory that won't die? *Journal of Motor Behavior, 3,* 193–203.

Welford, A. T. (1973). Stress and performance. *Ergonomics, 16,* 567–580.

Part Three Anxiety and Intervention in Sport

Anxiety, stress, and worry about the athletic experience on the part of athletes is a major area of concern. It is estimated that many young athletes drop out of organized sport each year due to frustration and fear of failure. Many young athletes thrive on the pressure and tension associated with competitive sport. However, far too many find that the experience precipitates feelings of apprehension and stress.

In this section I discuss the phenomenon of anxiety and how it affects the athletic experience. I present numerous strategies designed to intervene and reverse the negative effects of anxiety on the athlete. Knowing how to use these strategies is based on an understanding of the neurophysiology of the nervous system as introduced in the previous chapter on arousal. To a large extent, intervention strategies are used to counter the effects of runaway anxiety and associated arousal. However, it is also important to realize that psychological intervention strategies can also be used to motivate and increase the attentional readiness of the athlete.

Two chapters are devoted to the broad topic of anxiety and intervention. Chapter 4 deals with anxiety from an informational point of view. Basic questions about the nature, cause, and measurement of anxiety are answered. These and many other issues related to the phenomenon of anxiety are addressed. In chapter 5 I discuss intervention and stress management strategies that control and reverse the harmful effects of anxiety. Intervention strategies such as relaxation training, visual imagery, and hypnosis are introduced and explained. Goal-setting strategies that are used to increase motivation and interest are also discussed within the context of intervention. ∎

4   **Anxiety in Sport**

Key Terms

anxiety
cognitive state anxiety
competitive A-state
competitive A-trait
competitive process
CSAI
CSAI-2
distress
ego threat
eustress
inverted-V pattern
objective competitive
   situation

objective demand
SAI
SCAT
somatic state anxiety
state anxiety
stress
stress process
subjective competitive
   situation
TAI
TMAS
trait anxiety

The following story about a young athlete illustrates the potential debilitating effects of anxiety on athletic performance: Ryan is a physically gifted sixteen-year-old athlete. He participates in several sports for his high school during the academic year and plays summer baseball as well. Some of the team sports he excels in are football, basketball, and baseball. However, his favorite sport is track and field, which is primarily an individual sport.

Ryan is a highly anxious young man with a tendency toward perfectionism. In Ryan's particular case, these traits had very little negative effect on his performance in the team sports that he played. He would often get uptight about a big game, but he could always rely upon his teammates to help him out. The fact that team games involved other players seemed to help control the negative impact that his anxiety could have had on his performance. Ryan occasionally "clutched" up during baseball games, but the outcome of the game was rarely affected. Usually, only Ryan and Ryan's parents were aware of the anxiety and tension that was boiling within.

However, track and field was a different matter. Ryan was a sprinter and hurdler. His physical power and mesomorphic build made him especially well equipped for running and jumping events that required speed and leg power. Unfortunately, his basic anxiety and worry about failing had a serious effect on his performance during competition. During practice, Ryan always did well. In fact, during three years of high school Ryan had never lost a race to a teammate during practice. In actual competition things were different. Ryan began preparing mentally for his races days in advance of the actual competition. During the days and hours preceding competition his anxiety would rise to fearful levels. By the time actual competition came, Ryan could hardly walk, let alone run or jump. Several times he had to vomit before important races. His coach talked to him a great deal about learning to relax and not worry about the race, but didn't give him specific suggestions on how to accomplish this. Finally, the coach decided to remove Ryan from his favorite events because he was actually a detriment to the team. This was more than Ryan could take. He approached the coach one day and announced that he was going to give up athletics altogether and concentrate on his studies.

This story actually has a successful conclusion, but I will wait until the beginning of the chapter on intervention strategies to share it with you. In this chapter I will address a number of important topics designed to help the reader to better understand anxiety and its potential effect on performance. I will first define anxiety and attempt to explain how anxiety relates to a number of other common and nearly equivalent terms. Second, I will discuss a number of pencil-and-paper and other techniques for measuring anxiety. Three other topics I will discuss include sport competition and anxiety, the multidimensional nature of anxiety, and precompetitive anxiety.

Defining Anxiety

In its simplest form, **anxiety** may be defined as a subjective feeling of apprehension and heightened physiological arousal (Levitt, 1980). It is closely associated with our concept of fear. An athlete who manifests anxiety before and during competition will experience an elevated level of arousal and feelings of tension and apprehension.

As we saw earlier, arousal is a neutral term that reflects activation of the sympathetic nervous system. It refers to the intensity of physiological activation, and does not indicate emotions. For example, both fear and joy can cause an increase in physiological arousal. However, fear is associated with negative affect, whereas joy is associated with positive affect.

Sport psychologists often use the terms *stress* and *anxiety* interchangably. This is very confusing to physiologists, because stress to the exercise physiologist refers more to the activation of the sympathetic nervous system. Hans Selye (1975), often referred to as the *father of stress,* defined **stress** as the "nonspecific response of the body to any demand made upon it." In other words, stress like arousal is a *neutral* physiological response to some sort of stressor. The stressor could be in the form of physical exercise, or it could be some sort of bodily harm threat. Selye (1975) and Humphrey (1986) further differentiated the nature of stress by referring to positive stress as **eustress** and negative stress as **distress.** Harris (1980b) referred to positive affect (joy, exhilaration, happiness) in sport as eustress, while Martens (1982) defined anxiety in terms of negative affect (fear, apprehension, worry). In other words, Selye's use of the term *distress* is virtually identical to Martens' use of the term *anxiety*.

Distress as defined by Selye is situation specific. That is, an athlete becomes distressed when a particularly disagreeable call is made by an official (anger). However, the degree to which an athlete responds to this situation with anger may be related to the athlete's predisposition toward being easily distressed. Charles Spielberger introduced the terms *trait* and *state anxiety* to represent these two conceptualizations. Spielberger defined **state anxiety** as an immediate emotional state that is characterized by apprehension, fear, and tension. State

The stress process

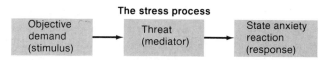

Figure 4.1 The stress process as adapted from R. Martens (1982). From R. Martens, *Sport competition anxiety test.* Copyright © 1982 Human Kinetics Publishers, Inc., Champaign, IL. Adapted by permission of the publisher.

anxiety involves acute feelings of apprehension and tension accompanied by physiological arousal. **Trait anxiety,** however, is a feature of personality. It is a predisposition to perceive certain environmental situations as threatening, and to respond to these situations with increased state anxiety (Spielberger, 1971).

In recent years, sport psychologists have tended to interchange the terms *state anxiety* and *distress*. However, in most cases the prefix *dis-* is dropped for the more common term *stress*. Stress as defined by Martens (1982) refers to the process that is associated with the occurrence of state anxiety. This process is explained in terms of an objective demand, a perceived threat, and a state anxiety reaction. The **objective demand** represents the situation that the athlete is placed in; it is considered a stimulus. Whether or not the athlete sees the objective situation as threatening depends on his or her subjective evaluation of the situation and the role of trait anxiety in his or her personality. The relationship between the objective situation and the response can also be explained in terms of an imbalance (McGrath, 1970). That is, stress will occur if the perceived demand is not balanced by the athlete's perception of his or her ability to respond. The **stress process** as described by Martens (1982) is illustrated in figure 4.1.

An anecdote attributed to Tuckman (1972) and related by Fisher (1976) serves to clarify the relationships illustrated in figure 4.1. Two researchers were studying the effects of fear of drowning on the physiological responses of a subject. The subject was strapped to the side of a swimming tank with the water steadily rising. For some reason the researchers left the test area and forgot about their subject. When they remembered, they were aghast and numb with fear. Dropping everything, they raced to the test area to find the water level dangerously high. Quickly, they unstrapped the subject and pulled him from the water. Safely on the pool deck they asked the subject if he was frightened. The subject responded that he wasn't at all worried, because it was just an experiment and he knew that the researchers wouldn't let any harm come to him! The subject perceived the test situation (objective demand) to be nonthreatening, and therefore the state anxiety reaction was not evoked.

1. **Principle** Whether or not an athlete responds to a threatening situation with high levels of state anxiety will depend entirely on the athlete's perception of the situation.

   Application Each athlete is different and should be treated as an individual. Do not attempt to predict an athlete's anxiety response to a competitive situation based on your own perception of the same situation. The athlete's own perception of the situation will determine the level of anxiety response, if any.

Measuring Anxiety

In this section I will discuss ways to measure trait and state anxiety. The meanings of the factors being measured are more easily understood when we see how they are used in anxiety tests.

Trait Anxiety

There are many references to tests of trait anxiety (A-trait) in the literature. However, we will only discuss the four that are most commonly used.

Taylor Manifest Anxiety Scale (TMAS) The TMAS was developed by Taylor (1951) from items in the MMPI that were indicative of manifest anxiety. The TMAS contains fifty items to which the subject's response is yes or no (Taylor, 1953). During the 1950s, the TMAS was by far the most commonly used measure of anxiety. A children's version of the test, the CMAS, has also been developed.

Spielberger Trait Anxiety Inventory (TAI) The TAI was developed by Spielberger, Gorsuch, and Lushene (1970) to measure general nontransitory anxiety. The test is composed of twenty items to which the subject responds using a four-item Likert-type scale. A children's version of the TAI for A-trait has also been developed. A revised version of the TAI was published in 1983 (Spielberger, 1983).

Sport Competition Anxiety Test (SCAT) SCAT is a situation-specific modification of the TAI for A-trait developed by Martens. Both a children's (ages 10–15) and adult form of SCAT were developed. Both forms contain fifteen items and require a three-choice Likert-type response (hardly ever, sometimes, often).

The adult form is called the Illinois Competition Questionnaire Form A, and the children's version is Form C (Martens, 1982, pp. 93–94). A sample question from Form A is "before I compete I feel uneasy." SCAT is recommended for measuring an athlete's trait anxiety in a competitive situation. Since its development in 1977, SCAT has been the subject of numerous research investigations and has been used in many studies involving the assessment of personality constructs (Gerson & Deshaies, 1978; Martens & Gill, 1976; Martens & Simon, 1976; Rupnow & Ludwig, 1981; Weinberg & Genuchi, 1980). Plans are currently underway to revise SCAT to reflect the multidimensional nature of trait anxiety (Vealy, 1988).

---

2. **Principle** High trait-anxious athletes tend to respond to competitive situations with higher levels of state anxiety.

   Application Make a point of ascertaining an athlete's general trait anxiety level and/or competitive trait anxiety level. This can be accomplished by using one of the trait anxiety inventories identified under the section on measurement of anxiety. The Sport Competition Anxiety Test is of special interest, since it represents a situation-specific measure of trait anxiety.

Cognitive Somatic Anxiety Questionnaire The CSAQ is a fourteen-item questionnaire designed to assess both cognitive and somatic modes of trait anxiety. The questionnaire was developed by Schwartz, Davidson, and Golemen (1978) and tested for use by Tamaren and Carney (1985). The test is composed of seven items that measure the cognitive or worry dimension of anxiety and seven that measure the somatic or bodily indicators of anxiety. The advantage of the CSAQ is that it takes into consideration the multidimensional nature of trait anxiety.

State Anxiety

Since arousal is associated with state anxiety (A-state), the electrophysiological indicators used to measure arousal can also be used to measure state anxiety. In addition, numerous behavioral indicators of state anxiety have been developed. One category of behavioral measurement is direct observation. In this system, the experimenter looks for objective signs of arousal in the subject and records them. Such things as nervous fidgeting, licking the lips, rubbing palms on pants or shirt, and change in respiration could all be interpreted as behavioral signs of activation. Such a system was developed and used by Lowe (1973) for ascertaining arousal through "on-deck activity" of batters in Little League baseball.

Table 4.1. Checklist for Monitoring Distress Related Behavioral Responses of the Athlete. From Harris, D. V., and B. L. Harris, (1984). *The athletes guide to sports psychology: Mental skills for physical people.* New York: Leisure Press. Adapted by permission of the publisher.

Butterflies in stomach	_____	Increased heart rate	_____
Clammy hands	_____	Increased respiratory rate	_____
Cotton mouth	_____	Irritability	_____
Desire to urinate	_____	Muscle tension	_____
Diarrhea	_____	Nausea	_____
Feeling of fatigue	_____	Resorting to old habits	_____
Flushed skin	_____	Sense of confusion	_____
Forgetting details	_____	Trembling muscles	_____
Heart palpitations	_____	Visual distortion	_____
Hyperventilation	_____	Voice distortion	_____
Inability to concentrate	_____	Vomiting	_____
Inability to make decisions	_____	Yawning	_____

Along these lines, Harris and Harris (1984) have prepared a list of overt behavioral responses that can be used by the athlete to identify indicators of distress or state anxiety. The list is arranged in alphabetical order in table 4.1 and may be used by the athlete as a checklist to monitor state anxiety response during practice, immediately before competition, and during competition.

3. **Principle** The state anxiety response to stressful situations can be observed and recorded through the use of a behavioral checklist.
   Application The athlete should systematically chronicle anxiety-related behavioral responses. Once recorded, the coach will be able to help an athlete identify and control competitive stress.

A second category of behavioral assessment of A-state is subjective in nature and is based on a short pencil-and-paper questionnaire. This technique for measuring A-state is by far the most common method used by sport psychologists. The use of pencil-and-paper indicators for measuring A-state is not without its critics (Landers, 1980b), especially if it is the only indicator used. However, other sport psychologists feel that the pencil-and-paper questionnaire is the most realistic and accurate approach to measuring A-state. Martens (1982), for example, points out that electrophysiological measures are impractical and do not lend themselves well to field research.

While Martens and Landers differ in their confidence in self-report techniques of measuring arousal, they agree that the researcher must be careful in the assessment of arousal regardless of the technique used. One may conclude that the answer to the measurement dilemma rests with the researchers or practitioners. Those responsible for assessing arousal must do so within the scope of available resources, test environment, technical knowledge, and practical implications. In other words, if it is reasonable to monitor heart rate, blood pressure, and skin resistance simultaneously as well as administer a self-report test, then do it. However, if it is not reasonable, this should not deter researchers from doing the best they can with the available resources.

It is also important to note that the relationship between physiological and psychological measures of state anxiety are quite low (Gershon, 1984; Karteroliotis & Gill, 1987; Morrow & Labrum, 1978). Consequently, if both physiological and psychological measures of state anxiety are recorded, it is very possible that conflicting results may be obtained. Gershon (1984) has outlined steps that the researcher may take to obtain better and more consistent physiological measurements. The steps identified by Gershon (1984) underscore the importance of closely monitoring the subjects' responses to specific stimuli.

Some of the more commonly used questionnaires designed to measure A-state will now be discussed.

Activation-Deactivation Checklist (AD-ACL) The AD-ACL was developed by Thayer (1967) to measure activation along four independent dimensions (general activation, general deactivation, high activation, and deactivation-sleep). Associated with each dimension are several adjectives that potentially describe the subject's activation and state anxiety level. Each adjective is scored on a four-point Likert-type scale (4, definitely; 3, slightly; 2, cannot decide; and 1, definitely not).

Autonomic Perception Questionnaire (APQ) The APQ as designed by Mandler, Mandler, and Urviller (1958) is divided into three sections. Section one is a free response section and requires subjects to describe in their own words how they feel in terms of apprehension and pleasure. Section two consists of thirty graphic-scale items dealing with the perception of bodily activity (heart rate, perspiration, temperature changes, respiration, gastrointestinal disturbance, muscle tension, and blood pressure). Section three is composed of thirty-four additional items on bodily perception.

Zuckerman's Affective Adjective Check List (AACL) The AACL, developed by Zuckerman (1960), was one of the first scales developed for measuring A-state. The scale is composed of twenty-one adjectives, eleven categorized as being anxiety-positive and ten anxiety-negative. Anxiety-positive words are scored +1 if checked and anxiety-negative words are scored +1 if not checked. Subjects are asked to check words that express how they feel at a specific point in time.

Spielberger State Anxiety Inventory (SAI) The SAI was developed by Spielberger et al. (1970). The SAI test of state anxiety and the TAI test of trait anxiety were conceived as companion tests. Like the TAI, the SAI is composed of twenty "how I feel" questions. To each question, subjects select one of four Likert-type responses to describe how they feel at any particular point in time. A children's form of the SAI is also available. A revised version of the SAI was published in 1983 (Spielberger, 1983).

Competitive State Anxiety Inventory (CSAI) The CSAI is based on the observation of Spielberger et al. (1970) that as few as five items from the twenty-item SAI inventory could be used as a subscale. Martens (1982) reasoned that a shorter ten-item competitive version of the parent test could be developed. The CSAI is composed of ten items from the parent test that are most closely associated with a competitive situation. Martens (1982) and Gruber and Beauchamp (1979) have reported that the CSAI is suitable for repeated assessment of competitive state anxiety of athletes in a competitive environment. The CSAI is widely used by sport psychologists for measuring state anxiety associated with competition in sport.

Competitive State Anxiety Inventory-2 The CSAI-2 was developed by Martens, Burton, Vealey, Smith, and Bump (1983) and appears in monograph form by Burton and Vealey (1989). The CSAI-2 was developed by the authors to assess the multidimensional nature and aspects of state anxiety. It is believed that a multidimensional approach to the measurement of A-state will provide more specific information about an athlete's response to the athletic experience. The inventory is composed of twenty-seven questions, to which the subject selects one of four Likert-type scale responses. The three dimensions of state anxiety that are assessed include cognitive state anxiety, somatic state anxiety, and self-confidence state anxiety. Cognitive and self-confidence state anxiety are viewed as being at different ends of the same continuum. In a study reported by Karteroliotis and Gill (1987), the multidimensional nature of the state anxiety construct and the independence of cognitive and somatic anxiety were confirmed.

---

4. **Principle** How an individual responds to an event is very often situation specific. The response is also often multidimensional in nature.

　　Application The CSAI-2 is the appropriate tool to use for measuring sport competition state anxiety. It is situation specific and accurately assesses three different dimensions or manifestations of state anxiety.

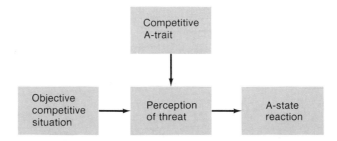

Figure 4.2 Competitive A-trait as a mediator between the competitive situation and the response to the situation. From R. Martens, *Sport competition anxiety test.* © 1982 Human Kinetics Publishers, Inc., Champaign, IL. Adapted by permission of the publisher.

Sport Competition and Anxiety

Since the early 1960s, the influence of anxiety in contemporary society has been increasingly recognized. This is especially true in competitive sports. Sport competition is one example of an objective situation that can result in increased state anxiety or stress. The stress process illustrated in figure 4.1 can be easily modified to fit the competitive situation illustrated in figure 4.2.

The "perception of threat" component of figure 4.2 is synonymous with Martens's (1975) notion of a **subjective competitive situation.** It has to do with how the athlete perceives the **objective competitive situation.** If the athlete perceives the situation to be threatening, heightened state anxiety will be the result.

The **competitive process** is the anxiety process that occurs within an individual as a result of a threatening objective situation. An important component of the competitive process is the influence of **competitive A-trait** upon the athlete's perception of threat. As illustrated, competitive A-trait is believed to be an important mediator between the competitive situation and the **competitive A-state** response.

Martens (1982) argued that the A-state reaction in an objective competitive situation could be predicted more accurately if competitive A-trait could be measured. It was with this goal in mind that he developed the SCAT. Development of the SCAT was based to a large degree on Sarason's work on test anxiety (Mandler & Sarason, 1952; Sarason, Davidson, Lighthall, Waite & Ruebush, 1960).

An early study on SCAT (Martens & Simon, 1976) demonstrates how well SCAT, A-trait measurement, and coaches' ratings of A-trait can predict state anxiety. The results are illustrated in figure 4.3. As can be observed, SCAT is nearly twice as effective in predicting state anxiety as A-trait measurement, and five times better than coaches' subjective opinions. Recall that a correlation coefficient is an estimate of the strength of the relationship between two variables,

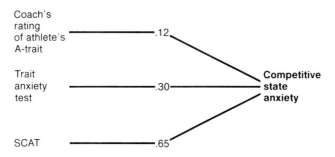

Figure 4.3 A comparison of three methods of predicting state anxiety in a precompetitive situation. From R. Martens and J. A. Simon, Comparison of three predictors of state anxiety in competitive situations. *Research Quarterly,* 1976, *47,* 381– 387. Reprinted by permission of the American Alliance for Health, Physical Education, Recreation and Dance, 1900 Association Drive, Reston, Virginia 22091.

with 1.0 being a perfect correlation. Clearly, if it can be assumed that state anxiety is related to skilled performance, then SCAT is an extremely important construct for estimating it.

---

5. **Principle** The objective competitive situation will result in heightened state anxiety if the situation is perceived as threatening to the athlete. Whether or not the athlete perceives a situation as threatening will often depend on the athlete's competitive trait anxiety.

    Application Two of the best psychological tools available to the coach are the SCAT and the CSAI-2. Both of these tests are easy to administer, easy to interpret, and are based on a solid theoretical foundation. In applied situations, the use of the tests to ascertain competitive A-trait and A-state is highly recommended.

Research on Competitive Anxiety

There has been much research interest in anxiety since the 1960s. Many studies have been published in recent years that attempt to explain the nature of anxiety and its effect upon the athlete. Some of this research will now be reviewed and summarized for its practical application. The research is organized here into four subdivisions: (a) the multidimensional nature of anxiety, (b) precompetitive anxiety, (c) the effects of competition on anxiety, and (d) the anxiety-performance relationship.

The Multidimensional Nature of Anxiety

The current view of anxiety is that it is multidimensional in nature. The development of the CSAI-2 with its three dimensions of anxiety reflects this line of reasoning. Fisher and Zwart (1982) analyzed athletes' responses to basketball situations and reported that an athlete's response pattern to anxiety is consistent with his or her perception of anxiety. In other words, one's response to anxiety is congruent with one's perception of the anxiety-eliciting capacity of the situation. This finding lends additional support to the stress process illustrated in figure 4.1, where the state anxiety reaction is shown to depend on the athletes' perception of how threatening the situation is.

Fisher and Zwart (1982) identified three factors associated with perceived anxiety. The first, the **ego threat** factor, occurs when the athlete is cast in a bad light. For example, an athlete who makes a bad play is criticized by the coach in front of the crowd. The second factor, the *positive anticipation* factor, includes situations in which the outcome has not been decided, but the potential for a desirable outcome exists. This type of anxiety response occurs during the pregame introductions, when both teams are hopeful of victory. Finally, the *negative outcome certainty* factor involves those anxiety-producing situations that are never in doubt, but have negative connotations for the athlete. This sort of anxiety is experienced by teams that have a losing record and fully expect to lose the game that they are preparing for.

Gould, Horn, and Spreeman (1983b) also studied the multidimensional nature of anxiety in a competitive situation. Using junior elite wrestlers as subjects, these researchers identified three dimensions of perceived anxiety. As did Fisher and Zwart (1982), Gould et al. identified ego threat or fear of failure as the greatest contributor to perceived anxiety. Thus it appears that one of the most significant sources of anxiety in competitive sports is the fear of failure and damage to the ego. These results certainly suggest to the practitioner and coach that perceived anxiety is very complex, and should not be dismissed as a minor problem. Anxiety can influence an athlete's performance as well as that athlete's decision to continue in competitive sports.

---

6. **Principle** An important source of anxiety is threat to the ego, or fear of failure.

   Application The coach should try to minimize situations that are particularly threatening to an athlete's ego. For example, the coach could de-emphasize the importance of winning compared to other factors, such as skill development and doing one's best.

Precompetitive Anxiety

In recent years a great deal of research on precompetitive anxiety has been conducted in field settings. This research has involved skydivers (Fenz, 1975; Powell & Verner, 1982), wrestlers (Gould, Horn & Spreeman, 1983a; Gould, Weiss & Weinberg, 1981; Highlen & Bennett, 1979), gymnasts (Mahoney & Avener, 1977), and racquetball competitors (Meyers, Cooke, Cullen & Liles, 1979).

The research on precompetitive anxiety has demonstrated a couple of important facts. The first is that the anxiety patterns of experienced athletes often differ markedly from those of inexperienced athletes. For example, precompetitive anxiety may be higher for experienced athletes than for less experienced athletes in gymnastics and racquetball. However, in wrestling and skydiving, the less experienced athletes are likely to have higher levels of anxiety.

A second important finding is that precompetitive anxiety seems to follow a very distinctive **inverted-V pattern.** This phenomenon is clearly illustrated in research by Fenz (1975, 1988) using skydivers and by Gould et al. (1983a) using elite junior wrestlers. The Fenz (1975) research demonstrated that for both experienced and inexperienced skydivers, state anxiety increased to an apex and decreased gradually until the actual jump occurred. For the experienced jumpers, the apex in anxiety occurred when the jumpers entered the plane at the airport. However, for the inexperienced jumpers the apex occurred at the "ready" signal immediately prior to the jump. The Gould et al. (1983a) research results, using junior elite wrestlers, are illustrated in figure 4.4. State anxiety increased steadily until just minutes before competition, and then dropped off rapidly. A significant difference between high and low trait-anxious athletes was also observed. Athletes high in competitive trait anxiety respond with greater levels of state anxiety than do those who are low in trait anxiety.

The basic inverted-V pattern has continued to be verified by other investigations (Karolezak-Biernacka, 1986). However, a study reported by Gould, Petlichkoff, and Weinberg (1984) clarified that the inverted-V pattern is primarily a function of somatic as opposed to cognitive state anxiety. Furthermore, Huband and McKelvie (1986) observed that the inverted-V pattern is flatter or less pronounced for low as opposed to high trait-anxious subjects.

---

7. **Principle** Athletes typically exhibit the inverted-V pattern of competitive anxiety prior to competition.

   Application The sooner an anxious athlete gets into the game, the sooner his or her competitive anxiety level will decline. This principle may help the coach decide who should be the starters. Pregame or match activities that closely approximate or mimic actual competition may also help to reduce anxiety.

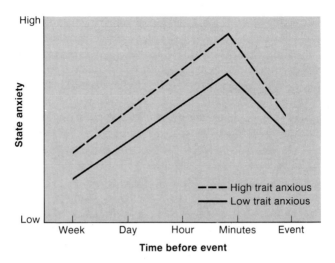

Figure 4.4 The inverted-V pattern of precompetitive anxiety for high trait-anxious and low trait-anxiety subjects. From D. Gould, T. Horn, and J. Spreeman, Competitive anxiety in junior elite wrestlers. *Journal of Sport Psychology,* 1983, *5,* 58–71. Adapted by permission of Human Kinetics Publishers, Inc., Champaign, IL.

The clear finding of a precompetitive inverted-V pattern suggests that anxiety prior to competition may be worse than that experienced during competition. Therefore, coaches should not extend the pregame buildup, since this may only increase their athletes' anxiety. The sooner the game can get underway, the sooner precompetitive anxiety will decline. The same situation is likely to occur if a basketball player is forced to wait a long time to shoot free throws in a game. No wonder coaches typically call one or even two time-outs immediately before an important free-throw attempt by the opposing team.

Research has also clarified a number of other anxiety-related factors during the precompetitive period. For example, the more important an impending match or contest is, the higher the level of precompetitive state anxiety (Dowthwaite & Armstrong, 1984). Furthermore, Gould and Weinberg (1985) observed that less successful athletes tend to worry a great deal more about pending competition than do successful athletes. The kinds of things that intercollegiate wrestlers worry most about include (1) concern about coaches' evaluation of their performance, (2) concern about losing, and (3) concern about making mistakes. The most salient of these three worries is concern about coaches' evaluation.

Effects of Competition on Anxiety

As illustrated in figure 4.2, perception of threat determines whether or not a competitive situation will cause an increase in state anxiety. An important mediator between the competitive situation and the athlete's response is competitive

A-trait. Athletes who display a high level of competitive trait anxiety generally display higher levels of state anxiety with competition than do athletes low in this trait (Gould et al., 1983a; Passer, 1983; Scanlan, 1978; Scanlan & Ragan, 1978).

Females exhibit higher levels of competitive trait anxiety than males (Segal & Weinberg, 1984). This suggests that females have a tendency to perceive competitive sport situations with greater feelings of fear and apprehension (A-state). It has also been observed that athletes who typically perceive themselves as being successful and satisfied with their performance exhibit low levels of competitive trait anxiety (Furst & Gershon, 1984). Boys who suffer from low levels of self-esteem also exhibit higher levels of competitive trait anxiety (Brustad & Weiss, 1987).

Another important line of research dealing with competition and anxiety is the effect of winning and losing upon state anxiety. The research indicates that state anxiety increases as the percentage of wins decreases. A-state remains relatively low in athletes who experience success most of the time. This finding is consistent with figure 4.2. If there is no perceived imbalance between the competitive situation and response capability, A-state will not increase (Scanlan, 1977). Research by Scanlan and Passer (1978), Scanlan (1978), and Scanlan and Ragan (1978) further reveals how success and failure affects state anxiety reactions of youth sports participants. They found that boys and girls participating in soccer competition experienced higher levels of postgame anxiety when they lost than when they won. Winning players experienced lower postgame than pregame A-state scores, while losing players experienced higher postgame than pregame A-state scores. Finally, A-state increased in young athletes who didn't find competition to be fun or who perceived that the coach felt a particular game was very important.

---

8. **Principle** Sports competition very often has the effect of elevating the state anxiety level of athletes.

   Application It is imperative that coaches of young athletes deemphasize the importance of winning and emphasize the importance of learning, effort, and having fun. In the long run the athlete will perform better and feel better about him- or herself if this goal can be accomplished.

From the foregoing review, it would appear that sports create a great deal of anxiety. Undoubtedly, many young athletes drop out of competitive sports because of the threat of failure and the elevated levels of anxiety (Martens, 1978). However, is the sports experience more threatening than other achievement situations? Apparently not. A study by Simon and Martens (1979) compared the

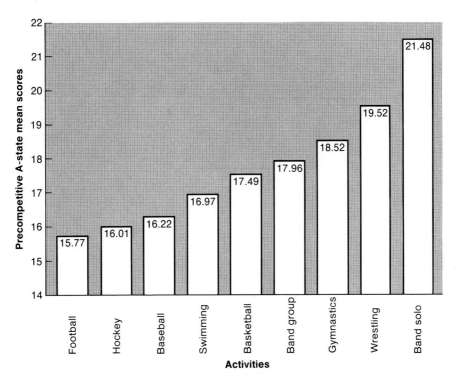

Figure 4.5 Precompetitive A-state levels in various competitive sports and evaluative activities. From J. A. Simon and R. Martens, Children's anxiety in sport and non-sport evaluative activities. *Journal of Sport Psychology,* 1979, *1,* 160–169. Adapted by permission of Human Kinetics Publishers, Inc., Champaign, IL.

precompetitive state anxiety of young people in both sport and nonsport activities. Some of the results of this study are displayed in figure 4.5. Interestingly, several nonsport activities are more threatening than most competitive sports. Specifically, precompetitive state anxiety for band solos is higher than for any of the sporting events. Also of interest is the observation that individual sports such as gymnastics and wrestling are more threatening than the team sports. The result is undoubtedly due to the greater evaluative potential involved in one-on-one competition.

Effects of Anxiety on Performance

In chapter 3 it was argued that the relationship between arousal and athletic performance took the form of the inverted-U. Evidence of this position was taken from research that primarily used paper-and-pencil tests of state anxiety as a

measure of arousal. Since state anxiety is associated with increased levels of physiological arousal, this is a defensible practice. However, this practice points out a very interesting observation about research purporting to test the inverted-U hypothesis. In virtually every reported case, it is negative stress (distress) or arousal that is compared with athletic performance. Sport psychologists actually know very little about the effect of positive stress (eustress) on athletic performance.

With this brief introduction, it would appear that the relationship between state anxiety and athletic performance takes the form of the inverted-U. However, in recent years, several studies have reported a linear but negative relationship between athletic performance and state anxiety. For example, in the case of swimming (Barnes, Sime, Dienstbier & Plake, 1986) and spiking in volleyball (Cox, 1986), performance decreases as state anxiety increases.

The development and field testing of the CSAI-2 has served to clarify the relationship between athletic performance and state anxiety. Recall that the CSAI-2 takes a multidimensional approach to the measurement of state anxiety. Using a design procedure popularized by Sonstroem and Bernardo (1982), Burton (1988) and Gould, Petlichkoff, Simons, and Vevera (1987) have demonstrated that the relationship between performance and state anxiety depends upon the dimension of anxiety being measured. Burton (1988) observed that the relationship between

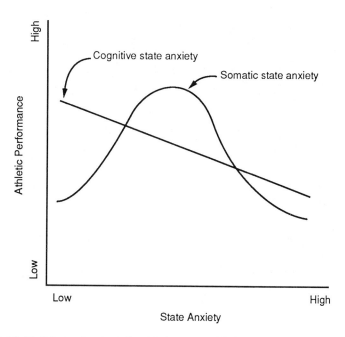

Figure 4.6 Multidimensional relationship between athletic performance and state anxiety.

performance in swimming and state anxiety was linear and inversely related when the cognitive or worry subscale was used and quadratically related (inverted U) when the somatic subscale was being used. Similarly, Gould et al. (1987) observed that the relationship between pistol-shooting performance and cognitive state anxiety was linear and negative, while the relationship between somatic state anxiety and pistol-shooting performance was curvilinear.

As can be observed in figure 4.6, the relationship between **cognitive state anxiety** and performance is linear and negative. As cognitive state anxiety increases, athletic performance decreases. This is consistent with the volleyball findings of Cox (1986) when a unidimensional measurement of state anxiety was used (CSAI-1). Conversely, the relationship between **somatic state anxiety** and performance is quadratic in nature and takes the form of the inverted-U. As somatic state anxiety increases, performance also increases up to an optimal level, and then decreases as somatic state anxiety continues to increase.

It would appear that the CSAI-2 has led to a major breakthrough in our understanding of the relationship between state anxiety and athletic performance. Worry and apprehension associated with cognitive state anxiety is a major hindrance to athletic performance. The lower the level of cognitive state anxiety the better the athlete will perform. The notion that a "little" anxiety is good for the athlete is not true if it is of the cognitive variety.

Conversely, an increase in the somatic indicators of state anxiety (increased heart rate, muscle tension, jittery, etc.) are associated with increased athletic performance up to an uncertain optimal level and then thereafter result in a decrement in performance. This is the classic inverted-U relationship between anxiety/arousal and performance.

---

9. **Principle** The relationship between somatic state anxiety and athletic performance takes the form of the inverted U, while the relationship between cognitive state anxiety and performance is linear and negative.

> **Application** The real threat to quality athletic performance is worry, self-doubt, and apprehension. Knowing this, the coach must help the athlete cope with these debilitating threats. At the same time, an optimal level of somatic-related state anxiety should be encouraged and maintained. Certainly, too much somatic-related state anxiety is bad, but so is too little.

Summary

Anxiety is defined as a subjective feeling of apprehension and heightened physiological arousal. An athlete who manifests anxiety before and during competition will experience an elevated level of arousal and feelings of tension and apprehension. Anxiety, arousal, and stress are discussed and explained. Trait anxiety is a personality disposition and reflects an individual's predisposition to behave in certain ways. State anxiety is a situation-specific manifestation of an athlete's response to a stressor.

Various pencil-and-paper tests of anxiety are identified. Tests that measure the trait anxiety construct include the Taylor Manifest Anxiety Scale, the Spielberger Trait Anxiety Inventory, and the Sport Competition Anxiety Test. Tests that measure state anxiety include the Activation-Deactivation Checklist, the Autonomic Perception Questionnaire, Zuckerman's Affective Adjective Checklist, Spielberger's State Anxiety Inventory, the Competitive State Anxiety Inventory, and the Competitive State Anxiety Inventory-2.

Marten's sport competition anxiety model is discussed. If the objective competitive situation represents a threat to the athlete, state anxiety will be the end result. An important factor that mediates the relationship between the situation and competitive state anxiety is competitive trait anxiety.

Research on the subject of competitive anxiety was classified under the headings of (1) the multidimensional nature of anxiety, (2) precompetitive anxiety, (3) the effects of competition on anxiety, and (4) the anxiety-performance relationship.

Review Questions

1. Discuss the terms *arousal, anxiety,* and *stress.* How are these terms similar? Dissimilar?
2. What is the difference between state and trait anxiety? Name three tests for each.
3. Define distress and eustress. How do these terms relate to stress and anxiety?
4. What is competitive trait anxiety and how is it measured?
5. What is competitive state anxiety and how is it measured?
6. What is the stress process? Relate the stress process to the competitive process.
7. Describe and diagram the various components of the competitive process.
8. What is the inverted-V pattern for precompetitive anxiety? Explain.
9. Discuss the multidimensional nature of anxiety.
10. Explain some of the effects of competition on an athlete's state anxiety response.
11. Discuss the relationship between anxiety and athletic performance.

Glossary

anxiety A feeling of apprehension and heightened physiological arousal.
cognitive state anxiety The worry and apprehension dimension of the state anxiety construct.
competitive A-state Situation-specific anxiety response to a threatening competitive situation.
competitive A-trait The personality disposition to respond with elevated levels of competitive A-state before, during, and after athletic competition.

competitive process Competition represents an objective demand situation; therefore, like the stress process, the competitive process may elicit a state anxiety reaction as a result of that objective situation.

CSAI The Competitive State Anxiety Inventory, a ten-item shortened version of Spielberger's SAI.

CSAI-2 Competitive State Anxiety Inventory-2, a multidimensional test of competitive state anxiety.

distress Negative stress or state anxiety.

ego threat A major source of competitive stress caused by fear of failure or loss of esteem.

eustress The positive or pleasant aspect of stress.

inverted-V pattern The observed relationship between precompetitive anxiety and amount of time to event. The pattern appears when the relationship is plotted on a graph.

objective competitive situation The competitive situation that the athlete is placed in.

objective demand Environmental situation or stimulus in the stress process.

SAI Spielberger's State Anxiety Inventory, a test of state anxiety composed of twenty "how I feel" questions.

SCAT Martens' Sport Competition Anxiety Test, an important test for estimating state anxiety based on measurement of trait anxiety.

somatic state anxiety Somatic or bodily related dimension of state anxiety measured by the CSAI-2.

state anxiety An emotional state characterized by apprehension, fear, and tension accompanied by physiological arousal.

stress Defined by Selye (1975) as the "nonspecific response of the body to any demand made upon it."

stress process The process by which an objective demand situation results in a state anxiety reaction, if the situation is perceived to be threatening.

subjective competitive situation The athlete's perception of the objective competitive situation. Synonymous with the perception of threat component of the competitive process.

TAI Spielberger's Trait Anxiety Inventory, a measure of trait anxiety and a companion test to the SAI.

TMAS Taylor Manifest Anxiety Scale, the test of anxiety most commonly used during the 1950s.

trait anxiety A relatively permanent personality disposition to perceive a wide variety of situations as being threatening or dangerous, and to respond to those situations with increased state anxiety.

Recommended Readings

Burton, D. (1988). Do anxious swimmers swim slower?: Reexamining the elusive anxiety-performance relationship. *Journal of Sport and Exercise Psychology, 10,* 45–61.

Cox, R. H. (1986). Relationship between skill performance in women's volleyball and competitive state anxiety. *International Journal of Sport Psychology, 17,* 183–190.

Fenz, W. D. (1975). Coping mechanisms and performance under stress. In D. M. Landers (ed.), *Psychology of sport and motor behavior II.* Penn State HPER Series, No. 10. University Park: Pennsylvania State University Press.

Gould, D., Horn, T., & Spreeman, J. (1983a). Competitive anxiety in junior elite wrestlers. *Journal of Sport Psychology, 5,* 58–71.

Gould, D., Petlichkoff, L., Simons, J., & Vevera, M. (1987). Relationship between competitive state anxiety inventory-2 subscales scores and pistol-shooting performance. *Journal of Sport Psychology, 9,* 33–42.

Humphrey, J. H. (1986). *Profiles in stress.* New York: AMS Press, Inc.

Karteroliotis, C., & Gill, D. L. (1987). Temporal changes in psychological and physiological components of state anxiety. *Journal of Sport Psychology, 9,* 261–274.

Martens, R. (1982). *Sport competition anxiety test.* Champaign, IL: Human Kinetics Publishers.

Martens, R., Burton, D., Vealey, R. S., Bump, L. A., & Smith, D. E. (1989). The competitive state anxiety inventory-2 (CSAI-2). In D. Burton & R. Vealey (eds.), *Competitive anxiety.* Champaign, IL: Human Kinetics Publishers.

Selye, H. (1975). *Stress without distress.* New York: New American Library.

Sonstroem, R. J., & Bernardo, P. (1982). Intraindividual pregame state anxiety and basketball performance: A re-examination of the inverted-U curve. *Journal of Sport Psychology, 4,* 235–245.

Spielberger, C. D. (1971). Trait-state anxiety and motor behavior. *Journal of Motor Behavior, 3,* 265–279.

5 Intervention Strategies

Key Terms

anxiety-prone
anxiety-stress spiral
autogenic training
autohyponosis
biofeedback
cognitive strategy
ergogenic aid
external imagery
fine motor skill
gross motor skill
heterohypnosis
hypnosis
hypnotic induction
hypnotic trance
imagery
internal imagery

intervention strategies
mantra
mental device
neutral hypnosis
posthypnotic suggestion
progressive relaxation
psyching up
relaxation response
SIT
SMT
stress management
transcendental
   meditation
VMBR
waking hypnosis

In the previous chapter on anxiety in sport, I began by introducing the case study of a young high school athlete by the name of Ryan. Recall that Ryan was an extremely gifted multiple-sport athlete who experienced difficulty in dealing with anxiety while competing in track events. Specifically, he would become so anxious prior to sprinting and hurdling events that he literally could not run efficiently. During practices, Ryan experienced little or no tension and anxiety. During three years of high school track he had never lost a race during practice with teammates.

It was clear that Ryan was going to be a track "drop out" if some sort of intervention wasn't provided. Ryan's father talked to a professor of sport psychology at the local college to find out if there was something psychological that could be done to help Ryan. After three weeks of studying Ryan's anxiety response to competition, the sport psychologist concluded that an individualized intervention program could be developed to help him. The program that was recommended was one very similar to the stress inoculation training (SIT) program that is described later on in this chapter. In this program, Ryan learned what caused his anxiety and learned how to cope with anxiety when it occurred. Ryan's success at reversing the damaging events of anxiety did not occur overnight. However, during his senior year he made up for many of his earlier failures by setting a state record in the 220-yard sprint.

In chapters 3 and 4, I discussed the concepts of arousal and anxiety in great depth. You are now familiar with both of these terms and aware of several theories that purport to explain the relationship between arousal/anxiety and performance. Too much or too little arousal may result in poor athletic performance. Consequently, the goal for the athlete and coach is to identify the optimal level of arousal for any particular event. In the case of cognitive or worry anxiety the goal is to completely eliminate it if possible.

The purpose of this chapter is to identify strategies to help athletes to intervene and alter their existing levels of arousal or anxiety. Perhaps one of the most famous examples of this occurred before the first heavyweight boxing match between Muhammad Ali and Ken Norton in 1973. Norton hired a professional hypnotist to help him with his self-confidence and anxiety. He won the match in a stunning upset, effectively calling attention to hypnosis as an intervention strategy.

Other famous athletes who have used intervention strategies such as imagery and relaxation include Dwight Stones in the high jump, Jack Nicklaus in golf, and Chris Evert in tennis. For the 1984 National Collegiate Athletic Association basketball championships, two teams employed professional sport psychologists to help their athletes with their concentration and relaxation. The psychologists were Dan Smith at the University of Illinois and Robert Rotella of the University of Virginia. Virginia went to the final four, and Illinois reached the final eight. Neither team was expected to do this well.

In this chapter, we will use the term **intervention** to refer to various cognitive and physiological strategies for altering existing levels of anxiety, arousal, and self-confidence. Other authors have chosen to use the term **stress management** to refer to much the same thing (Zaichkowsky & Sime, 1982). The important thing to remember is that certain strategies are available to the athlete to change the existing level of arousal and tension in the body. The term *tension* will be used to mean much the same thing as anxiety. Tension specifically refers to the tightness that we feel in certain muscle groups as a result of excessive worry and frustration.

Another term that has been used interchangeably with *intervention* is *ergogenic* or **ergogenic aid.** An ergogenic aid is any sort of technique or substance, beyond actual training regimens, that is employed to improve performance (Williams, 1983). In the case of sport psychology, these ergogenic aids are referred to as *psychological ergogenic aids.* Some of the ergogenic or intervention techniques that will be introduced in this chapter include relaxation, autogenic training, hypnosis, imagery, and goal setting.

Numerous books, monographs, and articles have been published that deal with various authors' perceptions of how intervention programs can be approached by and developed for the athlete (e.g., Gauron, 1984; Harris & Harris, 1984; Martens, 1987; Nideffer, 1985; Orlick, 1986). In addition, various sport psychologists have reported on the application and development of specific intervention regimens. For example, Hellstedt (1987a) described a psychological-skills training program that was developed for students enrolled in an alpine ski academy. Skills taught included anxiety control, imagery, relaxation, and goal setting. In a similar vein, Mahoney, Gabriel, and Perkins (1987) describe the development of a Psychological Skills Inventory for Sports (PSIS). The PSIS ascertains an athlete's knowledge relative to mental preparation skills. The authors reported that the PSIS effectively discriminates between high-and low-skill athletes.

Coaches have been looking to the sport psychologist to help learn how to maintain optimal levels of arousal in athletes. This is a most promising development, since many coaches have improperly prepared their athletes for competition. The typical approach has been to "psych up" the athlete through various kinds of pep talks and activation techniques. There is, of course, a proper time to get athletes excited and aroused, but often these techniques are applied at the wrong time. It is commonplace, for example, to see high school volleyball coaches leading their players in cheering and psyching-up sessions immediately before a match. Generally, these athletes have only an intermediate level of skill, and the extra arousal serves only to induce unforced errors. This problem is illustrated in figure 5.1. Each athlete in this figure begins with a different initial level of arousal. Increasing arousal affects each athlete differently. In most cases, intervention

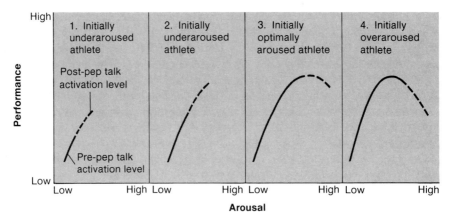

Figure 5.1 The effects of a pep talk on the activation levels of four different athletes.

procedures are best applied on an individual basis; each athlete should be treated differently. Some will need a pep talk, but others may need an entirely different form of intervention.

As can be observed in figure 5.1, using a pep talk to increase the arousal level of four different athletes has interesting ramifications. Only in situations 1 and 2 did the pep talk have the desired effect. In situation 3, the athlete was already at an optimal level of activation and it was destroyed by the coach's pep talk. In situation 4, the athlete was overactivated to begin with; the intervention was totally inappropriate. How many coaches overactivate their athletes by their pregame locker room pep talks?

---

1. **Principle** Group activation strategies such as pep talks may help some athletes reach an optimal level of arousal but may cause others to become overaroused.

   Application Indiscriminate use of activation procedures to psych up athletic teams should be avoided. Instead, help each athlete to find his or her own optimal arousal level.

This chapter contains four major sections. The first deals with relaxation procedures designed to lower and control physiological arousal, anxiety, and muscular tension. The second identifies three different cognitive strategies designed to alter and improve an athlete's competitive-readiness level. In section three, various relaxation and cognitive intervention strategies are combined and discussed in terms of "packaged" or formal intervention and stress-management programs. Finally, in section four, various strategies used by coaches and athletes to get psyched for competition are discussed.

Relaxation Procedures

I think a lot of it has to do with me pressing. It's in my head. I'm trying harder, and the harder I try, the worse it goes. I've just got to try and relax. But the more I miss, the harder it is to relax, so it's just a vicious circle.

Jeff Jaeger
Place Kicker, Cleveland Browns, 1987

While some athletes may suffer from low levels of arousal, the more difficult problems occur with athletes who experience excessively high levels of anxiety and tension. For these athletes, any strategy calculated to heighten arousal can only cause greater anxiety and tension. Typically, what happens is an initial increase in anxiety leads to a decrease in performance. This decrease in performance itself results in even greater anxiety, resulting in the so-called **anxiety-stress spiral.** There is only one way out of this spiral, and that is to reverse the process by reducing the anxiety and tension. *Relaxation procedures* can effectively reduce tension and anxiety associated with sport. In this section, we will discuss some of them.

Four popular relaxation procedures can be adequately categorized under the broad heading of relaxation. These are (1) progressive relaxation, (2) autogenic training, (3) transcendental meditation, and (4) biofeedback. Each procedure is unique in its own way, but they all yield essentially the same physiological result. That is, they all result in the **relaxation response.** The relaxation response consists of physiological changes that are opposite the so-called fight or flight response of the sympathetic nervous system. Specifically, procedures such as progressive relaxation, autogenic training, and transcendental meditation result in decreases in oxygen consumption, heart rate, respiration, and skeletal muscle activity while they increase skin resistance and alpha brain waves. The research supporting the effectiveness of the various relaxation procedures is outlined in table 5.1.

Benson, Beary, and Carol (1974) explained that four different factors are necessary for eliciting the relaxation response. Each of these factors is present to some degree in the specific relaxation techniques that we will discuss. These four elements or factors are (1) a **mental device,** (2) a passive attitude, (3) decreased muscle tonus, and (4) a quiet environment. The mental device is generally some sort of word, phrase, object, or process used to shift attention inwardly. We will now turn to a brief discussion of the specific relaxation procedures.

Table 5.1 Physiologic Reactions to Various Mental Techniques. Adapted from Benson, H., Beary, J. F., & Carol, M. P. The relaxation response. *Psychiatry, 1974, 37,* 37–46. Reprinted by special permission of the William Alanson White Psychiatric Foundation, Inc. Copyright © 1974 by the William Alanson White Psychiatric Foundation, Inc.

Parameter	Relaxation Techniques	Autogenic Training	Hypnosis*	Transcendental Meditation	Zen and Hatha Yoga
Oxygen Consumption	D(4)	N.M.	D(8)	D(13,14)	D(12)
Respiratory Rate	D(4)	D(11)	D(3)	D(1,14)	D(2,12)
Heart Rate	N.M.	D(11)	D(3)	D(13,14)	D(2,12)
Alpha Waves (EEG)	N.M.	I(11)	N.M.	I(13,14)	I(12)
Skin Resistance (GSR)	N.M.	I(11)	I(6, 9)	I(13,14)	I(2)
Blood Pressure	D(7)	?(11)	?(5)	0(14)	0(2, 12)
Muscle Tension	D(10)	D(11)	N.M.	N.M.	N.M.

Key: N.M.—not measured D—decrease
I—increase ?—inconclusive results
0—no change

1. Allison (1970)
2. Bagchi & Wenger (1957)
3. Barber (1971)
4. Beary, Benson, & Klemchuck (1974)
5. Crasilneck & Hall (1959)
6. Davis & Kantor (1935)
7. Deabler, Fidel, Dillenkoffer, & Elder (1973)
8. Dudley, Holmes, Martin, & Ripley (1963)
9. Estabrooks (1930)
10. Jacobson (1938)
11. Luthe (1969)
12. Sugi & Akutsu (1968)
13. Wallace (1970)
14. Wallace, Benson, & Wilson (1971)

*Suggestion given of deep relaxation.

2. **Principle** An important part of any relaxation procedure is to focus attention on a mental device.

   Application Two mental devices are highly recommended for the athlete. The first is to take a deep breath and exhale slowly, and the second is the use of a mantra or key word or phrase. Athletes can focus on the key phrase and slow air release as they relax.

Progressive Relaxation

Modern progressive relaxation techniques are all variations of those outlined by Edmond Jacobson (1929, 1976). Jacobson began his work with progressive relaxation in the early part of the twentieth century. It was Jacobson's basic thesis that it is impossible to be nervous or tense in any part of the body where the muscles are completely relaxed. In addition, Jacobson believed that nervousness and tenseness of involuntary muscles and organs could be reduced if the associated skeletal muscles were relaxed.

Jacobson's **progressive relaxation** procedure requires that subjects lie on their backs, with their arms to the side. Occasionally a comfortable chair and a sitting posture is recommended. In either case, the room should be fairly quiet and arms and legs should not be crossed; this is to avoid unnecessary stimulation. While the goal of any progressive relaxation program is to relax the entire body in a matter of minutes, it is essential that in the beginning the subject practice the technique for at least one hour every day. Once the relaxation procedure is well learned, the relaxation response can be achieved in a few minutes.

Jacobson's method calls for the subject to tense a muscle before relaxing it. The tensing helps the subject to recognize the difference between tension and relaxation. Once the subject can do this, he or she should be able to relax a limb completely without tensing it first. Jacobson warns that only the first few minutes of any relaxation session should be devoted to muscle tensing. The rest of the time should be devoted to gaining complete relaxation. For a muscle to be considered relaxed, it must be completely absent of any contractions and must be limp and motionless.

Jacobson's full progressive relaxation procedure involves systematically tensing and relaxing specific muscle groups in a predetermined order. Relaxation begins with the muscles of the left arm and proceeds to the right arm, left and right legs, abdomen, back, chest, and shoulder muscles, and concludes with the neck and face muscles. The full training procedure lasts many months. In the beginning stages, an entire session should be devoted to the total relaxation of a single muscle group. While it probably is unrealistic to expect an athlete to devote this much time to learning to relax, Jacobson's point is well taken. A well-developed relaxation training program requires a great deal of practice in the beginning. It is unrealistic to expect an athlete to elicit the relaxation response at will after only one or two fifteen-minute practice sessions. However, after several months of practice and training, it should be possible to evoke the relaxation response in a matter of seconds (Nideffer, 1981).

The ultimate goal of any relaxation training program is to evoke the relaxation response to counter stress in a specific situation. For example, a professional golfer does not have thirty minutes to relax prior to a fifteen-thousand-dollar putt. The golfer must be able to accomplish this while waiting to putt. This ability takes many hours of practice to master.

Most of the progressive relaxation research has verified the relaxation response. An athlete who learns to evoke the relaxation response through progressive relaxation procedures can reduce state anxiety, physiological arousal, and muscular tension. However, this says nothing directly about improving athletic performance. Based on the inverted-U theory, we can expect an athlete whose arousal level is initially too high to perform better after evoking the relaxation response. However, this is difficult to demonstrate scientifically. If the relaxation response brings arousal below the optimal level, we may actually observe a decrement in performance. Consequently, most research on performance and progressive relaxation has been case studies. Nideffer and Deckner (1970) reported one such study, in which a shot-putter's performance improved significantly after the athlete was taught how to relax. Winter (1982) has claimed that sprinters at San Jose State have broken thirty-seven world records by learning how to relax. However, researchers such as Bennett and Stothart (1980) and Weinberg, Seabourne, and Jackson (1981) have failed to observe a performance effect using relaxation procedures alone. More recently Griffiths, Steel, Vaccaro, Allen, and Karpman (1985) observed both anxiety reduction and performance facilitation as a result of relaxation and mental-rehearsal strategies. Divers in the experimental group enjoyed a reduction in state anxiety and an increased ability to perform a standard SCUBA "bail-out" procedure as a result of stress management training.

3. **Principle** Learning how to relax the muscles of the body is a foundation skill for all stress management and intervention strategies.

   Application As a first step in learning how to control anxiety and stress the athlete must become proficient at relaxing the mind and the body.

Autogenic Training

In many ways, **autogenic training** is very similar to Jacobson's progressive relaxation training. However, greater emphasis is placed upon how various limbs and parts of the body feel (e.g., arm feels heavy and warm) rather than how relaxed they are. According to Ulett and Peterson (1965), self-hypnosis plays an important role in autogenic training. Autogenic training procedures were developed by Johannes H. Schultz, a German physician (Schultz & Luthe, 1959).

Autogenic training as outlined by Schultz and Luthe is composed of six psychophysiologic exercises. Each exercise must be practiced until the desired results are obtained, and only then may the subject move on to the next exercise. After about four months of training, the individual should be able to complete all six steps in a matter of minutes. The end result is the relaxation response and its accompanying changes in various physiological parameters.

Vanek and Cratty (1970) have reported the widespread use of autogenic training by athletes in Europe. The technique is practiced on willing athletes using a wide range of variations. To use the technique successfully, athletes must be intelligent, extremely attentive, and reasonably open to suggestion. Once the technique is thoroughly mastered, it is applied in stressful situations to help reduce tension and anxiety. Vanek and Cratty outline the following basic steps: (1) athlete is placed in a comfortable position (usually on his or her back), (2) athlete is taught to breathe deeply and to concentrate on his or her own breathing, (3) athlete tenses and relaxes all of the muscles in the body several times, (4) athlete concentrates on relaxing specific parts of the body and experiencing feelings of heaviness in each limb, (5) athlete experiences feeling of warmth in limbs and abdomen and coolness of the forehead, and (6) athlete repeats to him- or herself statements such as, "I feel quite relaxed." An example of autogenic training being practiced with frogmen is provided by Spigolon and Annalisa (1985).

Various authors have outlined autogenic training and relaxation programs that can be adopted by the athlete (Harris & Harris, 1984; Nideffer, 1985; Orlick, 1986). In addition, numerous relaxation and autogenic training cassette tapes can be commercially purchased or developed (Rotella, Malone & Ojala, 1985). In table 5.2, I have outlined a series of statements that can be used for teaching athletes to relax. In this list, I freely intertwine statements and principles that may be considered integral parts of progressive relaxation, autogenic training, or both.

Table 5.2 Suggested Statements That May Be Included in an Autogenic Training Presentation.

1. Find a comfortable position where you can sit or lie down.
2. Do not cross your arms or legs; try to get comfortable.
3. Close your eyes and put away thoughts of the outside world.
4. I want you to concentrate on your breathing as you inhale and exhale.
5. "Inhale," "exhale," "inhale," "exhale," "inhale," "exhale."
6. Each time you exhale I want you to *feel* the tension being expelled from your body.
7. "Inhale," "exhale," "inhale," "exhale," "inhale," "exhale."
8. You are beginning to feel very relaxed and very calm.
9. Now, as you continue your breathing, I want you to systematically tighten and then relax all of the muscles in your body.
10. Let's first start with your left leg. Tense the muscles of your left leg and left foot. Now, totally relax the muscles in that leg.
11. As you relax the muscles of your left leg, notice how heavy and warm your foot feels.
12. Continue on your own to tense and relax all of the muscles in your body. Start with your lower extremities and move upward.
13. "Tense and relax," "tense and relax," "tense and relax. . . ."
14. At this time your muscles feel very relaxed. Your arms and legs feel heavy.
15. Your hands and feet feel warm and your forehead feels very cool.
16. Let's return now to concentrating on your breathing.
17. "Inhale," "exhale," "inhale," "exhale," "inhale," "exhale."
18. You feel very relaxed and calm.
19. Each time you exhale you are expelling anxiety and tension from your body.
20. Think to yourself, "I feel quite relaxed and quite calm."

Transcendental Meditation

Transcendental meditation (TM) is a meditation procedure with religious and mystical overtones. Transcendental meditation, along with Zen and Hatha Yoga, had their origins in India more than four thousand years ago. The procedure uses devices such as concentration on breathing, visualization, relaxation of muscles, and the repetition of the **mantra** to gain the desired effect. The mantra is a simple sound selected by the instructor as a mental concentration device. One such sound, "om or ahhom," has been a popular one (Nideffer, 1976a). The modern founder of the transcendental meditation movement was Maharishi Mahesh Yogi of India.

In practice, the subject sits in a comfortable position with eyes closed. The subject concentrates on deep breathing while at the same time repeating the mantra silently. Reportedly, the sound of the mantra soon disappears as the mind experiences subtler levels of thought and finally arrives at the source of the thought. While most Oriental approaches teach a sitting meditation position, both Zen and transcendental meditation emphasize that standing or sitting are acceptable (Layman, 1980).

From a physiological point of view, the practice of meditation results in the relaxation response (Wallace & Benson, 1972). In fact, when stripped of its religious and mystical overtones, transcendental meditation is essentially identical to the four elements identified by Benson et al. (1974) for eliciting the relaxation response.

While it is clear that transcendental meditation can reduce anxiety and tension by evoking the relaxation response, it is not clear whether its practice has a facilitative effect on athletic performance. Again, while it seems clear that a reduction in arousal and muscle tension should help the anxiety-prone athlete, this is very difficult to verify. The evidence is typically anecdotal or based on single case study reports (Layman, 1980). However, since 1976 several scientific investigations have related transcendental meditation with motor performance. Reddy, Bai, and Rao (1976) randomly assigned subjects to control and experimental TM training conditions for six weeks. At the end of the training period, the subjects were tested on various motor tasks. Results showed a significant difference in improvement for the TM group on the fifty-meter dash, an agility test, standing broad jump, reaction time, and coordination. Reliable differences were not noted between the two groups on a strength test and the shot put. The investigators concluded that transcendental meditation helps the athlete develop a broad range of qualities essential to motor performance: agility, speed, endurance, fast reactions, and mind-body coordination.

While the research by Reddy et al. (1976) suggests that transcendental meditation has a facilitative effect upon **gross motor skills**—skills that require large muscle involvement—research by Williams and associates (Williams, 1978; Williams & Herbert, 1976; Williams, Lodge & Reddish, 1977; Williams & Vickerman, 1976) showed no such effect for **fine motor skills,** those that require delicate muscle control. Subjects trained in transcendental meditation techniques did not demonstrate superior learning or performance on fine motor tasks compared to control subjects. Williams (1978) concluded that certain physiological effects attributed to the practice of transcendental meditation, such as lowered anxiety and arousal, are not manifested in terms of learning and performance of a novel perceptual fine motor skill such as mirror tracing or rotary pursuit.

---

4. **Principle** Teaching athletes how to elicit the relaxation response will help them avoid or curtail the anxiety-stress spiral.
   Application Athletes should be taught to relax in a matter of seconds using progressive relaxation, autogenic training, or transcendental meditation.

Biofeedback

It has been proven that humans can voluntarily control functions of the autonomic nervous system. Research on animals by DiCara (1970) and on humans by Benson et al. (1974) has verified this. **Biofeedback** is a relatively modern technique that is based upon this principle.

Biofeedback training uses instruments to help people control responses of the autonomic nervous system. For example, a subject monitors an auditory signal of his or her own heart rate and experiments with different thoughts, feelings, and sensations to slow the heart rate. Once the subject learns to recognize the feelings associated with the reduction of heart rate, the instrument is removed, and the subject tries to control the heart rate without it. This is the goal of the biofeedback therapist. People suffering from chronic anxiety or illnesses caused by anxiety can often benefit from biofeedback training, because when they learn to reduce functions of the sympathetic nervous system, they are indirectly learning to reduce anxiety and tension (Brown, 1977; Danskin & Crow, 1981). Biofeedback is essentially the same as progressive relaxation, autogenic training, and meditation. Using the latter three techniques, the subject relaxes, which lowers arousal and decreases the activity of the sympathetic nervous system. With biofeedback, the subject begins by lowering certain physiological measures with the help of an instrument. This decreases arousal and increases relaxation.

Instrumentation

Theoretically, biofeedback can be very useful to athletes who suffer from excessive anxiety and arousal. If athletes could be trained to control their physiological responses in the laboratory, they should be able to transfer this ability onto the athletic field. The main drawback to biofeedback in athletics is expense. The cost of purchasing a machine for measuring heart rate, EEG, EMG, or GSR changes is out of reach for the average school's athletic budget. However, not all biofeedback measurement techniques are expensive, and many are still in the experimental stages. Some of the basic measurement techniques used in biofeedback training will be listed (Danskin & Crow, 1981; Schwartz, 1987).

Skin Temperature The most commonly used and least expensive form of biofeedback is skin temperature. When an athlete becomes highly aroused, additional blood is pumped to the vital organs. Part of this additional blood supply comes from the peripheral blood vessels, leaving the hands feeling cold and clammy. Thus, the effect of stress is to decrease the skin temperature of the extremities. Subjects can monitor skin temperature to discover what kinds of responses, thoughts, and autogenic phrases are most effective in increasing it.

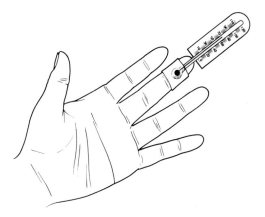

Figure 5.2 Skin temperature can be monitored with a cardboard-backed thermometer. From *Biofeedback: An introduction and guide* by David Danskin and Mark Crow. Reprinted by permission of Mayfield Publishing Company. Copyright © 1981 by Mayfield Publishing Company.

Typically, subjects are trained to use progressive relaxation techniques and autogenic phrases to assist them in the biofeedback process. Although sophisticated instruments are available, a simple and inexpensive cardboard-backed thermometer can be used to monitor skin temperature. For use, the cardboard is cut off just above the bulb and the thermometer is taped to the finger as illustrated in figure 5.2.

Electromyography Another very popular biofeedback technique employs the use of an electromyographic feedback instrument (EMG). Electrodes are attached to a particular group of muscles in the forearm or forehead, and the subject tries to reduce muscular tension by using auditory or visual cues of muscle electrical activity. Auditory cues typically come through earphones in the form of clicks. Visual cues come through a meter that the subject watches.

Electroencephalogram A third major instrument used for biofeedback is the electroencephalogram (EEG). Use of the EEG is commonly called brainwave training. Tiny electrical impulses from billions of brain cells can be detected by electrodes placed on the scalp and connected to an EEG. Four basic types of brain waves are associated with EEG recordings. Beta waves predominate during periods of excitement and of high arousal. Alpha waves predominate when the subject relaxes and puts his or her mind in "neutral." It is the alpha waves that the subject tries to produce. The other two types are theta waves, which predominate during drowsiness, and delta waves, which are associated with deep sleep (Fisher, 1976).

Other Methods While skin temperature, EMG, and EEG are the most common methods used in biofeedback training, several others are used to a lesser degree. These are the galvanic skin response (GSR), heart rate, and blood pressure. Some other methods of biofeedback training techniques are still in the experimental stages. One of these is the use of a stethoscope to monitor heart rate. Others include monitoring respiration rate, vapor pressure from the skin, stomach acidity, sphincter constriction, and blood chemistry.

Biofeedback and Performance

In a laboratory setting, the athlete learns to control the autonomic nervous system. The feelings and experiences associated with learning how to reduce sympathetic nervous system responses in the laboratory are then transferred to the athletic environment. In some cases biofeedback may be practiced in the athletic environment. For example, Costa, Bonaccorsi, and Scrimali (1984) reported the use of biofeedback training with team handball athletes to reduce precompetitive anxiety.

As observed by Wenz and Strong (1980), the difference between success and failure of two equally matched athletes often depends on an individual's ability to cope with the perceived stress of competition. Biofeedback provides a way for athletes to determine their levels of physiological arousal and to learn how to make conscious changes calculated to reduce anxiety and improve performance. A number of scientific investigations have been conducted to determine the effect of biofeedback on athletic performance. The following three studies are representative of the research conducted in this area.

DeWitt (1980) reported two studies in which biofeedback significantly enhanced performance. In the first, six football players received twelve weeks of biofeedback, relaxation, and mental rehearsal training in two one-hour sessions per week. The results showed a significant reduction in muscle tension (EMG), and the coaching staff felt that four of the six improved in football-playing ability. In the second study, twelve basketball players were assigned to either a control or biofeedback treatment condition. The results showed that biofeedback subjects significantly reduced heart rate and EMG levels as a result of training. Also, posttest performance ratings of biofeedback subjects were superior to those of the control subjects. The author concluded that biofeedback training reduces anxiety and arousal and facilitates athletic performance as a result of stress management.

French (1978) tested thirty college males on the stabilometer test of balancing and recorded their EMG scores. The subjects were then assigned into three matched groups according to their performance scores. Experimental groups 1 and 2 received a combination of relaxation, autogenic, and biofeedback training prior to a posttest on the stabilometer. During the posttest, only experimental group 1 received auditory EMG feedback. All groups received a posttest on the stabilometer while EMGs were being monitored. The results revealed that biofeedback training effectively reduced EMG recordings, but that stabilometer scores were unaffected.

Daniels and Landers (1981) compared a group of shooters receiving verbal instructions with an experimental group receiving biofeedback training. The results showed that the subjects who received biofeedback training significantly improved shooting accuracy and pattern consistency while showing greater control over the autonomic pattern. This research demonstrated that shooting performance can be improved using biofeedback.

In summary, it seems clear that the relaxation procedures introduced in this section effectively reduce anxiety and arousal. Theoretically, this should help the athlete to reduce anxiety and tension during competition. However, the indiscriminate use of these procedures does not guarantee better athletic performance. Just as pep talks can overarouse an athlete, relaxation can underarouse an athlete if improperly applied.

---

5. **Principle** Biofeedback is an effective and powerful tool for reducing the debilitating effects of anxiety and stress.
   Application If an athlete can't control anxiety and stress using progressive relaxation, autogenic training, or meditation, then biofeedback training should be tried. To get started with feedback training, it may be necessary to identify a professional therapist. Equipment necessary for biofeedback training may not be readily available to the athlete or coach.

Cognitive Strategies

Cognitive strategies are psychological procedures used by athletes to mentally prepare themselves for competition (Ravizza & Rotella, 1982). In that they are used to alter the existing anxiety, frustration, confidence, and arousal levels of the athlete, they are also classified as intervention strategies. The cognitive strategies discussed in this section may be used to reduce the debilitating effects of anxiety and stress upon athletic performance. However, many of these procedures can also be used either to elevate or to reduce arousal levels. A case in point would be imagery. Depending on the kinds of images that are attended to, the athlete could be either aroused or relaxed. For example, imagining yourself sitting on a

California beach is much different than imagining a scene of aggression in professional hockey. The cognitive strategy of goal setting is primarily used to motivate athletes by directing their attention to specific aims and objectives. Three of the most common cognitive intervention strategies are discussed in this section (imagery, hypnosis, and goal setting).

Imagery

Game six of the 1987 baseball World Series provided an excellent example of the use of imagery by a professional athlete. During game six, Don Baylor, the Minnesota Twins' designated hitter, faced pitcher John Tudor of the St. Louis Cardinals. It was the bottom of the fifth inning; St. Louis was leading 5 to 3; and there were no outs and one man on second base. Baylor had last faced Tudor in 1983 when he was with the Yankees and Tudor was with the Red Sox. Preparing to face Tudor in this classic match-up of game six, Baylor recalls, "I reminisced about the last time he pitched me then. Let's just say I was somewhat more ready for him than he was for me." (Wulf, 1987). History records that Baylor took Tudor's first pitch deep into the left-field stands for a two-run homer.

Block (1981) identified human **imagery,** the use of visualization to imagine situations, as one of the most important topics in cognitive science. Two general theories have evolved. The first states that when we imagine a scene in our mind's eye, we are scanning an actual image that has somehow formed in our brain. This is not to say that a brain surgeon could find actual physical pictures lodged in our brains, but that the images are as real to us as an image taken from the retina of the eye. This position is held by the so-called pictorialists. The second position is that of the descriptionist. The descriptionist argues that there is no such thing as a mental image. That is, when we imagine a physical scene in our mind's eye, we are not really seeing an internal image, but the graphic and de-tailed nature of our language makes it seem so. Our thoughts, as it were, actually manufacture an image so clear that we think we are seeing one (Block, 1981).

Regardless of which view one takes, the images we see are vivid enough, and therefore it makes little difference whether they are pictorial by nature or de-scriptively represented in our minds. Some experimental findings about imagery are (1) mental images can be scanned, (2) small mental images are hard to see, (3) when images are expanded, they eventually overflow, (4) and images overflow from a roughly elliptical shape (Kosslyn, Pinker, Smith & Schwartz, 1981).

Consistent with Block's (1981) notion of the nature of imagery, Fisher (1986) clarifies that imagery is the language of the brain. In a real sense, the brain really can't tell the difference between an actual physical event and the vivid visual-ization of the same event. For this reason, imagery can be used by the brain to provide repetition, elaboration, intensification, and preservation of important ath-letic sequences and skills.

Smith (1987) identified five basic principles of the application of imagery to sport. These five principles are (1) imagery skills can be developed, (2) the ath-lete must have a positive attitude relative to the effectiveness of imagery, (3) imagery is most effective when used by skilled athletes, (4) knowing how to relax is a necessary precursor to the effective use of imagery, and (5) there are two kinds of imagery, internal and external. Using the principles outlined by Smith (1987), Fenker and Lambiotte (1987) reported a case study in which a perfor-mance enhancement program, based on the development of imagery skills, was implemented for a major college football team. The program used imagery training techniques to help the team achieve its best record in twenty years. The mere fact that a major football program was willing to adopt an imagery per-formance enhancement program is evidence that imagery is being taken seriously by coaches and athletes.

Sport psychologists have identified two methods of sport performance imagery: *internal* and *external* imagery (Mahoney & Avener, 1977). **Internal imagery** is considered to be primarily kinesthetic in nature. That is, athletes pretend to be within their own bodies while performing. Athletes feel themselves performing, and can see the object of attention, but cannot see their own bodies. **External imagery** is considered to be primarily visual in nature. That is, athletes pretend to watch themselves perform from outside. The research by Mahoney and Avener (1977) seemed to indicate that the first-person or internal type of imagery was superior. Their conclusions were based on elite gymnasts who claimed a reliance upon internal imagery as opposed to a group of less successful gymnasts who relied upon external imagery. One explanation for the supposed superiority of kinesthetic (internal) imagery is that it actually results in subliminal muscle activity in the muscles associated with the imagined actions. This concept was first demonstrated by Jacobson (1931) and was verified by Hale in 1982. Hale showed that weight lifters who used an internal imagery style experienced greater biceps muscle activity than those who used an external style. Likewise, Harris and Robinson (1986) demonstrated that internal imagery elicited greater EMG activity in the deltoid muscle group than external imagery during a lateral arm-raising task. They further demonstrated that advanced karate students not only used internal imagery to a greater degree than beginning karate students, but that the internal imagery generated greater EMG activity.

These findings provide evidence that a physiological difference exists between the two types of imagery. Internal imagery generates greater muscle EMG activity than does visual imagery. Whether or not internal imagery is actually better than external imagery in terms of facilitating physical performance is still open to debate. The Harris and Robinson (1986) findings suggest that internal imagery may be superior, since higher-skilled karate athletes favored its use. However, Epstein (1980) reported research showing that neither method is superior in terms of dart-throwing performance. In fact, the research is uncertain on this point (Rotella, Gansneder, Ojala & Billings, 1980). Because of this, it would seem reasonable to assume that some type of guided combination of the two styles would be most beneficial. Certainly the athlete can benefit from both visual and kinesthetic image rehearsal.

---

6. **Principle** Two kinds of imagery are available to the athlete.
   Application Internal imagery allows athletes to kinesthetically experience the correct execution of a skill, while external imagery allows them to see themselves performing the skill. Athletes should develop skill in both internal and external imagery.

Current interest in imagery makes one wonder why this has all occurred so recently. The fact is that interest in the topic has always been strong, but it was previously known as mental practice, not imagery or visualization. The current findings regarding imagery are consistent with earlier published information. Representative of some of this research are selected studies by Clark (1960) and Corbin (1967a, 1967b). Clark compared the effect of mental practice with that of physical practice in the learning of the Pacific Coast one-hand foul shot. He placed 144 high school boys into physical and mental practice groups on the basis of varsity, junior varsity, or novice experience. All subjects were given a twenty-five–shot pretest before and a twenty-five–shot posttest after fourteen days of practice (thirty shots per day). Results showed that mental practice was almost as effective as physical practice for the junior varsity and varsity groups, but physical practice was far superior to mental practice for the beginners. Corbin (1967a, 1967b) observed similar results using a wand-juggling task. From the results of these studies, it seems clear that for mental practice or imagery to facilitate performance, a certain amount of skill is necessary. In other words, a coach or teacher should not expect imagery training to be effective with athletes who are unskilled in their sports. The more skillful they are, the more useful mental rehearsal techniques will be for them. In support of this position, Landers, Boutcher, and Wang (1986) observed that skilled archers use imagery to a significantly greater extent than lesser-skilled archers.

---

7. **Principle** The more skillful and experienced an athlete is, the more he or she will be able to benefit from the use of imagery.

  Application To avoid discouraging young athletes from the use of imagery, make sure that he or she is familiar enough with the activity to know the difference between a good or bad performance. An athlete must know both what the skill looks like and how it feels in order to effectively use imagery.

Imagery or mental practice is most effective for activities that require some thought—those that have a large cognitive component (Ryan & Simons, 1981). For example, a balancing task would have a small cognitive component, while a finger maze would have a large cognitive component. In terms of sport, one should expect better results using imagery for tennis than for a rope-pulling contest.

As a general rule, the use of mental practice and imagery to enhance performance is supported by the literature. In a meta-analysis (summary analysis) conducted by Feltz and Landers (1983), a reveiw of over one hundred studies revealed that mental practice is better than no practice at all. Price and Meacci (1985) demonstrated that relaxation and imagery is as effective as physical practice in improving putting in golf. However, it is important to note that negative outcome imagery is more powerful in causing a decrement in performance than positive outcome imagery is for facilitating athletic performance (Woolfolk, Murphy, Gottesfeld & Aitken, 1985.) This is why it is so important that the athlete master the technique of *thought stopping* and *centering* as introduced in chapter 2. The more competent an athlete is in mastering imagery skills, the more effective its application (Kohl, Roenker & Turner, 1985).

Developing Imagery Skills

As with relaxation training, imagery abilities can be improved with practice. Hickman (1979, pp. 120–121) listed thirteen steps to effective training in mental imagery and rehearsal. These are summarized in the following six steps:

1. Find a quiet place where you won't be disturbed, assume a comfortable position, and relax completely.
2. Practice imagery by visualizing a circle that fills the visual field. Make the circle turn a deep blue. Repeat the process several times, imagining a different color each time. Allow the images to disappear. Relax and observe the spontaneous imagery that arises.
3. Create the image of a simple three-dimensional glass. Fill it with a colorful liquid, add ice cubes and a straw. Write a descriptive caption underneath.
4. Select a variety of scenes and develop them with rich detail. Include sport-related images such as a swimming pool, tennis court, and a beautiful golf course. Practice visualizing people, including strangers, in each of these scenes.
5. Imagine yourself in a sport setting of keen interest to you. Visualize and feel yourself successfully participating in the scene. Relax and enjoy your success.
6. End the session by breathing deeply, opening your eyes, and adjusting to the external environment.

The potential of imagery as an effective cognitive strategy is enormous. An athlete can physically practice shooting basketball free throws for years, and yet never feel comfortable or confident doing the same thing in a game situation. Generally, practice conditions do not match the anxiety and fear associated with the real-life situation. In an effective mental imagery session, athletes can imagine themselves successfully making basket after basket in pressure-packed game situations.

Stress management strategies using imagery have proven effective in improving athletic performance. Perhaps the strongest evidence comes from Suinn's (1972) visual-motor behavior rehearsal program (VMBR). This program will be discussed in greater detail later in this chapter. A body of supporting literature that speaks well of the use of imagery to improve athletic performance is continuing to emerge (Kolonay, 1977).

If there is a shortcoming to research involving imagery, it is in terms of determining whether or not an athlete is using it. For example, how can you be sure that an athlete who is supposed to be practicing visual imagery really is? And how can you be sure that control subjects are not using the technique? These and other methodological problems present challenges to the researcher.

---

8. **Principle** Imagery allows the anxiety-prone athlete to practice relaxation skills in a stressful situation.

    Application Since actual practice situations are rarely as stressful as competition, the athlete should use imagery to create numerous anxiety-provoking situations.

Hypnosis

Of all the intervention strategies, hypnosis is the least understood. Yet a close analysis reveals that in many important ways hypnosis (especially self-hypnosis) is identical to relaxation training and transcendental meditation. This is especially true during the induction phase of hypnosis. Once an individual is hypnotized and is asked to perform some act (waking hypnosis), then certain physiological differences may emerge. For example, if while hypnotized, the subject is asked to imagine that a raging tiger is approaching, you can expect that the person's heart rate and respiration rate will go up, not down. Yet in table 5.1 we can see that hypnosis yields the same type of relaxation response as do the other intervention strategies. This is because suggestions of deep relaxation were given to the subjects. This pattern also emerges before hypnotic suggestions are given.

A case study in which hypnosis was used to help an amateur boxer was documented by Heyman (1987). In this chronology, a single-case experimental design was presented in which hypnosis was systematically used as an intervention strategy. The athlete was described as suffering a performance decrement due to anxiety caused by crowd noise. As a result of the controlled and professionally applied use of hypnosis, the athlete was able to show some improvement. While there may be some potential risks associated with the indiscriminate use of hypnosis by an untrained therapist (Morgan & Brown, 1983), most concerns about hypnosis are unfounded. It is probably fair to say that hypnosis is clouded by more myths and misconceptions than any other form of psychological intervention (Clarke & Jackson, 1983).

The following discussion should demystify hypnosis to some degree and explain its relationship to sport performance. The subject is divided into four subsections. They are (1) defining hypnosis, (2) obtaining the hypnotic trance, (3) self-hypnosis, and (4) the effect of hypnosis on athletic performance.

Hypnosis Defined

Ulett and Peterson (1965) define **hypnosis** as the uncritical acceptance of a suggestion. This is a definition that almost all psychologists can agree upon, since it does little to explain what causes hypnosis or how it differs from the waking state. Four events occur when a subject is hypnotized. First, the subject elicits the relaxation response and becomes drowsy and lethargic. Second, the subject manifests responsiveness to suggestions. Third, the subject reports changes in body awareness and feeling. Finally, the subject knows that he or she is hypnotized (Barber, Spanos & Chaves, 1974).

There are at least two theoretical explanations for the phenomenon of hypnotism. (Barber, et. al., 1974). The first represents the hypnotic trance viewpoint, while the second represents the cognitive-behavioral viewpoint. The traditional or hypnotic trance viewpoint is that the hypnotized subject is in an altered state or hypnotic trance. The cognitive-behavioral viewpoint rejects the notion of a trance and simply bases the hypnotic phenomenon on the personality of the subject. That is, subjects carry out hypnotic behaviors because they have positive attitudes, motivations, and expectations that lead to a willingness to think and imagine with the themes suggested by the hypnotist. Since only about 16 percent of subjects who go through the hypnotic induction procedure can reach a deep trance (Edmonston, 1981), the cognitive-behavioral viewpoint is certainly plausible.

From the hypnotic trance viewpoint, the trance has also been referred to as a state of cortical inhibition (Orne, 1959). The cortical inhibition viewpoint is supported by the work of Watzlawick (1978). According to this explanation, hypnosis appeals directly to the functioning of the nondominant cerebral hemisphere. The process of hypnosis inhibits the functions of the dominant hemisphere (thinking, logic, language, details) and allows the nondominant hemispheric functions (whole movements, whole ideas, picture rather than words, music rather than ideas) to take over (Pressman, 1980).

A third explanation for the phenomenon of hypnosis was proposed by Orne (1959). According to Orne, a simple increase in suggestibility results from the hypnotic induction procedure. The weakness of this explanation is that it does not say how or why the subject becomes more responsive to suggestions. This is undoubtedly why Barber et al. (1974) did not include it. Consequently, we can agree that hypnosis is a state of uncritical acceptance of suggestions, but we are torn between two divergent explanations of how this is brought about.

The acceptance of Barber's cognitive-behavioral viewpoint certainly would tend to demystify hypnosis. However, by itself it may be too simplistic an explanation. Regardless of which position one takes, the end result is the same: A subject is extremely responsive to suggestions when he or she was not as responsive during the waking state.

Achieving the Hypnotic Trance

Five phases are associated with inducing the **hypnotic trance** in a subject. They are preparation of the subject, the induction process, the hypnotic phase, waking up, and the posthypnotic phase.

When subjects are prepared for hypnotism, they must be relieved of any fears and apprehensions they have about hypnotism. Some myths may need to be exposed. For example, subjects may be under the impression that they will lose control, that they will be unaware of surroundings or will lose consciousness. They must have complete trust in the hypnotist and must want to be hypnotized. They also must be told that they will remain in control at all times and will be able to come out of the hypnotic trance if they want to.

It is during the **hypnotic induction** phase that the hypnotist actually hypnotizes the subject. There are many induction techniques. The best ones are associated with relaxation, attentional focus, and imagery. In fact, the steps involved in eliciting the relaxation response using these techniques are essentially identical to those in hypnosis. The only difference is that the word hypnosis is never used in eliciting the relaxation response. It should also be pointed out that in terms of physiological responses, hypnotic induction is identical to the relaxation responses associated with progressive relaxation, transcendental meditation, and autogenic training. Coleman (1976) verified this in a study in which he compared the physiological responses associated with hypnotic induction and relaxation procedures.

Generally, induction procedures are fairly standard. They are typically comprised of a series of suggestions aimed at eliciting the subject's cooperation and directing his or her attention to thoughts and feelings about being relaxed and peaceful. The selection of an induction technique is generally based on the hypnotist's comfort with it or because he or she believes the subject's attentional style or personality is compatible with it. Some of the more common techniques involve fixation on an object, monotonous suggestions ("you feel sleepy"), and imagery. Regardless of which technique is used, the effect is the same. The subject becomes very lethargic, experiences the relaxation response, and becomes very susceptible to suggestions. The hypnotist can use a number of techniques to make the subject become more responsive to hypnotism. Most of these are associated with relaxing the subject and gaining his or her confidence. Others include using the word *hypnotism* to define the situation and the manner in which suggestions are given. For example, a good time to suggest to the subject that he or she is becoming tired is when the hypnotist observes that the subjects' eyelids are drooping. The hypnotist must also avoid making suggestions that the subject may fail.

Once the hypnotic state has been induced, the subject is in **neutral hypnosis.** In this state, physiological responses are identical to those of the relaxation response. The hypnotized subject is generally asked to respond either in imagination or physically to suggestions of the hypnotist. Typically, these suggestions are alerting and arousing, and bring about the "alert" trance, or **waking hypnosis** (Edmonston, 1981). If subjects are asked to carry out suggestions while in a trance, they are doing so in the state of waking hypnosis. Subjects may, of course, be given suggestions of deep relaxation while in the hypnotic state. This will result in the relaxation response as illustrated in table 5.1. Generally, subjects will be given suggestions to carry out after they are awake. These are referred to as **posthypnotic suggestions.** Ken Norton was given posthypnotic suggestions for his fight with Muhammad Ali.

The fourth phase of hypnosis is coming out of the trance. Actually, a hypnotized subject can come out of the trance anytime. The only reason subjects do not come out on their own is because they don't want to. The relationship between the hypnotist and the subject can be a very pleasant one. When the hypnotist wishes to bring a subject out of a trance, he or she does so simply by suggesting that the subject wake up on a given signal. For example, the hypnotist might say, "Okay, when I count to three you will wake up." Occasionally a subject will resist coming out of the trance. If this happens, the subject is taken back into a deep trance and asked why he or she doesn't want to come out. After a few minutes of discussion and another suggestion to wake up, the subject will generally do so.

Suggestions given to subjects during hypnosis are often designed to influence them during the posthypnotic phase, or after they have come out of the hypnotic trance. Posthypnotic suggestions given to athletes should focus on the way they should feel in certain competitive situations. For example, a baseball player may be told that "when you get into the batter's box, you will find that you feel relaxed and confident." Specific suggestions such as "you'll be able to get a hit almost every time," should be avoided, since failure will tend to undermine the effectiveness of the suggestions (Nideffer, 1976a).

Autohypnosis

There are two kinds of hypnosis. The first kind is **heterohypnosis,** and the second is called **autohypnosis,** or self-hypnosis. Our discussion up to this point has dealt primarily with heterohypnosis, that which is induced by another person, usually a trained hypnotist or psychologist. Heterohypnosis should only be practiced by trained professionals. Even though an attempt has been made in this text to demystify hypnosis, this does not mean that potential dangers do not exist. Heterohypnosis is based upon a rather delicate rapport between the hypnotist and the subject. Consequently, if heterohypnosis is to be practiced on athletes, it should be done so by a competent psychologist (Morgan & Brown, 1983).

---

9. **Principle** A trained psychologist should be present if heterohypnosis is used as a cognitive strategy.

   Application The hypnotized person is very susceptible to suggestions. For this reason, failure to employ a professional may do more harm than good.

Autohypnosis is not based on a relationship with another individual. Yet all of the effects that can be achieved through heterohypnosis can be achieved through autohypnosis. It should also be emphasized that in one sense, all hypnosis is self-hypnosis, since people cannot be hypnotized unless they want to be. Furthermore, hypnosis is a natural state of consciousness that we slip into and out of dozens of times a day (Pulos, 1979).

As explained by Ulett and Peterson (1965), there are two kinds of autohypnosis. The first is self-induced, and the second is induced as a posthypnotic suggestion following heterohypnosis. The latter method is easier to achieve. In this method, subjects are told during hypnosis that they will be able to hypnotize themselves anytime they wish simply by following some relaxation and attentional focus induction procedures. Because they have already been hypnotized, they know how it feels and they enjoy the feeling. Therefore, it is much easier for them to hypnotize themselves. With each repetition of self-hypnosis, it becomes easier and easier to achieve. What will initially be relaxation will later become effective hypnosis as subjects learn to narrow their field of attention.

The phases involved in autohypnosis are identical to those outlined for hypnosis generally. If a coach or teacher wishes to employ autohypnosis as an intervention strategy for reducing anxiety and improving concentration and imagery, he or she should go over these steps with the athlete. First, the athlete must be completely comfortable regarding the use of hypnosis. The athlete should begin with the reminder (suggestion) that he or she is in complete control and can disengage from the hypnotic trance at any time. The induction procedures are the same as for heterohypnosis. Some common strategies for induction are to sit in an easy chair and stare at a spot on the wall, imagine a blank screen, or look into a mirror.

Posthypnotic suggestions given during autohypnosis should always be couched in positive terms, stressing what is to be accomplished rather than dwelling on negative things to be eliminated. For example, the athlete may wish to concentrate on being more positive when he or she prepares to receive a tennis serve from a tough opponent. A suggestion such as "I will feel relaxed and agile," would be better than, "I'm going to hit a winner." The second suggestion contains the seeds of defeat, since you can't always hit a winner. Suggestions such as "I won't feel nervous," are negative because they only call attention to the problem. The athlete should have specific suggestions already in mind before the hypnotic phase begins. In some cases, the athlete could have the suggestions written on a card (perhaps by the coach) to read during the hypnotic trance.

---

10. **Principle** Self-hypnosis or autohypnosis is just as effective as heterohypnosis, and does not place the athlete in a situation of dependence.

   Application If hypnosis skills are taught, autohypnosis is preferred to heterohypnosis. Autohypnosis is very similar to autogenic training and is safe.

Hypnosis and Athletic Performance

Since 1933, several important reviews have been published on the relationship between hypnosis and motor performance. These reviews have centered primarily on the literature comparing hypnosis and muscular strength and endurance. None of these early reviews (Gorton, 1949; Hull, 1933; Johnson, 1961; Weitzenhoffer, 1963) resulted in clear-cut conclusions about the effectiveness of hypnosis in facilitating motor performance. All of the reviews identified research design problems and lack of standardization procedures as factors that led to the inconsistent results. However, Johnson (1961) made several important conclusions. These are very important and remain valid.

1. The deeper the hypnotic trance, the more likely it is that suggestions will work.
2. General arousal techniques are more useful in enhancing muscular strength and endurance than hypnotic suggestions.

3. Negative suggestions invariably work to the detriment of the performer.
4. Hypnosis can help a successful athlete, but it can't make a good performer out of a poor one.
5. Hypnotizing athletes may do more harm than good.

---

11. **Principle** Giving negative suggestions to a hypnotized athlete will likely result in a performance decrement.

    Application If an athlete under hypnosis is told that she will be successful, that may or may not happen. However, the athlete who is told under hypnosis that he or she will fail probably will. Negative suggestions must be completely avoided when working with athletes.

Probably the most important review conducted to date on this subject was done by Morgan (1972a). Morgan reviewed the literature in two phases. First, he took a second look at the research already reviewed prior to 1963, and second, he reviewed the literature from 1963 to 1971. His review included the literature about muscular strength and endurance as well as the rather scanty research dealing with athletic performance. Morgan's conclusions for both types of tasks were remarkably similar to Johnson's (1961). He indicated that positive suggestions were effective in facilitating performance regardless of whether or not the athlete was hypnotized, and that negative suggestions almost always caused a decrement in performance.

Since Morgan's review was published, several investigations have been conducted on the relationship between hypnosis and athletic performance. We will consider three of them. As we shall see, the results of these three studies are generally consistent with the conclusions drawn by Johnson (1961) and Morgan (1972a).

Ulrich (1973) conducted a study to determine the effect of hypnotic and non-hypnotic suggestions on archery performance. Using archery students (forty-three males and nine females), he assigned each student to one of four treatment conditions. First of all, the subjects were tested on their susceptibility to hypnosis and categorized as high or low on this variable. The highly susceptible subjects were matched in terms of archery skill and assigned to either a hypnotism-plus-positive-suggestions group or to a positive-suggestions-only group. Likewise, the less susceptible subjects were matched according to skill and assigned to either a positive-suggestions-only group or a control group receiving neither suggestions nor hypnotism. Statistically, the groups were compared on shooting performance from distances of 15, 20, and 25 yards. The results revealed no reliable differences among the groups. The researcher concluded that identical suggestions given in the normal waking state appeared to be as effective as the same suggestions given in the hypnotic state.

Baer (1980) studied the effect of time-slowing hypnotic suggestions on volleying in a video tennis game. Fourteen female subjects were screened for hypnotic suggestibility, but only three of them were retained for being high in suggestibility. After establishing both a waking and a hypnotic baseline for length of volleys, subjects were given alternating suggestions for ball slowing and quickness of response. Results revealed that the initial suggestions for ball slowing did not result in improved volleys, but in subsequent presentations, longer volleys were made. The author concluded that highly suggestible subjects could improve volleying performance as a result of hypnotic suggestions.

Ito (1979) further investigated the relative effect of suggestibility upon motor performance. Ito studied the effects of hypnosis and motivational suggestions on muscular strength. In this experiment, thirty male subjects performed a hand dynamometer strength task under four different conditions. The four conditions were performance in the waking state, motivating instructions in the waking state, hypnosis alone, and performance in the hypnotic state with motivating instructions. The results showed that the subjects who received motivating instructions did the best, regardless of whether they were hypnotized or not. At this point, Ito categorized his thirty subjects as being high, medium, or low on hypnotic suggestibility. With this further manipulation, it was discovered that the highly suggestible subjects who were both hypnotized and who received motivating instructions had the highest strength scores ($p = .05$). We can conclude that the question of susceptibility to hypnosis was the critical factor in research involving hypnosis.

The reviews by Johnson (1961) and Morgan (1972a) explain quite well the relationship between hypnosis and motor performance. Little has been reported since 1972 that would alter Morgan's conclusions. In a more recent work, Morgan and Brown (1983) reiterate many of the conclusions derived from the early review but with greater emphasis on the need for a psychotherapist when dealing with heterohypnosis. Finally, the question of susceptability to hypnosis as mentioned by Ito (1979) seems to be a viable issue, and perhaps future research involving hypnosis should pay particular attention to this variable.

Goal Setting

While the notion of goal setting to enhance achievement is not new, its specific application to athletic performance has become an important cognitive strategy in recent years. A study by Dmitrova (1970) involving sprinting, and a more recent study by Wankel and McEwan (1976) involving a 450-meter run, verifies

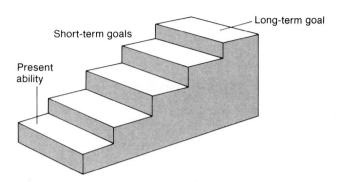

Figure 5.3 A goal-setting staircase showing the relationship between short- and long-term goals. From Gould, Dan, Developing psychological skills in young athletes, in *Coaching science update.* Copyright © 1983 Coaching Association of Canada, Ottawa, Canada. Reprinted by permission.

the utility of goal-setting procedures in sport. In the study by Wankel and McEwan, eighty-four high school boys were evenly divided into three treatment conditions based upon a pretest on the 450-meter run. Subjects in the control group were given knowledge of results (KR) of their first run and told to do their best on the posttest. Subjects in a private goal-setting condition were also given KR for their first run and asked to set private goals for their second run. Finally, those in the public goal condition met as a group and were asked to write down their goals on a piece of paper for the second run. They were informed that their goals would be posted for everyone to see. The results of the second run revealed significant differences favoring the public goal-setting group over the other two.

This study confirms our expectation that goal setting is an effective psychological strategy for improving performance. Research also shows that the nature of the goals being set is very important (Gould, 1983). Several factors make goal setting more effective. First, in order to obtain a long-term goal, such as becoming a varsity basketball player, an athlete must meet several short-term goals along the way. The relationship between long- and short-term goals is illustrated in figure 5.3. The best way to reach the top step is to take each step one at a time.

A second important characteristic of effective goal setting is to set hard but realistic goals. A goal that is not realistic and cannot be reached may discourage the athlete. For example, setting a goal to run one hundred meters in less than nine seconds is certainly unrealistic. On the other hand, if you can run the mile in six minutes and you set a season goal to run it in five minutes, this is a hard goal, but certainly realistic.

Another important characteristic of good goal setting is to set specific behavioral goals that can be measured. We can easily determine if we are meeting our behavioral goals. For example, if a basketball player's goal is simply to become a good shooter, how does one determine when this goal has been met? It cannot be determined. On the other hand, if this player's goal is to hit eight out of ten 15-foot jump shots, the accomplishment of this goal can easily be determined.

A fourth important characteristic of goal setting is to outline a specific strategy or plan for meeting the goal. Many goals are not reached simply because there is no systematic plan for achieving them. For example, exactly how does one achieve the goal of becoming an 85 percent free-throw shooter? If left to chance, it will probably never happen. The coach and athlete together must devise a plan for achieving this goal. The athlete may have to stay after practice every day and shoot an extra one hundred baskets. Other strategies such as increasing wrist and arm strength may also be considered.

Finally, a good goal-setting program requires constant monitoring and evaluation by player and coach. A day should not go by without the athlete considering goals and evaluating progress. It may be that a particular goal cannot be achieved. In this case the athlete should redefine that goal in a more realistic manner. However, in most cases the regular evaluation of progress will help athletes see improvements that will provide them additional motivation to achieve their goals.

---

12. **Principle** Athletes who practice good goal-setting skills are more
    successful than those who do not.
    Application Goal-setting skills should be an integral part of an
    athlete's psychological skill development. Good goal-setting skills
    do not come naturally; they must be taught.

The foundation for research associated with goal setting to enhance human performance comes from Edwin Locke. The basic premise of Locke's theory is that conscious intentions in the form of goals regulate subsequent actions and behaviors (Locke, 1968). More specifically, the setting of realistic but difficult goals will result in greater performance than no goals, easy goals, or "do your best" goals. Prior to turning his attention to goal setting in sport, Locke reported that of 110 studies reported between 1969 and 1980, 99 of them showed positive or partially positive effects favoring goal setting in industrial and related environmental settings (Locke, Shaw, Saari & Latham, 1981).

In testing the utility of employing goal-setting strategies in sport, researchers initially had difficulty in demonstrating the superiority of goal setting over a "do your best" strategy (Weinberg, Bruya & Jackson, 1985). However, researchers

Table 5.3 Principles of Goal Setting Derived from Research. From E. A. Locke and G. P. Latham, The application of goal setting to sports. *Journal of Sport Psychology, 1985, 7,* 205–222. Adapted by permission of Human Kinetic Publishers, Inc.

1. Specific goals direct activity more effectively and reliably than vague or general goals.
2. Difficult or challenging goals produce better performance than moderate or easy goals.
3. Short-term goals can be used as a means of attaining long-term goals.
4. Goal setting forces the athlete to focus attention on relevent activities.
5. Goal setting has the effect of regulating expenditure of effort.
6. Goal setting enhances persistence.
7. Goal setting promotes the development of new strategies.
8. Goal setting only works if there is timely feedback available showing progress in relation to the goal.
9. Goals must be accepted by the athlete in order to be effective.
10. Goal attainment is facilitated by a plan of action or strategy.
11. Competition, a key element in sports, can be viewed as a form of goal setting.

quickly recognized that the inability to demonstrate the superiority of the goal-setting strategy was due to the researchers failure to control variables such as competition and social evaluation (critical evaluation by peers and others) that are prevalent in sport (Hall & Byrne, 1988). When problems associated with field experiments (as opposed to laboratory experiments) were taken into consideration, researchers were able to demonstrate the importance of goal setting in the obtaining of athletic success (Hall, Weinberg & Jackson, 1987; Weinberg, Bruya, Longino & Jackson, 1988).

That athletes and coaches currently employ goal-setting strategies in sport is quite obvious. Coaches are very fond of stating that their goal for a team is to make the playoffs or to win a certain number of games in a particular season. What is not so obvious is that the goal-setting strategies employed by coaches and athletes are often very general and unmeasurable. In applying his theory of goal setting to sport, Locke has suggested eleven specific principles that the coach or athlete can use to refine goal-setting strategies (Locke & Latham, 1985). These eleven principles are based on previous research and are presented in table 5.3.

Package Intervention Programs

Numerous stress management and cognitive intervention programs may be identified for reducing competitive anxiety and increasing athletic performance. Using karate as the athletic medium, Seabourne, Weinberg, Jackson, and Suinn (1985) demonstrated that individualized and packaged intervention programs are more effective than a nonindividualized program in which participants select their own strategies. Athletes benefit most from intervention strategies when designed to fit their needs or presented in a systematic and organized fashion. Merely informing an athlete about various cognitive strategies is not particularly effective.

In this section I will describe four intervention programs that have received attention from psychologists, sport psychologists, and researchers. However, there are several other programs that are quite similar and should be briefly mentioned. Included among these are Suinn's (1983) seven steps to peak performance; Kirshenbaum, Wittrock, Smith, and Monson's (1984) criticism inoculation training; Murphy and Woolfolk's (1987) cognitive-behavioral stress reduction program; and Llewellyn and Blucker's (1982) mental self-improvement program. All of these programs, including those to follow, are based on many of the relaxation and cognitive strategies outlined previously in this chapter.

Visual-Motor Behavior Rehearsal

Visual-motor behavior rehearsal (VMBR) was developed by Suinn(1972) as an adaptation of Wolpe's (1958) desensitization procedures for humans. The process of desensitization was used to help patients to overcome phobias. For example, a patient fearing heights would be desensitized to this phobia through a series of systematic approximations to the fearful stimuli. Although Suinn used VMBR to treat people with depressions, he was especially interested in applying the techniques to athletes. His particular method of training consisted of (1) relaxing the

athlete's body by means of a brief version of Jacobson's (1929) progressive relaxation techniques, (2) practicing imagery related to the demands of the athlete's sport, and (3) using imagery to practice a specific skill in a lifelike stressful environment (Suinn, 1976, 1980).

Basically, VMBR combines relaxation and imagery into one procedure. It also requires the athlete to mentally practice a specific skill under simulated game conditions. Theoretically, this would be better than actual practice, since the practice environment rarely resembles a game situation. Coaches and teachers typically go to great lengths to minimize distractions to their athletes during practice sessions. VMBR teaches the athlete to use relaxation and imagery techniques to create lifelike situations. Going through these stressful experiences mentally should make it easier to deal with the stress of actual competition. Suinn generally recommends the use of internal kinesthetic imagery for VMBR training, but suggests that in addition the athlete should use external imagery to identify performance errors.

In testing the VMBR program, Suinn experimented with alpine skiers (Suinn, 1972); Olympic Nordic and biathlon athletes (Suinn, 1976); and a long-distance kicker in American football (Titley, 1980). While the results of these anecdotal reports were impressive in terms of perceived results, they were admittedly lacking in scientific controls.

Because of the need for statistical evidence for the theory, Kolonay (1977) conducted a scientific investigation of VMBR. The results of this study provided evidence in favor of VMBR. Kolonay used four groups of male college basketball players. Each group was assigned to a different treatment condition: a VMBR group, a relaxation-only group, an imagery-only group, and a control group. Before and after the six-week training period, each player's free-throw shooting percentage was recorded. Improvement in free-throw shooting was essentially used as the dependent variable. Kolonay's results showed a significant improvement in free-throw shooting percentage for the VMBR group.

The Kolonay study represented the first scientific investigation to study visual-motor behavioral rehearsal as a technique to improve athletic performance. However, the study had weaknesses that tended to throw some doubt on the conclusions. Recognizing the limitations of the Kolonay research, several other investigators studied VMBR. Noel (1980) researched the effect of VMBR training on the tennis-serving performance of high- and low-ability players. While a significant difference was not noted between the VMBR and control groups on serving accuracy, an interaction between skill level and stress management suggested that the performance of high-ability VMBR subjects improved with mental imagery, while the low-ability VMBR group performed worse. This finding is consistent with the basic mental practice research findings reported earlier by Clark (1960). Specifically, skilled performers use mental imagery and rehearsal better than do unskilled performers.

Weinberg, Seabourne, and Jackson (1981) replicated the Kolonay study with an effort at improving the statistical analysis and better defining the dependent variable. Subjects in this study were college-age males enrolled in a karate club. They were matched according to skill and assigned to one of four treatment conditions. As with the Kolonay study, the four treatments were VMBR training, relaxation training, imagery training, and a control group. In terms of anxiety, the results of the study showed that all subjects reduced their trait anxiety scores and that the VMBR and relaxation subjects had lower A-state scores at the end of the six-week training session than did the control or imagery training subjects. In terms of performance scores, the results were broken down into three categories—skill, combinations, and sparring. The results showed no reliable differences among the treatments in terms of skill and combinations. However, in terms of sparring scores, the VMBR group performed significantly better than the other three groups.

Seabourne, Weinberg, and Jackson (1982) did another study using karate students as subjects. Subjects were eighteen male and twenty-six female college-age students enrolled in one of two karate classes. Each class met twice a week for sixteen weeks. One class was randomly assigned to a VMBR training condition (in-class and at-home practice), while the other class served as a placebo control group studying the tradition and art of karate. The dependent variables used in the research were trait anxiety, state anxiety, and karate performance (skill, combinations, and sparring). The results of the research showed that both groups decreased their trait anxiety scores. The VMBR group also showed a significant reduction in state anxiety compared to the placebo group, and the VMBR group performed significantly better in all aspects of karate performance than the control group.

The effectiveness of VMBR with karate performers was further verified by a follow-up study by Seabourne, Weinberg, and Jackson (1984). In this investigation, VMBR was observed to effectively reduce state anxiety and improve karate performance over time.

Hall and Erffmeyer (1983) introduced a modeling strategy to enhance the effectiveness of VMBR. They reasoned that a performance effect was not observed in studies in which subjects had not mastered the VMBR technique. Highly-skilled female basketball players were randomly assigned to one of two treatment conditions. Treatment 1 used traditional imagery and relaxation techniques, while treatment 2 featured a film of expert performers shooting free throws. After watching the film, treatment 2 subjects imagined themselves executing a perfect free throw. The results showed that the addition of the model enhanced the effectiveness of the VMBR procedure, since treatment 2 (with model) resulted in higher posttest shooting percentages than treatment 1.

In summary, it appears that VMBR training is extremely effective in reducing an athlete's trait and state anxiety levels. This is certainly important in terms of stress management. The potential for VMBR training to improve athletic performance is very good, but its effectiveness depends on the type of task, skill level of the performer, and the athlete's ability to relax and use imagery. The study by Hall and Erffmeyer (1983) highlights the importance of skill level in the use of imagery and the additional effectiveness of VMBR if a skilled model is used. Highly-skilled athletes are more effective in using VMBR training and mental practice to enhance performance than are the unskilled.

---

13. **Principle** VMBR is an effective intervention program that incorporates principles derived from relaxation training and imagery to reduce anxiety, focus attention, and enhance performance.

   Application An athlete who suffers from the debilitating effects of anxiety as well as nonaffected athletes can benefit from visual motor behavior rehearsal.

Stress Inoculation/Management Training

In addition to VMBR, two other stress management training programs will now be addressed. The first is called *Stress Inoculation Training* and was developed by Meichenbaum (1977). The second was developed by R. E. Smith (1980) and is called the *Cognitive-Affective Stress Management Training* program. The key element associated with Stress Inoculation Training is the progressive exposure of the athlete to situations of greater and greater stress. The key element of Stress Management Training is that, through imagery, the athlete experiences feelings identical to those experienced during competition.

According to Long (1980), **Stress Inoculation Training** (**SIT**) involves four phases. In phase 1, the trainer talks with the athlete about the athlete's stress responses. During this phase, the athlete learns to identify and express feelings and fears. The athlete is also educated in lay terms about stress and the effect it can have upon athletic performance and psychological well-being. In phase 2, the athlete learns how to relax and use self-regulation skills. This is done in small groups, using a problem-solving approach, with members of the group helping each other find solutions. Stressful experiences are described in detail, and potential hazards identified. In phase 3, the athlete learns specific coping self-statements designed to be used in stressful situations. For example, in preparation for a wrestling match, the athlete may learn to say, "I'm okay, just relax. Take a deep breath, let it out slow. Slow things down, I'm in control here, and

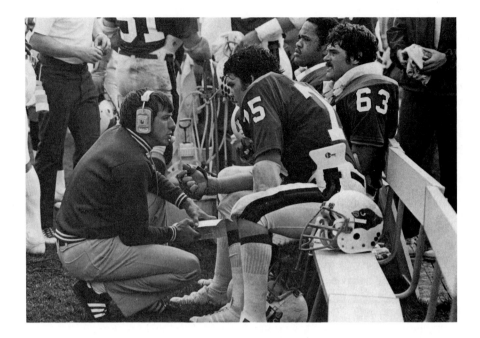

I'm in top condition." In the important final phase, the trainer guides the athlete through a series of progressively more threatening situations. As the athlete learns to cope and confront a relatively mild situation, he or she is immediately exposed to a situation of greater stress. In each situation, the athlete practices relaxation and coping statements. The threatening situations are presented through imagery, films, role playing, and real-life situations. For example, if the fear of competition is stressful, the athlete is allowed to experience competition in small gradations. The first grade may be a friendly game of "horse" in basketball. As soon as the athlete is able to cope with a low level of stress, the situation is changed, and a more stressful situation is presented. In this way, the athlete becomes inoculated to progressively increasing levels of stress. Eventually, the athlete's fear of competition is minimized to the degree that he or she can cope with it.

Smith's (1980) Cognitive-Affective **Stress Management Training (SMT)** program is quite similar to Suinn's (1972) anxiety management training program, the precursor to VMBR. SMT is also quite similar to the first three phases of SIT. The fundamental difference between SMT and SIT is in the final phase. Basically, the SMT program involves three phases. In phase 1, the athlete learns to conceptualize the stress experience. This phase is educational in nature, as the athlete learns to understand the stress response and what causes it. This typically entails a discussion between the trainer and the athlete. Phase 2 of the SMT program involves the development of psychological skills for coping with stress.

The athlete learns progressive relaxation techniques with particular emphasis on deep breathing to facilitate relaxation. The final phase requires the athlete to practice stress coping skills in stressful situations. As with SIT, stress is induced through imagery, films, electric shock, and real-life situations. Regardless of the type of situation, it is critical that the athlete actually experience the affect associated with stress, which distinguishes SIT from SMT. In SMT the feelings experienced in the actual stress situation are induced. In this way, the athlete learns how to cope with the stress of actual competition, even if it is only being visualized.

These two stress management programs were tested in a study by Ziegler, Klinzing, and Williamson (1982). The purpose of the study was to determine the effects the two stress management programs have on the heart rate and oxygen consumption of cross-country runners. Subjects in the treatment groups met with an experimenter twice a week for five-and-a-half weeks for stress management training. Results of a twenty-minute postsubmaximal run indicated significant differences in cardiorespiratory efficiency between the stress management training groups and a control group. Reliable differences were not noted between the SMT and SIT programs.

Reports by Boutcher and Rotella (1987) and Mace and Carroll (1985) provide additional support for the effectiveness of SIT. In the report by Boutcher and Rotella (1987), SIT was incorporated into the final phase of a four-phase psychological skills education program. In the study reported by Mace and Carroll (1985), SIT was effectively used to reduce anxiety levels of subjects involved in repelling from the roof of a 70-foot building.

Psychological Skills Education Program

The Psychological Skills Education Program (PSEP) was developed by Boutcher and Rotella (1987) for athletes who perform closed-skills such as weight lifting (clean-and-jerk) or a closed skill such as free-throw shooting in a sport that is primarily open-skill in nature (basketball). Open-skill sports such as basketball and football are classified as such because they are open to the environment. An opponent cannot interfere with an athlete's attempt at a clean-and-jerk in weight lifting, but an opponent can alter or interfere with a pass, dribble, or jump shot in basketball because they are open to the environment. The program was conceived as a four-phase program in which various intervention strategies are applied in the final phase.

In phase one, the *sport analysis* phase, the sport psychologist does a thorough analysis of the characteristics of the closed-skill that is involved. If the athlete is trying to improve his or her golf swing, the sport psychologist must become familiar with the important biomechanical elements of the golf swing as well as physiological and psychological requirements. The important point is that the sport psychologist should not prematurely attribute all problems to a psychological cause.

In phase two, the *individual assessment* phase, the psychological strengths and weaknesses of the athlete must be determined from a psychological perspective. It is at this point that various psychological inventories should be administered and interpreted. Appropriate inventories might include the Sport Competition Anxiety Test (SCAT), the Profile of Mood States (POMS), and Cattell's 16 Personality Factor Questionnaire. If after interpreting the selected inventories it is concluded that the athlete demonstrates abnormal clinical symptoms, he or she should be referred to the appropriate professional sources.

In phase three, the *conceptualization/motivation* phase, the sport psychologist discusses with the athlete the kind of commitment that is needed in order to change inappropriate behaviors. It is during this phase that the athlete must come to grips with his or her own desire to excel. Whether or not an athlete has the desire to develop effective psychological skills must be determined prior to entering into phase four.

In phase four, the *development of mental skills* phase, the athlete learns specific intervention techniques that can influence anxiety and performance. These mental skills include relaxation, imagery, and thought-stopping. In learning various invervention strategies the athlete is taken through three training stages. In the first stage, the athlete practices and learns a psychological skill such as imagery in a general environmental setting. In stage two, the athlete applies the psychological skill to a situation-specific visualized setting. Finally, in stage three, the athlete develops appropriately designed performance routines. These performance routines are similar to the ritualistic steps that many professional baseball players go through in the batter's box. All good athlete's have well-developed preperformance routines they go through in preparation for skill execution. The rather precise routine that a professional golfer goes through each time he or she addresses a golf ball is another example. These performance routines are important to the athlete to help him or her direct attention to appropriate stimuli.

---

14. **Principle** Package intervention programs that are individualized for the athlete are more effective than nonstructured and nonindividualized approaches.

   Application Select an intervention program that the athlete feels comfortable with. Apply the principles and practices of the program in an organized and systematic fashion.

Psyching-Up Strategies

Generally speaking, **psyching-up** strategies are techniques designed to increase an athlete's arousal and activation level. While overanxiety and overarousal may be a major stumbling block for the **anxiety-prone** athlete, too little activation can also be a problem. This is especially so for highly-skilled athletes who must defeat a relatively weak team in order to play a better team in a tournament. Under-arousal causes the downfall of talented teams every year in the National Collegiate Athletic Association basketball tournament. Invariably, one or two highly seeded teams will be beaten by weaker teams simply because they were not ready for them.

Many of the cognitive stategies already discussed in this section can be used to heighten arousal as well as lower it. For example, both imagery and self-hypnosis can be used to stimulate an athlete to greater levels of arousal and motivation, simply by selecting or suggesting stimuli that promote the activation of the sympathetic nervous system. It is also interesting that when a group of athletes are asked to "get psyched," they report using all kinds of different cognitive strategies not normally associated with activation. For example, in a study by Caudill, Weinberg, and Jackson (1983) using track athletes, 25 percent reported using relaxation/distraction procedures to psych up. These are cognitive strategies normally reserved for reducing activation. Other psych-up strategies reported by these subjects were preparatory arousal (7 percent), imagery (16 percent), self-efficacy statements (25 percent), and attentional focus procedures (16 percent).

It is important that athletes learn to prepare for competition using the strategy best for them. This may involve using one strategy to control anxiety and another to get psyched up. However, for a team rather than an individual, a different strategy may need to be used. For example, if a coach determines that his team is not taking an opponent seriously, he or she must do something to get the players prepared. The coach runs the risk of overactivating a few anxiety-prone members of the squad, but this is usually better than running the risk of an uninspired effort from the whole team. And if the coach identifies the players with very high trait anxiety profiles, he or she can work with them individually.

Oxendine (1970) indicated that an above-average level of arousal is essential for optimal performance in gross motor activities involving strength, endurance, and speed. We would expect psyching-up strategies to facilitate strength and muscular endurance activities. The research supports this conclusion. Shelton and Mahoney (1978) demonstrated that psyching up facilitated performance on a static strength task (hand dynamometer). In a similar study, the effects of psyching up on three different motor tasks were investigated by Weinberg, Gould, and

Jackson (1980). The three tasks were dynamic balancing, dynamic leg strength, and an arm movement task for speed. For each task, the subjects were encouraged to select their own cognitive psyching-up strategy. Only in the case of leg strength was a significant effect observed between control and experimental subjects. Gould, Weinberg, and Jackson (1980) conducted another investigation in which they concluded that in the first experiment, preparatory arousal and imagery were the best psyching-up techniques for enhancing leg strength, and in the second experiment, only preparatory arousal was effective in enhancing leg strength. In a study involving hypnosis (Ikai & Steinhaus, 1961), it was discovered that subject's static elbow flexion strength was enhanced on trials in which subjects either shouted or performed immediately after a gunshot. Caudill, Weinberg, and Jackson (1983) reported that psych-up procedures used by sprinters enhanced performance. Most recently, Wilkes and Summers (1984), using an isokinetic exercise system, and Weinberg and Jackson (1985), using selected muscular endurance tasks (sit-ups, push-ups, pull-ups), confirmed that mental preparation strategies effectively increase muscular strength and endurance when used to psych up the athlete.

It seems clear that heightened arousal can facilitate performance on strength, speed, and muscular endurance activities. It would also follow that heightened arousal would help any athlete whose precompetitive arousal level was below optimal. The key, regardless of the activity, is the inverted-U. If the athlete is either overaroused or optimally aroused for a particular activity, then psych-up procedures are inappropriate. However, if the athlete is underaroused, then psych-up procedures are called for.

Coaches can use a number of specific strategies to psych up their athletes (Voelz, 1982). If these strategies are properly planned and not overused, they can help get a team fired up for competition.

Goal Setting

Goal setting was discussed in some detail in a previous section as a cognitive strategy. Goal setting is also an extremely effective tool for psyching up an athlete or a team. Athletes rarely need to be psyched up for high visibility games such as city or state rivalries. However, how does an athlete get excited about playing a team that his or her team has defeated ten times in a row? How does a professional baseball player get psyched up to play the last twenty games of a season when the team is fifteen games behind in the standings? These and situations like these present a tremendous challenge to athletes, coaches, and managers. The solution lies in effective goal setting.

In preparing a top-ten–rated basketball team with twenty-five wins and two losses to play an unranked team in the NCAA playoffs, the coach must do something to keep his or her team from overlooking a potential "giant killer." One useful strategy is to help each member of the team to set personal performance goals for the game. The star rebounder might be challenged to accept the personal goal of getting thirteen "bounds" in the game. Similarly, the guards might be challenged to keep their turnovers below three between them. With each member of the team working to achieve realistic but difficult goals, it is likely that the team as a whole will perform well.

Pep Talks

A pep talk by the coach or a respected member of the team is the most effective method now used to increase the activation level of athletes. But like any verbal communication, it can be either effective or ineffective. Perhaps the most important element of the pep talk is an emphasis on the ingredient that is lacking in the team. If the team is obviously taking an opponent lightly, it must be impressed upon them that on a given night, any team can be a "giant killer." Some of the elements of an effective pep talk may include personal challenges, stories, poems, silence, reasoning, and voice inflections.

Bulletin Boards

In many ways the visual messages on a bulletin board are identical to a pep talk, but they are visually rather than verbally conveyed. Poster board displays should be placed where team members cannot miss them. Such places as locker room dressing areas and confined training areas are ideal. The bulletin board should always convey positive motivating thoughts and ideas. Catchy phrases such as "when the going gets tough, the tough get going" can be effective. Athletes remember these simple phrases and will repeat them later when they need reinforcement. Other messages on the display board might include personal challenges to members of the team. One such display for a volleyball team might look like the one in figure 5.4. This poster could reflect either great performances for the season or challenge performances for the next match.

Challenging or inflammatory statements by opposing teammates or coaches should also appear on the bulletin board. If an opponent is quoted as saying that he or she will dominate a certain player, this should be posted for all to see. It will give the team something to get excited about.

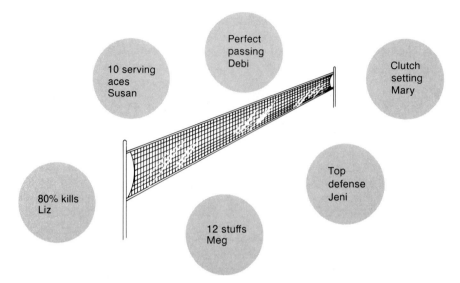

Figure 5.4 Poster showing performance goals for a women's volleyball team. From C. Voelz, *Motivation in coaching a team sport*. Reprinted by permission of American Alliance for Health, Physical Education, Recreation and Dance, 1900 Association Drive, Reston, Virginia 22091.

Publicity and News Coverage

The school newspaper and other advertisements can be very helpful in generating a team spirit. If the members of the team sense that the student body is behind them, they will work harder to get prepared. Ads can be placed in the newspaper by the coach to call attention to an important game or contest. These same ads can be used to recruit new players for the team. For many teams, publicity comes easy, but for others it does not. It may be necessary to cultivate a close relationship with the media and school sports reporters. Invite them to games and send them positive information about players and upcoming contests.

Fan Support

Those who enjoy sport for its recreational value do not need people watching in order to enjoy the game. However, if you practice ten to fifteen hours a week and have a twenty-game schedule, it doesn't hurt to have fan support. Fans tell the athletes that what they are doing is important to someone other than themselves. A full season of daily basketball, football, or tennis can burn out many players. Those responsible for promoting the team must do all they can to get people to support the team by coming to watch them.

Self-Activation

Often, lethargic activity on the part of an athlete can be reversed through the application of mental strategies to increase activation. Over the years I have observed Jimmy Conners's psych up in a tennis match by slapping himself on the thigh and by using positive self-statements. Research has clearly shown that specific attempts to "get psyched" using various internal cogitive strategies is effective in enhancing strength and muscular-endurance activities (Weinberg & Jackson, 1985).

Coach, Athlete, and Parent Interaction

The interaction among an athlete's parents, the athlete, and the coach is an often overlooked source of motivation for an athlete (Hellstedt, 1987b). Coaches are often wary about the overinvolved and demanding parent. However, often just the opposite is true and parents are excluded from active involvement in motivating a young athlete. Parents provide tremendous support for an athlete's involvement that sometimes goes completely unnoticed. Parents provide transportation for games and practices, and sacrifice vacations and leisure time to watch their son or daughter perform. When called on, they are observed serving as scorekeepers, water "boys," bus drivers, and sometimes as assistant coaches. What a tremendous source of support and motivation a parent can be when properly nurtured!

Precompetition Workout

In the mid-sixties when the Japanese were dominating the international volleyball scene, I observed an interesting phenomenon. Prior to an international men's match between the United States and Japan, the Japanese team came out two hours early and went through a full workout. This was no warm-up as typically observed prior to competition, but a full-blown practice session to exhaustion. The Japanese team went on to defeat the U.S.A. in three relatively easy games. I have often wondered if this was an effective strategy that would have proven effective against the powerful U.S.A. men's team of the 1984 and 1988 Olympics.

Husak and Hemenway (1986) were apparently thinking along similar lines when they tested the effects of competition day practice on activation and performance of collegiate swimmers. In this investigation, members of a collegiate swimming team engaged in brisk workouts four to six hours prior to competition. The results did not yield a significant performance effect, but they did show a reduction in feelings of tension and anxiety on the part of the precompetition workout group. Because tension and anxiety could easily hamper performance in swimming competition, precompetition workouts could be an effective tool for preparing an athlete for competition. Precompetition workouts that enhance and increase activation are apparently effective in reducing precompetitive anxiety.

---

15. **Principle** Athletes are sometimes underaroused, and psych-up strategies are necessary in these situations.

    Application Goal setting, pep talks, bulletin boards, news coverage, fan support, parental involvement and self-activation measures are all effective for getting athletes psyched up for competition. However, these techniques should not be overused or indiscriminately applied.

Summary

Intervention strategies can help athletes find and maintain the optimum level of arousal for high performance. Relaxation techniques reduce anxiety and tension by eliciting the relaxation response. The relaxation response counters the effects of the sympathetic nervous system. Progressive relaxation, autogenic training, transcendental meditation, and biofeedback all elicit the relaxation response.

Cognitive strategies can help athletes improve their psychological skills and improve athletic performance. These cognitive skills are used in conjunction with relaxation techniques to bring about the desired result. Cognitive strategies discussed in this chapter included imagery, hypnosis, and goal setting. Internal imagery provides athletes with a kinesthetic feel for the skill, while external imagery allows them to see themselves perform. If heterohypnosis is used, a trained psychologist should be present. Autohypnosis may be practiced by the athlete without supervision. Both kinds of hypnosis are equally effective in reducing anxiety and in enhancing performance.

Four different kinds of packaged intervention programs were discussed. These programs, VMBR, SMT, SIT, and the Psychological Skills Education Program, all employ combinations of the relaxation and cognitive strategies discussed earlier. Intervention programs are extremely effective in controlling stress and in many cases enhance athletic performance. Individualized intervention and stress management programs are more effective than nonindividualized programs.

Techniques proven effective in psyching up the athlete were also discussed. The use of goal setting, pep talks, bulletin boards, news coverage, fan support, self-activation, parent involvement, and precompetition workouts were identified as being effective strategies for increasing the activation level of athletes.

Review Questions

1. What is the relaxation response, and how can it be elicited?
2. Name the four elements involved in evoking the relaxation response. Describe each element in some detail.
3. What is a cognitive strategy?
4. Name two kinds of imagery, and explain the difference between them. Which is more effective in terms of facilitating performance?
5. Give a concrete example of centering or thought stopping.
6. What is hypnosis? How does it differ from transcendental meditation?
7. How does autohypnosis differ from heterohypnosis? Which method is preferred in sports, and why?
8. Describe the principles of good goal setting.
9. What does VMBR stand for? What strategies are employed in VMBR, and how effective is it for reducing anxiety and improving performance?
10. What is the difference between SIT and SMT? Which one do you prefer, and why?
11. Describe Boutcher and Rotella's Psychological Skills Education Program.
12. When are psych-up strategies effective? Name some psych-up strategies, and explain how they can be appropriately applied.

Glossary

anxiety-prone A condition in which an athlete has a predisposition toward responding to competitive situations with elevated A-state.

anxiety-stress spiral The circular effect of anxiety causing poor performance, which results in even more anxiety.

autogenic training A relaxation training program in which the athlete attends to body feedback.

autohypnosis Hypnotizing oneself as opposed to being hypnotized by another.

biofeedback A program in which the athlete learns to elicit the relaxation response with the aid of physiological measurement equipment.

cognitive strategy A mental strategy designed to control anxiety and improve performance.

ergogenic aid Technique or substance employed to improve or enhance athletic performance.

external imagery Imagery in which athletes watch themselves perform.

fine motor skill A skill, such as putting in golf, that requires delicate muscle control.

gross motor skill A skill, such as tackling in football, that requires large muscle involvement.

heterohypnosis Hypnosis requiring the assistance of a hypnotist or psychologist.

hypnosis The uncritical acceptance of a suggestion.

hypnotic induction The process of bringing a subject into the hypnotic trance.

hypnotic trance The state of being hypnotized or willing to uncritically accept suggestions.

imagery Use of visualization to imagine situations.

internal imagery Kinesthetic imagery in which the subject is "within" his or her own body.

intervention strategies Various cognitive and physiological strategies for altering existing levels of anxiety, arousal, and self-confidence.

mantra A key phrase or mental device used in transcendental meditation to help the athlete focus attention internally.

mental device A word, phrase, object, or process used to help elicit the relaxation response.

neutral hypnosis A hypnotic state in which the athlete's physiological responses are identical to the relaxation response.

posthypnotic suggestion Suggestion given during the alert hypnotic trance that is to be carried out when awake.

progressive relaxation Muscle relaxation procedure in which skeletal muscles are systematically tensed and relaxed.

psyching up Cognitive strategies designed to increase an athlete's activation level.

relaxation response Physiological changes that reverse the effect of the sympathetic nervous system.

SIT A four-phase stress management program called Stress Inoculation Training, whose goal is to "inoculate" an athlete against stress by guiding the athlete through progressively more stressful situations.

SMT A stress management program called Cognitive-Affective Stress Management Training in which the athlete practices stress-coping skills in stressful situations.

stress management Programs and procedures designed to manage or reduce stress (see intervention strategies).

transcendental meditation A relaxation procedure that originated in India and features the repetition of a mantra to elicit the relaxation response.

VMBR A stress management program called Visual-Motor Behavior Rehearsal that uses imagery and relaxation techniques to help athletes deal with stress.

waking hypnosis Stage of hypnosis during which the athlete is asked to carry out suggestions that are alerting and arousing.

Recommended Readings

Barber, T. X., Spanos, N. P., & Chaves, J. F. (1974). *Hypnosis, imagination, and human potentialities.* New York: Pergamon Press.

Benson, H., Beary, J. F. & Carol, M. P. (1974). The relaxation response. *Psychiatry, 37,* 37–46.

Block, N. (ed.). (1981). *Imagery.* Cambridge, MA:MIT Press.

Boutcher, S. H., & Rotella, R. J. (1987). A psychological skills education program for closed-skill performance enhancement. *The Sport Psychologist. 1,* 127–137.

Danskin, D. G., & Crow, M. A. (1981). *Biofeedback: An introduction and guide.* Palo Alto, CA: Mayfield Publishing Company.

DiCara, L. V. (1970). Learning in the autonomic nervous system. *Scientific American, 222,* 30–39.

Edmonston, W. E., Jr. (1981). *Hypnosis and relaxation: Modern verification of an old equation.* New York: John Wiley and Sons.

Jacobson, E. (1929). *Progressive relaxation.* Chicago: University of Chicago Press.

Johnson, W. R. (1961). Hypnosis and muscular performance. *Journal of Sports Medicine and Physical Fitness, 1,* 71–79.

Kolonay, B. J. (1977). "The effects of visual-motor behavior rehearsal on athletic performance." Unpublished master's thesis, Hunter College, New York.

Locke, E. A., & Latham, G. P. (1985). The application of goal setting to sports. *Journal of Sports Psychology, 7,* 205–222.

Mahoney, M. J., Gabriel, T. J., & Perkins, T. S. (1987). Psychological skills and exceptional athletic performance. *The Sport Psychologist, 1,* 181–199.

Morgan, W. P. (1972a). Hypnosis and muscular performance. In W. P. Morgan (ed.), *Ergogenic aids in muscular performance.* New York: Academic Press.

Morgan, W. P., & Brown, D. R. (1983). Hypnosis. In M. H. Williams (ed.), *Ergogenic aids in sport.* Champaign, IL: Human Kinetics Publishers.

Nideffer, R. M. (1976a). *The inner athlete: Mind plus muscle for winning.* New York: Thomas Y. Crowell Company.

Nideffer, R. M. (1981). *The ethics and practice of applied sport psychology.* Ithaca, NY: Mouvement Publications.

Schultz, J. H., & Luthe, W. (1959). *Autogenic training: A psychophysiological approach in psychotherapy.* New York: Grune and Stratton.

Smith, D. (1987). Conditions that facilitate the development of sport imagery training. *The Sport Psychologist, 1,* 237–247.

Suinn, R. M. (1972). Removing emotional obstacles to learning and performance by visuo-motor behavior rehearsal. *Behavioral Therapy, 31,* 308–310.

Wallace, R. K., & Benson, H. (1972). The physiology of meditation. *Scientific American,* 85–90.

Zaichkowsky, L. D., & Sime, W. E. (1982). *Stress management for sport.* Reston, VA: AAHPERD Publications.

Part Four   **Theories of Motivation**

In parts two and three we discussed attention, arousal, and anxiety in terms of their impact on athletic performance. We now understand that attention is critically important to skilled performance and that an optimal level of arousal exists for most sport situations. Arousal is an important source of motivation; it is an energizer for human behavior. However, it is not goal-directed. The direction that behavior takes is a function of the person's fundamental needs, goals, and personality. Martens (1974) made an important distinction between arousal and goal-directed behavior. Just as a car engine can be running at full throttle and not go anywhere until the clutch is engaged, an athlete may be highly aroused and not accomplish anything until a worthwhile goal is identified. Part four deals with the goal-directed behavior aspect of motivation.

There are two basic approaches to explaining motivation as goal-directed behavior. The first is achievement motivation theory and the second is attribution theory.

In a review of achievement motivation sport literature, Roberts (1982) categorized attribution theory as perhaps the most important subdivision of achievement motivation. However, here we will deal with achievement motivation and attribution separately, mainly because their theoretical constructs are strikingly dissimilar.

In chapter six I will discuss achievement motivation as it relates to athletes generally; the chapter also contains sections on women in sport, effects of competition on children, and strategies to enhance motivation. I will also discuss attribution theory in terms of how an athlete's cognitive attributions can affect feelings of confidence and self-worth and attribution as it relates to the effects of external rewards on intrinsic motivation. ∎

6 Achievement Motivation

Key Terms

achievement motivation
achievement situation
androgyny
BSRI
competence motivation
competition
cross sex-typed
extrinsic motivation
   (M_{ext})
femininity
FOF
FOS
incentive value of
   success (I_s)
intrinsic motivation
M_{af}
M_s
M_{-s}

masculinity
McClelland-Atkinson
   model
n Ach
PAQ
participatory modeling
PCSC
perceived contingency
probability of success
   (P_s)
risk-taking behavior
self-confidence
self-efficacy
sex-typed
social comparison
sport confidence
test-anxiety approach
WOFO

Two young boys were asked to participate in a sandlot baseball game. One of them happily joined in and became active in team selection, competition, skill development, and socialization. The other youngster's immediate reaction was to follow his friend. However, after a few seconds of deliberation he declined, citing school work and chores. He feared that if he participated, he would be shamed by being the last player chosen, and would be ridiculed for making errors.

As this story suggests, not everyone approaches an achievement situation with the same enthusiasm. An **achievement situation** is one in which someone expects that their performance is going to be evaluated (Atkinson, 1964). This occurs regularly in sport and is referred to by Martens (1982) as **competition.** Competition is nothing more than a sport-specific achievement situation.

Achievement Motivation

Achievement motivation can be defined as the athlete's predisposition to approach or avoid a competitive situation. However, in a broader sense I would like to define achievement motivation as including the concept of desire or desire to excel. The athletic literature and folk history is full of examples of athletes who have excelled because of an internal desire as opposed to physical attributes such as size and strength. Boston Celtics' Larry Bird may be a case in point. Bird has never been accused of possessing great quickness, speed, or vertical jumping ability, yet he remains one of the greatest players of all time. Much of his greatness is attributed to an intense internal desire to work hard and to achieve success. In introducing the topic of achievement motivation, I am addressing a psychological construct that is much more than merely getting psychologically aroused or motivated for a single competitive event. I am talking about the fundamental internal drive that motivates athletes to literally commit a large portion of their lives to achieve a particular goal.

From the mid-1950s through the mid-1970s, the theory of achievement motivation that received the most attention in the psychological literature was the McClelland-Atkinson theory. During that time, two other basic theories competed with the McClelland-Atkinson model for general research appeal. Excluding attribution theory, Roberts (1982) identified these two as the **test-anxiety approach** (Sarason, Hill & Zimbardo, 1964) and the Crandall approach (1963). Simply stated, the test anxiety approach merely hypothesized that fear of test taking or fear of failure (test anxiety) was the critical factor in determining whether or not an individual would approach or avoid an achievement situation. Children who suffer from high levels of anxiety might be expected to avoid achievement situations. By contrast, the Crandall approach placed the emphasis upon an individual's expectation for reinforcement and on an individually determined standard of excellence. In practice, the child compares social expectations with minimal standards for success. If expectations are too high or reinforcements too few, the child drops out of the achievement situation.

In the first part of this chapter I will discuss in greater detail the psychological constructs associated with the McClelland-Atkinson model. While interest in this model has waned in recent years, the tenents of the theory provide a useful framework for considering more current approaches to explaining the phenomenon of achievement motivation. In a subsequent section I will introduce a second class of cognitive theories that have dominated the sport psychology literature since the late 1970s.

The McClelland-Atkinson Model

The **McClelland-Atkinson model** of achievement motivation is a complex behavioral mathematical approach to explaining the need to achieve, abbreviated as **n Ach** (Arkes & Garske, 1982). For our purposes, we will only consider a simplified version of the model. Basically, the model proposes that two factors determine an athlete's n Ach (McClelland, Atkinson, Clark & Lowell, 1953). These two factors are the **motive to achieve success** (M_s) and the **motive to avoid failure** (M_{af}).

$$\text{n Ach} = M_s - M_{af} \tag{1}$$

The motive to achieve success has traditionally been measured by the Thematic Apperception Test (TAT). Another test that has also been used a great deal to measure M_s is Mehrabian's (1968) Scale of Achievement. Fineman (1977) identified twenty-two different tests that have been used to determine a person's motive to achieve success.

The motive to avoid failure (M_{af}) has traditionally been measured using the Mandler and Sarason (1952) Test Anxiety Questionnaire (TAQ). However, other anxiety tests such as Taylor's Manifest Anxiety Scale (TMAS) and Spielberger's State-Trait Anxiety Inventories have also been used. Table 6.1 summarizes the n Ach constructs of the McClelland-Atkinson model.

The motive to achieve success is believed to represent an athlete's **intrinsic motivation** to approach a competitive situation. It is roughly equivalent to the terms self-confidence, self-efficacy, and personal competence. People high in this construct are more likely than those who are not to enter into a situation in which they will be evaluated by others. The second factor that determines whether an athlete will engage in competition is the motive to avoid failure. This factor is represented by the subject's personality disposition for anxiety. A highly anxious person is more likely to avoid competition than one who is low in this construct.

Table 6.1 McClelland-Atkinson Achievement Motivation Constructs. From *Psychological Theories of Motivation*, 2d Ed., by H. R. Arkes and J. P. Garske. Copyright © 1977, 1982 by Wadsworth, Inc. Reprinted by permission of Brooks/Cole Publishing Company, Pacific Grove, CA 93950.

Factor	Description	Symbol
Need achievement	Achievement motivation	n Ach
Motive to succeed	Motivation to engage in achievement tasks	M_s
Motive to avoid failure	Motivation to avoid or delay engaging in an achievement situation	M_{af} (FOF)
Probability of success	Perceived probability for success	P_s
Incentive value of success	Perceived satisfaction associated with success	I_s
Extrinsic motivation	External rewards such as money, praise, status, and trophies	M_{ext}
Motive to avoid success	Fear of success, experienced primarily by women	M_{-s}(FOS)

The motive to avoid failure (M_{af}) has also been referred to as **fear of failure** (FOF) by some authors (Richardson, Jackson & Albury, 1984).

The motive to achieve success (M_s) prompts the athlete to enter into the activity with enthusiasm. However, fear of failure (FOF) may cause the young athlete to withdraw entirely or to approach with caution; this is the classic approach-avoidance conflict (Watson, 1986). Theoretically, if the motive to achieve success is stronger than the fear of failure, the individual will enter into the achievement situation; otherwise, he or she may withdraw.

1. **Principle** According to the McClelland-Atkinson model, people's motives to achieve and their fear of failure are the primary factors determining whether they will approach or avoid an achievement situation.

    Application Since the motive to achieve (M_s) and the motive to avoid failure (M_{af}) are independent constructs, coaches must treat them as such. For example, it would be a mistake to assume that an athlete high in M_s would always enter into competition with enthusiasm. The athlete may have great desire but be restrained by fear of failure.

Other important components of the McClelland-Atkinson model are the **probability of success** (P_s) and the **incentive value of success** (I_s) notions about an achievement situation. Athletes approaching a competitive situation will form a subjective perception about their chances of succeeding (P_s). The incentive value associated with the competitive situation is equal to one minus the probability of success.

$$I_s = 1 - P_s \qquad (2)$$

From formula 2, it should be clear that the incentive value of success increases as the probability of success decreases (Arkes & Garske, 1982). This makes sense, because an athlete should place more value upon succeeding at a hard task than an easy one. The relationship of all of the constructs we have discussed thus far is illustrated in formula 3.

$$\text{n Ach} = (M_s - M_{af})\,(P_s \times I_s) \qquad (3)$$

Notice in formula 3 that a multiplicative relationship exists between the constructs M_s and M_{af} with the constructs P_s and I_s. What this means is that if either the construct P_s or I_s is equal to zero, then n Ach will necessarily equal zero.

Consider the following example: An athlete is asked to enter into a competitive situation in which he or she is 100 percent sure that he or she will win. This being the case, the athlete's incentive motivation for competing at a high level of performance will be zero. In fact, for a highly motivated athlete, the situation that will result in the greatest level of n Ach is one in which the probability of success is 50 percent. This fact is easily demonstrated by simply inserting various probabilities for P_s into formula 2 and 3 above. The observation that a 50 percent expectation for success elicits the greatest potential for high n Ach is often referred to as *risk-taking behavior.*

Essentially, **risk-taking behavior** predicts that highly motivated athletes seek out achievement situations that are challenging (50 percent chance of failure). Athletes low in the motive to achieve success will seek out situations that offer little risk, such as when P_s is very high or low. Highly motivated athletes have difficulty getting excited about playing opponents they know they can beat. They prefer playing someone as good as they are. This is risk-taking behavior. However, athletes who are motivated to avoid failure will likely prefer either opponents they know they can beat or opponents who are so good that they would expect to lose. Losing to a vastly superior opponent does not threaten self-esteem.

The risk-taking behavior notion is important to the McClelland-Atkinson model of achievement motivation. Many researchers have studied the validity of that notion. Generally, the research on the subject has been very favorable, providing strong support for the McClelland-Atkinson model among male subjects (Atkinson & Litwin, 1960; Brody, 1963; Feather 1961; Isaacson, 1964; Roberts, 1974).

2. **Principle** The probability of success and incentive value of success are factors that influence an athlete's n Ach.

   Application When confronted by a competitive situation that is not challenging, athletes who are generally high achievers will experience diminished n Ach. Consequently, high need achievers must be challenged to the degree that the probability of success is about 50 percent.

3. **Principle** Athletes who are low in M_s and high in M_{af} should be guided into situations of high or low probability of success.

   Application An athlete who fears failure and lacks the motive to achieve success will avoid situations involving risk-taking behavior. These athletes will be more likely to have fun and participate if there is more than a 50 percent chance of success. The coach may be able to build confidence and n Ach by carefully selecting achievement situations.

In summary, the basic McClelland-Atkinson model is extremely useful in conceptualizing the phenomenon of achievement motivation. The motive to achieve success (M_s) and the motive to avoid failure (M_{af}) are personality variables. On the other hand, the probability of success (P_s) and incentive value of success (I_s) represent situational variables. Consequently, the McClelland-Atkinson model is consistent with the interaction model of personality discussed in chapter 1.

Performance Expectations

It seems reasonable to predict that if two athletes are equal in ability but unequal in terms of n Ach, then the person high in n Ach will exhibit the better performance. However, research evidence shows that the relationship between n Ach and performance is not quite this simple. This makes sense in light of our earlier discussion of personality in chapter 1. It is very difficult to predict athletic success based on personality dispositions alone. The motive to achieve success and the motive to avoid failure are personality dispositions.

While it is true that a number of studies have found that higher levels of n Ach are associated with superior performance (Atkinson, 1958; Atkinson & Raphelson, 1956; Cox, 1962; McClelland, Atkinson, Clark & Lowell, 1953), the tasks involved were primarily of the nonmotor variety. Research carried out with motor skills has revealed a rather complex relationship between motor performance and n Ach. One set of studies found a relationship between n Ach and motor performance, but only in the early stages of learning. Roberts (1972) formed two extreme groups of n Ach subjects by administering the French Test of Insight (FTI) and TAQ to 278 undergraduate males, then selecting subjects from those high and low on n Ach. Subjects practiced and later performed a shuffleboard task for a score. Results showed no difference between groups in terms of performance, but a significant difference favoring high n Ach subjects during their preperformance practice phase.

Healey and Landers (1973) similarly divided subjects on the basis of extreme high- and low-need achievement scores and had them perform a stabilometer task. The results revealed no performance differences in terms of n Ach, but the subjects high in test anxiety ($M_s < M_{af}$) demonstrated a lower level of performance consistency on the initial learning scores. In a related study, Ostrow (1976) used four-walled handball competition to demonstrate the relationship between n Ach and motor performance. His results showed that high n Ach subjects set more realistic goals and performed better under competitive conditions than low n Ach subjects, but only in the first of four tournament contests.

Carron (1980) offered a plausible explanation for the consistent finding that subjects high in n Ach perform better than those low in n Ach during the early phases of competition or practice, but not in later trials. Carron reasoned that high levels of n Ach facilitate performance in the early and relatively easy learning trials, but thereafter, differences in n Ach disappear. Subjects initially high in n Ach become bored with the relatively easy task and their motivation decreases. Conversely, subjects initially low in n Ach are motivated by their unexpected success, and thence n Ach increases. At this point the situation-specific n Ach of the two groups is identical, and performance results are identical.

Another factor that seems to affect the relationship between motor performance and n Ach is competition. Ryan and Lakie (1965) tested subjects on the motive to succeed and the motive to avoid failure and observed the relationship between n Ach and performance on a ring peg task in competitive and noncompetitive situations. The results revealed that in a noncompetitive situation, low n Ach subjects perform better than high n Ach subjects, but in a competitive situation the opposite is true. Ryan and Lakie concluded that anxious individuals ($M_s < M_{af}$) tend to do well in a relaxed, nonthreatening environment, but not in a pressure-packed competitive situation. Competition enhances the performance of high n Ach subjects while it causes a decrement in the performance of low n Ach subjects.

While there is some evidence that athletes high in achievement motivation will perform better than those low in the construct, the relationship is complex and often uncertain. For example, Fodero (1980) demonstrated that a reliable relationship does not exist between n Ach and the performance of elite gymnasts. It

seems unlikely that athletic performance can be predicted solely on the basis of n Ach. However, as DeCharms and Carpenter (1968) point out, the real value of measuring n Ach is in predicting long-term patterns of motivation, not in predicting success in a specific event.

---

4. **Principle** The real value of measuring n Ach is in predicting long-term patterns of motivation, not in predicting success in a specific event.

   Application Personality tests of achievement motivation are valuable indicators of long-term motivation, but should not be used to make predictions of success in a specific athletic event. For example, the coach should not cut a player from the team because of a low n Ach score.

Elaborations of the McClelland-Atkinson Model

Since its inception, three basic elaborations or additions to the McClelland-Atkinson model of n Ach have been proposed. These include (1) the motivational value of extrinsic motivation, (2) perceived contingency, and (3) the motive to avoid success (fear of success). Each of these elaborations will be briefly introduced and discussed.

Extrinsic Motivation

Recognizing that some athletes who are low in M_s and high in M_{af} still enter into achievement situations, Atkinson (1964) conceded that **extrinsic motivation (M_{ext})** might make the difference. Extrinsic motivation comes in many forms, usually in terms of praise, money, or trophies. To take into consideration the additive factor of extrinsic motivation, Atkinson recommended that the basic formula be revised as follows:

$$\text{n Ach} = (M_s - M_{af})(P_s \times I_s) + M_{ext} \qquad (4)$$

5. **Principle** Contrary to predictions of the McClelland-Atkinson model, individuals whose motive to succeed is low and fear of failure is high may still enter into a competitive situation if some sort of extrinsic motivation is promised.

    Application Participation ribbons and awards for effort may be effectively used to encourage children who are fearful and high in the motive to avoid failure to participate in sport.

Perceived Contingency

Raynor's (1969) notion of **perceived contingency** takes into account the fact that many achievement situations have implications for future goals and aspirations. For example, if a boy playing Little League baseball aspires to play high school baseball, then his opportunity to do so will depend on his performance as a Little League player. If he aspires to play intercollegiate baseball, his opportunity to do so will depend on his performance as a high school player. And his chances of becoming a professional baseball player will depend on his collegiate performance. At each step, the athlete recognizes that performance affects his opportunity to reach his ultimate goal of becoming a professional athlete.

    Raynor (1969) argued and demonstrated (Raynor, 1968) in a three-step mathematics task that a contingent achievement situation requires greater levels of n Ach than does a noncontingent situation. He also demonstrated that subjects in whom M_s was less than M_{af} would do worse in a contingent than in a noncontingent situation. Thus, Raynor suggested the following adjustment in the model for a contingent achievement situation:

$$\text{n Ach} = (M_s - M_{af})[(P_{s1} \times I_{s1}) + \ldots + (P_{sn} \times I_{sn})] \qquad (5)$$

In essence then, the principle of Raynor's elaboration is that performance in any achievement-related activity is a function of both immediate and future expected success and failure. Thus, someone who feels that their future opportunities depend on present performance will reveal a greater desire to achieve (Weinberg, 1977). Raynor's elaboration of perceived contingency simply recognizes that future success is tied to present achievement. For the athlete high in the motive to achieve success, this tends to increase motivation. For the athlete low in the motive to achieve success, the pressure of future expectations and dreams will merely lower the athlete's n Ach. Raynor's elaboration has been an important and realistic addition to the basic achievement motivation model. It has also received significant research support (Raynor, 1968, 1969, 1970; Raynor & Rubin, 1971; Weinberg, 1977).

---

6. **Principle** If future opportunity depends on present performance, the athlete's n Ach can be either enhanced or diminished. It will be enhanced if the motive to succeed is greater than the motive to avoid failure ($M_s > M_{af}$), but diminished if $M_s < M_{af}$.

   Application The pressure to succeed at Little League baseball could be devastating to young athletes who have career aspirations in baseball. This is especially true if they suffer from fear of failure ($M_s < M_{af}$). Coaches must find ways to help young aspiring athletes to concentrate on making small daily improvements and not dwell on success or failure.

Fear of Success

One of the serious shortcomings of the McClelland-Atkinson model of achievement motivation is that it has failed to accurately and consistently account for n Ach in women. Sarason and Smith (1971) observed that in studies with female subjects, results were both inconsistent and dissimilar to those for males. This deficiency in the model prompted Horner (1968) to propose the **motive to avoid success** (M_{-s}), or simply **fear of success** (FOS). This elaboration of the basic McClelland-Atkinson model was conceived to account for an apparent lack of motivation to succeed in women competing with men. Ignoring Raynor's perceived contingency elaboration and extrinsic motivation, the addition of M_{-s} to the basic McClelland-Atkinson model yields:

$$\text{n Ach} = M_s - M_{af} - M_{-s} \tag{6}$$

As can be observed in this equation, the motive to avoid failure and the motive to avoid success are subtracted from the motive to succeed in order to get n Ach.

According to Horner (1972), otherwise high-achievement–oriented women may suffer a self-inflicted decrement in performance and motivation when competing against men for traditional masculine goals. The female fears that if she succeeds in a male-dominated environment she will suffer a perceived loss of femininity and social rejection by members of both sexes.

In Horner's (1968) research, college-age subjects were tested on the fear of success motive (FOS) using a thematic projective test in which they wrote stories in response to verbal leads. From this research, Horner concluded that (1) women show more evidence of the fear of success motive than do men, (2) subjects exhibiting FOS perform better when working in a noncompetitive environment, and (3) the n Ach pattern for women was ambiguous until the motive to avoid success was identified and included in the model.

Since Horner first conceived M_{-s} there has been a flurry of interest in the construct. The notion that the measurement of M_{-s} could solve the contradictions involved in female n Ach is very appealing. The validity of the FOS construct received empirical support from Zuckerman and Allison (1976). Zuckerman and Allison (1976) developed the Objective Fear of Success Scale (FOSS) and administered it to male and female subjects. Their results confirmed that (1) females scored higher on fear of success than males, and (2) subjects scoring low in FOS outperformed subjects scoring high on FOS in a competitive achievement situation. Similarly, Silva (1982) categorized 193 female and male college students by sex and athletic participation (athlete versus nonathlete) and gave them the Zuckerman and Allison test. The results showed that the FOSS scores for the male athletes were significantly lower than the other three groups. However, no reliable differences were observed between the male nonathletes and the two categories of women. This result provides only partial support for the FOS construct, since the female subjects were not unusually high in fear of success.

An important study by McElroy and Willis (1979) tested the FOS construct in a sport setting and found no evidence to justify its inclusion in a sport-specific achievement environment. The authors composed a series of yes-no statements reflecting sport-specific situations and administered them to 262 female athletes from five different sports. Factor analytic procedures were used to isolate and identify two significant n Ach dimensions, M_s and M_{af}. The analysis failed to support the presence of a fear of success (M_{-s}) dimension for female atheles. McElroy and Willis suggested that the sport setting may be one area where women's achievement is accepted, and fear of success is not a salient factor.

The McElroy and Willis (1979) study is important because it suggests that female athletes do not view success as a masculine accomplishment. According to the original M_{-s} construct proposed by Horner, women should fear success when competing against men for a traditional masculine goal. If athletic achievement was viewed by the subjects in this research to be associated with masculinity, a fear of success response pattern should have emerged. The fact that it did not is good news, since athletic participation is a positive experience that should not be sex-typed.

With the exception of the Zuckerman and Allison (1976) and Silva (1982) studies, the McElroy and Willis study is consistent with the vast majority of research involving the motive to avoid success (M_{-s}). For example in twenty-two studies reviewed by Tresemer (1974, 1976), the median rate of fear of success was 47 percent for women and 43 percent for men. This is not a significant difference. And in over half of the studies, fear of success was actually more common among men than women. Since Horner first introduced the FOS construct in 1968, researchers have consistently failed to demonstrate that FOS is a personality disposition in women independent from M_{af} (Arkes & Garske, 1982).

While women do not seem to have a personality disposition to avoid success to a greater degree than men, they do appear to fear activities inappropriate to their sex role (Peplau, 1976). A young women may avoid such activities as boxing, football, and wrestling, but feel perfectly comfortable playing tennis or volleyball.

---

7. **Principle** It is unlikely that women suffer from a fear of success (FOS) to any greater degree than men.

   Application A female athlete's reluctance to excel in certain achievement situations is probably due more to the masculine nature of the task than to fear of success. Fear of success is not an independent personality disposition. In choosing competitive activities for women, organizers should carefully consider whether the task is sex-role appropriate.

Models of Self-Confidence

Since the late 1970s a number of motivational theories have been proposed and researched that are based on the broad notion of **self-confidence** (Vealey, 1986). As observed by Arkes and Garske (1982), researchers have recognized that the critical factor that discriminates between individuals high or low in achievement motivation is self-confidence. Athletes who are self-confident and expect to succeed are the same athletes who generally do succeed.

Increased interest in self-confidence research parallels a declining interest in the achievement motivation theory of McClelland and Atkinson. However, this should not be construed as a dismissal or rejection of the basic constructs identified in the McClelland-Atkinson model. Clearly, the construct of self-confidence is very similar to the n Ach notions of the motive to succeed (M_s) and probability of success (P_s). The confident athlete has a high motive to succeed and a high expectation of success.

The three basic motivational models that I will briefly introduce in this section include (1) Bandura's (1977) self-efficacy theory, (2) Harter's (1978) effectance motivation theory, and (3) Vealey's (1986) conceptual model of sport-confidence.

Bandura's Theory of Self-Efficacy

The notion of **self-efficacy** is synonymous with an individual's belief that he or she is competent and can succeed at a particular task. An individual who enjoys a high level of self-efficacy enters into a competitive situation with enthusiasm and self-confidence. The degree of self-efficacy possessed by an individual will determine whether that person will approach or avoid an achievement situation. While the concepts of self-confidence and self-efficacy may not be absolutely identical, it is clear that they are very similar. Bandura's theory of self-efficacy (1977, 1982) proposes that self-efficacy is fundamental to competent performance. In competitive situations, the higher the level of self-efficacy, the higher the performance accomplishments and the lower the emotional arousal (Bandura, 1982).

Bandura's (1977) model of self-efficacy states that self-efficacy is enhanced by successful performance, vicarious experience, verbal persuasion, and emotional arousal. The most important of these four factors is successful performance. According to Bandura, successful performance raises expectations for future success; failure lowers these expectations. Once strong feelings of self-efficacy develop through repeated success, occasional failures will be of small consequence. Feelings of self-efficacy lead to improved performance, while a lack of those feelings results in slackening performance.

The most critical aspect of Bandura's theory is repeated success through **participatory modeling.** In participatory modeling, the subject first observes a model perform a task. Then, the model assists the subject in successfully performing the task. The subject is not allowed to fail. As a result of repeated success, strong feelings of self-efficacy develop. Considerable support for Bandura's model exists in sport-related research (Feltz & Mugno, 1983; Gould & Weiss, 1981; Kavanagh & Hausfeld, 1986; Lan & Gill, 1984; Weinberg, 1985).

---

8. **Principle** The development of self-efficacy in young athletes is closely associated with the level of success that they are able to experience.

   Application Participatory modeling should be used by teachers and coaches to assure that young athletes "feel" and experience repeated success. This will result in the athlete feeling personally competent in an achievement situation.

Harter's Competence Motivation Theory

Patterned after White's (1959) theory of effectance motivation, Harter (1978) proposed a theory of achievement motivation that is based on an athlete's feeling of personal competence. According to Harter, individuals are innately motivated to be competent in all areas of human achievement. In order to satisfy the urge to be competent in an achievement area such as sport, the person attempts mastery. An individual's self-perception of success at these mastery attempts give rise to feelings of positive or negative affect. As illustrated in figure 6.1, successful attempts at mastery gives rise to self-efficacy and feelings of personal competence, which in turn gives rise to high **competence motivation.** As competence motivation increases, the athlete is encouraged to make further mastery attempts.

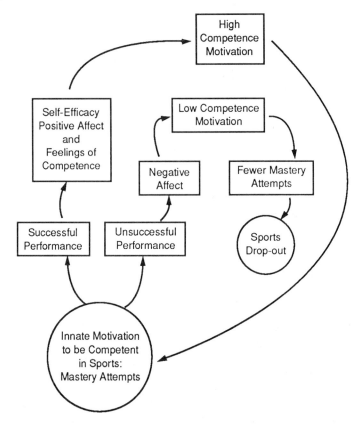

Figure 6.1 Harter's competence motivation theory. From S. Harter, Effectance motivation reconsidered. *Human Development,* 1978, *21,* 34–64. Adapted by permission of S. Karger AG, Basel.

Conversely, if a young athlete's attempts at mastery results in perceived rejection and failure, then low competence motivation and negative affect will be the end product. It is hypothesized that low competence motivation will result in a youth sport dropout (Klint & Weiss, 1987).

Several sport-related studies have provided support for Harter's competence motivation theory (Feltz & Mugno, 1983; Klint & Weiss, 1987; Roberts, Kleiber & Duda, 1981; Ulrich, 1987). In each of these investigations the tool for measuring competence was Harter's (1982) **Perceived Competence Scale for Children** (PCSC). In this instrument, emphasis is placed on the assessment of a child's competence in three domains; cognitive (school competence), social (peer-related competence), and physical (skill at sports). A general measure of self-worth is also obtained from the twenty-seven-item scale of perceived competence.

---

9. **Principle** Competence motivation may be enhanced in children through repeated successful mastery attempts.

   Application Redefining success to include positive outcomes other than winning will allow more children to succeed. Success may come in the form of skill improvement, trying, and in just having fun.

An extension of Harter's competence motivation theory is Nicholls' (1984) developmentally based theory of achievement motivation. As explained by Duda (1987), Nicholls' theory is very similar to Harter's except greater emphasis is placed on a child's developmental level. Nicholls' theory also gives greater emphasis to the concept of ability in the development of competence motivation.

Vealey's Sport Specific Model of Sport Confidence

Vealey's (1986) model of **sport confidence** is a unique and relatively untested approach to conceptualizing achievement motivation and self-confidence in sport. Perhaps the real strength of Vealey's proposed model is that it is situation specific and represents a legitimate attempt at theory development within the discipline of sport psychology. All other theories discussed in this chapter have been borrowed from the parent discipline of psychology and then applied to sport.

In the model illustrated in figure 6.2, Vealey defines sport confidence as "the belief or degree of certainty individuals possess about their ability to be successful in sport" (p. 222). The athlete brings to the objective competitive situation a personality trait of sport confidence (SC-trait) and a particular competitive orientation. These two factors are then predictive of the level of situational state specific

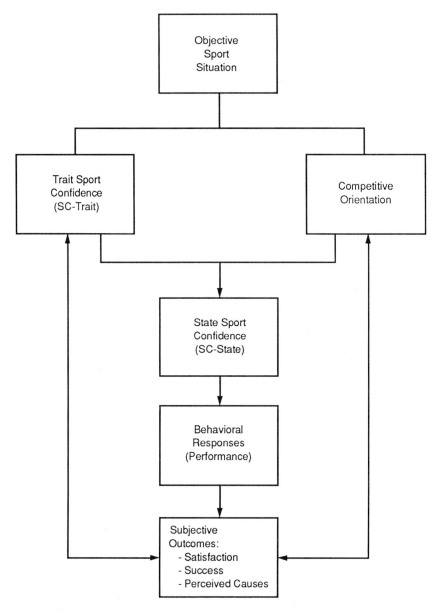

Figure 6.2 Vealey's Model of sport confidence. From R. S. Vealey, Conceptualization of sport-confidence and competitive orientation: Preliminary investigation and instrument development. *Journal of Sport Psychology,* 1986, *8,* 221–246. Adapted by permission of Human Kinetics Publishers, Inc., Champaign, IL.

sport confidence (SC-state) that the athlete exhibits during competition. Situation-specific sport confidence (SC-state) is then predictive of performance or overt behavioral responses. Behavioral responses give rise to subjective perceptions of outcome. Examples of subjective outcomes include such things as satisfaction, perception of success (independent of win or lose), and causes given for outcomes. Subjective outcomes in turn influence and are influenced by the athlete's competitive orientation and personality trait of sport confidence.

Vealey (1986) tested the basic tenets of her proposed model and found them to be viable. In doing so, she also developed instruments for measuring SC-trait (Trait Sport-Confidence Inventory), SC-state (State Sport-Confidence Inventory), and competitive orientation (Competitive Orientation Inventory).

Vealey's sport confidence model is very useful for explaining the relationship between general sport confidence and situation-specific sport confidence. An athlete who is very successful at one sport transfers much of the confidence derived from his or her success to other sport situations.

---

10. **Principle** An athlete who enjoys a general feeling of sport confidence will be able to transfer that predisposition to new and different situation-specific events.

    Application It is important that each youth sport participant find success and a feeling of competence in at least one sport or activity. A situation-specific success experience will have the effect of enhancing the athlete's general perception of sport confidence. As the personality trait of sport confidence is developed, the athlete will experience greater levels of situation-specific sport confidence as new events are attempted.

Women and Sex-Roles

As mentioned briefly in a previous section in which the fear of success (FOS) was discussed, women tend to suffer reduced levels of self-confidence in situations that they perceive to be sex-role inappropriate. Women and men perceive certain selected activities to be **sex-typed** or appropriate for only one sex. For example, American football is considered to be a male sex-typed activity, ballet a female sex-typed activity, and swimming a neutral sex-typed activity (Sanguinetti, Lee & Nelson, 1985). Women suffer a decrement in self-efficacy when asked to perform motor tasks that they perceive to be male sex-typed. They do not suffer a decrement when asked to perform neutral or female sex-typed activities. Both males and females enjoy higher ability self-estimates in gender appropriate tasks (Gill, Gross, Huddleston & Shifflett, 1984; Sanguinetti et al., 1985). The work of Lenney (1977) supports these conclusions, and suggests two other insights about women and self-confidence.

Lenney (1977) observed that previous reviewers suggested that women display lower self-confidence than men across almost all achievement situations. Lenney analyzed the empirical validity of this suggestion and concluded that while this was often the case, it was not true in all achievement situations. Women are often low in self-confidence, a frequent and potentially debilitating problem. However, Lenney points out that whether a woman will respond with lower levels of self-confidence depends on certain situational variables. She then identified three important variables that influence sex differences in self-confidence.

The first of these is the nature of the task. While it is not clear exactly what types of tasks yield this effect, it is clear that women respond to some tasks with a great deal of confidence, but to others with little confidence. For example, a woman might be expected to respond with a low level of confidence to a task that was inappropriate to her sex role (Corbin & Nix, 1979). Bodybuilding might be such a task, although this is changing rapidly.

Second, the nature of sex differences in self-confidence depends on the availability of clear and unambiguous information. Females provided with clear feedback regarding their performance will exhibit as much self-confidence as men. However, if the feedback is unclear and ambiguous, women tend to have lower opinions of their abilities and to respond with lower levels of self-confidence than men. For example, women might be more likely to show a lack of confidence if they were asked to execute a sideward roll in volleyball without being told what was good or bad or for what purpose they were doing it.

Finally, the third factor that influences a sex difference in self-confidence is that of **social comparison** cues. When women work alone or in a situation not involving social comparison, they are likely to respond with self-confidence levels equal to those of men. However, when placed in a situation where their performance is compared with others in a social context, they typically respond with lower levels of self-confidence (Corbin, 1981). This notion is not entirely foreign to Horner's concept of fear of success.

In summary it appears that the potential for women to exhibit lower levels of self-confidence than men in a competitive achievement situation is very real. Many sport-related situations are sex-typed, ambiguous, or involve social comparison. However, it could also be argued that both men and women would prefer to avoid such situations.

11. **Principle** Women are self-confident when competing with men if the activity is unambiguous, is not a "masculine" task, and does not involve social comparison.

> **Application** Women are not necessarily less confident than men. To make sure that women do not develop feelings of inadequacy, carefully select activities that women consider appropriate. For example, women will not be confident of their ability if they must compete in strength activities with men.

A Multifaceted Approach

To study women and achievement motivation, Spence and Helmreich (1978) have proposed a multifaceted approach. Whereas the McClelland-Atkinson model represents a unitary approach to n Ach, achievement motivation is much more complex than this. Because of this, Spence and Helmreich (1978) developed the **Work and Family Orientation Questionnaire** (WOFO). Based on Mehrabian's (1968) scale of achievement, WOFO is a multifaceted approach to measuring n Ach composed of four separate components. These components are

1. *Work orientation:* desiring to do one's best in whatever one undertakes.
2. *Mastery:* persistence in accomplishing tasks, in doing difficult things.
3. *Competitiveness:* enjoying the challenge of situations involving skill and competition.
4. *Personal unconcern:* lack of concern about what others think.

The test itself (second version) is composed of fourteen questions to which the subject responds using a five-point Likert-type scale of agreement. For example, question 4 reads, "I would rather do something at which I feel confident and relaxed than something which is challenging and difficult."

In addition to developing a multifaceted approach to the measurement of n Ach, Helmreich and Spence (1977) also felt it was important to develop a test that would classify people according to their own perceived sex roles. Thus, they created the **Personal Attributes Questionnaire** (PAQ). Development of the PAQ was based on several theoretical concepts proposed by Bakan (1966). Bakan contended that all people are characterized by two fundamental qualities that he labeled *agency* and *communion.* Agency reflects an awareness of self and is manifested in self-assertion, self-protection, and self-expansion. Communion, on the other hand, implies selflessness and a concern for others. Bakan linked agency to

masculinity and masculine principles, and communion to **femininity** and feminine principles. Thus, masculinity and femininity are separate dimensions. Possession of one neither logically nor psychologically precludes the possession of the other. An individual may possess factors associated with either or both of these dimensions of masculinity and femininity.

The development of the PAQ, then, was based on Bakan's concept of agency (masculinity) and communion (femininity). The guiding principles for its development were

1. Masculine attributes are those characteristics considered to be socially desirable to both sexes, but found in greater abundance in males.
2. Feminine attributes are those charateristics considered to be socially desirable to both sexes, but found in greater abundance in females.

The PAQ is composed of twenty-four items (Spence & Helmreich, 1978, pp. 231–232). For each item, subjects are asked to rate themselves along a five-point scale. For example, item number 4 reads as follows:

Very Submissive				Very Dominant
A	B	C	D	E

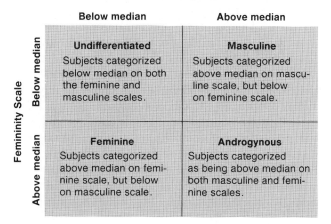

Masculinity Scale

	Below median	Above median
Femininity Scale — Below median	**Undifferentiated** Subjects categorized below median on both the feminine and masculine scales.	**Masculine** Subjects categorized above median on masculine scale, but below on feminine scale.
Femininity Scale — Above median	**Feminine** Subjects categorized above median on feminine scale, but below on masculine scale.	**Androgynous** Subjects categorized as being above median on both masculine and feminine scales.

Figure 6.3 Classification system used by Helmreich and Spence (1977) when they analyzed scores from the Personal Attribute Questionnaire. From R. Helmreich and J. T. Spence, Sex roles and achievement. In *Psychology of motor behavior-1976 (Vol. 2),* R. W. Christina & D. M. Landers (Editors). Copyright © 1977 by Human Kinetics Publishers, Inc. Adapted by permission of the publishers.

Each subject receives three scores. One is a femininity score, in which a high score reflects femininity. A second is a masculine score, in which a high score reflects masculinity. The third score is sex-specific and denotes a bipolar pattern between the sexes. The sex-specific scale (masculine-feminine) is derived from questions that are considered to polarize the response as either masculine or feminine. A high score on the sex-specific scale implies masculinity.

Helmreich and Spence (1977) also developed a simple classification system for the masculine and feminine scores. This scale is used widely by researchers studying women and n Ach. It is displayed in figure 6.3. Subjects are first pooled according to their scores on the feminine and masculine scales. Next, the median score for each pool is established and subjects are classified as high or low according to the median split.

Female subjects classified as high in femininity and low in masculinity would be categorized as feminine. Women low in femininity but high in masculinity would be categorized as masculine. High scores in both masculinity and femininity indicate **androgyny.** Since the items in both the feminine and masculine scales are considered socially desirable for both sexes, the androgynous classification should be very desirable for both men and women. Finally, subjects scoring low on both the feminine and masculine scales are classified as undifferentiated, since they are not high in either dimension.

In preliminary research using the PAQ, Helmreich and Spence (1977) tested male and female scientists, male and female college students, and female athletes, and classified them according to the four categories displayed in figure 6.3. The results revealed that female athletes and scientists are quite similar in terms of androgny, but both differed from female students on this factor.

Harris (1980a), using both the PAQ and WOFO, tested 240 female athletes in order to examine the relationship between the PAQ sex-role classification and the WOFO n Ach components. Results revealed superior WOFO scores for androgynous and masculine subjects compared to feminine and undifferentiated subjects. There was also a tendency for the masculine subjects to exhibit higher levels of motivation than the androgynous subjects. These results suggest that female athletes differ in achievement motivation consistent with differences in perceived sex roles. Female athletes exhibiting perceived masculinity or androgyny score higher in n Ach than those who have a feminine perception.

---

12. **Principle** The androgynous female athlete is likely to be higher in achievement motivation than the athlete who considers herself feminine.

   Application Many feminine qualities, such as compassion and empathy, are desirable human qualities. And many masculine qualities, such as assertiveness and independence, are desirable human qualities. Athletes must be taught that to be feminine does not mean that desirable masculine qualities are to be shunned.

Gender Role and Competitive Trait Anxiety

The Helmreich and Spence (1977) approach to measuring perceived sex roles is not the only approach. Bem (1974) also developed a test for measuring psychological androgyny. Bem's test is called the **Bem Sex-Role Inventory** (BSRI). The BSRI asks people to indicate on a seven-point scale how well each of sixty masculine, feminine, and neutral items describes them. On the basis of these responses, the subjects receive a femininity, masculinity, and androgyny score. The masculinity and femininity scores indicate the extent to which a person endorses masculine and feminine personality characteristics. The androgyny score indicates the degree to which the individual has both masculine and feminine characteristics.

As indicated above, Bem originally used the BSRI to categorize individuals as being feminine, masculine, or androgynous. However, after considerable criticism from Spence, Helmreich, and Stapp (1975), Bem (1977) recommended

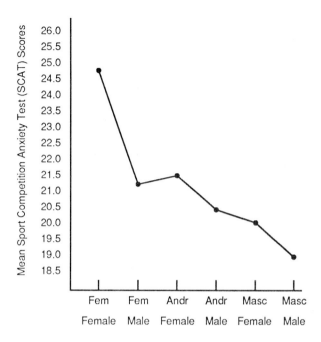

Figure 6.4 Mean sport competitive anxiety scores by gender role classification and sex. From M. B. Anderson and J. M. Williams, Gender role and sport competition anxiety: A re-examination. *Research Quarterly for Exercise and Sport,* 1987, *58,* 52–56. Reproduced by permission of the American Alliance of Health, Physical Education, Recreation and Dance.

that a fourth category of undifferentiated be included. An individual scoring high on both the feminine and masculine scales would be labeled androgynous, while those scoring low on both scales would be labeled undifferentiated.

In a study designed to investigate the relationship between gender role (BSRI) and competitive trait anxiety (SCAT), Anderson and Williams (1987) classified male and female subjects as being feminine-female, feminine-male, androgynous-female, androgynous-male, masculine-female, and masculine-male. Undifferentiated males and females were excluded. As discussed, individuals with the same sex and gender role orientation are referred to as sex-typed (feminine-female and masculine-male), while individuals having different sex and gender role orientation are referred to as **cross sex-typed** (feminine-male and masculine-female). Androgynous persons are those individuals who endorse both gender roles (androgynous-female and androgynous-male).

As illustrated in figure 6.4, the Anderson and Williams (1987) results show a linear relationship between competitive trait anxiety (SCAT) and a person's sex and gender role classification. The greatest degree of competitive trait anxiety is exhibited by female subjects who endorse a feminine gender role. Conversely, the lowest level of competitive trait anxiety is exhibited by male subjects who endorse a masculine gender role. Wittig, Duncan, and Schurr (1987) observed similar results involving 270 undergraduates.

These results suggest that gender role may be a powerful predictor of sport nonparticipation. If feminine females participate in sport, they are more likely to experience high levels of anxiety than other sex and gender role groups. As predicted by the McClelland-Atkinson model of achievement motivation, individuals with high levels of fear of failure (anxiety) may be reluctant to enter into a competitive situation.

---

13. **Principle** Girls and women who endorse a feminine gender role are more likely to experience feelings of anxiety and fear of failure than other gender role groups when thrust into a sport environment.
     Application Coaches and teachers of sport-related activities should anticipate the nature of the relationship between gender orientation and anxiety. With this in mind, special assistance should be given to vulnerable individuals in order to minimize anxiety and nonparticipation.

Developing Achievement Motivation

Research on Bandura's self-efficacy theory suggests that n Ach can be enhanced through repeated experiences of success. Coaches and teachers can help young people develop their achievement motivation by making sure they are not confronted with repeated failure. When the importance of winning is deemphasized and success is viewed in terms of effort and improvement, youth sports can be a positive experience for each participant.

---

14. **Principle** Self-efficacy, and hence achievement motivation, can be developed through performance mastery.
     Application Children involved in sports must experience success. If success is viewed in terms of performance mastery, then everyone can experience it. If success means winning, then most will fail.

Classic research by Winterbottom (1953) and Rosen and D'Andrade (1959) point to the important role of parents in the development of achievement motivation. The following principles summarize much of their research:

1. Parents should encourage independence and reinforce a child's efforts at becoming independent.
2. Parents (especially mothers) should be warm and encouraging to their children.
3. Parents should comfort and support their children when setbacks, fear, and discouragement occur.
4. Parents should expect their children to be able, competent, and responsible.
5. Parents can demonstrate confidence in their children's ability by resisting the urge to "take charge" when they experience difficulty in mastering a task.
6. Parents should allow and expect many trials for a child to master a task. Do not keep track of trials. Appreciate small steps.
7. Keep track of a child's successes and applaud them. Do not dwell on failures.
8. Parents should pay attention to their child's efforts. Listen to their problems and pay attention to their feelings.

There can be no doubt about the importance of developing self-confidence in children. Parents, coaches, and teachers must be willing to go to extreme lengths to make sure that every youth sports participant has a positive experience. One cannot guarantee success, but specific steps can be taken to make sure that failure is not the dominant outcome.

There are many positive outcomes associated with sport participation. Each positive outcome serves to reinforce the child's self-confidence and hence achievement motivation. Some of the positive outcomes associated with sport have been identified by Passer (1981). They include the following:

1. Opportunity to affiliate and associate with others.
2. Opportunity to develop skill in selected sports and activities.
3. Opportunity to experience the excitement, thrill, and challenge of sports participation.
4. Opportunity to enjoy increased status associated with participation and success in sports.
5. Opportunity to enjoy enhanced levels of physical fitness and vigor as a result of sports participation.
6. Opportunity to use sports participation as an energy release and catharsis.

The young athlete who benefits from the positive outcomes associated with sport will enjoy increased motivation to achieve and will continue his or her sports participation (Man & Hondlick, 1984; Miller & McAuley, 1987; Richman & Heather, 1986).

Summary

The McClelland-Atkinson theory is a mathematical model based upon the motive to succeed and the motive to avoid failure. If M_s is greater than M_{af}, then the resultant need for achievement (n Ach) will be high and the athlete should be likely to enter into an achievement situation. Competition is a situation-specific example of an achievement situation.

A weak but significant relationship exists between athletic performance and achievement motivation. Achievement motivation is a good predictor of long-term success, but may not be a reliable predictor of immediate success. Raynor's elaboration to the McClelland-Atkinson model demonstrates that perceived contingency is a contributing factor to n Ach. Women are not affected by the fear of success more than men are. Women fear success when they perceive that it will result in a loss of femininity or social rejection.

Categorized under the heading of self-confidence, three additional theories of motivation were introduced and discussed. These include Bandura's Theory of Self-Efficacy, Harter's Theory of Competence Motivation, and Vealey's Sport Specific Model of Sport Confidence. In each of these theories, it is predicted that the individual will increase in self-confidence as he or she experiences task mastery and an expectation of success.

Women do not necessarily have less self-confidence than men, but ambiguous tasks, "masculine" tasks, and fear of social comparison can dampen their self-confidence. We can use a multifaceted approach to measure achievement motivation and can identify perceived sex-related attributes to help clarify the relationship between women and achievement motivation. Women high in androgyny and masculinity exhibit higher levels of n Ach than women high in femininity. Women who endorse a feminine gender role exhibit higher levels of competitive trait anxiety than other sex and gender role groups.

Bandura's self-efficacy theory explains how self-esteem and confidence can be developed in young athletes. Self-efficacy develops as a result of successful performance, vicarious experience, verbal persuasion, and emotional arousal. The most important of these is successful performance.

Review Questions

1. What is an achievement situation?
2. Describe McClelland and Atkinson's basic achievement motivation model. According to the model, when will an athlete approach or avoid a competitive situation?
3. What is the meaning of M_s, M_{af}, M_{ext}, and M_{-s}?
4. What are some ways of measuring the motive to succeed and the motive to avoid failure?
5. What is risk-taking behavior? Which type of athlete is likely to engage in risk-taking behavior?
6. Explain Raynor's perceived contingency elaboration.
7. What is the relationship between athletic performance and n Ach?
8. What is the motive to avoid success? How does it relate to achievement in women?
9. Describe Bandura's Theory of Self-Efficacy. How is achievement motivation developed within this theory?
10. Describe Harter's Theory of Competence Motivation. How is achievemnt motivation developed within this theory?
11. Show the relationship and commonality of Bandura's, Harter's, and Vealey's models relative to self-confidence and n Ach.

12. What factors contribute to low levels of self-confidence in women?
13. Describe the Work and Family Orientation Questionnaire.
14. What is androgyny, and how does it relate to achievement motivation in women?
15. How may gender roles be categorized? Describe two sex role inventories and how they may be used.
16. What is the relationship between gender role and competitive trait anxiety? Explain.
17. Discuss ways in which achievement motivation can be enhanced in young athletes.

Glossary

achievement motivation An athlete's predisposition to approach or avoid an evaluative situation.

achievement situation Situation in which there is an expectation that a person's performance will be subject to evaluation.

androgyny A condition in which an individual has both masculine and feminine characteristics.

BSRI The Bem Sex-Role Inventory for measuring femininity and masculinity.

competence motivation The motivation and drive to become competent.

competition An achievement situation in which performance in a sport is evaluated.

cross sex-typed Individuals having different sex and gender role orientations.

extrinsic motivation (M_{ext}) External rewards such as praise, money, or trophies.

femininity A term that describes those qualities desirable in both sexes, but found in greater abundance in women.

FOF Fear of failure.

FOS Fear of success.

incentive value of success (I_s) The perceived value of being successful.

intrinsic motivation Roughly equivalent to the need to achieve.

M_{af} The motive to avoid failure.

M_s The motive to achieve success.

M_{-s} The motive to avoid success, or fear of success.

McClelland-Atkinson model A mathematical model of achievement motivation based on n Ach, M_s, and M_{af}.

masculinity A term used to describe those qualities desirable in both sexes, but found in greater abundance in men.

n Ach Shorthand for the need to achieve.

PAQ Personal Attribute Questionnaire, used to measure sexual orientation.

participatory modeling Modeling in which the model helps the athlete to experience success.

PCSC Perceived competence scale for children.

perceived contingency Situation in which success at a future activity depends upon success in a present activity.

probability of success (P_s) The perceived probability of succeeding at a task.

risk-taking behavior The notion that athletes high in n Ach seek out challenging achievement situations, while those low in n Ach do not.

self-confidence A feeling or perception of belief or confidence in one's self.

self-efficacy A feeling of personal competence, self-esteem, and self-confidence.

sex-typed Individuals with the same sex and gender role orientation.

social comparison Comparison of one person with another in terms of social cues.

sport confidence The perception of confidence in a sport situation.

test-anxiety approach Sarason's theory of achievement motivation based on test anxiety.

WOFO Work and Family Orientation Questionnaire used to measure four facets of achievement motivation.

Recommended Readings

Arkes, H. R., & Garske, J. P. (1982). *Psychological theories of motivation* (2d ed.). Monterey, CA: Brooks/Cole.

Bandura, A. (1977). Self-efficacy: Toward a unifying theory of behavioral change. *Psychological Review, 84,* 191–215.

Bem, S. L. (1974). The measurement of psychological androgyny. *Journal of Consulting and Clinical Psychology, 42,* 155–162.

Harris, D. V. (1980). Assessment of motivation in sport and physical education. In W. F. Straub (ed.), *Sport psychology: An analysis of athlete behavior* (2d ed.). Ithaca, NY: Mouvement Publications.

Harter, S. (1978). Effectance motivation reconsidered: Towards a developmental model. *Human Development, 21,* 34–64.

Harter, S. (1982). The perceived competence scale for children. *Child Development, 53,* 87–97.

Horner, M. S. (1972). Towards an understanding of achievement-related conflicts in women. *Journal of Social Issues, 28* (2), 157–175.

Klint, K. A., & Weiss, M. R. (1987). Perceived competence and motives for participating in youth sports: A test of Harter's competence motivation theory. *Journal of Sport Psychology, 9,* 55–65.

Lenney, E. (1977). Women's self-confidence in achievement situations. *Psychological Bulletin, 84,* 1–13.

McClelland, D. C., Atkinson, J. W., Clark, R. W., & Lowell, E. L. (1953). *The achievement motive.* New York: Appleton-Century-Crofts.

Raynor, J. O., & Rubin, I. S. (1971). Effects of achievement and future orientation on level of performance. *Journal of Personality and Social Psychology, 17,* 36–41.

Roberts, G. C. (1982). Achievement motivation in sport. In R. Terjung (ed.), *Exercise and sport science reviews* (Vol. 10). Philadelphia: Franklin Institute Press.

Scanlan, T. K. (1982). Motivation and stress in competitive youth sports. *Journal of Physical Education, Recreation, and Dance, 53*(3), 27–28.

Spence, J. T., & Helmreich, R. L. (1978). *Masculinity and femininity.* Austin: University of Texas Press.

Vealey, R. S. (1986). Conceptualization of sport-confidence and competitive orientation: Preliminary investigation and instrument development. *Journal of Sport Psychology, 8,* 221–246.

Weinberg, W. T. (1977). Future orientation and competence motivation: New perspectives in achievement motivation research. In R. W. Christina & D. M. Landers (eds.), *Psychology of motor behavior and sport, 1976* (Vol. 2). Champaign, IL: Human Kinetics Publishers.

7   Causal Attribution Theory

Key Terms

additive principle
attribution theory
Causal Dimension Scale
cognitive evaluation
   theory
controllability
controlling aspect
covariation principle
discounting principle
ego-enhancing strategy
ego-protecting strategy
external control
extrinsic motivation
illogical models
informational aspect

internal control
intrinsic motivation
learned helplessness
locus of control
logical model
multiplicative principle
open-ended attribution
origin-pawn relationship
overjustification
   hypothesis
reinforcement
self-serving hypothesis
stability
structural rating scale

The key element in *attribution theory* is perception. When athletes are asked, "To what do you attribute your great success?" they are being asked for their perceptions. The fact that their perceptions of why they are successful may be completely erroneous is beside the point. The manner in which athletes answer questions like these reveals their perceptual biases.

Consider the following scenario: Two experienced volleyball players were matched against a pair of less experienced players in intramural doubles competition. The outcome was predictable; the experienced team won the match 15–1, 15–3. After the match the losers explained to the victors that they lost because one of them had injured his shoulder and they had had a bad day. In point of fact, they lost because they played a team with far more ability. However, this was not apparent to the losers, since they attributed their loss to bad luck and an injured shoulder. In so doing, they were subconsciously protecting their egos. While this may not have made them better volleyball players, it served to protect their feelings of self-esteem.

Attribution theory is a cognitive approach to motivation. It assumes that people strive to explain, understand, and predict events based on their cognitive perception of them. Other theories of motivation, such as the McClelland-Atkinson theory of achievement motivation and perhaps drive theory, attempt to explain behavior through complex formulas and constructs. Not so with attribution theory, according to which the intent of every human being is to explain his or her own actions in terms of their perceived causes. Fritz Heider (1944, 1958), the originator of attribution theory, described his theory as one of common sense or naive psychology.

However, as viewed by Weiner (1985) and Roberts (1982), attribution theory is far more than a layperson's theory of perceived motivation. It is a complex theory in which perceived attributions are viewed as greatly influencing a person's actions, feelings, confidence, and achievement motivation. How an athlete feels about him- or herself is directly related to the athlete's perception of cause and effect.

Most of the research that uses attribution theory deals with understanding when and why people select certain categories of attribution. For example, if an athlete systematically attributes failure to bad luck, we might suspect an unwillingness to accept responsibility. The attributions that athletes select reveal their motivational structures. Furthermore, helping athletes to change their perceptions can have a significant effect on their motivation to achieve. For this reason, n Ach and attribution theory are very closely related. For example, some young people feel that they fail because they lack innate ability. Since innate ability is relatively permanent, it is hard for those children to see that things will ever change for the better. However, if young athletes can be encouraged to consider bad luck or lack of effort as a cause for their failure, they need not feel that things cannot change. After all, luck can improve, and one can always try harder.

---

1. **Principle** Attributions that athletes select to explain their outcomes reveal much about their motivational structures.

   Application Coaches should not disregard the kinds of attributions athletes use to explain their outcomes. Instead, coaches should analyze them to understand the athletes' basic attribution structures. Athletes who give inappropriate attributions may need help in explaining their outcomes.

This chapter deals with attribution theory under four broad categories: model development, causal attributions in n Ach situations, egocentrism in attribution, and the effect of extrinsic rewards upon intrinsic motivation.

The Attribution Model

Heider (1944, 1958) proposed the basic attribution model. However, several significant contributions by Weiner (1972, 1979) have made it much more useful. Most recently, a contribution by Russell (1982) has improved research on the subject.

Fritz Heider's Contribution

Fritz Heider is the acknowledged founder of attribution theory (Arkes & Garske, 1982). The basis for Heider's model was that people strive for prediction and understanding of daily events in order to give their lives stability and predictability. Heider's (1958) basic model is depicted in figure 7.1.

According to Heider, outcomes are attributed to the person (personal force) or to the environment (environmental force) or to both. Effective personal force is composed of the factors *ability* and *trying* (effort). Trying in turn is composed of the factors *intention* and *exertion*. Intention is the qualitative component and represents what the person is trying to do, while exertion is the quantitative component and represents how much effort is expended.

As shown in figure 7.1, environmental force is composed of the factors *task difficulty* and *luck*. Heider considered task difficulty to be the more important of these two. As the figure indicates, the personal force dimension of ability and

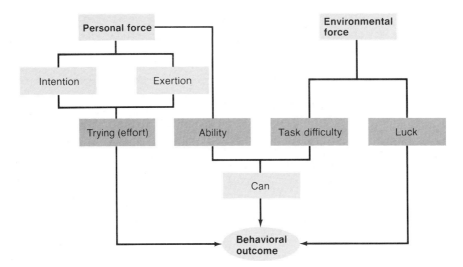

Figure 7.1 Schematic of Heider's (1958) basic model of causal attributes. From Fritz Heider, *Psychology of interpersonal relations.* Adapted with permission of Lawrence Erlbaum Associates, Inc., Hillsdale, New Jersey.

the environmental force factor of task difficulty interact to yield a separate dimension referred to as *can* (or *cannot*). This makes sense. If a task is difficult and yet is accomplished, it must be due to great ability. Conversely, if a person has ample ability but fails, it must be due to great difficulty. Depending on the difficulty of the task and the ability of the subject, several other attributions can give rise to the can or cannot dimension.

The highly unstable factor of luck also enters into many attribution situations. Luck is a variable environmental factor that can favorably or unfavorably change an outcome in an unsystematic way. However, we must keep in mind that what one person calls luck another person may call ability. For example, a tennis player who consistently places the first serve into the deep back-hand corner of the opponent's serving area should be considered skilled. However, the opponent may continue to attribute the event to luck. Consequently, what appears to be very simple can become very complex. All of these factors (trying, ability, task difficulty, and luck) combined result in a behavioral outcome, to which an individual attributes a cause. Heider reasoned that the relationship between the personal and environmental components of causation were additive. Thus, the following formula represents his reasoning:

Behavioral outcome = Personal force + Impersonal force

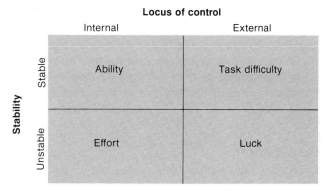

Locus of control

	Internal	External
Stable	Ability	Task difficulty
Unstable	Effort	Luck

Stability

Figure 7.2 Weiner's classification scheme for causal attributions. From Bernard Weiner, *Theories of motivation: From mechanism to cognition.* Copyright © 1972 by Houghton Mifflin Company. Used with permission.

Bernard Weiner's Contributions

Using Heider's basic formulation, Weiner (1972) made several significant contributions to the attribution model that made it easier to understand and apply in achievement situations. Weiner took Heider's four main factors and restructured them into two main causal dimensions. These two dimensions he labeled *stability* and *locus of control*. As can be observed in figure 7.2, **stability** is composed of stable and unstable attributes, while **locus of control** includes internal and external locus of control. Locus of control is a psychological construct that refers to people's belief about whether they are personally in control of what happens to them. Athletes who exhibit **internal control** tend to believe their behaviors influence outcomes. Those who exhibit **external control** tend to attribute their outcomes to outside forces such as fate, chance, and other people.

Weiner then incorporated Heider's four main factors (trying, ability, task difficulty, and luck) into his classification scheme for causal attribution. Ability was classified as a stable internal factor, while trying or effort was classified as an unstable internal factor. Both ability and effort are internal or personal in nature. However, ability is relatively unchanging or stable, while effort is constantly changing or unstable. A soccer player's ability may not change much from game to game, but the effort expended might fluctuate a great deal.

Conversely, task difficulty and luck are external in terms of locus of control. Task difficulty is relatively stable and unchanging (ability of an opponent, for example), while luck is unstable and variable.

Within this four-choice framework, Weiner envisioned that people would generally attribute their successes and failures to one of the four factors depicted in figure 7.2. If a female sprinter loses a race to a faster opponent and then reasons that the loss is due to bad luck, what she is really saying is that the cause is external and unstable, and given another chance she would win. But if she loses and attributes the loss to a lack of ability, she is saying the cause is internal, and is not going to change; if she ran the race a second time, she would still lose.

Weiner's original conceptualizations included only the four specific classes of attribution shown in figure 7.2. Frieze (1976) provided evidence to support the four category system. She found that 85 percent of the open-ended attributions reported in her research could be easily categorized in terms of stability and locus of control. However, Roberts and Pascuzzi (1979) reported that only 45 percent of the open-ended attributions that children use in a sport setting can be easily categorized in terms of effort, ability, difficulty, and luck. **Open-ended attribution** systems allow subjects to identify their own causes without any suggestions or constraints from the experimenter.

Weiner (1972), however, never meant to imply that there could not be more than four categories for classifying attributions. Consequently, he later identified another dimension, **controllability** (Weiner, 1979). Under this dimension, attributions are classified as being either controllable or uncontrollable. A controllable attribution is one in which the athlete's perception is under his or her personal control; an uncontrollable attribution is not. One drawback to the controllability dimension is that it is difficult to conceive of an attribution that is both external and controllable. Thus, two of the eight potential cells would have to be empty.

Due to the similarity of the terms *locus of control* and *controllability,* the introduction of the controllability dimension is confusing. For this reason Weiner (1985) suggested that the locus of control dimension be changed to *locus of causality.* As explained by Weiner (1985), the distinction between locus of causality and controllability is a subtle one. An athlete may perceive that failure is due to ability and therefore internal, yet feel little control over ability. For example, I might lose a 100-meter race to a faster opponent, attribute the loss internally to low ability (speed), yet feel that I don't have control over how fast I can run.

Dan Russell's Contribution

Traditionally, there have been three different ways of measuring causal attribution. The first is the **structural rating scale** method, in which the athlete is asked to rate several attributions in terms of how they apply to an event. The list of attributions usually includes ability, effort, difficulty, and luck. The second method is the structural percentage rating scale method. With this the attributions are again supplied, but the subject must rate them in terms of percentage of contribution. The third method is referred to as an open-ended system. The athletes make their own attributions or select them from a long list of potential attributions. The researcher then assigns the open-ended statements to specific categories of the attribution model shown in figure 7.2.

The weakness of the two structural methods of assessing attributions is that they are too constrained. Subjects are forced to select attributions from a list that may not contain a statement that matches their perception of what caused an event. The weakness of the open-ended system is that it leaves the experimenter with the task of assigning attributions to the appropriate dimensions. The researcher and the athlete may not agree on the meaning of a causal attribution, and too often the open-ended attributions are ambiguous (Ross, 1977).

To deal with attribution distortion and misclassification, Russell (1982) developed the **Causal Dimension Scale** (CDS). In using the CDS, athletes are asked to indicate their perceived cause for an outcome, and then to rate the cause relative to nine questions. The scale is composed of three questions for each of the dimensions of locus, stability, and controllability. The score range for each dimension is between 3 and 27. The higher the score, the more internal, stable, and controllable the athlete perceives the attribution to be. Thus, if an athlete attributed his or her outcome to "I had a good day" and then received a locus score of 25, a stability score of 21, and a controllability score of 10, you could label his or her attribution as internal, stable, and uncontrollable. Using the three-dimensional model shown in figure 7.3, you could also classify the attributional response in the *ability* category.

Russell avoided the problem of empty cells for the external/controllable interactions by slightly modifying the dimensions of controllability. He redefined a controllable cause as one that could be controlled, changed, or affected by either the athlete or some other person. Others affecting an outcome could be teammates, opponents, coaches, or fans. This modification resulted in eight possible categories of attributions based on the three dimensions of locus of control, stability, and controllability.

According to Russell's classification system, the attributions of ability, task difficulty, and luck are uncontrollable. In addition, mood has replaced effort as one of the original four attributions listed by Weiner. Effort, formerly considered to be an internal/unstable attribution, is the only attribution that Russell classifies as controllable. However, within the controllable category it may be further categorized in terms of stability and locus of control. This conceptualization places a great deal more emphasis on effort as a viable attribution. This is reasonable, since it would include the efforts of other people such as referees, coaches, and judges. Athletes often attribute their successes and failures to other people, such as referees and umpires (Roberts & Pascuzzi, 1979).

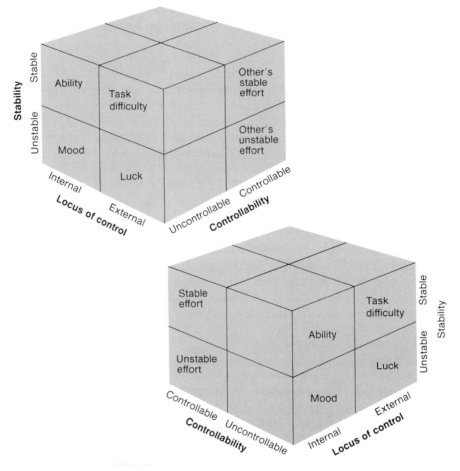

Figure 7.3 Two views of a three-dimensional model that Russell (1982) used to illustrate causal perceptions in terms of locus of control, stability, and controllability. From Russell, D., The causal dimension scale: A measure of how individuals perceive causes, *Journal of Personality and Social Psychology, 42,* 1137–1145.

2. **Principle** Formal attempts to measure an athlete's attribution structure should employ an open-ended system in conjunction with the Causal Dimension Scale.

   Application Open-ended attributions allow freedom of choice. In conjunction with the Causal Dimension Scale, these freely selected attributions can be correctly categorized. Although usually reserved for researchers, the practice of gathering data on perceived causality can be a valuable source of information for the coach.

Other Considerations

The process of identifying and categorizing causal attributions has come a long way since Heider first defined it. However, a number of conceptual problems persist. For instance, researchers and practitioners may fail to recognize that the kinds of attributions people make are based on a socialization process that may vary across cultures. Socialization plays an important part in the emphasis that we place on attributions. Attributions depend on what we learn to value. For example, ability is very important for Iranian children, and it consequently evolves as an important attribution regardless of whether a child fails or succeeds. American children, on the other hand, tend to value effort and intent regardless of innate ability (Salili, Maehr & Gillmore, 1976). These socialization differences will undoubtedly affect the kinds of attributions made.

A second problem that has often plagued attribution research is that the experimenter can bias a subject's perception of outcome (Halliwell, 1980). In many sports-related attribution studies, subjects do not perceive themselves to be succeeding or failing until the researcher biases their perceptions by asking, "To what do you attribute your success (or failure)?" Sometimes success and failure are perceived differently by researcher and athlete. For example, let's say I play tennis with one of the world's best players. I don't expect to win, but if I can win one or two games, I would consider myself a success.

Spink and Roberts (1980) studied this problem in a sport setting and demonstrated that a person's causal attributions are affected by the ambiguity of the outcome. They determined that clearly perceived wins or losses were attributed to internal factors such as ability or effort, while ambiguous results were attributed to external factors such as task difficulty and luck. An ambiguous outcome was defined as one in which the athlete's subjective perception of success differed from the objective outcome.

For a more in-depth analysis of the attributional model, refer to Arkes and Garske (1982), Rejeski and Brawley (1983), and Roberts (1982). We will now discuss attribution in specific need achievement situations.

Causal Attributions in Need Achievement Situations

In recent years, attribution theory has become instrumental in clarifying some of the research on achievement motivation theory. The two theories complement each other in many important ways. This section will identify several areas associated with achievement motivation in which attribution theory has been particularly useful.

Internal/External Attributions

Regarding the internal and external dimensions of attribution, several lines of research have evolved. Three of them are of particular interest to us in this section. One of them has dealt with the notion of locus of control at the exclusion of the stability dimension. Another has investigated the relationship between affect and attribution. The third has concentrated on the notion of covariation.

Locus of Control

Locus of control, or the extent to which people believe they are responsible for their behavioral outcomes, has often been cited as an important factor in achievement-oriented behavior (Chalip, 1980). As we discussed earlier, people with an internal locus of control tend to believe their behaviors influence outcomes, while those with an external locus of control tend to attribute outcomes to outside forces such as fate, chance, and other people. This dichotomy closely resembles DeCharms and Carpenter's (1968) **origin-pawn relationship.** People who are origins like to be in control and originate their own behavioral outcomes. Those who are pawns feel powerless and acted on by external sources.

Perhaps the person most responsible for developing the conceptual framework for the locus of control dimension in attribution was Julian B. Rotter (1966, 1971). Rotter (1966) developed the twenty-nine item Internal-External Locus of Control Scale to measure the extent to which people believe they possess some control over their lives. The Rotter scale has been used by many researchers to classify subjects on the basis of the locus of control dimension. After using the scale for many years, Rotter (1971) stated the following generalities about locus of control: (1) children coming from a lower socioeconomic environment tend to be external, (2) children tend to become more internal with age, and (3) highly external people feel they are at the mercy of their environment, they are continually being manipulated by outside forces.

Some interesting findings have been reported on the subject of locus of control in a sport setting. Martens (1971b) found that children who differ in locus of control do not respond differently to the presence of social reinforcement. Studies by Hutchinson (1972) and DiGuiseppe (1973) are in agreement that team sport and individual sport athletes do not differ in locus of control. Finn and Straub (1977) compared the locus of control of highly skilled Dutch and American female softball players and discovered that the American athletes were significantly more internally oriented. Duke, Johnson, and Nowicki (1977) monitored the locus of control of 109 children ages six to fourteen during an eight-week sport fitness camp, and observed a significant shift towards internal control as a result of the experience. Scheer and Ansorge (1979) observed that gymnastics coaches typically rank-order their gymnasts from poorest to best. Their natural expectation is that scores should improve for performers at the highest rank in the order. The purpose of this study was to determine to what degree female judges were influenced by the within-team position of gymnasts, based on the judges' own locus of control. The results showed that the externals were influenced by order while internals were not. Finally, Aguglia and Sapienza (1984) tested male and female amateur adult volleyball players and their team captains relative to locus of control. They observed that team captains tend to be more internal than the more external team members.

Research suggests that an internal locus of control is better than an external locus of control. However, very little research has been conducted on the influence of locus of control on performance. Chalip (1980) suggests that internals demonstrate less performance disruption under stress than externals and are better able to use task-centered coping behaviors. Anshel (1979) observed that internals perform better than externals on the pursuit rotor task when feedback is positive, but worse when feedback is negative.

From a developmental point of view, the research suggests that an internal orientation is more mature (Rotter, 1971). Furthermore, the research indicates that sport involvement can help shift a person's locus of control from external to internal. This is not to imply, however, that all external attributions are immature. Sometimes external attributions are appropriate and expected. For example, it may be completely normal for athletes to complain that they lost because of poor officiating if their team was called for twice as many fouls as the other.

---

3. **Principle** An internal locus of control is preferred to an external locus of control.

    Application Externals can be identified by using Rotter's Internal-External Locus of Control Scale or by observing that the athletes attribute most outcomes to external causes. These athletes can be encouraged to become more internal through the development of self-confidence and through encouragement to attribute outcomes internally when appropriate.

Attribution and Affect

The kinds of attributions that we make in response to outcomes are closely associated with affect, or emotion (Weiner, 1985). An internal attribution generally results in greater affect than an external attribution (Riemer, 1975; Weiner, Heckhausen, Meyer & Cook, 1972). For example, imagine that you have just scored a 68 on a new eighteen-hole golf course. You feel elated! You have never done so well before; your true ability has finally shown itself. But when you check some other people's scores, you discover that everyone has scored in the 60s, even your friend who never gets below an 80! You can no longer attribute your success internally, because the low score is obviously due to a lack of difficulty, an external attribution.

Weiner (1981) and McAuley, Russell and Gross (1983) suggested some specific cause-and-effect relationships among attribution, outcome, and affect. In terms of locus of control, the expected pattern of emotional responses, given success or failure, is illustrated in figure 7.4. When people attribute success to internal causes, they typically respond with pride, confidence, and satisfaction. Conversely, if after succeeding, they attribute success externally, then they will probably experience gratitude and thankfulness.

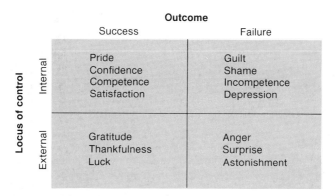

Figure 7.4 The influence of outcome and locus of control upon affect.

While the affect for success, regardless of attribution, tends to be positive and enthusiastic, the affect for failure is typically negative and sometimes subdued. For example, an athlete who fails at a task and attributes the failure internally is likely to feel guilty, especially if other teammates are involved. On the other hand, failure that is explained externally might result in an outburst of anger or surprise. Consider the tennis player who loses an important point due to a line call. If the athlete feels that the line judge was in error, the response may predictably be anger.

Weiner, Russell, and Lerman (1979) extend the attribution-affect connection one step further and suggest that attributions may be surmised from observing affect. In other words, one ought to be able to determine to what cause a child attributes failure or success by simply observing the emotional response. For example, if a child strikes out in a baseball game and responds with a look of surprise, one can predict that the child attributed failure to an outside source (the umpire, perhaps).

The kinds of attributions that young athletes make in response to success and failure is closely linked with our discussion in chapter 6 on achievement motivation. Children who exhibit self-confidence and pride about their performance are typically high in n Ach. Consequently, internalizing success is of great value in developing self-efficacy (Bandura, 1977). However, as can be observed in figure 7.4, internalizing failure results in feelings of incompetence and shame. This is certainly counterproductive to the development of n Ach. Children who continually experience feelings of shame, guilt, and incompetence are likely to withdraw completely from competitive sports (Roberts, 1980).

4. **Principle** The kinds of attribution that athletes make for success and failure are closely associated with their emotions.

    Application Coaches should learn to recognize athletes' unspoken attributions from the athletes' emotional responses. If an athlete hides emotions, the coach should be able to predict how that person is feeling based on the attributions the athlete makes.

Consistent with our discussion on affect, the most fundamental finding about n Ach and attribution is that people high in achievement motivation tend to attribute successes to internal causes more than those who are low in n Ach. Following a success, athletes high in n Ach will feel very good, because such people attribute success to their ability. Under the same circumstances, low n Ach people typically attribute their success to an external source such as luck (Ames, 1978; Gillis, 1979; Lefebvre, 1979; Roberts, Kleiber & Duda, 1981).

Covariation Principle

A person's attributions for success or failure can be predicted on the basis of the performance of others on the same task (Arkes & Garske, 1982). This phenomenon has been named the **covariation principle.** According to this principle, when the performance of others agrees (covaries) with the performance of the subject, attributions will be external. If the performance of others disagrees (lacks covariation) with the performance of the subject, attributions will be internal. For example, if I beat someone in tennis whom everyone else has lost to, I will certainly attribute my victory to an internal cause such as superior ability. The covariation principle has received experimental support from Weiner and Kukla (1970) and Frieze and Weiner (1971).

5. **Principle** According to the covariation principle, outcomes that agree with the performance of others usually result in external attributions, while outcomes that disagree usually result in internal attributions.

    Application This principle can help the coach tell when the athlete is making inappropriate attributions for success and failure. For example, if an athlete hits a home run off a pitcher who strikes most batters out, this outcome should be attributed internally.

Stability Considerations

In the previous section our concern was with locus of control and affect. In this section we will turn to a discussion of research related to the stability dimension of causal attribution.

Attribution and Expectancy

Suppose an athlete with a history of success is unexpectedly defeated. To what is this athlete likely to attribute the failure? Or suppose an athlete who consistently loses suddenly experiences success. To what is this athlete likely to attribute the success? One might expect both athletes to attribute their unexpected outcomes to some type of unstable factor such as luck, officiating, or effort. In other words, we might expect an ascription to an unstable attribution whenever an outcome is different than what should be expected based on previous experience. We should expect a stable attribution to be selected in response to an expected outcome (success or failure). For example, if an athlete with a history of success defeats another who has a history of failures, we should expect both of them to attribute their outcomes to some type of stable attribution such as ability or task difficulty.

Frieze and Weiner (1971) provided research evidence to support these logical expectations. They asked subjects to ascribe hypothetical successes and failures to ability, effort, task difficulty, or luck as a function of past performance on the same task. The results are illustrated in figure 7.5. The figure indicates that when present performance agrees with past performance, stable attributions score high.

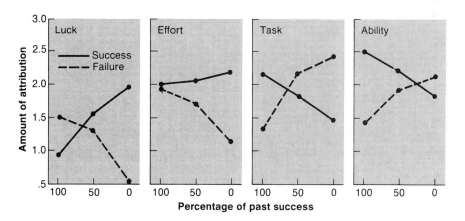

Figure 7.5 Attribution as a function of past performance. From I. Frieze and B. Weiner, Cue utilization and attributional judgements for success and failure. *Journal of Personality, 39,* 591–605. Copyright 1971 by Duke University Press. Adapted with permission.

And when present performance disagrees with past performance, unstable attributions score high. Consider the luck attribution. For success, the causal attribution to luck (an unstable attribution) is highest when the individual succeeds even though the percentage of past successes is zero. Furthermore, the causal attribution to luck is lowest when the individual fails, consistent with past experiences. These same generalizations were also observed by Spink (1978b) in basketball and by Roberts (1977) and Iso-Ahola (1977b) in Little League baseball. Thus, past experience significantly affects the kinds of causal attributions given for success and failure. If the outcome is consistent with past experience, then attributions tend to be stable. If the outcome is inconsistent with past experience, attributions tend to be unstable. This information should be of great value to the coach or teacher who is trying to help athletes cope with success and failure.

Given these generalizations, it follows that we can predict athletes' future expectations about performance based on the kinds of attributions they give for their present performance. If an athlete attributes a loss to bad luck, he or she is saying that things may be different next time. But if the loss is attributed to a lack of ability, the athlete is saying that the result will be the same next time. This observation points to the utility of ascribing failures to unstable causes, since it does not imply repeated failure. It would be wise to encourage a young athlete to attribute a failure to lack of effort. This will suggest that more effort can change the outcome from failure to success. Experimental support for these conclusions has been provided by Duquin (1978), Roberts (1980), and Ryan (1981).

---

6. **Principle** Athletes tend to give stable attributions in response to expected outcomes and unstable attributions in response to unexpected outcomes.

    Application Attributions along the stability dimension should suggest to the coach the kind of performance expectations the athlete has for the future. An unstable attribution suggests that the athlete expects future outcomes to change, while a stable attribution suggests that future outcomes are expected to remain the same.

Learned Helplessness

In need achievement situations, some people act as if events are out of their control, that failure is inevitable. The person who displays these characteristics in achievement situations is suffering from **learned helplessness** (Seligman, 1975). This is a psychological state in which people feel that events are out of their control.

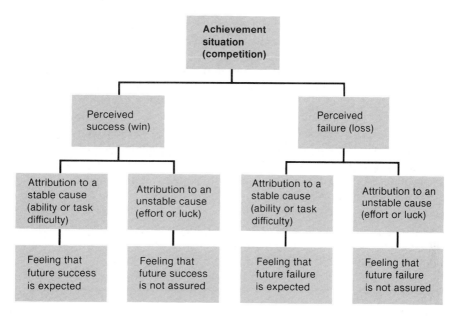

Figure 7.6 Flow chart showing the results of both stable and unstable attributions for success and failure.

Learned helpless children who show a deterioration of performance under the threat of failure tend to attribute their failure to stable factors, such as lack of ability. Those who show enhanced performance under the threat of failure tend to choose unstable factors such as luck or lack of effort (Dweck, 1980; Valle & Frieze, 1976). Attributing success to stable factors suggests to the child that success is a realistic expectation for the future; attributing failure to stable factors suggests to the child that failure is a realistic expectation for the future (Duquin, 1978; Dweck, 1980; Valle & Frieze, 1976, Weiner, 1985). These and other attributional predictions about stability are illustrated in figure 7.6.

A coach or teacher should promote feelings of self-efficacy and self-confidence by encouraging children to make appropriate attributions to success and failure (Valle & Frieze, 1976). Children who succeed should be encouraged to view the success as both stable and internal—internal, because the child needs to feel pride in this accomplishment; stable, because the child needs to feel that success is likely to occur again. Attributing success to ability should be beneficial—it is both internal and stable. Children who experience repeated failure should be encouraged to select an unstable and perhaps internal attribution (Grove & Pargman, 1986). Such an attribution will assure the child that failure is not inevitable because the cause is not stable. But an internal attribution will help the child accept responsibility for the results. It would not be wise to continually encourage an external/unstable attribution, because the child may come to feel that bad luck or poor officiating are the cause of all disappointments. However, a good mix of internal and external unstable attributions would be beneficial.

Dweck (1975) proposed and tested such a therapeutic strategy. A sample of learned helpless children were categorized into a failure deprivation condition and an attribution retraining condition. In the deprivation condition, the children's confidence was bolstered through programmed success. The children in the attribution retraining condition were told after experiencing a failure to attribute the failure to an unstable cause such as effort. The results showed that by the end of the training period, the attribution retraining children fared far better than the success-only children in the face of a contrived failure. Therefore, helping children to change their attributions may be more beneficial than merely manipulating success. This does not mean that experiencing success is not important. It is. But performance and self-efficacy can also be enhanced by helping children to make confidence-building or -protecting attributions.

---

7. **Principle** Attributing failure to an internal/stable cause is potentially damaging to a young athlete's self-esteem.
   Application Young athletes should be encouraged to attribute failure to unstable causes that can be expected to change. For example, effort would be an ideal attribution for failure.

---

8. **Principle** Attributing success to an internal/stable cause such as ability is good for a young athlete's self-confidence.
   Application The development of self-confidence is the most important goal of any youth sport program. Coaches should encourage athletes to take credit for their successes.

The relationship between learned helplessness and the stability dimension is also documented in achievement motivation research. Subjects who are high in the motive to succeed ($M_s > M_{af}$) tend to attribute failures more to lack of effort (an unstable dimension) and less to lack of ability than do subjects who are low in this motive ($M_s < M_{af}$) (Arkes & Garske, 1982). These findings are consistent with our earlier discussion on learned helplessness and the stability dimension.

Sex Differences

The literature on motor tasks and the sport setting does not reveal a consistent difference between the causal attributions of men and women. That is, males do not attribute winning or losing to any particular cause any more than females do (Gillis, 1979; Iso-Ahola, 1979; Roberts, Kleiber & Duda, 1981). One exception to this general pattern was a study by Duquin (1978) involving soccer, volleyball, and touch football, in which males used more ability attributes than did females. In the Iso-Ahola (1979) study, boys and girls did not differ significantly in attributions for success or failure, but an interesting sex-stereotype finding was reported. Specifically, if a boy lost to a boy, he was willing to attribute the loss to lack of ability, but if the opponent was female he was not willing to do so. Bird and Williams (1980) observed differential patterns of attributions as a function of age and sex. Most striking was that by age 13, male outcomes were usually explained on the basis of effort, while female outcomes were usually explained in terms of luck.

Several important findings outside the sport psychology literature, however, provide convincing evidence about attributional tendencies and the subject's sex. Ickes and Layden (1978), for example, asked male and female undergraduate students to attribute their successes to various causes. The results showed that males were far more likely than females to attribute their successes to internal causes. Males and high n Ach individuals tend to attribute success to internal causes more so than do females and low n Ach individuals. Ickes and Layden also found that males were likely to attribute their losses to no cause at all. They apparently viewed failure as being highly unlikely! In her book *Inside Volleyball for Women,* Mary Jo Peppler (1977) commented on this characteristic of male athletes. As an Olympic volleyball player and all-American, she promoted volleyball by giving demonstrations and clinics at high schools. As part of her exhibition she and another female athlete would challenge any group of six young men to a game. She marveled that, no matter how badly the boys were beaten, they were always ready to try again with complete confidence that they would win the next time. She suggested that young female athletes should develop this characteristic.

Similar results with younger subjects have been reported by Nicholls (1975) and Dweck and Reppucci (1973). In these studies, young girls tended to attribute their failures to low ability (internal attribution), while young boys attributed their failures to bad luck or to low effort (unstable attributions). A quick review of figure 7.6 suggests that this pattern of attribution would be disastrous for the females and highly desirable for the males. Women or girls who tend to attribute their losses to an internal stable cause are likely to conclude that failure is inevitable. Conversely, the boys' practice of attributing failure to the unstable factors of effort and luck suggests that they will view failure as transitory.

Dweck and Goetz (1978) suggest that this pattern of ascribing failure to low ability may be the reason that females often suffer from low self-confidence and self-esteem. Why would females tend to ascribe failure to low ability rather than to effort or luck as the boys do? To find an answer, Dweck and Goetz carefully observed classroom interactions between teachers and students. They observed that boys received more negative feedback than girls, but it was unrelated to their intellectual ability. On the other hand, they observed that 88 percent of the negative feedback the girls received pertained to their intellectual ability. Dweck and Goetz suggested that this may cause girls to make internal attributions to failure much more often than boys do. These conclusions are, of course, speculative. However, they provide an important clue for explaining the low levels of n Ach often displayed by women and girls compared to the n Ach of men and boys.

---

9. **Principle** Young women and girls who lack self-confidence tend to ascribe internal and stable causes to their failures, while young men and boys tend to attribute failure to unstable causes or to no cause at all.

    Application As with the learned helpless child, girls and women who suffer from perceptions of low self-esteem should be encouraged and coached to consider unstable causes such as effort or luck for their failures in sport.

Typical Attributions in Sport

We have learned a great deal about the kinds of attributions that athletes make in various n Ach situations. However, we have said little about the general patterns of attributions made by athletes in response to success and failure. Investigations by Gill, Ruder, and Gross (1982) and by McAuley and Gross (1983) provide valuable insight into this area.

In the Gill et al. (1982) investigation, 352 open-ended attributions for winning and losing were obtained from female volleyball players and male and female kinesiology students. The attributions from the volleyball players were based on actual volleyball competition, while the attributions for the kinesiology students were based on motor maze performance. Each attribution was categorized according to the dimensions of locus of control, stability, and controllability. Each was also categorized according to whether it referred to self, teammates, team as a whole, or other factors. The results indicated that (1) the typical pattern of attributions, regardless of outcome, was internal, unstable, and controllable; (2) members of winning teams used the controllable as opposed to uncontrollable attributions much more than the losing teams did; (3) attributions generally referred to the team as a whole; and (4) teamwork, or lack of teamwork, was by far the most frequently used attribution for success or failure.

The basic shortcoming of the Gill et al. (1982) study was that the researchers were left with the impossible task of correctly assigning open-ended attributions to the various dimensions. In the McAuley and Gross (1983) investigation, this problem was resolved by employing Russell's (1982) Causal Dimension Scale for categorizing attributions. Subjects were table tennis players who were asked to make open-ended attributions about the outcome of a 21-point game. The results of this study revealed that winners' attributions tended to be more internal, stable, and controllable than those of losers, a finding that is consistent with results reported by Duncan and McAuley (1987), McAuley (1985) and Tenenbaum and Furst (1985). The research by Tenenbaum and Furst (1985) also revealed that individual sport athletes use internal attributions to a greater extent than team sport athletes.

---

10. **Principle** Winners tend to attribute their outcome to internal, stable, and controllable causes to a greater extent than losers.
    Application It is possible to identify winners and losers based on the kind of attributions given for a perceived outcome.

Egocentrism in Attribution

People are assumed to follow logic when they make attributions to behavioral outcomes. For example, in regard to the covariation principle, it was observed that people tend to make attributions consistent with a certain logic. That is, if a person "aces" a test, but then realizes that everyone else did too, that person will ascribe the cause externally (e.g., an easy test). This is considered to be a **logical model** for making attributions to outcomes.

However, evidence suggests that people are not always entirely logical in making causal attributions for their behavior. Instead of making logical attributions, they often make blatantly self-serving ones. In this regard, a person might attribute successes to internal causes and failures to external causes. Attributing all successes to internal causes is called **ego-enhancing strategy,** while attributing all failures to external causes is called **ego-protecting strategy.** Both strategies are self-serving and are considered **illogical models** of attribution (Fontaine, 1975). Mann (1974) observed this strategy among football fans. Mann found that fans of winning football teams tended to attribute game outcomes to internal causes, such as ability, while fans of losing teams tended to attribute game outcomes to external causes, such as luck and biased officiating.

Perhaps the first serious review of the available literature on the **self-serving hypothesis** we have just described was conducted by Miller and Ross (1975). In their review, they pointed out that in order for the illogical model to be true, it must be shown that people indulge both in ego-protective attributions under conditions of failure and ego-enhancing attributions under conditions of success. Their basic conclusion was that the self-serving bias proposition was largely unsupported, since the literature provided strong evidence that people use ego-enhancing strategies under conditions of success, but only minimal evidence that they use ego-protective strategies under conditions of failure.

A review of the sport psychology literature since Miller and Ross's (1975) signal work reveals a significant interest in the self-serving hypothesis, but does little to clarify the issue. Of fourteen articles reviewed, not a single one of them demonstrated unambiguous support for the illogical hypothesis for both the ego-enhancing and ego-protecting notions. As with the Miller and Ross (1975) conclusions, all of the studies showed that people experiencing success typically attributed their success to internal factors such as effort and ability. But when it came to the ego-protecting bias, the results always tended to be qualified in terms of some situational factor.

For example, Kimiecik and Duda (1985) observed that the self-serving hypothesis was supported for children involved in one-to-one basketball competition when a forced choice attribution model was used (ability, effort, difficulty, or luck).

However, when an open-ended attribution model was used, winners selected internal and external causes equally and losers primarily selected internal attributions. Additionally, Brawley (1984) provided evidence to support his contention that self-serving attributions may not be necessarily self-serving after all. An athlete's ability to assign accurate causes to outcomes may be limited by memory. Athletes recall events about their own behavior to a much greater extent than they recall events about their opponents' or teammates' behavior, both of which may be responsible for outcome.

Even though the literature does not clearly support the self-serving bias hypothesis, several interesting factors are worth noting. Iso-Ahola (1977a), Spink (1978a), and Spink and Roberts (1980) studied the relationship between the self-serving hypothesis and decisiveness of outcome. All three of these studies hypothesized that subjects would attribute clear success and failure to internal causes, but ambiguous outcomes to external causes. The Spink and Roberts (1980) research supported this hypothesis, although success and failure were determined subjectively as a function of subjects' perceptions of "desirable qualities in themselves." Thus, for some people a loss at racquetball, for instance, could be perceived as a success. The results of the other two studies were identical to each other. Clear wins and ambiguous wins were attributed to internal causes (a familiar result), while clear losses and ambiguous losses were attributed to low effort and task difficulty. Thus, losers selected both internal and external causes. However, Iso-Ahola (1977a) noted that subjects tended to view lack of effort as an external attribution rather than an internal one. That is, the subjects reasoned that they didn't try very hard because of some external factor (e.g., poor officiating). With this interpretation of the effort attribution, the results support the self-serving hypothesis.

In another investigation, Iso-Ahola (1978) identified still another situational factor that could affect the interpretation of attributional results. In this study, subjects were asked to imagine that they either agreed or disagreed with an objective assessment of their performance on a motor maze task. The results indicated that subjects tended to use a self-serving strategy for selecting attributions under the objective success-failure conditions. However, when the subject's own perceptions of success and failure were considered, the attributions were generally logical and non-self-serving.

In an interesting study by Gill (1980b), the question of self-serving bias was investigated in regard to team outcomes rather than individual outcomes. Subjects were members of women's basketball teams. After winning or losing, players were asked to assign primary responsibility for success or failure either to their own team or to their opponents. Results showed that players attributed success to their own team and failure to the other team. Thus, in terms of group attributions, the self-serving hypothesis seemed to be supported. In another part of the study, players were asked to assign primary responsibility for success or failure to themselves (an internal attribution) or to their teammates (an external attribution). The results failed to support the self-serving hypothesis. Members of winning teams assigned primary responsibility to their teammates and members of losing teams assigned primary responsibility to themselves. Thus in this case, a reverse egocentric pattern emerged.

Bradley (1978) summarized the situation somewhat by suggesting that the attributional process is probably neither purely logical nor purely illogical (self-serving). Rather, the disposition to use a self-serving strategy is within each individual to some degree. Some people will rarely use it, preferring to accept responsibility for their own actions in most cases. However, others may find it comforting to reject personal responsibility for outcomes in order to protect a delicate ego.

It is good to remember at this point in our discussion that Dweck (1980) suggested that helpless children can be helped by teaching them to attribute their failures to unstable internal factors such as low effort.

It is also important to keep in mind that an ego-enhancing/protecting approach to attribution may be better from the standpoint of improving n Ach and self-efficacy. Athletes should learn to accept responsibility for their own performances, but not at the expense of their self-confidence. I personally would rather hear young athletes state that they struck out in baseball because of a bad call or because of a great curve ball, than because of a lack of ability (even if they do lack ability). It is healthy for athletes to ascribe failure to ability if they perceive ability to be something they can improve on. In this case, ability would be an unstable attribution, since it could be changed. Unfortunately, young athletes often fail to see skill as dynamic and changing.

---

11. **Principle** Athletes are not always completely logical in their attributions. They will often engage in illogical or ego-enhancing strategies to explain events.

    Application Athletes who make self-serving attributions for every event are in danger of losing contact with reality. After all, losing isn't always something or someone else's fault. However, to a certain extent, self-enhancing and self-protecting strategies are probably good for the athlete's self-confidence.

Effects of Extrinsic Rewards on Intrinsic Motivation

When someone engages in an activity for its own sake and not for any other reason, we may conclude that they engage in the activity from an **intrinsic motivation.** On the other hand, if it can be argued that someone has an external reason for engaging in the activity, we would agree that they have an **extrinsic motivation** to engage in it. If the external motivation is a reward, then it can be assumed that the reward may be part of the reason the person is participating.

It is appealing to assume that extrinsic rewards can enhance motivation. But what happens to an athlete's motivation if the rewards are withdrawn? Can extrinsic rewards actually damage rather than enhance motivation? Research on attribution theory has led to the conclusion that extrinsic rewards can damage a young athlete's intrinsic desire to compete. The kinds of attributions that people give for receiving external rewards may have a negative impact on their intrinsic motivation.

In our earlier discussion on achievement motivation theory, we noted that the motive to achieve success (M_s) is essentially equivalent to what we now are calling intrinsic motivation. Atkinson and McClelland pointed out that people who are higher in the motive to avoid failure (M_{af}) than in the motive to achieve success

(M_s) theoretically should not enter into achievement situations. However, since it is obvious that they often do, Atkinson (1964) argued that it must be due to the added incentive of extrinsic motivation. In other words, intrinsic motivation (M_s) and extrinsic motivation combine to create need achievement. Otherwise, as Atkinson points out, people whose M_s was less than their M_{af} would not engage in achievement-related situations.

According to this **additive principle,** a young athlete who is low in n Ach will participate in an achievement situation if there is sufficient reward or extrinsic motivation for doing so. Yet a great deal of research evidence seems to cast doubt on the additive principle. Specifically, it has been argued that the relationship between intrinsic and extrinsic motivation is multiplicative, not additive. That is, extrinsic rewards can either add to or detract from intrinsic motivation. This principle is illustrated in the story of an elderly man who wanted to chase away some noisy children who liked to play near his home (Siedentop & Ramey, 1977).

The man was bothered by the noise made by a group of young boys who liked to play in an area near his house. The man tried several strategies to get the boys to play elsewhere, but to no avail. Finally, he came up with a new and interesting strategy. He decided to pay the boys to play near his house! He offered them twenty-five cents apiece to return the next day. Naturally, the boys returned the next day to receive their pay, at which time the man offered them twenty cents to come the following day. When they returned again he offered them only fifteen cents to come the next day, and he added that for the next few days he would only give them a nickel for their efforts. The boys became very agitated, since they felt their efforts were worth more than a nickel, and they told the man that they would not return!

The boys in this story came to believe that the reason they were playing near the man's house was for pay and not for fun. Therefore their perceived locus of control shifted from an internal to an external source. When this happens, the activity can lose its intrinsic value. Is it possible that this is happening today in professional baseball? There are no doubt many highly paid athletes who have shifted their locus of control from an internal source—love of the game—to an external source. If the high salaries were withdrawn, how many would continue playing the game?

A similar thing could be happening to our young athletes as they receive trophies, money, pins, and awards for athletic participation. Is the relationship between intrinsic and extrinsic rewards additive as suggested by Atkinson (1964), or is it multiplicative as suggested by Lepper & Greene (1976)? The **multiplicative principle** suggests that the interaction between intrinsic and extrinsic rewards could either add to or detract from intrinsic motivation.

12. **Principle** The notion that intrinsic motivation and extrinsic rewards are always additive is a myth.

Application Extrinsic motivation in the form of awards and trophies may enhance achievement motivation, but such rewards may also diminish it. Coaches should carefully consider what they intend to accomplish by giving rewards for athletic performance.

There is little doubt that those who promote ever-larger trophies, awards, and purses do so out of a desire to increase motivation. However, is that actually what happens? Whether or not a person discounts the value of intrinsic motivation depends on perception of causality (Kelley, 1972). The solution to the problem rests with attribution theory and locus of control.

Deeply seated in attribution theory and the *discounting principle* is Lepper and Greene's concept of an **overjustification hypothesis.** According to this hypothesis, people's intrinsic motivation may be decreased by inducing them to engage in an otherwise interesting activity in order to receive some extrinsic reward or goal (Greene & Lepper, 1974a, 1974b; Lepper & Greene, 1975, 1976; Lepper, Greene & Nisbett, 1973). For example, if a child plays baseball for fun but then is induced to do so for a trophy, this trophy may represent an overjustification for playing baseball. Remember the story of the elderly man and the boys. As a result of this overjustification, the intrinsic motivation of the baseball game is discounted—this is the **discounting principle**—and the child stops playing in the absence of a reward. The child's intrinsic motivation has been undermined due to the presence of the extrinsic reward. The child comes to perceive that he or she is playing for the purpose of receiving a trophy rather than for any intrinsic reasons.

Perhaps the single most important contribution to our understanding of the relationship between intrinsic motivation and extrinsic rewards comes from the work of Deci and associates (Deci, 1971, 1972, 1975, 1978, 1980; Deci, Cascio & Krusell, 1975). Deci's **cognitive evaluation theory** is deeply seated in attribution theory, and in the locus of control origin-pawn relationship discussed earlier in this chapter (DeCharms & Carpenter, 1968).

Deci theorized that extrinsic rewards can affect intrinsic motivation in two ways. The first results in a decrement in intrinsic motivation, and occurs as people perceive a change in locus of control from internal to external. That is, when people come to perceive that their behavior is controlled by external forces, they respond with decreased levels of intrinsic motivation. This is referred to as the **controlling aspect** of extrinsic motivation, and serves to place an athlete in the position of a pawn who is acted on. The second effect of extrinsic rewards is informational in nature and results in an increase in intrinsic motivation. If an external award provides feedback to the person and enhances that person's sense of competence and self-determination, increased intrinsic motivation will be the end result. This is referred to as the **informational aspect** of extrinsic motivation, and it places an athlete in the position of an originator who does the acting.

As Halliwell (1978) pointed out, there are several important points to remember about cognitive evaluation theory. The first is that every external reward has two potential aspects, a controlling aspect and an informational aspect. The second is that a change in locus of control from internal to external is associated with a loss of self-determination and control. Finally, it is not the actual strength of the reward that is critical, but the *perceived* strength of the controlling or informational aspect that makes the difference.

Consider the following situation: A ten-year-old boy agrees to run in a five-mile road race with his father. As further incentive to train and finish the race, the father promises the boy ten dollars. Later on, the boy passes up a second opportunity to run in a race with his father because, as he puts it, "Why, what's in it for me?" This seems like an extreme example, yet situations like this occur all the time. Why did this boy lose interest in this intrinsically interesting activity? Because he came to perceive that the primary reason for his running in the race was for money. The money became the source of his motivation, not the intrinsic fun of running. Once the shift in locus of control was made from the internal cause to the external cause, the boy came to feel controlled by the external reward. He was running for the money and not for the intrinsic value of the experience; consequently, when the salient external motivation was withdrawn, intrinsic motivation was insufficient.

---

13. **Principle** An extrinsic reward that encourages athletes to attribute their participation to external causes can reduce intrinsic motivation.
   Application Coaches should discourage any form of extrinsic reward that athletes may perceive to be more important than athletic participation itself.

Let us consider a second example. A twelve-year-old girl competed in a singles tennis tournament and won an award for accomplishment. The inscripton on the award said, "In recognition of your placing in the top ten of the City Tournament." This positive feedback about her performance gave the girl a feeling of competence and self-determination. She was proud of the award and went on to participate in several more tennis tournaments that year. Because she perceived that the award provided her positive information about her ability as a tennis player, it became intrinsically motivating.

---

14. **Principle** Extrinsic rewards such as praise, awards, ribbons, and trophies that the athlete views as rewarding excellence and encouraging further participation will enhance intrinsic motivation.

    Application Coaches and teachers should carefully consider the perceptions that young athletes have about extrinsic rewards. If the rewards are perceived to represent excellence, they can be valuable. However, if they become more important than the sport itself, they can be damaging.

These two examples illustrate the controlling and informational aspects of external rewards. The critical factor in both cases was how the individual perceived the reward. If the reward was perceived to be controlling, intrinsic motivation declined. If the reward was perceived to be conveying positive information about performance, intrinsic motivation increased. An important study by Ryan (1980) further illustrates this point. Ryan hypothesized that collegiate female athletes who received scholarships would view their awards as being informational in nature, and as a result they would exhibit greater intrinsic motivation than nonscholarship athletes. Ryan also hypothesized that male athletes on wrestling and football scholarships would view their awards as being controlling in nature, and would suffer a loss in intrinsic motivation compared to nonscholarship athletes. The results generally confirmed the hypotheses. Females who recived scholarships were higher in intrinsic motivation than those who did not. Also, as predicted, football players who received scholarships suffered a loss in intrinsic motivation compared to those athletes who did not have scholarships. However, the wrestlers who had scholarships increased in intrinsic motivation. Apparently wrestlers and football players perceive scholarships differently. The football players felt the scholarships controlled their behavior—evidently many coaches hold a scholarship over the athlete's head like a club. However, women and wrestlers felt that the scholarships provided important motivational information about their performance.

Another factor that seems to enter into the formula is whether or not the rewards are contingent on performance. Research indicates that rewards that are contingent on the quality of performance yield more intrinsic motivation than do noncontingent rewards (Ross, 1976). Our example of the female tennis player is a case of a contingent reward, since her receiving the award was contingent on a good performance. On the other hand, if every participant received a similar award, it could not be perceived the same way.

In terms of athletic competition, Deci (1978) explains that since competition is very similar to working for a reward, it also contains an informational and a controlling aspect. The overwhelming desire to win can be a controlling factor. Conversely, the results of competition provide direct feedback, which has informational value. Deci (1978) conducted a study using puzzles and undergraduate subjects in which the independent variables of competition, sex of subject, and reward were manipulated. Generally, the results showed that subjects instructed to compete displayed significantly less intrinsic motivation during a free choice period than subjects who did the same thing without being told to compete. This difference was very large for females. Deci also observed an interesting interaction among the three independent variables. Males told to compete for money were more intrinsically motivated then males told to compete without the additional reward. However, for females, just the opposite was true. Females told to compete for money were less intrinsically motivated than those told to compete without the reward. Males' orientation in regard to competition is to compete for some reward, and without the reward they lose interest in the activity. For females, being told to compete decreases intrinsic motivation, and adding extrinsic rewards decreases intrinsic motivation even more.

Building upon Deci's original formulations, Weinberg and associates (Weinberg, 1979; Weinberg & Jackson, 1979; Weinberg & Ragan, 1979) conducted a series of studies involving male and female undergraduates and the motor task of balancing on a stabilometer. In all three of these studies, Weinberg argued that competition can either enhance or detract from intrinsic motivation. If someone succeeds at a competitive task, this provides information that suggests they are competent. On the other hand, if someone fails during competition, intrinsic motivation should decrease, since failure suggests that they are not competent. Weinberg used an experimental design similar to those of other intrinsic motivation studies. The results tended to underscore the importance of perceived attribution in the development of intrinsic motivation. And Deci's basic postulates about extrinsic rewards and competition were upheld. Competition enhanced intrinsic motivation in males more than in females, and competition was generally viewed as informational in nature.

The importance of Deci's cognitive evaluation theory cannot be overemphasized (Vallerand & Reid, 1984). It clearly points out the potential danger of extrinsic rewards, but also underscores their informational value. Rewards that are perceived to indicate superior performance often lead to greater intrinsic motivation. This is closely tied to the important concept of reinforcement. **Reinforcement** serves as an encouragement for a rewarded event to be repeated. Thus, if an athlete does well in a game of basketball and is praised by the coach, the desire to continue to do well is reinforced.

However, youth leaders and sports directors must continually monitor the practice of giving awards and trophies to make sure that the awards do not become more important than the sports. It does not make good sense to give a five-foot trophy to a five-foot boy for running a race. There is a very good chance that he will come to attribute his desire to run to the potential reward rather than to the fun of running.

---

15. **Principle** The development of an athlete's intrinsic motivation is the ultimate goal of youth sport programs.
Application Coaches and administrators should define program goals in terms of the intrinsic values the participants will gain.

Interestingly, research by Wankel and Kreisel (1985) identifies intrinsic factors as being more important to youth sport participants than extrinsic factors. Eight hundred and twenty-two children were asked to indicate their reasons for participating in sport. The following intrinsic factors were listed as being most enjoyable and important:

Excitement of sport
Personal accomplishment
Improving skill
Testing skills against others
Just doing the skills
Pleasing others
Being with friends

Extrinsic factors such as "winning the game" and "getting rewards" were identified as being least enjoyable or important.

To assist coaches, teachers, and researchers to assess intrinsic and extrinsic motivation of children, Weiss, Bredemeier, and Shewchuk (1985) developed and tested a motivation scale specifically designed for this purpose. The scale effectively identifies six main factors associated with children's motivation. The six factors were labeled challenge, interest, skill improvement, mastery, judgment, and criteria.

Summary

Attribution theory is based on the kinds of perceptions that people make for why they succeed or fail. Attributions are causal explanations for outcome. Fritz Heider is the acknowledged founder of attribution theory, but Bernard Weiner is credited with making significant contributions to it in terms of interpretation and usefulness. People are believed to make attributions along three dimensions: locus of control, stability, and controllability.

Attribution theory is very useful in understanding behavior exhibited in need achievement situations. Locus of control is a basic dimension used by athletes in explaining causality. People who believe that they are in control of their own destinies exhibit internal control, while those who feel at the mercy of outside forces exhibit external control. The kinds of attributions that people give for outcome are related to previous experience. Future expectations can also be predicted from attributions. Emotions are closely associated with attribution. Internal attributions for success result in feelings of self-confidence, while the same attributions for failure result in feelings of shame and guilt. Making stable attributions about failure promotes a loss of confidence; making unstable attributions about the same outcome gives one the feeling that failure can be reversed. Low n Ach in young females may be due in part to their tendency to make internal/stable attributions about failure.

Egocentrism in attribution occurs when athletes routinely assign failure to external causes and success to internal causes. This is a self-serving strategy and is considered to be an illogical model of attribution. The self-serving strategy of assigning attributions is not universal among athletes, but it is used occasionally by most people.

If an athlete comes to believe that an extrinsic reward for participation is more important than the sport itself, then intrinsic motivation will be diminished. Deci's cognitive evaluation theory explains that rewards are perceived as being either informational or controlling. If controlling, then intrinsic motivation is diminished. If informational, intrinsic motivation is enhanced.

Review Questions

1. Who are the three people responsible for the development and refinement of attribution theory? What were their contributions?
2. Name the three dimensions used for causal attribution. What are the categories of each? Name the basic attributions identified by Weiner.
3. What is the Causal Dimension Scale and why is it valuable? Who developed it?

4. What types of attributions do people typically give for situations in which outcome is consistent with previous performance? Inconsistent?
5. What is the covariation principle? Explain.
6. What is learned helplessness? What causes it? Using an attributional approach, how can it be minimized?
7. In what way are affect and attribution related? Give specific examples.
8. Discuss ways in which achievement motivation can be enhanced through attribution ascription.
9. Explain the phenomenon of egocentrism in attribution. Is it desirable or undesirable? Explain.
10. Explain the relationship between perceived causality and extrinsic motivation.
11. Explain Deci's theory of cognitive evaluation.
12. Using Deci's theory, explain how and when extrinsic rewards can be damaging to intrinsic motivation.

Glossary

additive principle The notion that intrinsic and extrinsic motivation combine to create need achievement.

attribution theory A cognitive approach to motivation in which perceived causation plays an important role in explaining behavior.

Causal Dimension Scale A scale developed by Russell for assigning attributions to one of three dimensions: locus of control, stability, and controllability.

cognitive evaluation theory A theory developed by Deci according to which extrinsic rewards are perceived to be either informational or controlling.

controllability Attributional dimension in which causes for events are perceived to be either within or beyond a person's control.

controlling aspect An important component of Deci's cognitive evaluation theory. It refers to the extent extrinsic rewards control a person's behavior.

covariation principle When the performance of others agrees (covaries) with the performance of the athlete, attributions about that performance will be external.

discounting principle According to this principle, if an extrinsic reward is percieved to be more important than the intrinsic value of participation, the value of intrinsic motivation is discounted.

ego-enhancing strategy A strategy by which one attributes all success to internal causes.

ego-protecting strategy A strategy by which one attributes all failures to external causes.

external control The perception that external factors determine outcomes.

extrinsic motivation The ability of external rewards, such as trophies, money, ribbons, and praise to motivate behavior.

illogical model Use of an ego-enhancing or ego-protecting strategy for selecting attributions.

informational aspect An important component of Deci's cognitive evaluation theory. It refers to the extent to which extrinsic rewards provide positive feedback about a person's performance.

internal control The perception that factors within a person determine that person's outcome.

intrinsic motivation The motivation to engage in an activity for its own sake and for no other reason.

learned helplessness A condition in which people feel that they have no control over their failures, and that failure is inevitable.

locus of control A psychological construct that refers to people's beliefs about whether they can control what happens to them.

logical model The notion that people make logical attributions about outcomes.

multiplicative principle The notion that intrinsic and extrinsic motivation are interactive and not additive.

open-ended attribution An attribution freely made by the athlete without any categorical constraints.

origin-pawn relationship A term coined by DeCharms and Carpenter (1968), who observed that some people (origins) like to control their outcomes, while others (pawns) feel powerless to control their outcomes.

overjustification hypothesis If a reward for participating in an otherwise interesting activity causes intrinsic interest in the activity to decrease, the reward may be perceived as an overjustification.

reinforcement A reward that is given so that the rewarded event will be repeated.

self-serving hypothesis The observation that people will sometimes make illogical attributions to enhance or protect their egos.

stability An attributional dimension that suggests that an outcome will either change or remain stable.

structural rating scale A method of selecting attributions in which options are structured and limited.

Recommended Readings

Arkes, H. R., & Garske, J. P. (1982). *Psychological theories of motivation* (2d ed). Monterey, CA: Brooks/Cole.

Atkinson, J. W. (1964). *An introduction to motivation.* New York: D. Van Nostrand Company.

Deci, E. L. (1980). *The psychology of self-determination.* Lexington, MA: Lexington Books.

Dweck, C. S. (1980). Learned helplessness in sport. In C. H. Nadeau, W. R. Halliwell, K. M. Newell & G. C. Roberts (eds.), *Psychology of motor behavior and sport, 1979,* Champaign, IL: Human Kinetics Publishers.

Rejeski, W. J., & Brawley, L. R. (1983). Attribution theory in sport: Current status and new perspectives. *Journal of Sport Psychology, 5,* 77–99.

Roberts, G. C. (1982). Achievement motivation in sport. In R. Terjung (ed.), *Exercise and sport science reviews* (Vol. 10). Philadelphia: Franklin Institute Press.

Rotter, J. B. (1971). External control and internal control. *Psychology Today, 5*(1), 37–42, 58–59.

Russell, D. (1982). The causal dimension scale: A measure of how individuals perceive causes. *Journal of Personality and Social Psychology, 42,* 1137–1145.

Vallerand, R. J., & Reid, G. (1984). On the causal effects of perceived competence on intrinsic motivation: A test of Cognitive Evaluation Theory. *Journal of Sport Psychology, 6,* 94–102.

Wankel, L. M., & Kreisel, S. J. P. (1985). Factors underlying enjoyment of youth sports: Sport and age group comparisons. *Journal of Sport Psychology, 7,* 51–64.

Weiner, B. (1985). An attributional theory of achievement motivation and emotion. *Psychological Review, 92,* 548–573.

Part Five

Social Psychology of Sport

In 1979, Thomas Tutko identified five broad areas of sport psychology. One of them was the social psychology of sport. Social psychology brings together a number of important topics that cannot be categorized as either purely psychological or sociological. In sport psychology we tend to deal with those areas of sport that affect the individual, while the sociology of sport deals more with groups and less with the individual. But it is often very difficult to separate the individual from the group in sport; hence the need for an area of study called social psychology of sport.

In this section I will discuss four broad areas of interest that can be best classified as social psychological in nature. Chapter 8 deals with the growing problem of aggression in sport. Chapter 9 is somewhat related to aggression in that it presents the important topic of audience effects on athletic performance. In chapter 10 I will deal with the interesting subject of team cohesiveness in terms of how it can facilitate team performance. Finally, in chapter 11 I introduce the topic of leadership in sport. ■

8   Aggression in Sport

Key Terms

aggression
archival research
assertiveness
Berkowitz's
   reformulation
Bobo doll
bracketed morality
Buss aggression
   machine
Buss-Durkee Hostility
   Scale
catharsis
circular effect
cognitive developmental
   approach
completion tendency

frustration-aggression
   (F-A) theory
hostile aggression
hostility
instinct theory
instrumental aggression
intent to harm
moral reasoning
readying mechanism
retaliation hypothesis
shock box
social learning theory
state aggression
trait aggression
violence

The setting was a rugby field on the outskirts of Honolulu, near Pearl Harbor. Two undefeated rugby teams were about to decide the Oahu league championship. These were volatile teams composed of Polynesian athletes from Fiji, Tonga, Samoa, Tahiti, and Hawaii. One team was the Tongan Vikings, a collection of proud Tongan athletes from the Honolulu area. The opposing team was from Laie, a small town on the windward side of Oahu. These athletes were a mixture of Tongans, Samoans, Fijians, and Hawaiians, all student athletes at Brigham Young University–Hawaii campus.

If the volatile nature of these warrior-athletes was not enough, a second factor evolved that threatened to push the contest into open conflict. A New Zealand merchant ship was anchored in the harbor. One of the ship's officers was an internationally respected rugby official. It was the consensus of both teams that this man should referee the match. However, the Rugby Federation of Hawaii ruled that the senior official in the league should be the referee. When the match finally began, emotions were near the boiling point, and each team was looking to the official for some sign of favoritism.

The first twenty minutes of the match were brutal, but fairly played. Some violations were called, but they were evenly administered and the game seemed to be under control. Then a relatively routine violation was called against the Tongan Vikings for unnecessary roughness. As the penalty was being marked off and the referee was standing with the ball, one of the Tongan Vikings approached him from behind and slugged him in the base of the skull. The referee never knew what hit him! Players and spectators alike were stunned. The official fell flat on his face and remained unconscious for ten minutes.

The offending player was thrown out of the game and barred from league play for one year. The game continued with the New Zealand referee as the head official. The Tongan Vikings lost the match in a very closely fought battle. Afterwards, the offending player was in tears over what he had done. He was very sorry and asked forgiveness of everyone. The injured official was taken to the hospital, where he was placed on observation and released a few hours later.

This was perhaps the single most repugnant and volatile act of sport aggression that I have personally observed. However, the newspapers and sports pages of America and Canada are full of stories such as this in which acts of aggression are routinely performed on the athletic field.

At New York's Shea Stadium during a 1978 Jets-Steelers football game, spectators overpowered a security guard and dropped him over a railing to a concrete walkway fifteen feet below (Gilbert & Twyman, 1983). In Toronto four members of the Philadelphia Flyers hockey team faced maximum penalties of up to three years in prison on assault charges stemming from a wild brawl during the Stanley Cup play-offs of 1975 (Yeager, 1977). Also in 1975, Henry Boucha suffered a severe beating from Dave Forbes during a Boston-Minnesota hockey game, causing Boucha to lose 70 percent of his sight in one eye (Noverr & Ziewaez, 1981). In professional basketball, on 9 December 1977, Los Angeles Laker Kermit Washington literally shattered the face of forward Rudy Tomjanovich of the Houston Rockets with a devastating punch (Noverr & Ziewaez, 1981). On 13 August 1978, football fans were shocked by the crushing blow Jack Tatum gave receiver Darryl Stingley in an exhibition match between the Oakland Raiders and the New England Patriots. The blow left Stingley a quadriplegic (Noverr & Ziewaez, 1981). A *Sports Illustrated* article chronicles a rivalry between two NHL professional hockey teams. The Calgary Flames took a brawling home-and-home series from archrival Edmonton Oilers. The Flames won the first game 5 to 4 and the second 6 to 3. While the first game was a reasonable facsimile of fair play, the second was nothing but a brawl. It was described as a three-hour slugfest composed of 60 penalties and 250 total minutes of penalty time (Murphy, 1987).

Fighting and violence among athletes is not reserved for men. After Missouri's 72 to 70 homecourt basketball victory over rival Oklahoma on 17 January 1987, a brawl erupted. The center of attention was Oklahoma's volatile coach. With players slugging and kicking, the coach was observed on her back kicking at an opposing player (Kirpatrick, 1987).

Most of the examples of aggression and violence described above involved participating athletes. However, numerous examples of violence can be cited that involve spectators. One of the most recent and repugnant examples of fan violence occurred in Europe, where a soccer riot in Brussels left 38 dead and 437 injured after English hooligans attacked panic-stricken Italian partisans. The riot occurred prior to the European Cup Soccer final in Heysel Stadium in Brussels between Liverpool and Juventus, the soccer team of Turin, Italy. Well-liquored Liverpool hooligans attacked Juventus fans with broken bottles, tin cans, flag sticks, and metal bars. Within minutes hundreds of Italian fans found themselves pressed against a chain link fence and a restraining wall. As more bodies pressed against the barriers, they collapsed, pitching hundreds of terrified fans into a hideous pileup in which thirty-one Italians, four Belgians, two Frenchmen, and one Briton were killed, most of them by suffocation. The event has since been referred to as Black Wednesday by shamed residents of Liverpool (Gammon, 1985).

Scott (1970) argued eloquently and optimistically that sport provides the ideal environment for young athletes to learn how to control their aggression and their emotions. On the other hand, Fisher (1976) criticized Scott's thesis on the grounds that competitive sport seems to *teach* aggression rather than eliminate or channel the emotions. Considering the examples of sport aggression just listed, Fisher's position would seem to be more realistic.

A number of critical questions come to mind as one contemplates the issue of sport aggression. Does participating in or observing violent sporting events serve as a *catharsis* or release from aggressive tendencies, or do these events merely teach and encourage further aggression on and off the playing field? If these two questions can be answered, then is it possible to eliminate aggression and violence from sports? If so, how?

These and other critically important questions will be discussed in this important chapter. We will deal with the following: definition of terms, techniques of measurement, theories of aggression, the catharsis hypothesis, conditions accompanying aggression, and situational factors associated with sport aggression.

Defining Aggression

Many definitions of **aggression** have evolved over the past seventy-five years. Dollard, Miller, Doob, Mourer, and Sears (1939) defined it as a sequence of behavior in which the goal is to injure another person (p. 9). Similarly, Kaufman (1970) defined aggression as a behavior directed against a living target, in which there is a probability greater than zero of imparting a noxious stimulus (pp. 10–11). Finally, Baron (1977, p. 12) defines aggression as any form of behavior directed toward the goal of harming or injuring another being who is motivated to avoid such treatment.

These definitions have three things in common. First, for an overt behavior to be labeled aggression it must be directed against a living target. In our case, we are talking about other human beings. Second, for an act to be labeled aggression, there must be an **intent to harm** the target. Finally, there must be a reasonable expectation that the aggression will be successful, and the target will be harmed. This definition effectively eliminates the following:

1. Doing destructive violence to an inanimate object such as a door.
2. Unintentionally injuring another person during athletic competition.
3. Aggressive behavior in which there is no chance for the intended victim to be injured (e.g., aggressor and victim separated by bars or teammates).

Aggression as defined above is often used interchangeably with the term **hostility,** and is very different from the type of assertive or aggressive play that is needed to perform effectively in competitive sports (Freischlag & Schmedke, 1980). Perhaps the term **violence** can be reserved for the more serious manifestations of aggression in sport (Feshback, 1971).

Over the years, two basic kinds of aggression have been identified: *hostile aggression* and *instrumental aggression* (Baron, 1977). These two types of aggression are distinguished in terms of their primary reinforcers, or in terms of the goals being sought. However, in both cases the intent is to harm another human being. If this is not the case, then the behavior is not aggression (Bandura, 1973; Berkowitz, 1962; Silva, 1980a, 1980b).

For individuals engaged in **hostile aggression,** the primary goal is the injury of another human being. The intent is to make the victim suffer, and the reinforcement is the pain and suffering that is caused. This sort of aggression is always accompanied by anger on the part of the aggressor. Other terms that have been used for hostile aggression include reactive aggression (Silva, 1980a) and angry aggression (Buss, 1971). A good example of hostile aggression occurs when a baseball pitcher throws a high inside fastball at a batter who has angered him. The clear attempt to injure is present, and the goal is to cause suffering. The outcome of the contest is not a factor to be considered. The goal is to harm, not to win.

Individuals engaged in **instrumental aggression** also intend to harm the target. However, their goal is not to observe the victim's suffering, but to receive some other external reward or goal. In sports this goal could be money, victory, or prestige. The aggressor views the aggressive act as being instrumental in obtaining the primary goal. Obtaining this goal reinforces the aggressive behavior. A parallel baseball example for instrumental aggression would be one in which the pitcher throws a high inside fastball for the purpose of establishing dominance of the strike zone. The pitcher is not necessarily angry at the batter, but sees hitting the batter as being instrumental in achieving his goal of winning the game. Other examples of instrumental aggression in sport are flailing the elbows while rebounding in basketball, disrupting a double play relay throw in baseball by sliding into the shortstop, and tackling a defenseless football quarterback a little harder than necessary just as he releases a forward pass.

In terms of the aggressive act itself, there is little difference between the two types of misbehavior. However, hostile aggression always involves anger, while instrumental aggression may not. Rebounders in basketball who flail their elbows need not be angry at their opponents. However, the outcome of the aggression is the same. In many cases these two types of aggression cannot be separated. For example, if the pitcher hits the batter with the high inside pitch, how can one determine whether it was instrumental aggression or hostile aggression? This discrimination problem is illustrated in figure 8.1. Generally, hostile aggression can be identified on the basis of emotion. That is, the pitcher will be openly angry at the batter or the opposing team. If his goal is only to win the game, he will never throw at a batter if it means putting the winning run into scoring position. However, the pitcher guilty of hostile aggression might. In some cases, only the pitcher could say whether the aggression was hostile or instrumental. In figure 8.1, this is represented by the overlapping of the two circles representing hostile and instrumental aggression.

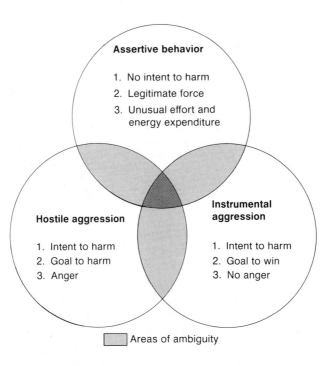

Assertive behavior

1. No intent to harm
2. Legitimate force
3. Unusual effort and energy expenditure

Hostile aggression

1. Intent to harm
2. Goal to harm
3. Anger

Instrumental aggression

1. Intent to harm
2. Goal to win
3. No anger

Areas of ambiguity

Figure 8.1 Schematic showing the possible difficulties in discriminating among hostile aggression, instrumental aggression, and assertive behavior. From J. M. Silva, III, Assertive and aggressive behavior in sport: A definitional clarification. In *Psychology of motor behavior and sport–1979* by C. H. Nadeau, Ed. Copyright © 1980 Human Kinetics Publishers, Inc., Champaign, IL. Adapted by permission.

Finally, it must be emphasized that neither type of aggression is acceptable. The aggressor is guilty of purposely inflicting harm with the intent to injure another person. This must be discouraged at all levels of competition, especially the professional level, because young athletes everywhere emulate the pros.

An example of a professional sport in which hostile and instrumental aggression are both continually present is boxing. Since the object of this sport is to inflict harm, it is by definition aggression. For this reason boxing is no longer included in NCAA athletic competition. Except when boxers become angry with each other, the sport is a pure example of instrumental aggression. Consequently, following the death of boxer Duk Koo Kim in November 1982, the American Medical Association urged a ban on boxing and sports journalist Howard Cosell called for stricter controls over boxing violence (Goldstein, 1983).

1. **Principle** The difference between hostile and instrumental aggression lies in the perceived goal of the aggressor and not in intent.

   Application Because the intent to harm is present in both forms of aggression, both must be discouraged from an ethical and moral reasoning standpoint.

A third category of behavior that is often confused with aggression and aggressiveness is the term *assertiveness* or assertive behavior. Generally, when coaches encourage their athletes to be more aggressive, what they really mean is to be more assertive. Coaches want their athletes to assert themselves and make their presence felt. **Assertiveness** involves the use of legitimate physical or verbal force to achieve one's purpose (Silva, 1980a). However, there is no intent to harm the opponent. If an opponent is harmed as a result of a tackle in soccer, it is not aggression. It is merely assertive play as long as it is within the spirit of the agreed-on rules and the intent to harm is not present. Assertiveness requires the expenditure of unusual effort and energy (Silva, 1980b), but if there is no *intent* to harm, then any resultant harm is incidental to the game. Let's go back to our baseball example. If the pitcher throws a slightly high inside fastball, with no intent to hit the batter, this is considered assertive play. The pitcher *must* establish control of the strike zone, or the batter will intimidate the pitcher into throwing either strikes or outside balls.

As can be observed in figure 8.1, there is an area of ambiguity between instrumental aggression, hostile aggression, and assertive behavior. This is to be expected, since at times only the athlete knows whether an "aggressive" act was intentional or unintentional. From a practical standpoint it is the job of the official to penalize any behavior that is in violation of the rules, regardless of the intent of the violator. However, most sports make provisions for extraordinary penalties if the behavior is deemed to be intentional and/or dangerous. For clarity, let's return to the baseball pitching example. If in the judgment of the umpire a pitcher purposely throws a pitch at a batter with intent to harm, he must be penalized regardless of why he did it. However, if a batter has his body over the strike zone, he is inviting an assertive pitcher to throw a fastball over the inside part of the plate. If the batter is hit, it is not the fault of the pitcher and it is not an example of sport aggression. Hollandsworth (1977) and Alberti (1977) further refined the distinction between assertiveness and aggression.

Finally, it should be stated that what has been labeled assertive behavior in this chapter has often been classified as instrumental aggression (Bredemeier, 1980; Cratty, 1981; Fisher, 1976; Martens, 1975). For this reason, much of the research in sport aggression has been misclassified. Assertive behavior in which injury is incidental to the play is not aggression, simply because there is no intent to harm the victim. Researchers must separate instrumental and hostile aggression from assertiveness. Merely tabulating fouls does not accomplish this, since many violations are a result of assertiveness and not aggression.

---

2. **Principle** There is a difference between aggression (the intent to harm) and assertiveness.

   Application From an ethical point of view, a coach must not teach or tolerate aggression. This should not impede efforts to teach athletes to be assertive in sports that require such behavior for success.

The Measurement of Aggression

In the previous section it was revealed that one shortcoming to a clear understanding of aggression has to do with how different people define the terms. In this section a similar problem will be identified. Specifically, there are many ways to measure aggression, but the correlations among the methods are very low. In other words, they may all be measuring something different (Leith, 1978). We will discuss some of the more common methods with regard to sport aggression, and we will examine the strengths and weaknesses of each.

Trait Measures of Aggression

You will recall that a personality trait is a relatively permanent disposition to behave in a certain manner. **Trait aggression** refers to a relatively stable personality disposition to respond in certain situations with acts of aggression. This disposition toward aggression is probable, but not necessary. We should also note that a pencil-and-paper measure of aggression can be either a state or trait measure, depending on the wording of the questions. A state measure of aggression ascertains a subject's immediate or situation-specific feelings about aggression while a trait measure ascertains a subject's general feelings about aggression.

Projective Techniques

Projective methods of measuring personality traits were discussed in detail in chapter 1. The two most common projective tests are the Rorschach ink blot test and the Thematic Apperception Test. The advantages of these tests are that the

true purpose of the test may be disguised. In the sport aggression literature, the Rosenzweig Picture Frustration Study Test has been used to assess various aspects of aggression (Martin, 1976).

Pencil-and-Paper Tests

Pencil-and-paper inventories have been devised to measure various aspects of personality, including aggressiveness. Perhaps the most often used and highly regarded is the Cattell 16 PF. In the aggression literature, several specific tests have been developed to measure the personality trait of aggressiveness. We will briefly discuss four of them.

The Buss-Durkee Hostility Scale The **Buss-Durkee Hostility Scale** was developed by Buss and Durkee (1957) to assess seven aspects of hostility and guilt. The seven aspects of hostility include: assault, indirect hostility, irritability, negativism, resentment, suspicion, and verbal hostility. The test is composed of seventy-five true-false items, sixty-six of which measure hostility, while nine measure guilt. A high score on the test suggests hostility.

The Anger Self-Report Test The Anger Self-Report (ASR) Test (Zelin, Adler & Myerson, 1972) differentiates between the awareness and the expression of aggression. The ASR is a Likert-type questionnaire yielding separate scores for awareness of anger, expression of anger, guilt, condemnation of anger, and mistrust. The test contains sixty-four items.

The Bredemeier Athletic Aggression Inventory The Bredemeier (1978) inventory of aggression (BAAGI) is a sport-related instrument for assessing instrumental and reactive (angry) aggression. The test is composed of one hundred items, fifty of which measure instrumental aggression while the remaining fifty measure hostile aggression. An analysis of the BAAGI identified two factors that were identified as the two types of aggression. The factor labeled reactive aggression appears to be a valid estimate of the personality trait of hostile aggression. However, the factor labeled instrumental aggression appears to measure both instrumental aggression and assertiveness.

A short form of the Bredemeier Athletic Aggression Inventory (BAAGI-S) has been developed by Wall and Gruber (1986). The BAAGI-S also measures instrumental and hostile aggression and is composed of twenty-eight items. Subjects respond to each item using a four-point Likert-like scale: strong agreement, agreement, disagreement, and strong disagreement.

Bredemeier Scale of Children's Action Tendencies Bredemeier's Scale of Children's Action Tendencies in Sport (SCATS) assesses children's self-reported aggression tendencies in sport-specific situations (Bredemeier, Weiss, Shields & Cooper, 1987). Bredemeier's SCATS is closely patterned after Deluty's (1979) Children's Action Tendency Scale (CATS). The Children's Action Tendency Scale is a thirty-item inventory that permits reliable and valid assessment of Children's aggressiveness, assertiveness, and submissiveness. The CATS takes approximately fifteen to twenty minutes to administer. It was designed by Deluty as a primary prevention tool in schools to help pinpoint children with preclinical levels of aggressiveness or submissiveness who might benefit from assertiveness training.

State Measures of Aggression

State measures of aggression fall into two categories: laboratory tests and field tests. **State aggression** is a transitory emotional condition characterized by consciously perceived feelings of aggression, often resulting in overt aggression. In the field measures, actual sport aggression is observed and recorded. In the laboratory, aggression is somewhat inferred. For example, in Bandura's research with modeling, how a child treats a Bobo doll is called aggression. It is situation specific and therefore a state measure of aggression, yet it is inferred that the child would behave in a similar fashion in the "real world."

Laboratory Measure of Aggression

Buss (1963) introduced the shock box as a tool for measuring aggression. The **shock box** or **Buss aggression machine** allows an experimenter to assess a subject's level of aggression in terms of the duration and intensity of electrical shock that the subject imparts to an accomplice. Of course, no shock is actually delivered, but the accomplice acts like it has been, and the subject's intentions are recorded in terms of buttons pushed (1 through 10) and the duration of time they are depressed. Since a shock is a noxious stimulus, delivering it satisfies our definition of aggression.

A study by Leith (1982) provides an ideal example of how the shock box may be used. The assessment of aggression was disguised as a learning study. The subject assumed the role of the teacher, while an accomplice was the learner. The teacher was instructed to shock the learner every time he or she made a mistake on a word association test. The teacher was told to use his or her own discretion in selecting shock intensity and duration. After completing the first phase of the research, with indicated baseline aggression, the subjects were all shown a film involving various intensities of physical activity. After the film had been shown, the subjects repeated the learning study. The shock intensities delivered in phase 1 were compared with those of phase 2. Significant changes were believed to have been caused by exposure to the films, suggesting that feelings of aggressiveness can be heightened by viewing scenes of aggression.

There are a number of reasons why the Buss aggression machine has been a favorite of laboratory researchers. First, it lends itself easily to experimental manipulation. Second, the notion of delivering an electrical shock fits in very nicely with the theoretical definitions of what aggression is. Finally, the resultant measures of aggression are objective and easy to interpret (Leith, 1978). However, the shock box is not without its critics. Some researchers question the relationship between aggression induced in a laboratory setting and actual aggression in a field setting (Leith, 1978).

The use of electrical shock in experimental research has declined in recent years for several reasons. The first involves concern for the safety and well-being of the subject. Even in cases in which shock is not actually delivered, severe psychological damage can result. Perhaps the most classic example of research abuse using a shock box occurred in the famous Milgram studies (Wheeler, 1970). In this research, subjects were led to believe that shocks they were ordered to deliver to an accomplice were so severe that recipients actually screamed in pain. The studies were conducted under the guise of obedience research.

Field Measures of Aggression

Field measures of aggression have been used a great deal by sport psychologists. This is to their credit, since the leap from the laboratory to the field is often a large one. The single disadvantage of field research is that the experimenter is often unable to control or identify all of the variables that might either cause or conceal an effect. Nevertheless, it is possible with care and planning to conduct field studies that are as well controlled as laboratory studies. Two of the most common measurement techniques used for field research in sport aggression are behavioral observation and archival studies.

Behavioral Observation This method of measuring aggression is perhaps the most difficult to use, but it is also the most valuable and relevant. It generally involves three stages. In stage one, the researcher develops a checklist with which relevant behaviors are identified and categorized. This is perhaps the most important stage since random observation of an athlete's aggressive responses would be meaningless. In the second stage, the researcher must train assistants to use the measurement tool. This could take several months. Trained observers must know what to look for and must be objective and consistent in their judgments. In stage three, the researcher must devise a plan for reducing the voluminous data into meaningful measurement scores. If this cannot be done, then the data are useless.

Harrell (1980) offers a good example of the behavioral observation approach. In this study, forty-five male high school basketball players were observed during actual competition in forty-five games. During each of these games, a single athlete was identified from the home team and systematically scrutizined by two trained observers. The dependent variables that were recorded and categorized included acts of overt aggression by the subject and number of penalties assessed. The independent variables included such things as turnovers, assists, field goal percentages, and acts of aggression against the subject.

In general, the great advantage of the behavioral approach is that the data are theoretically relevant and occur in a natural setting. On the other hand, the technique is limited by the classification system adopted, and by the lack of control of variables that cannot be controlled.

To effectively use behavioral observation, the observers must be trained to recognize the intent to harm, and therefore must separate aggression from assertiveness. Merely recording fouls fails to discriminate between the two.

Archival Studies The archival approach to studying aggression is based on actual data gathered during the contest but not systematically studied until a later time. The statistical information in **archival research** is based on game information recorded by official scorers. The advantage of this approach is that a great deal of information can be gathered from official score sheets during a season or even over several years of competition. The disadvantage is that the information is limited to the official records. And the researcher is not present to determine the validity of the records. For example, there would be no way for the researcher to determine if a foul was due to aggression or merely assertiveness on the part of the athlete. In the case of ice hockey, where penalties are assessed in terms of severity (e.g., time in the penalty box), this problem is somewhat rectified, but not eliminated. Indeed, it is not clear at all that number of penalties or time in the penalty box are valid measures of aggression. This approach has been used by Volkamer (1972) with soccer, and by McCarthy and Kelly (1978b) and Russell (1981a, 1986) in ice hockey.

---

3. **Principle** Trait measures of aggression merely indicate the disposition to aggress in a certain situation, while state measures of aggression represent actual overt acts of aggression.
   Application You must use valid and reliable measuring instruments to avoid inaccurately labeling behavior as aggression.

Theories of Aggression

A number of theories have arisen to explain the phenomenon of aggression. Basically, they fall into three categories: instinct theory, frustration-aggression theory, and social learning theory. Each of these theories will be briefly discussed in this section. Basic tenants of the three theories are displayed in table 8.1.

Instinct Theory

Instinct theory is based upon the writings of Sigmund Freud and ethologists such as Konrad Lorenz. Freud (1950) viewed aggression as an inborn drive similar to sex or hunger. Aggression was unavoidable since it was innate, but as with any

Table 8.1. Theories of Human Aggression

Theory	Basic Tenets of Theory
Instinct Theory	1. Aggression is an innate biological drive. 2. Aggression results in a purging or venting of pent-up emotions. 3. Sport provides a safe and socially acceptable outlet for aggression.
Frustration-Aggression Hypothesis	1. Aggression is a natural consequence of frustration. 2. The strength of the tendency to aggress is related to the strength, degree, and number of frustrations. 3. Overt aggression *may* act as a catharsis or release against further aggression.
Social Learning Theory	1. The need for aggression is a learned response. 2. Aggression begets further aggression. 3. Aggression does not serve as a vent or catharsis against further aggression.

drive it could be regulated through discharge or fulfillment. Likewise, Lorenz (1966) argued that humans have the same aggressive instincts as animals. We are born with the instinct to defend territory and to fight for survival.

According to biological instinct theory, human beings are aggressive animals and must fulfill this biological instinct. The solution to aggression in our society is not to ignore this aspect of our nature, but to provide positive outlets for it. Thus it behooves society to promote athletic sports and games that provide a safe and socially acceptable outlet for aggression.

An important corollary of the biological instinct theory is the notion that aggression results in a purging or release of the drive to be aggressive, just as a hungry animal that finds food will no longer be hungry. The aggressive human who finds an outlet for aggression will no longer be aggressive—until the instinctive drive for aggression builds up and requires another release. This purging of pent-up aggression is known as **catharsis.** The subject of catharsis will be discussed in detail later in this chapter.

There is little doubt that the biological instinct theory has great appeal to the average sport enthusiast. It is commonplace to hear a weekend rugby or football player talk of the psychological release provided by a hard tackle. However, instinct theory has received very little support from the researchers or the academic

community. This is primarily due to the observation that true aggression rarely leads to a catharsis. Instead it leads to further aggression (Berkowitz, 1972).

Perhaps the greatest support for instinct theory comes from our knowledge of the physiology of aggression. It is clear that brain mechanisms exist that, when stimulated, cause aggression or tranquility. For example, it is known that stimulation of the hypothalamus facilitates aggression, while stimulation of the amygdala inhibits it (Scott, 1975). However, as Moyer (1973) points out, the fact that the human animal is "wired" for aggression does not mean that aggression is inevitable. He argues that the brain mechanisms merely dictate the threshold at which a stimulation from the environment will result in aggression. The threshold for aggression is a function of both heredity and learning. Learning can interact with the brain mechanism and override a drive to be aggressive.

Perhaps the most telling argument against biological instinct theory comes from an article by Berkowitz (1969b) in which he critically reviews the works of Ardrey (1966), Lorenz (1966), Morris (1968), and Storr (1968). Berkowitz charges these authors with lack of controlled systematic research, use of ill-defined terms, gross analogies, oversimplifications, and the use of casual anecdotes. He also points out that research has shown that certain societies do not display aggressive behavior or include aggressive games in their play culture. In this respect I am reminded of a badminton class I once taught in which a female student from the orient was totally unable to relate to the concepts of "smash" and "kill shot" as used in that sport. It appears that biological instinct theory, standing alone, is a weak and pessimistic explanation for aggression in sport.

---

4. **Principle** The biological instinct theory of aggression is woefully inadequate when applied to humans. Acts of aggression rarely, if ever, serve as a catharsis resulting in a reduction in aggression.
   Application Athletes should be encouraged to deal with their aggressive tendencies from an ethical and moral standpoint and not attempt to rationalize them from a biological perspective.

Frustration-Aggression Hypothesis

The original **frustration-aggression (F-A) theory** was developed by Dollard, Miller, Doob, Mourer, and Sears (1939) as a response to Sigmund Freud's writings on frustration and aggression. The original F-A theory stated that *aggression was always a consequence of frustration* (Dollard et al., 1939, p. 1). The theory was severely criticized. It should be clear to anyone who observes human behavior that frustration does not *always* result in an overt aggressive response (Berkowitz, 1969a). It is also clear that every act of aggression cannot *always* be traced to some original frustration.

It would seem unfair, however, to dismiss the F-A theory on the basis of this point, especially since the authors seemed to have something else in mind. For example, the authors clearly stated in their original work (p. 28) that aggression can take many different forms. Thus, a batter who strikes out may not be overtly aggressive against the umpire or the pitcher but may attack the water cooler, fantasize about abusing the umpire, or even antagonize an innocent fan. It may be true that frustration always results in some form of aggression if your definition of aggression includes fantasy and displacement (attacking something or someone besides the offender). In a clarifying article, Miller (1941, p. 338) stated that frustration produces instigations to a number of different types of responses, one of which is some form of aggression. Nevertheless, according to our earlier definition of what constitutes aggression, fantasized aggression or aggression against inanimate objects does not qualify.

A second basic postulate of the F-A hypothesis is that the strength of instigation to aggression varies directly with (1) the strength of the frustration, (2) the degree of frustration, (3) the number of frustrations, and (4) the amount of punishment anticipated as a response to aggression. A corollary of these principles is that the strongest instigation for aggression will be toward the source of the frustration. Thus, if frustration results in aggression, it will most likely be directed against the person who caused the frustration. Failing in this, the aggressor may attack a secondary target. Thus, in application, a basketball player continually frustrated in attempts to drive for the bucket due to defensive holding is likely to focus aggression against the offending defensive player. However, if this is likely to result in a penalty, the frustrated player may instead take out this frustration on the basketball, by slamming it against the floor.

Is the instigation toward aggression due to frustration based on some sort of innate mechanism, or is it learned? Berkowitz (1965) argues that the F-A mechanism is built in but that it is amendable to learning. Miller's (1941) original statements on the theory do not take a position on this point, but he contends that the F-A mechanism is present early in infancy. I will say more on this later.

Finally, an important component of the F-A theory is that overt aggression acts as a catharsis for further aggression; that is, pent-up emotions can be purged or discharged by expressing one's feelings through aggression (Berkowitz, 1970). Once this has been achieved, the individual will have no further need for aggression. Yet there is considerable evidence against the catharsis hypothesis, and in light of this evidence, this part of the theory would seem to be suspect. However, the F-A hypothesis deals with this problem in a number of qualifications mentioned by Dollard et al. (1939) and clarified by Berkowitz (1958). Specifically, the theory proposes that a frustrated person's need for aggression will be reduced through catharis *unless one of three things occurs:* (1) the frustration persists, (2) the aggressive behavior becomes a *learned* response, or (3) aggression leads to anxiety, which is frustrating and will lead to further aggression.

The frustration-aggression hypothesis is not easily disproven. For this reason it has been a major focal point of research since 1939. With a number of minor adjustments, which have come to be called *Berkowitz's reformulation,* it remains viable. Perhaps this is due to the fact that the revised F-A hypothesis takes into consideration both learning and the notion of an innate mechanism.

Berkowitz's reformulation takes the position that innate determination and learning can coexist. A frustrating event creates a readiness for aggression. For aggression to actually occur, certain stimuli associated with aggression must be present (Berkowitz & Alioto, 1973). These stimuli are cues that the frustrated person associates with aggression. One general example would be the "red flag" for the enraged and frustrated bull. A more relevant example might be the frustrated basketball player who continually avoids aggression until an opponent utters a few choice words that are associated with aggression. Berkowitz and Le Page (1967) aptly demonstrated this point in a study in which frustrated and angry subjects were placed in a room where either weapons or badminton rackets were openly displayed on a table. The subjects who observed the guns—the aggressive cue—exhibited greater aggression than the control subjects, who observed the badminton rackets. Aggression was measured through the use of a shock box.

Berkowitz's reformulation of the F-A hypothesis argues that frustration does not have to lead to aggression. It only heightens the predisposition to aggression. And the F-A response can be modified by learning. An athlete can learn not to respond to frustration with aggression. Regarding catharsis, Berkowitz rejects the notion that aggression can lower a person's basic inclination to aggression. Instead he allows that aggression begets further aggression. Nevertheless, he contends that there is a certain satisfaction in what he calls the **completion tendency** (Berkowitz, 1964). That is, the frustrated person does not feel satisfied or fulfilled until the urge for aggression is completed. Thus, at least momentarily, "completing the ongoing aggressive sequence . . . leads . . . to a pleasurable reduction in the experienced tension" (p. 104). However, if this aggressive act becomes reinforced or learned, it will only lead to further aggression. Berkowitz (1981) has also stated that the legitimacy of a frustration also is an important factor in aggression. A frustration is considered "legitimate" if it is no fault of the person who caused it. In such a case the tendency toward aggression is minimal. For example, a wide receiver drops the quarterback's perfect pass because of freezing rain, not because of lack of concentration. The latter case would represent a case of "legitimate" frustration to the quarterback.

---

5. **Principle** A frustrating event creates a readiness for aggression.
   Application Coaches must look for game situations that could result in aggression. When an athlete becomes frustrated and angry, the coach should immediately take that athlete out of the game to give him or her a few minutes to cool down.

Social Learning Theory

Perhaps the strongest advocate of **social learning theory** as an adequate explanation for aggression is Albert Bandura. Social learning theory, unlike biological instinct theory, regards aggression as a learned response. Proponents such as Bandura (1973) acknowledge the presence of physiological mechanisms for aggression and rage, but totally dismiss the instinct or the F-A notion of aggression. They feel that people behave aggressively because they have learned to do so, and not because of biological instinct or frustration.

The fact that people can learn aggression is clearly documented in the experimental literature. Many studies have shown that children's play behavior will change after they have watched models display acts of aggression and hostility (Bandura, Ross & Ross, 1961; Christy, Gelfand & Hartmann, 1971; Nelson, Gelfand & Hartmann, 1969; Walters & Brown, 1963). In these studies, children generally observed an adult model acting either aggressively or nonaggressively toward a **Bobo doll.** Following the presentation of the model, the children would be allowed to play with the Bobo doll. The results clearly showed that the children who watched an aggressive model abuse the Bobo doll later exhibited much greater aggression than those who watched the passive model. In this kind of research, the Bobo doll is an inflated plastic figure that can provide reinforcement to the subject. The reinforcement comes from the eyes, which light up when the doll is punched, and from colored glass marbles that are dispensed when the doll's stomach is punched.

Bandura has argued that aggression has a **circular effect.** That is, one act of aggression leads to further aggression. This pattern will continue until the circle is broken by some sort of positive or negative reinforcement. Smith (1980), for instance, argues that violence in ice hockey is due to modeling. Youngsters learn aggression by watching their role models, the professionals, on television or in person. As long as aggression in professional sports is tolerated, children will continue to have adult models of aggressive behavior.

The most striking difference between the two previously discussed theories and social learning theory is their view of catharsis. For Bandura, the notion of catharsis is simply nonsense. Aggression results not in lowered aggression, but in further aggression. An athlete who engages in aggression on the athletic field will not become more passive as a result, but will probably continue to be aggressive. As we shall see in the next section, there is ample evidence to support this contention. There is no question that social learning theory differs completely from biological instinct theory. However, in view of Berkowitz's reformulation of F-A theory, the F-A hypothesis and social learning theory are not incompatible. This

---

6. **Principle** The athletic experience does not provide an outlet for pent-up aggression.

   Application Aggressive behavior on the athletic field leads to further aggression. It is a behavior that is learned and often tolerated. Coaches and teachers must teach their athletes that an act of aggression will neither make them feel better nor help the team.

---

is because Berkowitz included a large social learning component in his reformulation of the F-A hypothesis. Nevertheless, social learning theory provides the single most viable explanation for the continued rise of aggression and violence in amateur and professional sports.

The Catharsis Hypothesis

Most of the research on aggression generally, and sport aggression specifically, has dealt with the notion of catharsis. In a very real sense, tests of the catharsis hypothesis are tests of the three basic theories of aggression. If aggression results in a purging of aggressive tendencies, then there must be some truth to the biological instinct and frustration-aggression hypotheses. Conversely, if aggression merely begets more aggression and violence, then social learning theory would seem to be the most viable explanation for what causes aggression. However, the finding that aggression begets further aggression would not totally damage the F-A hypothesis, since Berkowitz's reformulation predicts that result if aggression becomes a learned behavior. The relationship between catharsis and the three theoretical explanations for aggression is illustrated in figure 8.2.

Research on catharsis in sport has concentrated on two different questions. First, does participating in aggression result in catharsis? Second, does observing others participate in aggression result in catharsis? Does participating in aggression during football and soccer games result in a purging of aggression, or does it teach aggression? Will the athlete be a less aggressive person, on and off the field, as a result of participatory aggression, or will that athlete actually become more aggressive? In the case of an observer, does observing violence on the athletic field result in a catharsis, or does vicarious violence actually teach and enhance aggression among sports fans?

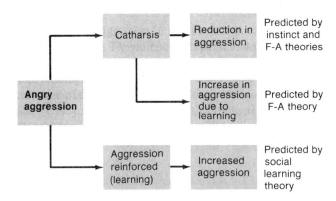

Figure 8.2 Does aggression result in a catharsis, or in further aggression?

Catharsis and the Participant

While the results are often contradictory, research tends to demonstrate that athletes who engage in aggressive kinds of activities exhibit more aggression than control groups. This would favor the social learning theory, because it indicates that aggression is not a catharsis that results in a decrease in aggression.

Ryan (1970) demonstrated that subjects who engaged in a vigorous "pounding" task, when compared to a control group, exhibited a greater willingness to administer electric shock to a victim. Zillman, Katcher, and Milarsky (1972) observed that subjects placed in an anger and high-exercise condition were more willing to exhibit heightened aggression on a shock box than were subjects in more passive groups. Leith (1977) reported similar findings. Admittedly, however, field research designed to investigate the relationship between overt aggression and future aggression on and off the field is critically lacking.

Catharsis and the Spectator

While applied sport research involving aggression and participants is scant, such is not the case with research on spectators. Many studies have demonstrated that viewing aggressive scenes tends to heighten, not lower, aggressive tendencies.

Research involving the viewing of violent and nonviolent films clearly demonstrates that higher levels of aggression result from watching aggressive scenes than from watching nonaggressive scenes (Berkowitz, 1972; Goranson, 1970; Leith, 1982). In the study by Leith (1982), high school boys were allowed to observe a film depicting boxing, tennis, or sailing. Scores obtained from before and after measures of aggression on a shock box revealed significantly greater increases in aggression for the boys watching the violent fight scenes than for the others. Fenigstein (1979) has also demonstrated that male subjects who engage in aggression are more likely to seek out aggressive films than neutral ones.

In several studies, the actual aggressive tendencies of subjects were measured before and after athletic contests. Each of these studies reported results contrary to the catharsis hypothesis (Arms, Russell, and Sandilands, 1980; Goldstein & Arms, 1971; Russell, 1981b; Turner, 1970). The study by Arms et al. (1980) represents a follow-up to the Goldstein and Arms (1971) study of aggressive and nonaggressive sporting events. The Arms et al. study involved 127 female and 87 male subjects who were randomly assigned to watch either an ice hockey game, professional wrestling, or a swimming meet. Pre- and postmeasures of aggressiveness were obtained through the administration of three pencil-and-paper tests of state aggression. As with the Goldstein and Arms research, this study concluded that contact sports such as football and ice hockey heighten, not lower, the perceived aggression of spectators. Thus, it appears clear that vicarious aggressive sport participation does not serve as a catharsis.

While the evidence in this section is certainly weighted against the catharsis hypothesis, the reader must bear in mind at least three important points. First, the research results of any study are only as good as the measurement tools used in the study. While studies using the shock box satisfy the "intent to harm" criteria for aggression, it is difficult to prove that a laboratory measure of aggression can be applied to a field setting. Also, viewing football and hockey games does not necessarily qualify as vicarious aggression. Most of the action in these contact sports falls under the heading of assertiveness, not aggression. Finally, the fact that subjects score high in perception of aggressiveness does not necessarily mean that they would participate in an act of aggression.

Summary of Catharsis

General reviews of the research (Berkowitz, 1972; Goranson, 1970) and studies discussed in this chapter do not support the notion of catharsis in sport. It is not reasonable to expect an act of violence to reduce the aggressive drive. Instead, aggression probably results in further aggression. These findings tend to support social learning theory at the expense of biological instinct theory. Even F-A theory as originally proposed by Dollard et al. (1939) is severely challenged. However, Berkowitz's reformulation of the F-A hypothesis is still tenable. Aggression can serve as a temporary catharsis through a momentary reduction in aggressive behavior or through feelings of guilt (Cataldi, 1980), but learning can override any cathartic benefit and result in further aggression. In Berkowitz's reformulation, aggression serves as a cue or stimulus for further aggression whenever the system is "readied" for aggression.

This means that aggression in sport must be avoided. Acts of aggression can only make matters worse; they can never effectively prevent future aggression. An athlete may feel momentary satisfaction in inflicting harm as a result of some frustration, but the feeling will not last. A barrier has been lowered, the aggressive stimulus is in place, and it will be easier to be aggressive next time.

---

7. **Principle** The notion that an act of aggression is a catharsis is false.
   Application The idea of getting it out of the system just doesn't work in the case of aggression. Aggression begets aggression, and seldom results in a reduced drive to be aggressive.

Psychological Constructs Related to Sport Aggression

In this section we will discuss several conditions that tend to be associated with aggression in sport. The presence of these conditions does not cause aggression, but the conditions tend to accompany overt acts of aggression.

Arousal

Physiological or undifferentiated arousal is a necessary precursor to hostile aggression. It serves as a **readying mechanism** for aggression, but not as a sufficient cause for it. To feel anger (a mood state) toward another person, an individual must be aroused. Remember that anger is a necessary component of hostile aggression but not of instrumental aggression. Yet even in a case of instrumental aggression, an aggressor will generally be physiologically aroused. It is unrealistic to imagine any kind of aggression without the activation of the sympathetic nervous system.

The importance of arousal as a readying mechanism for aggression cannot be overemphasized. The aroused person is in a situation where some sort of frustration could, in the presence of an aggressive stimulus, trigger an aggressive response. Research shows that hostile aggression is more likely to occur in the presence of arousal (Geen & O'Neal, 1969; Lefebvre, Leith & Bredemeier, 1980). Russell (1981b) reported an excellent sport-related study that illustrates this principle. Two ice hockey games were studied. The first game was violent, involving a total of 142 minutes of assessed penalties. The second game was well played but lacking in violence, with only 46 minutes of assessed penalties. At predetermined times during each contest, the Mood Adjective Checklist (Nowlis, 1965), which measures aggression and arousal, among other variables, was administered to randomly selected spectators. The results showed a clear increase in arousal as aggression increased on the field of play, and the parallel pencil-and-paper measure of aggression also increased.

In terms of actual participants, the study by Zillmann et al. (1972) provides additional evidence for an arousal-aggression link. Subjects who were both aroused by exercise and angered by shock delivered the highest levels of electric shock to an accomplice. These results lead us to expect the probability of aggression to be highest in sports that involve the most physiological arousal. Such team sports as basketball, football, and ice hockey would be far more prone to violence than, say, cricket, softball, and baseball, although these sports are not without their violent moments.

8. **Principle** Athletes are more likely to engage in aggression when they are physiologically aroused.

   Application Optimal arousal is important to successful sport participation. Consequently, the coach must be aware of the increased probability of aggression occurring during a sporting event.

Moral Reasoning

Bredemeier's (1983) **cognitive development approach** to explaining aggression is based on Jean Piaget's stage theory of moral judgment and reasoning (Ginsburg & Opper, 1969). Just as a child goes through distinct stages in recognizing the permanence of a concrete object, individuals also go through distinct stages in the development of **moral reasoning.** At a low level of moral reasoning a person is unable to conceive of an act of aggression as being immoral. However, as the individual passes through successively higher stages of moral reasoning he or she comes to possess the underlying thought structures necessary for high moral reasoning. When a moral conflict arises we attempt to resolve it using our present stage of moral reasoning. Our present stage of moral reasoning may be incomplete, resulting in conflicting answers. Individuals at a low stage of moral reasoning cannot make highly moral decisions. At the highest level of moral reasoning, right is defined by the conscience in accord with ethical principles.

Bredemeier's research on moral reasoning relies heavily on theoretical frameworks developed by Kohlberg (1969) and Haan (1982) relative to Piaget's basic theory of intellectual development. In both cases, it is reasoned that children and adults pass through several distinct stages of moral development before they reach an enlightened or highly moral stage. Since human aggression is viewed as being unethical, Bredemeier reasoned that a relationship should exist between level of moral reasoning and overt acts of athletic aggression. Support for this basic model was forthcoming in several investigations. Bredemeier and Shields (1984) and Bredemeier (1985) observed that the moral reasoning of basketball players was inversely related to overt acts of athletic aggression. In another investigation, boys' participation in high-contact sports and girls' participation in medium-contact sports was positively correlated with less mature moral reasoning (Bredemeier, Weiss, Shields & Cooper, 1986).

As a result of her research in aggression and moral reasoning, Bredemeier and associates (Bredemeier & Shields, 1986; Bredemeier, Weiss, Shields & Cooper,

1987) have concluded that contact sport, because it legitimizes acts of aggression, may actually retard a person's moral development. The high level of morality necessary for everyday life is often partially suspended during athletic competition. Bredemeier refers to this suspension of ethical morality as **bracketed morality.**

Sport participants must be taught that it is unethical to assume that society's standards for moral behavior can be suspended during sport competition. If aggression is immoral in everyday life, then it is also immoral in the athletic arena.

---

9. **Principle** A relationship exists between an athlete's level of moral and ethical reasoning and his or her willingness to engage in acts of aggression.

    Application Coaches and teachers can best control athletes' aggression by appealing to their sense of right and wrong.

    Athletes must be taught that aggression during an athletic contest is just as wrong as it is in normal everyday life.

Guilt

Psychologists generally believe that aggression, especially hostile aggression, results in feelings of guilt. These feelings of guilt are expected to cause a decrease in further aggression (Mosher, 1966). This temporary reduction in aggression caused by guilt is often misinterpreted as a catharsis (Cataldi, 1980).

It does seem that athletes often experience genuine feelings of guilt as a result of violent acts. However, it does not appear that these feelings of guilt necessarily have a long-term effect on further instigations of violence. Furthermore, Silva (1979) demonstrated that acts of aggression may not result in the expected feelings of guilt, because athletes may feel their violent acts are permissible in sport (Feigley, 1983). Silva assigned 122 college-age male subjects to one of four treatment conditions based on pretests of guilt proneness. The assignments were made so that all treatments were equal in terms of the disposition towards guilt. The design involved the manipulation of aggression and assertiveness in both nonsport (peg board) and sport (basketball) settings. Following these manipulations, in which subjects in the hostile aggression conditions were incited to hostile acts by confederates, all subjects were again tested on their feelings of guilt with the Mood Adjective Checklist. The results showed that the *nonsport* hostile aggression group experienced the highest level of guilt. The subjects in the hostile aggression *sport* condition did not experience high levels of guilt. Therefore, in the sporting environment, aggression may not be inhibited due to guilt. The explanation for this is that the athletes perceive that violence in sport is not only legitimate, but sometimes expected (Silva, 1983). In the final analysis, while guilt may inhibit acts of aggression, it probably will not if the athlete perceives that it is "part of the game."

10. **Principle** Guilt about aggression is a potential deterrent to future aggression.
    Application Athletes should be taught that aggression is wrong. If they believe that it is wrong, they will avoid it. However, athletes often are taught that aggression is "part of the game." In this situation, feelings of guilt will not develop.

Personality and Aggression

It is very difficult to demonstrate a significant and meaningful relationship between an athlete's predisposition to aggression and that athlete's actual willingness to engage in acts of aggression. Several authors have contended that a correlation exists between the personality trait of aggression and actual instigations of overt hostile aggression (Cratty, 1981; Lefebvre, Leith & Bredemeier, 1980). However, as with the relationship between personality traits and athletic performance, the relationship between the personality trait of aggressiveness and overt aggression is tenuous.

Several investigations have inadvertently demonstrated the lack of such a relationship. McCarthy and Kelly (1978a) studied the relationship between ice hockey aggression and a pencil-and-paper measure of aggressiveness and discovered that the two were unrelated. Similar findings have been reported by Lipetz and Ossorio (1967), Bird (1972), and Russell (1974). Consequently, it is doubtful that one can obtain a trait measure of someone's aggressiveness and infer from this that they are likely to engage in aggression in a particular situation. However, the weakness of the observed relationship may be partly due to the methods used for assessing overt aggression on the field of play. In most examples of reported sport aggression research, aggression is defined in terms of fouls and penalties. These are not necessarily good indicators of aggression. They often reflect little more than assertiveness, misplaced exuberance, and overarousal.

Female Aggression

Nearly all of the research dealing with sport aggression has been conducted using male subjects. It is as if aggression is not something that women and girls engage in. This is probably not the case; it's just that females seldom participate in the kinds of sports that tend to trigger aggression, such as ice hockey, American football, and boxing. In fact, most sport-related research on this topic has used ice hockey athletes as subjects. Ice hockey is a male-dominated sport.

Research involving nonsport-related findings are unequivocal regarding female aggression. Early reports suggested that men are more aggressive than females. However, Baron and Bell (1976) and Harris (1974) failed to support this conclusion. Gender differences are observed in those studies in which strong provocation for aggression is lacking. When sufficiently strong provocation is present, men and women behave the same in terms of aggression (Baron, 1977). Men may have a lower threshold or "boiling" point for aggression than womem.

Sport-related research suggests that men and women perceive the legitimacy of aggressive acts differently. Men tend to believe that aggression during athletic competition is legitimate while women do not. This observation is based on research by Silva (1983) in which 203 male and female athletes were shown slides depicting rule-violating behavior (including aggressive acts) and asked to rate the legitimacy of the behavior in the sport context. The results of this research clearly demonstrate that males consider aggressive acts and rule violating behavior to be much more acceptable than females. For males, legitimacy of rule violation increases as the degree of body contact, years of participation, and level of participation increases. However, for females, potential body contact, years of participation, and level of participation are poor predictors of whether or not rule-violating behavior is perceived as being legitimate. Gilligan (1977) theorized that differences in the socialization of males and females contributes to the way in which aggressive acts are perceived in sport.

---

11. **Principle** Female athletes are not immune to acts of aggression in sport. They also must be taught that aggression is unacceptable behavior.

    Application Coaches of women's sports have not traditionally faced the problem of aggression as often as coaches of men's teams have. However, as the women's sport movement continues to grow and spectators come to expect more and more from them, aggression may become more of a problem.

Situational Factors in a Sport Setting

Much of the recent research in sport-related aggression has dealt with situation-specific factors. These are factors that occur in conjunction with aggression. We now turn to a discussion of several of them.

Perception of Victim's Intent

If an athlete perceives that the intent of an opponent is to inflict harm, then the athlete is more likely to respond with aggression against the opponent than if he or she perceives otherwise (Epstein & Taylor, 1967; Greenwell & Dengerink, 1973). This means that perception of an opponent's aggressive intentions may be more salient than such things as defeat and competition. Basketball players who perceive that their opponents' rough play is intentional and designed to inflict harm are more likely to respond with aggression than if they perceive that the

roughness is accidental. A study by Harrell (1980) using male high school basketball players demonstrated this point. The most significant factor in predicting player aggression was the amount of aggression directed against the subject. The athlete who perceives that an opponent is trying to inflict harm will respond in kind.

Fear of Retaliation

It might be argued that a player's level of aggression is somewhat tempered by fear of retaliation. If an athlete fears retaliation from a prospective victim, then the aggressor will resist becoming the aggressor. This seems to be a common theme of current international politics. In terms of interpersonal aggression, it may well be true. Baron (1971) studied the **retaliation hypothesis** and determined that subjects who had low expectations of victim counteraggression tended to deliver stronger electric shocks to a victim than subjects who expected strong retaliation. It appears that if punishment or perceived retaliation is probable, acts of aggression may be retarded. However, this basic notion was also tested by Knott and Drost (1972) with very different results. Knott and Drost observed that attack-escalating behavior was self-defeating, because the opponent tended to become more aggressive as a result. Thus, a circular effect can be observed. As the level of aggression increases, the victim tends to counter-aggression with even higher levels of aggression. In the final analysis, it appears that initial aggression can be inhibited by fear of retaliation, but once aggression and counteraggression have begun, further escalation will only result in heightened aggression.

Structure of the Game

Two of the earliest studies of game variables and aggression were conducted by Volkamer (1972) with soccer and Wankel (1972) with the ice hockey. These studies were quickly followed by investigations by Lefebvre and Passer (1974) with soccer, Cullen and Cullen (1975) with ice hockey, Martin (1976) with basketball and wrestling, and Russell and Drewery (1976) with soccer. Following is a summary of the findings with respect to game variables:

1. *Point differential.* More aggressive penalties occur as the game score differential increases (Volkamer, 1972; Wankel, 1972). When teams are tied or the scores are close, aggression is at a minimum. The penalty for aggression in a critical game situation is so high that players, coaches, and managers go out of their way to avoid aggression. Aggression often results in penalties, and these penalties can spell the difference between victory and defeat. Conversely, when score differentials are great, players may engage in aggression without seriously affecting the game's outcome.

2. *Playing at home or away.* Whether home or visiting teams display more aggressive behavior may depend on the nature of the aggression and the type of game involved. Lefebvre and Passer (1974) and Volkamer (1972) both observed that visiting soccer teams play more aggressively than home teams. However, Russell and Drewery (1976) and Wankel (1972) found no differences between the aggressive play of home and visiting hockey teams. Varca (1980) observed that home basketball teams were more assertive in rebounds, blocked shots, and steals, but visiting teams were whistled for more fouls, which suggests dysfunctional assertiveness.

3. *Outcome of participation.* Consistent with the frustration-aggression hypothesis, we can expect losing teams and players to be guilty of more overt aggression than winners. Certainly, it is more frustrating to lose than to win, although events can occur during a contest that can be frustrating to winner and loser alike. Research by Volkamer (1972) in soccer and by Martin (1976) in wrestling tend to support this position.

4. *League standings.* Studies by Volkamer (1972) and Russell and Drewery (1976), both with soccer, concluded that aggression is related to overall league standings. According to Volkamer, the lower a team is in the standings, the more its members tend to engage in aggression. Russell and Drewery, however, reported that teams trailing the front runner by only one or two games tended to display the highest level of aggression. These two studies do, however, agree that the lowest incidence of aggression occurs with the teams in first place.

5. *Periods of play.* Studies in which ice hockey athletes were used as subjects showed that the number and frequency of aggressive penalties tended to increase as the game proceeded (Cullen & Cullen, 1975; Russell & Drewery, 1976). This conclusion was somewhat qualified by Cullen and Cullen. They observed that the number of aggressive penalties increased in a linear fashion for winning teams, but for losing teams the relationship was curvilinear. The highest incident of aggression occurred at the midway point of the game for losers and at the end of the game for victors.

---

12. **Principle** Acts of aggression occur more frequently among teams that lose, during games that are not close, on the part of visiting teams, and after the first quarter of play.
    Application Athletes who have a history of aggression should be closely monitored during these situations.

The Performance-Aggression Relationship

Silva (1980b) has argued that sport aggression tends to inhibit athletic performance rather than enhance it. He gives two reasons for this. First, a performance decrement occurs when athletes shift their attention from the performance goal to that of attacking an opponent. Second, the heightened arousal associated with hostile aggression may cause a shift in activation past the optimal level of arousal for best performance. Both of these explanations seem reasonable, but they clash to some degree with the results of sport-related research. For example, Russell (1974) studied the relationship between hostile aggression in ice hockey and successful goals and assists and found rather low but in many cases significant correlations. The correlation between number of successful goals and hostile aggression was .191, while the correlation between hostile aggression and assists was a respectable .434. McCarthy and Kelly (1978a, 1978b) also concluded that a positive relationship exists between hostile aggression and performance in ice hockey.

From Silva's writings it would appear that aggression hinders performance, while the studies just mentioned suggest a modest positive relationship between the two. How can this conflict be resolved? Perhaps the solution lies in our understanding of the inverted-U hypothesis and in the techniques used to measure aggression.

Silva (1980b) argued that aggression would cause a decrement in performance because of too much arousal. Recall that arousal is a necessary mediator of hostile aggression. It is also likely to be associated with instrumental aggression. The increased arousal associated with aggression could cause a decrement in performance if the activation level became too high. However, suppose the activation level associated with the aggression was optimal for best performance of the task. For ice hockey, a high level of arousal would seem to be ideal for many of the skills involved—speed, body checking, power plays.

A second possible explanation involves the manner in which aggression was measured by Russell (1974) and McCarthy and Kelly (1978a, 1978b). Hostile aggression was defined as penalties awarded and challenge to authority. Thus, it is likely that much of the observed aggression was nothing more than assertive

---

13. **Principle** True aggression does not help but hinders a team's chances for victory.

   Application Coaches who want to be successful will not encourage aggression. An unpenalized act of aggression may help a team or individual win an athletic contest once or twice, but over the long run it will be a serious handicap and a distraction.

---

behavior. It may be that what these authors were observing is that assertive *and* aggressive behavior is modestly related to athletic performance. It is likely that if the truly aggressive acts were separated from the assertive acts, performance would be negatively related to aggression as Silva suggested.

Reducing Violence in Sport

Hostile aggression in sport can be curtailed, or at least minimized, if all concerned are interested in doing so. The sad part is that some of the most influential people actually promote rather than discourage violence because they believe it sells tickets (Russell, 1986). As long as this attitude is allowed to continue, there is little hope of solving the problem. And if it is allowed to continue on the professional level it will continue to be promoted on the lower skill levels. Athletes in the youth leagues emulate their heroes on the collegiate and professional levels. They see their sport heroes receive awards, applause, money, and adulation for behavior that borders on open aggression, and they want to become like them. In this section we will discuss ways to reduce aggression on the part of participants and spectators.

Curtailing Aggression in Athletes

In this section let us consider what can be done to curtail aggression on the part of the athlete. Based on the literature, we can make the following recommendations (Lefebvre, Leith & Bredemeier 1980; Nighswander & Mayer, 1969):

1. *Young athletes must be provided with models of nonaggressive behavior.* Great athletes who do not engage in aggression should be brought to the attention of young athletes. Athletic greatness should be associated with self-control and correct behavior as well as performance.

2. *An athlete who engages in an illegal act of aggression must be severely punished.* Fining a professional athlete who makes a half million dollars a year three hundred dollars for slugging an opponent can hardly be considered punishment. Similarly, a high school athlete who engages in an act of aggression must receive a more salient punishment than being sent to the showers. An athlete must be taught that an act of aggression is an unacceptable behavior that will result in severe punishment. For example, in the Kermit Washington/Rudy Tomjanovich case mentioned at the beginning of this chapter, Washington was fined ten thousand dollars and suspended without pay for two months for shattering Tomjanovich's face in an NBA

basketball game. Tomjanovich also sued Washington for 3.3 million dollars in damages. Nearly two years later, on 29 August 1979, the jury was dismissed and a settlement was made out of court. Part of the agreement was that the terms of the settlement would not be made public (Noverr & Ziewaez, 1981; Weber, 1978).

3. *Coaches who encourage or even allow their athletes to engage in acts of violence should be fined, censored, and/or suspended from their coaching duties.* The coach or manager who allows athletes to engage in acts of aggression must share the blame and the penalty for such acts. If the penalties for aggression were quick and sure, it is doubtful that a coach would allow the aggression to continue. In the Kermit Washington case, the Los Angeles Lakers were also found guilty of neglect for the manner in which they handled a player with a tendency for violence (Coakley, 1982). Cases such as this should make management think twice before they encourage aggression in order to promote ticket sales.

4. *External stimuli capable of evoking hostile aggression on the field of play should be removed.* Some athletes, coaches, fans, or even referees serve as aggressive stimuli to the athletes. If these people are removed from the scene, the chances of aggression will be greatly diminished. One popular college basketball coach was quoted as saying that "defeat in sports is worse than death because you have to live with defeat." Such an attitude is bound to promote a situation ripe for aggression, especially if that coach's team is suffering a defeat! This type of person should either change that philosophy or get out of coaching. In fact, the author of that statement was the lightning rod for several acts of aggression that occurred in collegiate basketball (Freischlag & Schmedke, 1980).

5. *Coaches and referees should be encouraged to attend inservice workshops for dealing with aggression and violence.* Such clinics would be very useful to referees of sports in which aggression is most likely to occur. Better referring can make a difference. Officials who have a "slow" whistle or who exhibit some sort of decision bias need to be retrained.

6. *Along with punishment for acts of aggression, athletes must also receive positive reinforcement for controlling their tempers in highly emotional situations.* Athletes who can sustain a punishing blow and continue to perform without seeking retribution should be praised. While this happens occasionally in sport, it does not occur as often as it should. These acts of great self-control *must* be identified and strongly reinforced.

7. Emotional control over acts of hostile aggression should be practiced.
The use of visual imagery and mental practice to improve performance was
discussed in chapter 4. These and other cognitive techniques can and should be
used to help volatile athletes cope with their aggressive tendencies.

Curtailing Aggression by Specators

The following practices would help to alleviate aggression on the part of spectators at sporting events (Freischlag & Schmedke, 1980):

1. *Limit the sale and distribution of alcoholic beverages at sporting events.*
It is well known that drugs and alcohol can facilitate violence and aggression
in many situations (Valzelli, 1981). For this reason, many organizers of
athletic events already take steps to cut down on alcoholic consumption, and
hence violence. All responsible organizers of sporting events should do this.

2. *Attendance at athletic events should be promoted as a family affair.*
Families can afford to attend athletic events together if tickets are offered for
reduced rates on a family plan. People are less likely to get caught up in
spectator violence if they are with their families.

3. *Responsible media can discourage aggression in sport by not
glamorizing it.* When TV stations show replays of aggressive acts they are in
fact encouraging and glamorizing the acts. In recent years, many TV stations
have made a point of not giving camera coverage to fan misbehavior. This is a
step in the right direction. They should do the same thing when player violence
occurs (Bryant & Zillman, 1983).

4. *The media should not attempt to promote friction or hatred between
two teams prior to competition.* Rather than pointing out all of the reasons
that two teams should dislike each other, the media should promote solidarity.
Winning or losing is certainly important, but the joy and excitement of
competition is a shared phenomenon, and should be promoted as such.

5. *Interaction between members of opposing teams should be encouraged
by coaches and managers.* Sport is not combat. Sport is a highly significant
event that promotes fitness and achievement. What is wrong with allowing
members of opposing teams to become familiar with each other as caring
human beings? It's much easier to be aggressive against a feared enemy than
against a respected and liked opponent.

6. *As with the athletes and coaches, acts of spectator aggression must be quickly and severely dealt with.* When a spectator is observed behaving in a manner that is not appreciated by the other fans, that spectator should be removed from the game. If the offense is severe enough, steps should be taken to bar the individual from future athletic events.

Summary

Human aggression is a problem in society as well as in sport. Aggression is any form of behavior directed to the goal of harming or injuring another being. The key element in this definition is the notion of intent to harm. We have identified two types of aggression. In hostile aggression, the aggressor's reinforcement is the suffering of the victim. In instrumental aggression, the reinforcement is an external reward such as winning. Assertive behavior involves the expenditure of unusual effort and energy, but injuries are incidental to the goal to win. Assertiveness involves no intention to injure another human being.

Aggression may be measured in terms of the personality trait of aggressiveness or through situation-specific state measures of aggression. Trait measures of aggression are generally ascertained through projective techniques and pencil-and-paper tests. Some of the common tests of state aggression include laboratory tests such as the shock box and field tests such as behavioral observation and archival records.

There are three basic theories that attempt to explain why athletes are aggressive. According to instinct theory, aggression is innate, and must be channeled and released through competitive activities such as sport. Frustration-aggression theory proposes that aggression occurs as a result of frustration; Berkowitz's reformulation of the F-A theory makes it clear that both learning and innate mechanisms are responsible for aggression. Social learning theory posits that aggression is learned and has little to do with biological instinct. One of the important by-products of aggression according to instinct theory and frustration-aggression theory is that it serves as a release or catharsis for further aggression. The catharsis hypothesis cannot be substantiated.

Several psychological factors are closely associated with acts of aggression. Hostile aggression is always associated with physiological arousal. Hostile aggression generally results in feelings of guilt and remorse. The association between the personality trait of aggressiveness and actual aggression in sport was discussed; it was determined that very little experimental evidence exists to postulate a positive relationship between the two. Finally, the relationship between aggression and gender was considered. Except that males have a lower threshold for aggression, there is no reason to believe that women are any less aggressive than men.

Various situational factors are believed to be related to aggression in sport. In a game situation an athlete's perception of an opponent's intentions is very important in determining whether or not aggression will occur. Athletic events in which the score differential is great result in more acts of violence. Losing is more frustrating than winning, and consequently losing results in more aggression. The relationship between performance and aggression is tenuous. Generally, true hostile acts of aggression will hamper the aggressor's athletic performance. This is due to distraction and overarousal.

Procedures designed to reduce violence in sport were discussed in reference to both participants and spectators. Violence and aggression in sport could be greatly minimized if all parties involved were interested in doing so. Perhaps the most salient factor is punishment. If the expected punishment for an aggressive act were severe enough, acts of aggression would be markedly reduced.

Review Questions

1. Describe the critical difference between aggression in sport and assertiveness. Give examples from several sports.
2. How does hostile aggression differ from instrumental aggression? Give some examples, and explain in what circumstances each might occur.
3. How can aggression be measured? Discuss both laboratory and field techniques.
4. Is a trait measure of aggression different from a state measurement? In what ways? Give examples and explain.
5. Which theory of aggression do you think best explains why athletes act aggressively? Give specific reasons for your answer.
6. Can aggression in sporting events result in a catharsis or purging of aggressive tendencies? Qualify your answer with reasons and specific examples.
7. Does viewing acts of aggression in sport result in catharsis or learned aggression? How about TV violence? Expand and explain.
8. What are some of the conditions associated with hostile aggression? How do these psychological constructs affect the athlete in terms of aggression?
9. What are some of the game factors that are known to be related to aggression? Can you describe sporting situations that would be likely to produce aggression based on these factors?
10. Discuss procedures to reduce violence on the part of athletes and spectators.

Glossary

aggression A form of overt behavior intended to harm a living being.

archival research Research in aggression based on game information recorded by official scorers.

assertiveness In sport, it is the expenditure of unusual effort and energy to achieve an external goal.

Berkowitz's reformulation A revision of the frustration-aggression hypothesis. Basically, the revision states that frustration creates a readiness for aggression. Aggressive responses can be modified by learning.

Bobo doll In social learning aggression research, an inflatable doll that provides reinforcement for acts of physical aggression against it.

bracketed morality Suspension of ethical morality during athletic competition.

Buss aggression machine The shock box or Buss aggression machine allows an experimenter to assess a subject's level of aggression in terms of the intensity of an electrical shock that a subject imparts to an accomplice.

Buss-Durkee Hostility Scale A pencil-and-paper questionnaire designed to measure a subject's personality trait of aggressiveness.

catharsis The notion that pent-up emotions, anger, and frustrations can be purged or discharged by expressing one's feelings through aggression.

circular effect The notion that aggression begets more aggression.

cognitive developmental approach A developmental view of how moral reasoning evolves based on Piaget's stage theory of intellectual development.

completion tendency In the frustration-aggression hypothesis, the notion that the frustrated individual does not feel satisfied or fulfilled until the urge or drive for aggression is completed.

frustration-aggression (F-A) theory As originally conceived by Dollard et al. (1939), the theory posits that frustration always results in aggression.

hostile aggression Aggression against another human being with the intent to harm; the reinforcement or goal is to inflict pain and suffering on the victim. It is always accompanied by anger.

hostility Used interchangeably with the term *hostile aggression.*

instinct theory The theory that human aggression is an innate biological drive that cannot be eliminated, but must be controlled for the good of humankind through catharsis.

instrumental aggression Aggression against another human being with the intent to harm; the reinforcement is to obtain some external goal such as victory or prestige.

intent to harm When a behavior includes the goal or intent to harm or injure another human being, it is aggression. There can be no aggression without intent to harm.

moral reasoning Process by which an individual comes to recognize right from wrong.

readying mechanism A mechanism, such as arousal, that prepares the organism for hostile aggression, but is not the cause of aggression.

retaliation hypothesis The notion that an athlete who fears counteraggression from a potential victim will not participate in aggression.

shock box See **Buss aggression machine.**

social learning theory As applied to aggression, social learning theory posits that aggression is a learned behavior.

state aggression A transitory emotional condition characterized by consciously perceived feelings of aggression, often resulting in overt aggression against a human target.

trait aggression A relatively stable personality predispostion to respond in certain situations with acts of aggression.

violence A term reserved for the more serious manifestations of overt aggression.

Recommended Readings

Berkowitz, L. (1969a). The frustration-aggression hypothesis revisited. In L. Berkowitz (ed.), *Roots of aggression.* New York: Atherton Press.

Berkowitz, L. (1972). Sports, competition, and aggression. In I. D. Williams & L. M. Wankel (eds.), *Proceedings of the Fourth Canadian Psychomotor Learning and Sport Psychology Symposium.* Waterloo, Ontario: University of Waterloo.

Bredemeier, B. (1978). The assessment of reactive and instrumental athletic aggression. *Proceedings of the International Symposium on Psychological Assessment.* Neyanya, Israel: Wingate Institute for Physical Education and Sport.

Bredemeier, B. J. (1983). Athletic aggression: A moral concern. In J. H. Goldstein (ed.), *Sports violence.* New York: Springer-Verlag.

Bredemeier, B. J., & Shields, D. L. (1986). Athletic aggression: An issue of contextual morality. *Sociology of Sport Journal, 3,* 15–28.

Buss, A. H. (1971). Aggression pays. In J. E. Singer (ed.), *The control of aggression and violence: Cognitive and physiological factors.* New York: Academic Press.

Buss, A. H., & Durkee, A. (1957). An inventory for assessing different kinds of hostility. *Journal of Consulting Psychology, 21,* 343–348.

Gammon, C. (1985, June 10). A day of horror and shame. *Sports Illustrated, 62,* 20–35.

Goldstein, J. H. (1983). *Sports violence.* New York: Springer-Verlag.

Goranson, R. E. (1970). Media violence and aggressive behavior: A review of experimental research. In L. Berkowitz (ed.), *Advances in experimental social psychology* (Vol. 5, pp. 1–31). New York: Academic Press.

Lefebvre, L. M., Leith, L. L., & Bredemeier, B. B. (1980). Modes for aggression assessment and control. *International Journal of Sport Psychology, 11,* 11–21.

Leith, L. M. (1978). The psychological assessment of aggression in sport: A critique of existing measurement techniques. *Proceedings of the International Symposium on Psychological Assessment.* Neyanya, Israel: Wingate Institute for Physical Education and Sport.

Russell, G. W. (1981b). Spectator moods at an aggressive sporting event. *Journal of Sport Psychology, 3,* 217–227.

Scott, J. P. (1970). Sport and aggression. In G. S. Kenyon (ed.), *Contemporary psychology of sport.* Chicago: The Athletic Institute.

Silva, J. M., III. (1980a). Assertive and aggressive behavior in sport: A definitional clarification. In C. H. Nadeau (ed.), *Psychology of motor behavior and sport, 1979.* Champaign, IL: Human Kinetics Publishers.

Silva, J. M., III. (1980b) Understanding aggressive behavior and its effects upon athletic performance. In W. F. Straub (ed.), *Sport psychology: An analysis of athlete behavior* (2d ed.). Ithaca, NY: Mouvement Publications.

Yeager, R. C. (1979). *Seasons of shame: The new violence in sports.* New York: McGraw-Hill.

9   Audience Effects

Key Terms

audience
audience density
audience hostility
audience intimacy
audience size
audience sophistication
coactive audience
coactor
dysfunctional
   aggressive behavior
evaluation apprehension
functional aggressive
   behavior

home court advantage
interactive audience
leveling effect
mere presence
motor maze
noninteractive audience
paradigm
psychological presence
self-attention
social facilitation
Zajonc's model

Perhaps no social-psychological effect is more important to athletic performance and outcome than the audience or spectator effect. The evidence is clear, for example, that there is significant advantage to playing at home in baseball, football, basketball, and ice hockey (Schwartz & Barsky, 1977). The perception of a home court advantage is especially evident in men's collegiate basketball. Many basketball conferences have adopted the policy of sending the winners of their postseason tournaments to the NCAA tournament. Thus, the conference championship has in many cases been reduced to a scramble for a home court advantage in the first round of the conference postseason tournament.

In professional sports two rather well publicized examples of the home court advantage may be cited. Sports writers have coined the phrase, "Celtic Mystique," when referring to the win-loss record of the Boston Celtics basketball franchise when playing at Boston Gardens. Prior to losing game number four to the Los Angeles Lakers in the 1987 NBA Championship series, the Celtics had won 94 of their previous 97 games in "friendly" Boston Gardens (McCallum, 1987). The 1987 World Champion Minnesota Twins baseball team won 70 percent of their regular season home games. The Twins won all of their home games when they defeated the heavily favored Detroit Tigers for the American League Pennant and the St. Louis Cardinals in the World Series.

While many variables might help create the home court or field advantage, none seem to be as important as the presence of a supportive audience. Determining exactly how and why presence of an audience affects athletic performance is the focus of this chapter. In the first part of the chapter I will address the concept of social facilitation from a theoretical perspective using noninteractive audiences. In this section I will deal with the *noninteractive* effects of an audience of one or more persons on athletic performance. I will introduce the contributions of Zajonc and Cottrell and will identify some of the ways that researchers have tested their theories. In the section on interactive audiences, I will turn to a discussion of the interactive effects of an audience on athletic performance. It is in this section that the home court advantage and other interactive variables will be discussed in an applied or real life setting. I will attempt to bridge the gap between the theory of *noninteractive audiences* with the reality of *interactive audiences.*

Social Facilitation

The term **social facilitation** has come to be associated with a rather limited range of audience effects. It is reserved for that area of research dealing with the noninteractive effect of an audience on performance. A **noninteractive audience** is one that does not interact with the athletes. Instead, the audience is said to be merely present.

In social facilitation research, the noninteractive audience eliminates many uncontrollable variables from the research paradigm. A **paradigm** is a scheme or model that helps the researcher to explain and test a theory. In social facilitation research, the goal is to control or eliminate all interactive variables, so that any observed effect can be attributed to the mere presence of the audience. For researchers, this strategy is very important.

Within the social facilitation paradigm, we also have the notion of an audience effect and a coactive audience effect. The audience effect has to do with the effect that a group of passive onlookers, the **audience,** has on performance. The **coactive audience** effect has to do with the effect that other participants have on athletic performance when those participants, the **coactors,** do not interact with the subject or with each other. For example, a group of rifle marksmen who independently fire at their own targets in close proximity with each other could be defined as a noninteractive coactive audience.

Historical Perspective

The earliest reported study of the social facilitation phenomenon was that of Triplett (1897). Triplett's research dealt exclusively with the effect of coaction on bicycling. Using official data from the Racing Board of the League of American Wheelman, he compared cycling times under three conditions: unpaced (cyclist alone but timed), paced (cyclist paced and timed), and paced competitive (cyclist paced, timed, and racing against another competitor who was also paced and timed). Triplett's results showed quite dramatically that the racing times for the paced and paced competitive conditions were significantly faster than those of riders in the unpaced condition.

The term *social facilitation* was first used by Allport (1924) to describe his research with coactive groups. Again, coaction represents a situation in which two or more individuals are performing side by side but independently of each other. Allport noted that when individuals worked on the same task in each other's presence, their performance was better than when they worked by themselves. He referred to the effect as *social facilitation* and defined it as "an increase of response merely from the sight or sounds of others making the same movement" (p. 262).

Dashiell's 1935 review of social facilitation research up to that point marked an end to an active interest in that field of study until 1965. This dropoff in interest may have resulted from researchers' inability to reconcile contradictory findings in the literature. However, in 1965, Robert Zajonc (pronounced zion) published his paper on social facilitation, in which he made several important generalizations and proposed hypotheses to account for them. Zajonc (1965, p. 269) defined social facilitations as "the consequences upon behavior which derive from the sheer presence of other individuals."

Zajonc's Model

Zajonc's paper on social facilitation remains the single most critical factor in the development of social facilitation as a field of inquiry. According to Zajonc (1965), the social facilitation literature prior to 1965 was replete with contradictions about the effects that the presence of others had on performance. For example, Bergum & Lehr (1963) observed that visual vigilance was significantly improved by the presence of a supervisor. However, Pessin (1933) found that college students could learn a list of nonsense syllables faster alone than in the presence of several observers. Conflicting results of this kind had exasperated researchers searching for a common thread since Dashiell (1935).

However, as Zajonc reviewed the results of social facilitation research over the previous half century, he identified what he felt was a subtle consistency in all of the conflicting reports. He observed that well-learned or simple responses are facilitated by the presence of spectators or coactors, while the acquisition of new responses is impaired. He concluded that the **mere presence** of an audience enhances the emission of the dominant response. In other words, Zajonc was suggesting that Hull-Spence drive theory could provide the theoretical framework for bringing order to chaos. We discussed drive theory in chapter 3 in reference to the arousal-performance relationship.

Zajonc included two experimental paradigms in his model of social facilitation. The first considers the behavior of performers in the presence of passive spectators (the audience effect), and the second considers their behavior in the presence of others engaged in the same activity (the coactive audience effect). In applying drive theory to social facilitation, Zajonc specified that the presence of others is psychologically arousing, and it is this arousal (loosely referred to as drive) that causes the emission of the dominant response. This hypothesis is called **Zajonc's model,** and is illustrated in figure 9.1.

The application of drive theory to social facilitation and to the sport scene is intuitively very appealing. Athletes who are in the process of learning new skills can be expected to suffer from the presence of an audience. Based on the predictions of drive theory, young, inexperienced athletes should be adversely af-

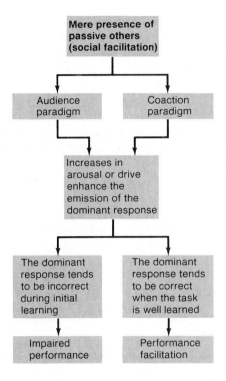

Figure 9.1 Zajonc's social facilitation model. From D. M. Landers and P. D. McCullagh, Social facilitation of motor performance. In *Exercise and Sport Science Reviews,* 1976, *4,* 125–162. Adapted with permission of Lawrence Erlbaum Associates, Inc., Publisher.

fected by the presence of an audience, while experienced athletes should benefit from the additional arousal. While the real world may not be quite as simple as this, this conclusion is very appealing. It is illustrated in figure 9.2.

---

1. **Principle** Beginning athletes can be expected to suffer a performance decrement when playing in front of an audience.
   Application The young athlete needs to be handled with sensitivity. Regardless of how talented they are, beginners when aroused, tend to make errors. Coaches should encourage beginners to accept errors as necessary for learning.

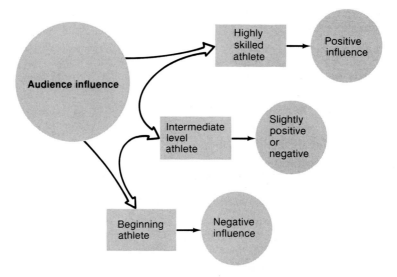

Figure 9.2 The effects of an audience on athletes at various levels of skill. Figure from *Myths and Truths in Sports Psychology* by Robert N. Singer. Copyright © 1975 by Robert N. Singer. Reprinted by permission of Harper & Row Publishers, Inc.

2. **Principle** The performance of the experienced and highly skilled athlete should be facilitated or unaffected by the presence of an audience.

   Application Give tough, pressure-packed assignments to experienced athletes. For example, late in the game, with the outcome in the balance, turn to your experience. If a technical foul has been called against the opposing basketball team, don't automatically send your best free throw shooter to the line. Select an athlete who has both a good free throw shooting record and who has been in the situation before.

A Critique of Social Facilitation

According to Zajonc (1965), the research on social facilitation prior to 1965 was characterized by equivocal findings. Some studies tended to find a facilitative effect in the presence of an audience, while others found just the opposite. Attempts to find consistent trends were believed to be a waste of time. However, Landers and McCullagh (1976) pointed out that this was not entirely correct. A critical review of the social facilitation research prior to 1965 indicates that the effect of an audience on motor performance depends to a great deal on the nature of the task. For example, simple speed and power tasks are generally facilitated by the presence of an audience, while continuous, fine-control accuracy tasks are also facilitated but late in the learning process.

3. **Principle** Simple speed and power tasks are generally facilitated by the presence of an audience.

   Application Coaches should identify those tasks that are readily facilitated by increased arousal. For such tasks, coaches should not try to minimize the audience effect.

Another of Zajonc's generalizations was that between 1930 and 1965 there was a general disinterest in social facilitation research. Consequently, few important studies were conducted on this subject during this time. This was apparently due to the inability of researchers to reconcile the contradictory findings in the literature. However, again, according to Landers (1975), even this conclusion was only partly true. There was a decided decline in animal research on social facilitation during this period, but the research dealing with humans continued somewhat unabated.

Finally, in applying drive theory to social facilitation research, Zajonc observed that the emission of well-learned responses is facilitated by the presence of spectators, while the acquisition of new responses is impaired. In other words, performance (meaning a well-learned response) is facilitated and learning (acquisition of new responses) is impaired by the presence of spectators. However, as with Zajonc's other statements, this one can only be partly verified by the literature. Landers (1975), for example, pointed out that Zajonc's 1965 conclusions were primarily based on animal research. Generalizing to humans was a more difficult task, especially since the literature at that time did not show that the mere presence of an audience could hamper learning among humans.

Arousal and Social Facilitation

Zajonc's (1965) model of social facilitation assumes that the "mere presence" of an audience is arousing. Zajonc's model equates the elevation in physiological arousal with the Hull-Spence concept of drive. Thus, as arousal increases, an organism's drive level also increases. Consequently, whether or not the mere presence of an audience does in fact increase a person's level of arousal is critical to Zajonc's model. Interestingly, when Zajonc published his research paper on social facilitation there was no evidence that the mere presence of an audience was arousing (Landers & McCullagh, 1976). Since then, however, a number of scientific reports have supported Zajonc's basic assumption that the presence of an audience increases drive.

Research since 1965 has consistently demonstrated that physiological arousal is greater for subjects who perform in the presence of an audience or coactors than for those who perform alone. Martens (1969) had subjects learn and perform a timing task with or without the presence of an audience. Palmar sweat prints administered throughout the study showed that the presence of others significantly elevated arousal. Chapman (1974) had subjects listen to a tape-recorded story while alone or in the presence of an audience of one. Arousal levels of subjects were monitored through EMG recordings from the subjects' frontalis muscles. Results clearly showed that subjects performing the task in the presence of a passive audience were significantly more aroused than subjects in the alone condition. Finally, McCullagh and Landers (1976) had subjects perform ball

rolling and simple reaction time tasks while in the presence of from one to six passive observers. Nervousness and activation levels were monitored through Thayer's Activation-Deactivation Checklist. Results indicated that activation and nervousness increased as the size of the audience increased.

---

4. **Principle** The presence of an audience increases the performers' levels of arousal.

   Application Athletes who suffer a performance decrement when playing in front of an audience should use intervention strategies to reduce anxiety and arousal.

Measuring Habit Strength

In applying drive theory to social facilitation research, Zajonc (1965) specified that increased arousal caused by the presence of an audience would elicit the dominant response among several possible responses. Thus, the clear implication is that responses can or should be arranged in hierarchical order so that the theory can be tested. Consequently, the researcher must demonstrate in some way that early in learning, the dominant response is the incorrect response. And the researcher must demonstrate in some way that late in learning, the dominant response is the correct response. In this section, several possible techniques for operationally defining habit strength for motor performance tasks are outlined. A more complete categorization of methods may be found in Carron (1980) and Cottrell (1972).

Learning Phase versus Performance Phase In the early stages of learning a motor task, the incorrect response is considered to be the dominant response. Conversely, during the later stages of learning a motor task, the correct response is considered to be the dominant response. Using Zajonc's terminology, we can argue that a learning curve can be divided into a learning phase and a performance phase. The performance phase begins when the curve becomes asymptotic and performance levels off. It is at this point that the dominant habit shifts from being the incorrect to the correct response.

The weakness of this approach is that the cutoff point for determining whether a response is dominant or nondominant is completely arbitrary. Martens (1969) used such a paradigm in a study using a timing task. In this study, *learning* trials were either the initial fifteen trials or the number required for the subject to reach a certain level of proficiency, whichever came later. After this point, the remaining trials were considered *performance* trials in which the dominant response shifted from the incorrect to the correct response.

Differential Reinforcement The differential reinforcement technique allows the researcher to predetermine which response is dominant and which is nondominant. The technique was first used in social facilitation research by Cottrell, Wack, Sekerak, and Rittle (1968). In motor performance research, Carron and Bennett (1976) used the differential reinforcement procedure with a four-choice reaction time task. The technique involves two phases, a pretest phase and a test phase. In the pretest phase, the subjects develop either a dominant or a nondominant bias for responding in a certain manner. For example, in the Carron and Bennett reaction time study, the subjects in the dominant response condition received extra practice on the correct response so that the correct response was *dominant*. The subjects in the nondominant condition received few practice trials on the correct response so that the correct response was *nondominant*. When the subjects entered into the test phase of the experiment they had a predetermined or learned bias for responding to a certain reaction time button. In this manner, the subject's bias to respond correctly or incorrectly was differentially reinforced.

Characteristics of the Task Perhaps the single best approach for determining habit hierarchy in motor performance research is to select a task that lends itself well to the hierarchical goal. The complex **motor maze** shown in figure 9.3 represents such a task. The motor maze has a specific number of correct and incorrect responses at each level. In completing the task, subjects must negotiate a penlike stylus through each of five levels. On each level, the subject must find the correct response in order to advance to the next level. In the motor maze depicted in figure 9.3, a subject could make 15 incorrect responses before passing through the five levels of the maze to the end. Landers, Brawley, and Hale (1978) used the complex motor maze in a social facilitation investigation. In this study, subjects were divided into five levels of social facilitation, and asked to practice the complex motor maze until they could complete the maze three times in a row without an error. The trials in which a subject made between eight and fifteen errors were labeled the incorrect response—dominant phase, while the trials in which the subject made between zero and seven errors were labeled the correct response–dominant phase.

Thus it was a simple matter to determine those trials in which the dominant response was correct or incorrect.

Research Evidence

Several important studies may be cited that provide experimental support for Zajonc's social facilitation model: Martens (1969); Hunt and Hillery (1973); Landers, Brawley and Hale (1978); and MacCracken and Stadulis (1985).

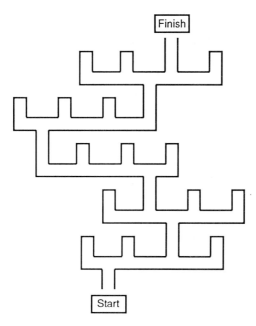

Figure 9.3 Example of a five-level, four choice per level complex motor maze (Landers, Brawley & Hale, 1978). From *Psychology of motor behavior and sport–1977*, D. M. Landers and R. W. Christina (Editors). Reproduced with the permission of Human Kinetics Publishers, Inc.

In the Martens (1969) research, subjects practiced a complex coincidental timing task until they reached a pre-established criterion. The criterion was either to perform three consecutive trials in which the error deviation was ninety milliseconds or less, or perform fifteen trials, whichever came later. At this point the subject was considered to have reached an asymptotic level of performance in which the dominant response shifted from being the incorrect response to the correct one. Zajonc's model was confirmed, since the presence of the audience during the learning phase caused a decrement in performance, while in the performance phase it facilitated performance.

The study by Hunt and Hillery (1973) provides even stronger support for the Zajonc model than did Marten's study. In experiment 1, subjects were randomly assigned to one of four conditions. Conditions 1 and 2 consisted of subjects performing ten trials on a simple motor maze either alone or in the presence of two coactors. In conditions 3 and 4 subjects practiced ten trials on a complex motor maze either alone or in the presence of coactors. Coactors could see each other, but could not see each other's motor maze. In the complex maze conditions, the dominant response was considered to be incorrect, since the probability of a correct response was only .25. In the simple maze conditions, the dominant response was considered to be correct, since the probability of a correct response was .50. The results of the experiment clearly supported drive theory; coacting subjects performed significantly better on the simple maze than those who were alone, while subjects who were alone performed better than coacting subjects on the complex maze.

In experiment 2 of the Hunt and Hillery (1973) investigation, subjects practiced on a four level complex motor maze. They were randomly assigned to either an alone or a coacting condition with two other coactors, and they practiced the task until they could negotiate the maze without any errors. The number of trials needed to navigate the maze with fewer than twelve errors was recorded. Subjects continued the practice trials until errors were reduced to zero. All trials with from six to twelve errors were plotted as stage I (learning phase). All trials with from zero to six errors were plotted as stage II (performance phase). In stage I the dominant response was the incorrect response, while in stage II the dominant response was the correct response. By comparing the slopes of the plotted lines, Hunt and Hillery concluded that the presence of coactors had a facilitative effect on the dominant response, hindering performance when the dominant response was incorrect and facilitating performance when the dominant response was correct.

Landers, Brawley, and Hale (1978) presented evidence of additional support for Zajonc's model. The task was a complex motor maze, and subjects were randomly assigned one of four treatment conditions (alone, coactor, audience, and noise stress conditions). Subjects were required to practice the motor maze until they could negotiate it three times in a row without an error. Trials in which subjects made between eight and fifteen errors were classified in phase 1, the incorrect response—dominant phase. Trials in which subjects made between zero and seven errors were classified in phase 2, the correct response—dominant phase. As predicted by drive theory, subjects in the experimental conditions made more errors in phase 1 and fewer errors in phase 2.

Consistent with Zajonc's model, MacCracken and Stadulis (1985) reported a developmental study in which the presence of an audience facilitated the motor performance of high-skilled children while causing a performance decrement in low-skilled children. Using several dynamic balancing tasks, the authors also reported a developmental effect relative to the presence of spectators. The presence of an audience has a greater effect on eight-year-old children than on younger children.

Cottrell's Evaluation Apprehension

Cottrell's notion of **evaluation apprehension** does not challenge Zajonc's basic model in its application of drive theory to social facilitation. But it challenges Zajonc's position that the mere presence of others is enough to cause a social facilitation effect. Cottrell (1972) reasoned that the mere presence of an audience is not enough to increase drive; in order for an audience to increase arousal, it must be capable of critically evaluating the subject's performance. Cottrell believed that this evaluation factor is a learned source of drive. That is, subjects react to evaluative audiences with increased levels of arousal because of previous experience with evaluation apprehension. To Cottrell, an audience that is merely present cannot evaluate and cannot cause an increase in arousal. Zajonc (1972), on the other hand, argued that the presence of an audience causes an increase in arousal by creating an atmosphere of uncertainty, not evaluation apprehension.

Evidence in favor of the evaluation apprehension notion was first presented by Cottrell, Wack, Sekerak, and Rittle (1968). In this study, which used nonsense syllables, subjects perceived blindfolded spectators differently than they perceived spectators who were capable of evaluating their performances. Blindfolded observers did not heighten physiological arousal, nor did they facilitate or inhibit performance. Subjects who performed in front of blindfolded observers exhibited results identical to those of subjects performing alone. Conversely, the subjects who performed in front of observers who were capable of evaluating their performances exhibited performance scores consistent with drive theory. During the initial phase of learning, performance was inhibited, while in the latter stages of learning, performance was facilitated.

Evidence supporting Cottrell's evaluation apprehension notion has also been documented in the motor domain using physical rather than verbal tasks (Haas & Roberts, 1975; Martens & Landers, 1972). In the Haas and Roberts experiment, subjects practiced the mirror tracing task under one of three audience conditions. The three audience conditions were alone, in front of blindfolded observers, and in front of a passive but evaluative audience. The results of this study were very supportive of drive theory, and mildly supportive of Cottrell's notion of evaluation apprehension. In one part of the experiment, the subjects practiced the mirror tracing task without any previous experience. Thus, the dominant response was considered to be the incorrect response. In a second part of the experiment, a different group of subjects did the same thing, but only after considerable practice on the mirror tracing device. Thus, the dominant response was considered to be the correct response. In the case of the initial learning part of the experiment, the alone condition exhibited superior performance scores, with no difference between the two audience conditions. In the case of the late-in-learning part of the experiment, subjects in the evaluative audience condition

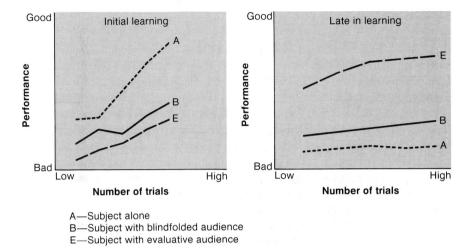

A—Subject alone
B—Subject with blindfolded audience
E—Subject with evaluative audience

Figure 9.4 Audience effects on subjects' performances in a mirror tracing task at two different points in the learning process. From J. Haas and G. C. Roberts, Effect of evaluative others upon learning and performance. *Journal of Motor Behaviour, 1,* 81–90, 1975. Reprinted with permission of the Helen Dwight Reid Educational Foundation. Published by Heldref Publications, 4000 Albemarle St., N.W., Washington, D.C. 20016. Copyright © 1975.

performed better than those in the other two conditions. However, those in the blindfolded condition also performed better than the subjects who were alone. These results conflict somewhat with Cottrell's evaluative apprehension theory, since according to Cottrell the blindfolded audience should have had an effect similar to the alone condition. If the critical factor in social facilitation was fear of being evaluated, the blindfolded audience in the Haas and Roberts research should have had no more effect on arousal and performance than if the subjects had been alone. Yet, subjects with a blindfolded audience performed better than those who were alone when the motor task was well learned, and performed the same as those with an evaluative audience when the task was novel. This suggests that the blindfolded audience contributes to heightened arousal in some manner other than fear of evaluation. The results of the Haas and Roberts (1975) research are illustrated in figure 9.4.

Psychological Presence

In explaining why a passive audience affects performance and elevates arousal, Zajonc speaks of the "uncertainty" caused by an audience (Zajonc, 1972), while Cottrell speaks of "evaluative apprehension." Perhaps the essence of these two

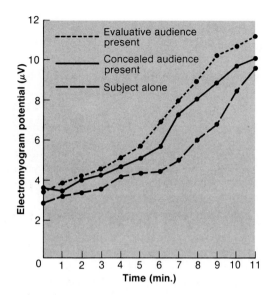

Figure 9.5 The effect of increased psychological presence upon arousal. From A. J. Chapman, An electromyographical study of social facilitation: A test of the mere presence hypothesis. *British Journal of Psychology, 65,* 123–128, 1974. Adapted with permission of the British Psychological Society.

concepts is captured by Chapman's concept of psychological presence. According to Chapman (1974), **psychological presence** represents the degree to which a performer feels the presence of an audience. With this concept, the results of the Haas and Roberts study can be easily explained. Placing the notion of psychological presence on a continuum, we can see that an evaluative audience would produce the greatest amount of arousal, followed by the blindfolded audience and the alone condition.

This is exactly what Chapman found in his 1974 study, in which he recorded muscle action potentials associated with three audience conditions. In this research, subjects were asked to listen to a tape-recorded story through headphones while EMG recordings were taken from the frontalis muscles of their foreheads. Subjects were assigned to either an alone condition, a concealed audience condition, or an evaluative audience condition. The results of this study are displayed in figure 9.5. As can be observed, as the *psychological presence* of the audience increased, the level of physiological arousal also increased.

5. **Principle** The level of arousal mediated by an audience is directly
   related to the psychological presence of the audience.

   Application Large but uninvolved audiences will have little effect
   of motivating athletes. When confronted with an uninvolved
   audience, the coach will need to find other ways to increase the
   activation level of underaroused athletes.

Alternatives to Zajonc's Model

At the present time, drive theory and Zajonc's model provide the best theoretical explanation for observed social facilitation effects (Geen & Gange, 1977). However, since the adequacy of the Zajonc model has been found wanting in some cases, researchers such as Landers (1980b) and Wankel (1980) have argued against it, suggesting that alternatives be sought.

Since it has been clearly demonstrated that the presence of an audience increases the level of physiological arousal (Chapman, 1974), it follows that any proposed alternative theory should address the arousal-performance relationship. In our earlier discussion on the relationship between arousal and performance (chapter 3), two basic theories were proposed. These two theories were *Drive Theory* (the basis of Zajonc's model) and *Inverted-U Theory*. Thus, if a viable alternative to drive theory is sought for explaining social facilitation, we might first look to Inverted-U Theory.

One explanation for the social facilitation phenomenon, as proposed by Landers and McCullagh (1976), is that audiences are distracting and lead to increased arousal on the part of the performer. In support of this notion, Baron, Moore, and Sanders (1978) demonstrated that subjects in the presence of an audience score higher on a distraction index than those who are alone. However, they also provided additional support for Zajonc's model and Drive Theory as opposed to Inverted-U Theory. Performance on a simple motor task was facilitated by the presence of a passive audience, while performance on a complex task was inhibited.

Closely related to the notion of audience distraction is the notion of attentional narrowing and cue utilization. According to Easterbrook (1959), increased arousal results in a narrowing of attentional focus. When arousal is low, attentional focus is very broad. The wide band of attentional focus allows the athlete to be distracted by irrelevant cues that could cause a decrement in performance. This would explain why subjects performing alone might perform at a lower level than subjects performing in front of an audience. When arousal is very high, attention narrows to the point that even relevant cues are gated out. This results in a decrement in performance as well. It could be caused by a severely distracting or arousing crowd. Finally, if arousal is just right, then only irrelevant cues are gated out and performance is at its best. This would explain why the presence of an audience often results in an improvement in performance compared to a control condition. Attentional narrowing predicts an inverted-U relationship between performance and arousal.

Easterbrook's cue utilization theory handles the problem of task difficulty by positing that the attentional band is much narrower for simple tasks than for complex tasks. Consequently, high arousal would gate out relevant cues much more quickly for a complex task than for a single or well-learned task.

Although a great deal of experimental evidence has accumulated on Easterbrook's cue utilization theory, it has seldom been linked with social facilitation theory. While it may be a viable alternative to drive theory for explaining social facilitation, there is no direct evidence to verify this.

Finally, signal detection theory has been proposed as an alternative to drive theory for explaining the social facilitation phenomenon (Landers, 1980b). As with Easterbrook's cue utilization theory, few studies have actually used signal detection as a theoretical model to explain social facilitation. One notable exception is an investigation by Kushnir and Duncan (1978).

Signal detection theory makes an operational distinction between a subject's actual sensitivity to an event (d') and the subject's response criterion for that event (beta). Drive theory, on the other hand, tends to look only at a subject's response bias. This is because of the dominant response notion in drive theory. Consequently, in many drive theory studies great care is taken to establish a response bias between two or more possible responses; that is, to establish which is the dominant response. Thus, in many cases it is only the subject's bias to respond in a certain manner that serves as the dependent variable. Signal detection theory, on the other hand, allows both the subject's sensitivity and response bias to be measured.

In the Kushnir and Duncan (1978) study, twenty-six undergraduates were randomly assigned to either an alone or an audience condition. Subjects were given a word cancellation task in which they were to cross out words that had 2, 3, 7, 8, or 9 letters in them. These words represented nonsignals or "noise" in the experiment. In this study, drive theory would predict more errors for the audience condition, since the task was decidedly complex. The results showed a significantly greater number of errors for the audience condition than for the alone condition. Drive theory would conclude that impairment occurred because of an increase in the number of incorrect dominant responses at the expense of the correct ones. However, an examination of the results according to signal detection theory revealed that the response biases for the two conditions were equal, while sensitivity favored the alone condition. Subjects who were alone were better able to discriminate between the "signal" and the "noise," although the response biases for the two conditions were identical.

Conclusion

Zajonc's model of social facilitation provides a credible explanation for the effect that a passive audience has on motor performance. In an athletic environment, the mere presence of an audience or coactors will increase an athlete's physiological arousal. The effect of increased arousal on performance depends on the

skill level of the athlete. If the athlete is highly skilled, the presence of an audience should facilitate performance. If the athlete is a beginner or relatively unskilled, the effect of an audience should be to cause a decrement in performance. If the task to be performed is relatively simple, increased arousal should enhance performance regardless of the athlete's experience.

It is unfair for a coach to expect a beginning athlete to perform like a veteran in front of an audience. Instead, the coach should allow the athlete to develop slowly. Errors will occur, and the athlete should be taught to expect this. The athlete who becomes more experienced and skilled will come to enjoy performing before an audience. The added arousal caused by the presence of an audience or coactors will facilitate performance as long as it does not become too high.

As the research evidence suggests, there are situations in which drive theory fails to explain the effects that an audience has on performance. For example, drive theory cannot easily explain why experienced athletes are sometimes negatively affected by the presence of an audience. In such situations it may be necessary to turn to cue utilization or signal detection theory for a more complete explanation.

Interactive Audiences

In the first part of this chapter, we discussed noninteractive audiences. This approach to studying audience effects was useful because uncontrollable variables were excluded. But while useful and necessary from a research design point of view, this approach presents problems for the practitioner and coach. Most athletic situations involve interactions among athletes and between athlete and spectator.

Therefore, an **interactive audience** is one in which the audience has verbal, visual, and emotional contact with the athletic participants.

In considering the effects that an interactive audience has on athletic performance, it is important for you to keep in mind the theoretical framework developed in the previous section relative to social facilitation. Factors to be considered in this section include the home court advantage, visiting team disadvantage, audience size and intimacy, the hostile crowd, audience sophistication, the home court disadvantage, gender, and competition among coactors.

Home-Court Advantage

Perhaps the most interesting topic associated with the interactive audience is that of the **home court advantage.** The fact that there is a home court advantage in such sports as basketball, baseball, football, and ice hockey is well documented (Schwartz & Barsky, 1977). However, what is not well documented is why it exists. Some authors have argued that it is related to such negative factors as travel, jet lag, unfamiliar surroundings, sleeping arrangements, and changed eating habits. While these factors may contribute to the home court advantage, most authors agree that the significant factor is related to whether the audience is supportive or hostile.

In recent years, several important studies have been conducted on the home court advantage phenomenon. The first, and perhaps most ambitious was that of Schwartz and Barsky (1977). These authors gathered statistical information on 1,880 major league baseball games, 1,092 professional and collegiate football games, 542 National Hockey League games, and 1,485 college basketball games. Their results clearly supported the home court advantage phenomenon, as the home team won 53 percent of the time in baseball, 60 percent in football, and 64 percent in basketball and ice hockey. In addition, their data showed that the home court advantage was due to audience support, and that a resulting improvement in the home team's offense was the critical underlying factor.

Varca (1980) proposed and tested a specific hypothesis for explaining the home court advantage. His theory was that the home court advantage was attributable to more functionally aggressive play on the part of the home team and dysfunctionally aggressive play on the part of the visiting team. Increased arousal caused by the crowd was believed to facilitate the aggression.

In Varca's terminology, **functional aggressive behavior** in basketball included the skills of rebounding, steals, and blocked shots, behavior that facilitated performance. **Dysfunctional aggressive behavior** was delimited to personal fouls, behavior that hampered performance. Skills such as turnovers and field goal and free throw shooting percentages were not categorized in terms of aggressive behavior. Theoretically, home and away teams should not differ on these three game statistics.

Based on our definition of aggression in chapter 8, Varca's notion of functional and dysfunctional aggression is somewhat misleading. Perhaps the terms functional and dysfunctional *assertive* behavior would be more accurate. The basketball skills of rebounding, shot blocking, and stealing rarely involve the intent to harm, although they could. Additionally, the dysfunctional statistic of fouling is as likely to be related to assertiveness as it is to aggression. There is no question, however, that personal fouls provide an excellent example of dysfunctional behavior.

Varca, using the archival method, collected game statistics for all men's collegiate basketball games played during the 1977–1978 season in the Southeastern Conference. The dependent variables included were field goal percentages, free-throw percentages, turnovers, steals, blocked shots, fouls, and rebounds.

As predicted by Varca's hypothesis, significant differences were noted between home and away teams on the functionally "aggressive" skills of stealing, blocking shots, and rebounding. The home teams enjoyed a superiority in these three important skills. Additionally, the visiting teams had significantly more fouls than the home teams. There were no observed differences between the home and away teams in terms of field goal percentages, free-throw percentages, or turnovers.

Based on the results, Varca concluded that the presence of a supportive crowd increased the arousal of the home team. This increased arousal was instrumental in enhancing performance on such functionally "aggressive" skills as rebounding, steals, and blocked shots. The presence of the crowd also increased the arousal level of the visiting team. However, in this case arousal was instrumental in producing increased dysfunctional behavior in the form of personal fouls. Varca explained this result in terms of the frustration-aggression hypothesis.

Varca's research is very helpful in explaining why the presence of a roaring crowd could facilitate the home team's performance but inhibit that of the visiting team. The skills involved in rebounding, stealing, and blocking shots are closely associated with strength and speed. These are the kinds of gross motor skills that would be facilitated by very high arousal. While trying to negate the functional "aggressive" behavior of the home team, the visiting team gets whistled for personal fouls. This causes increased frustration, and more dysfunctional behavior results.

Varca's research is based primarily on the notion that home and visiting teams differ in terms of functional and dysfunctional "aggressive" behavior. This is borne out by his data, because the home and away teams did not differ in terms of field goal and free-throw shooting percentages.

Other studies that have reported a clear win-loss advantage for the home team include Silva and Andrew (1987), Silva, Andrew, and Richey (1983), and Snyder and Purdy (1985). In the Snyder and Purdy (1985) study the home team in the Mid-American Conference won 66 percent of the basketball contests during the 1982–1983 season. In the Atlantic Coast Conference, Silva and Andrew (1987) also reported that the home team won 66 percent of their basketball games between 1971 and 1981. It is clear that a home-team advantage exists for the sports of basketball, ice hockey, football, and baseball. There is little reason to doubt that this advantage also exists for other team sports such as soccer and rugby as well as many individual sports (Edwards, 1979). However, the home-field advantage does seem to be a little stronger for professional and college sports rather than high school sport teams (McCutcheon, 1984).

6. **Principle** The presence of a supportive and emotionally arousing crowd translates into a home court advantage in many situations.
Application Since the home court advantage is a function of fan support, it is important to capitalize on this advantage by filling the stadium or fieldhouse. Additionally, the band, the cheering squad, and publicity should be used to generate excitement and enthusiasm.

The Away-Court Disadvantage

While it is clear that a home court advantage exists for many team sports, it is not entirely clear that the win-loss advantage enjoyed by the home team is due to increased performance on the part of the home team. From a theoretical perspective, it is reasonable to assume that an aroused and supportive crowd will have a special facilitory effect on the home team. However, it is also possible that the home field or court advantage is due to a decrement in performance on the part of the visiting team rather than an increment in performance on the part of the home team.

In a study designed to determine if a home or away court disadvantage exists in the Atlantic Coast Conference, Silva and Andrew (1987) examined archival data on 418 basketball games from 1971 to 1981. Performance indicators included field goal percentage, free throw percentage, turnovers, personal fouls, and rebounds. Performance comparisons indicated that the home team enjoyed a higher field goal shooting percentage, fewer turnovers, fewer personal fouls, and more rebounds than the visiting team. A significant difference was not observed between the free throw shooting percentages of home and visiting teams.

Silva and Andrew (1987) also compared each team's actual performance with a standardized estimate of average performance. The standardized estimates of team performance were supplied by the coaches prior to each contest. By comparing actual performance with expected performance, it was possible to determine if home or away game performance was better than expected (facilitation), worse than expected (decrement), or no different than expected (no change).

Silva and Andrew (1987) reported that an away court disadvantage existed for field goal shooting percentage, turnovers, and personal fouls. Only in the case of rebounding was there an indication of a home court advantage. In most cases, the home team outperformed the visiting team, but not because the home team was performing better than expected. Rather, the visiting team suffered a decrement in performance in terms of fouls committed, turnovers, and field goal shooting percentage.

---

7. **Principle** Winning on the road can be enhanced by understanding the nature of the home court advantage.

   Application When playing away from home, it is important that the coach develop a careful game plan and stay with it. The game plan should emphasize patience on offense, tactics to keep the crowd calm, and careful avoidance of penalties and fouls.

Audience Size and Intimacy

One might expect that increasing the size of an audience or the number of coactors would automatically increase arousal level and hence amplify the social facilitation effect. This conclusion has received empirical support in the coaction literature (Burwitz & Newell, 1972; Martens & Landers, 1969, 1972). For example, Martens and Landers (1969) observed that a leg extension muscular endurance task was enhanced when subjects performed in groups of four instead of singly or in pairs. Similarly, performance on a complex "roll-up game" task was inhibited when subjects performed in groups of four as compared to one, two, or three per group.

Laboratory research on the subject of **audience size**—the number of people in an audience—and motor performance is equivocal. Studies by McCullagh and Landers (1976) and Wankel (1977) have shown that motor performance tasks are largely unaffected by the number of observers. But it was demonstrated that arousal levels increased as the number of onlookers increased.

Schwartz and Barsky (1977) demonstrated that audience size is related to performance in baseball. They observed that the winning percentage of home teams increased as the size of the crowd increased. This effect is most pronounced when first-division home teams play visiting teams from the second division. Data from other sports such as basketball, football, and ice hockey are virtually nonexistent on this subject.

The Schwartz and Barsky (1977) research show that basketball and ice hockey enjoy a greater home court advantage than baseball and football. Since baseball and football normally accommodate a far greater number of fans than basketball and/or ice hockey, factors such as **audience density** and **audience intimacy** may be more important than size for creating the home court advantage (Edwards, 1979). In basketball and ice hockey the fans are often very close and intimate with the athletes.

---

8. **Principle** The home court advantage is related to audience size and intimacy.

   Application The more people there are in the audience and the more intimate and close the audience is to the athletes, the greater the home court advantage. For this reason, filling the stands and creating an intimate environment is a good strategy, even if it means lowering ticket prices.

The Hostile Crowd

It is generally accepted that a supportive and friendly crowd will help the home team (Singer, 1975). However, what is the effect of a seemingly hostile and protesting crowd on player performance? Early research by Laird (1923) demonstrated that **audience hostility** had a detrimental effect on a subject's performance in a controlled laboratory situation. Relatively recent research by Greer (1983) demonstrated that sustained hostile spectator protest has a clearly negative impact on the visiting team. Home basketball games of two Division I basketball teams were monitored and studied. Observations of sustained spectator protest were identified and studied relative to subsequent skill performance. Following episodes of sustained fan protest (usually directed at officials) the performance of athletes were monitored for five minutes of running game time. The results of the research showed a slight improvement in the performance of the home team paralleled by a more significant and pronounced decline in performance of the visiting team following spectator protest.

Arie Selinger, former head coach of the women's national volleyball team, can attest to the devastating effect of a hostile audience (Steers, 1982). Arie took his heavily favored women's team to Peru in 1982 to compete in the World Championships. Everything went according to plan until the USA team played Peru. That was when the crowd took over. For two hours, it was impossible to communicate verbally with players, coach, or officials. The highly unsportsmanlike fans were armed with whistles and noisemakers. Each time a USA player went back to serve, the noise was deafening. "The sound came down like thunder. You could feel the vibrations. You're totally disoriented. It's a terrible experience," said Coach Selinger. A father of one of the athletes summed it up this way: "The team prepared for nine months to win the World Championships and they were beaten by a wireless microphone and fifteen thousand plastic whistles."

---

9. **Principle** A supportive audience is important for the home team. However, the home team should make sure that the mood of an audience does not turn ugly and hostile.

   Application It is unethical and unsportsmanlike to promote fan hostility in support of the home team. Coaches, managers, and team officials are morally obligated to avoid such a situation.

Audience Sophistication

Audience sophistication is related to the degree of knowledge and understanding that an audience possesses. Research evidence suggests that when performers are aware that observers are highly skilled and knowledgeable, the psychological presence or evaluative potential of the situation is very high. According to drive theory, this would result in elevated drive and hence facilitation or inhibition of the dominant response (Gore & Taylor, 1973; Henchy & Glass, 1968). For example, playing a game of basketball in front of spectators who do not understand the game would not involve as much evaluative potential as playing in front of experts. The naive audience would not know if you were playing well or not. The same principle should apply in the case of coactors. Playing alongside other athletes who are skilled should be more arousing than playing novices.

10. **Principle** Audience sophistication is related to the important concept of psychological presence identified in figure 9.5.

    Application Fans must be educated about the subtleties of the sport they are watching. A stadium full of uninformed spectators will not be as effective as a stadium full of sophisticated fans. A slam dunk in basketball would be rather unimpressive without the associated roar from the partisan crowd.

The Home-Court Disadvantage

Is the home court or field always an advantage, or is it sometimes a disadvantage? From a drive theory perspective, the home field could easily translate into a disadvantage for young and/or less skillful players. For example, Snyder and Purdy (1985) reported that when second division teams in the Mid-American Conference play at home against first division teams, the home team only wins 40 percent of the time. Playing before the home crowd can be very arousing. Since increased arousal causes the elicitation of the dominant response, according to drive theory, less skillful players may revert to past bad habits or incorrect responses.

In addition, the evidence suggests that even highly skilled players may suffer from a home court disadvantage due to a state of **self-attention.** In some cases, the presence of a supportive audience increases the cost of not winning when one is expected to win (Baumeister & Steinhilber, 1984). In a sense, the athlete begins to "press," which interferes with the execution of a skillful response.

Support for the self-attention concept comes from research with professional baseball and basketball. Baumeister and Steinhilber (1984) analyzed archival data from World Series games played between 1924 and 1982 and National Basketball Championship and semifinal games between 1967 and 1982. The data for

11. **Principle** In baseball and basketball, a home court disadvantage may exist during critical final games when the favored team is "expected to win."

    Application In a critical game situation, when the home team fans expect a win, the coach must devise a game plan that takes the pressure off the athletes. For example, athletes could be coached to focus on external factors associated with a team strategy rather than themselves.

both baseball and basketball shows that the home team tends to win the early contests (60 percent in baseball and 70 percent in basketball) but lose the last or final games when played at home. For example, when the World Series went to seven games, the home team only won the final game 38.5 percent of the time. In basketball, when the NBA series went to the seventh and final game, the home team again only won 38.5 percent of the time.

Gender

Performing alone or in front of an audience does not affect men and women differently (Murray, 1983). However, during coaction, women are more susceptible to the social facilitation effect than are men (Chapman, 1973).

In terms of the sex of the subject and the sex of the observer, it has been observed that preadolescent boys perform better in the presence of a male adult than in the presence of a female adult (Fouts, 1980). Crable and Johnson (1980) obtained similar results in a study involving competitive coaction. Thus, it appears that if the audience or coactors are of the opposite sex, the potential for an audience effect increases.

Competition among Coactors

In Triplett's (1897) classic research, cyclists in paced competition had faster times than unpaced or paced racers. However, Moede (1914) observed a leveling effect among subjects of varying ability who were engaged in competitive coaction. This effect has also been observed more recently in research by Carment (1970) and Hunt and Hillery (1973). The **leveling effect** simply means that when coactors of unequal ability compete with each other, there is a tendency for the performance level of the coactors to become more alike. The performance of the less skilled subjects improves, while the performance of the more skilled subjects declines. Thus, rivalry does not always result in enhanced performance. However, if coactors are of equal ability, competition should enhance motivation, and results should be generally consistent with the predictions of drive theory (Church, 1962).

In application, this means that competition between two competitors will not always result in increased drive on the part of both athletes. This is especially true in the case of a large difference in skill level between competitors. The less skilled athlete will be motivated to try hard, but the highly skilled athlete may be content to play just well enough to win. This results in both athletes playing near the same level. This explains why less skilled athletes often have their best matches against vastly superior opponents.

12. **Principle** When coactors of unequal ability compete with each other there is a tendency for the performance level of the coactors to become more alike. This is referred to as the leveling effect.

   Application The leveling effect is beneficial to the less skilled performer but may prove detrimental to the higher skilled performer. In team sport situations, this is a good time for the coach of the superior team to substitute. In individual sport situations the superior athlete should use this time to work on a weak or largely ignored part of his or her game.

Summary

Audience effects are considered either as noninteractive or interactive situations. Social facilitation research is considered under the noninteractive classification. Factors considered under the interactive classification include home court advantage, audience size, spectator mood, audience sophistication, gender, and competition.

Zajonc's model of social facilitation is based on drive theory. The model considers the effects of the mere presence of coactors or an audience on a subject's performance and physiological arousal. According to Zajonc, increased drive enhances the emission of the dominant response.

According to Cottrell's evaluation apprehension theory, the presence of an audience is arousing only if the audience is capable of evaluating performance. Thus, the mere presence of blindfolded subjects would not be arousing. The notion of psychological presence explains the apparent contradiction between Zajonc's model and Cottrell's reformulation.

The home court advantage in sport is a function of fan support. Teams that play at home tend to be more assertive in terms of functional "aggressive" behavior. Visiting teams may suffer a decrement in performance because of the increase in dysfunctional behavior, which results in more fouls called against them.

Other factors that may affect the home court advantage or visiting team disadvantage include audience size and intimacy, crowd hostility, audience sophistication, home court disadvantage, gender, and competition among coactors.

Review Questions

1. Outline Zajonc's model of social facilitation in terms of drive theory and type of audience.
2. Discuss the difficulty of testing Zajonc's model with regard to the notion of a dominant response.
3. How does Zajonc's model compare to other explanations for social facilitation? Compare research findings.
4. What does Cottrell's notion of evaluative apprehension add to the usefulness of Zajonc's model? Explain.
5. Explain the notion of psychological presence relative to evaluation apprehension and the mere presence of an audience.
6. Identify audience factors that contribute to the home court advantage.
7. What can the visiting team do to minimize the effect of the home court advantage?
8. Discuss functional and dysfunctional "aggression" in relation to assertiveness, arousal, and the home court advantage.
9. What is the nature of the away court disadvantage? How does it relate to the notion of a home court or field advantage?
10. What is the effect of audience size and/or number of coactors on athletic performance?
11. What effect does a hostile audience have on the outcome of a sporting event? Explain.
12. What effects do audience mood and sophistication have on athletic performance?
13. In some cases playing at home can be a disadvantage. Discuss situations in which this might be true. How does the concept of "self-attention" enter into the possibility of a home disadvantage?
14. What are the effects of audience or coactor gender on athletic performance?

Glossary

audience Observers or spectators of an athletic event.
audience density The number of fans crowded into a fieldhouse or stadium.
audience hostility The level of hostility that the audience expresses toward officials and visiting team.
audience intimacy The closeness of the crowd to the athlete.
audience size The number of spectators in an audience.

audience sophistication How knowledgeable the fans are about the sport.

coactive audience An audience of one or more people who are performing the same task as the subject, independent of the subject.

coactor An individual who is performing the same task as the subject, but independent of the subject.

dysfunctional aggressive behavior Aggressive or assertive behavior, such as fouling, that interferes with successful performance.

evaluation apprehension Cottrell's notion that an audience is arousing only if it is perceived to be evaluating performance.

functional aggressive behavior Aggressive or assertive behavior such as rebounding, stealing, and shot-blocking in basketball that facilitates successful performance.

home court advantage The notion that playing at home is an advantage because of fan support.

interactive audience An audience that interacts verbally and emotionally with the athletes.

leveling effect The effect observed when highly skilled athletes compete with less skilled athletes. The highly skilled athletes perform beneath their abilities, while the less skilled opponents are at their best.

mere presence Term used by Zajonc to describe the facilitative effect of a noninteractive audience.

motor maze Apparatus used in social facilitation research that allows the experimenter to discriminate between dominant and nondominant responses.

noninteractive audience An audience that is passive and does not interact verbally or emotionally with the performer.

paradigm An example or pattern that explains a theory or model.

psychological presence The degree to which a performer feels the presence of an audience.

self-attention The degree to which an athlete begins to "press" and worry about execution of skills.

social facilitation The benefits or detriments associated with the presence of a noninteractive audience.

Zajonc's model A model of social facilitation based on drive theory.

Recommended Readings

Baumeister, R. F., & Steinhilber, A. (1984). Paradoxical effects of supportive audiences on performance under pressure: The home field advantage in sports championships. *Journal of Personality and Psychology, 47,* 85–93.

Chapman, A. J. (1974). An electromyographic study of social facilitation: A test of the "mere presence" hypothesis. *British Journal of Psychology, 65,* 123–128.

Cottrell, N. B., Wack, D. L., Sekerak, G. L., & Rittle, R. H. (1968). Social facilitation of dominant responses by the presence of an audience and the mere presence of others. *Journal of Personality and Social Psychology, 9,* 245–250.

Geen, R. G., & Gange, J. G. (1977). Drive theory of social facilitation: Twelve years of theory and research. *Psychological Bulletin, 84,* 1267–1288.

Greer, D. L. (1983). Spectator booing and the home advantage: A study of social influence in the basketball arena. *Social Psychology Quarterly, 46,* 252–261.

Hunt, P. J., & Hillery, J. M. (1973). Social facilitation in a coaction setting: An examination of the effects over learning trials. *Journal of Experimental Social Psychology, 9,* 563–571.

Landers, D. M. (1975). Social facilitation and human performance: A review of contemporary and past research. In D. M. Landers (ed.), *Psychology of sport and motor behavior II.* University Park: Pennsylvania State University Press.

Landers, D. M. (1980b). The arousal-performance relationship revisited. *Research Quarterly for Exercise and Sport, 51,* 77–90.

Landers, D. M., & McCullagh, P. D. (1976). Social facilitation of motor performance. *Exercise and Sport Sciences Reviews, 4,* 125–162.

Schwartz, B., & Barsky, S. F. (1977). The home advantage. *Social Forces, 55,* 641–661.

Silva, J. M., III, & Andrew, J. A. (1987). An analysis of game location and basketball performance in the Atlantic coast conference. *International Journal of Sport Psychology, 18,* 188–204.

Snyder, E. E., & Purdy, D. A. (1985). The home advantage in collegiate basketball. *Sociology of Sport Journal, 2,* 352–356.

Varca, P. E. (1980). An analysis of home and away game performance of male college basketball teams. *Journal of Sport Psychology, 2,* 245–257.

Zajonc, R. B. (1965). Social facilitation. *Science, 149,* 269–274.

10   Team Cohesion

Key Terms

coactive sports
competitive social
   situation
conceptual model of
   team cohesion
consequences
cooperative social
   situation
cross-lagged panel
   design
determinants
direct measure
group cohesion
Group Environment
   Questionnaire
group integration
high means
   interdependence
indirect measure
individual attraction
individualistic behavior
interactive sports

low means
   interdependence
meta-analysis
multidimensional
   approach
satisfaction
social cohesion
sociogram
sociometric measure
Sport Cohesion
   Instrument
Sports Cohesiveness
   Questionnaire
task cohesion
team cohesion
Team Cohesion
   Questionnaire
team homogeneity
team stability
unidimensional
   approach

Fundamental to the study of team cohesion is the understanding of group dynamics (Fisher, 1982). Members of a team or group begin to interact with each other the moment the group is first formed. Once a group is formed, it ceases to interact with outside forces in the same manner that a collection of individuals would. The team becomes an entity in and of itself. From a Gestalt perspective, the whole (group or team) is greater than the sum of its parts.

In sport, it is a well-established principle that a group of individuals working together are far more effective than the same individuals working independent of one another. On a basketball team, there may be several individuals capable of scoring 20 or more points a game. However, out of interest of team success, the coach may require that one or more of these athletes assume nonscoring roles. For example, a point guard has the primary responsibility of setting up plays and getting the offense started, while the power forward must "crash" the boards and get offensive and defensive rebounds. Athletes who play these specialized roles rarely score as many points as a shooting guard or forward. Yet, out of a desire to be a "team player" these athletes accept less glamorous roles for the common good of the team. Thus, as a group or team evolves, a certain structure develops. This structure varies from group to group and situation to situation, but it is critical for team success.

Not only do members of successful teams have the ability to work together (teamwork), but they also enjoy a certain attraction to one another. In this respect, it seems logical that teams composed of members who like each other and who enjoy playing together will somehow be more successful than teams lacking this quality. In 1979, the Pittsburgh Pirates won the World Series. Their theme was "We are Family," suggesting that they owed their success to this ability to get along and work together for a common goal. Ironically, the Oakland Athletics of the early 1970s and the New York Yankees in 1978 also enjoyed World Series success, but with well-publicized disharmony within their ranks.

The team attraction or "chemistry" necessary to bring the best out of a group of athletes appeared to be lacking in the 1988 Cincinnati Reds major league baseball team. After being picked to win the National League West, the Reds led by Pete Rose suffered a lackluster season. In attempting to explain how the talent-laden team could perform so poorly, Rob Murphy, a relief pitcher reportedly made the following observation (Kay, 1988):

> We've got a funny chemistry here. It's a strange mixture of guys. They're all good guys: I don't have any personal problems with any of them. They are guys who have great talent and good dispositions, but the mix—something's not there. I can't really explain it other than it's a strange chemistry (p. 15).

Early research on the subject of team cohesion often resulted in contradictory findings. For example, Lenk (1969) reported that Olympic and world championship rowing teams can experience success despite strong internal conflicts. However, Klein and Christensen (1969) demonstrated that in three-on-three basketball, team performance was related to team cohesion.

While the relationship between team cohesion and performance is not crystal clear, we can make the apparent contradictions easier to explain. For example, we now know that team cohesion is a *multidimensional* as opposed to a *unidimensional* variable. Different results can be obtained depending on which aspect of team cohesion is considered.

In the balance of the chapter, I will discuss team cohesion under the following broad headings: defining team cohesion, measurement of team cohesion, determinants of team cohesion, consequences of team cohesion, and developing team cohesion.

Defining Team Cohesion

Our basic understanding of team cohesion comes from the study of small groups and group interaction relative to the parent discipline of sociology and social-psychology (McGrath, 1984; Zander, 1982). From a sociological perspective, an effective group is much more than a collection of individuals. Individuals working together toward a common goal are much more effective than the same individuals working independently. This observation certainly applies to athletic teams such as soccer, basketball, and football where team success is dependent on how the total team performs as opposed to how individuals perform independently. In retrospect, it would appear that the 1977 Portland Trail Blazers led by Bill Walton provided a good example of a team that worked well together. Portland defeated a very talented Philadelphia 76ers basketball team for the 1977 NBA Championship. While Philadelphia seemed to have had the best athletes, Portland had the best team. The manner in which individual members of a group interact with each other constitutes the study of group cohesion or what I will refer to in this chapter as **team cohesion.**

There have been a number of definitions proposed to explain the nature and meaning of the term team cohesion. For example, Festinger, Schachter, and Back (1950) defined **group cohesion** as the total field of forces that act on members to remain in a group. Similarly, we could refer to *team cohesion* as the total field of forces that act on members to remain on a team.

From a sport-specific perspective, the Festinger, et al. definition is not very satisfying, since it fails to take into consideration either the dynamic nature of team cohesion or the importance of team goals and objectives. For this reason,

Albert Carron, a prominent sport social-psychologist defined team cohesion as "a dynamic process which is reflected in the tendency for a group to stick together and remain united in the pursuit of goals and objectives" (Carron, 1982, p. 124). It is the Carron definition that has been adopted for my discussion of team cohesion in this chapter.

Cartwright's Basic Model

In this chapter I will discuss several factors that are believed to lead to increased team cohesion and the results of effective team cohesion. The foundation for this theoretical approach comes from the important work of Cartwright (1968). A simple schematic of the Cartwright (1968) model is illustrated in figure 10.1.

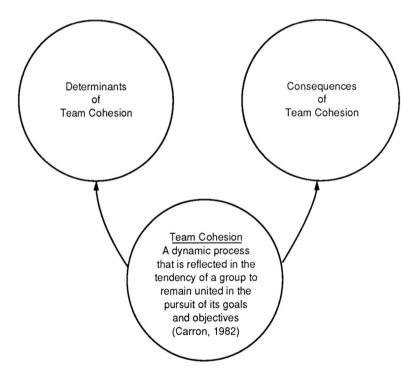

Figure 10.1 Cartwright's basic determinants and consequences model of cohesion, showing the inclusion of Carron's definition of team cohesion. The model is from *Group Dynamics: Research and Theory,* third edition, by Darwin Cartwright and Alvin Zander. Copyright © 1953, 1960 by Harper and Row, Publishers, Inc. Copyright © 1968 by Darwin Cartwright and Alvin Zander. Reprinted by permission of Harper & Row Publishers, Inc. Definition is from Cohesion in sport groups: Interpretations and considerations. *Journal of Sport Psychology, 4,* 123–138, 1982. Quoted by permission of Human Kinetics Publishers, Inc.

The model proposes that there are forces that determine the strength and effectiveness of team cohesion. Cartwright labeled these forces **determinants** of team cohesion. In addition, as a result of a team's or group's ability to work together, Cartwright proposed that there would be certain **consequences** associated with effective team cohesion.

Task and Social Cohesion

Hagstrom and Selvin (1965), Mikalachki (1969), and Peterson and Martens (1972) have all demonstrated that there are at least two distinct and independent dimensions associated with team cohesion. One dimension is related to interpersonal attraction, and is identified as *social cohesion*. **Social cohesion** reflects the degree to which the members of a team like each other and enjoy each other's company.

The second major dimension of team cohesion was called *task cohesion*. **Task cohesion** reflects the degree to which members of a group work together to achieve a specific and identifiable task. The task is usually associated with the purpose for which the team or group was formed. For example, the task in baseball is to score runs and to prevent the opposition from scoring runs.

It is quite easy to see how these two types of team cohesion could operate independently. Consider the world champion New York Yankees of 1978. This team was the best in the world in task cohesion. They could turn double plays, hit cut-off men, advance runners, and work together better than any other baseball team in the world. Yet in terms of social cohesion they were very low. Team members fought with each other, cliques were formed, and angry words were exchanged. Lenk's (1969) study of world-class rowers presents a similar example.

Research by Mikalachki (1969) suggests that groups that are high in task cohesion identify closely with formal group goals and experience success in obtaining these goals. Groups that are high in social cohesion tend to consider social interaction and member attraction to be more important than group goals. It is therefore possible for a person to score very high on at least one dimension of team cohesion (social) and still not identify closely with team goals.

It is certain that there are at least two basic dimensions of team cohesion. However, Yukelson, Weinberg, and Jackson (1983, 1984) demonstrated that there may be as many as four. Thus, while team or group cohesion was once considered to be **unidimensional**—having only a single construct—it most likely is **multidimensional**—composed of several independent factors. Therefore, the manner in which team cohesion is measured is of great importance to both the researcher and the practitioner.

1. **Principle** Team cohesion is a multidimensional construct and not a unidimensional construct.

   Application A coach must recognize that a team can be low in one dimension of cohesion and high in another. Task cohesion is a worthwhile goal to strive for, while social cohesion is of small consequence to performance.

Conceptual Model of Team Cohesion

Building on the distinction between task and social cohesion (Mikalachki, 1969) and the distinction between group integration and individual attraction, Carron, Widmeyer, and Brawley (1985) developed a **conceptual model of team cohesion.** According to Carron et al. (1985), individuals are bound and attracted to a group for two basic reasons. The first reason is labeled **group integration** and refers to how the group functions as a group or team. Group integration takes into consideration the athlete's perception of closeness, similarity to other team members, and bonding to the group as a whole. The second reason is labeled **individual attraction** and refers to those factors that personally attract an athlete to a team. Individual attraction to the group takes into consideration how a team member feels about teammates, quality of member interaction, and the degree to which team members identify with the team.

The conceptual dichotomy between group integration and individual attraction and between social and task cohesion is fundamental to understanding the multidimensional nature of team cohesion (Carron & Chelladurai, 1981). Team cohesion is not a unidimensional construct. For purposes of clarity Carron, Widmeyer, and Brawley's conceptual model of team and group cohesion is illustrated in figure 10.2.

Measurement of Team Cohesion

Cartwright (1968) is responsible for the first serious attempt to categorize the various methods of measuring group cohesion. Cartwright proposed four major approaches to measuring group cohesion: interpersonal attraction among members, group satisfaction, group commitment, and desire to remain in the group. These approaches are primarily related to social cohesion as opposed to task cohesion (see figure 10.2). Two entirely different methods of measuring interpersonal attraction among members are also addressed. The **indirect approach** to measuring interpersonal attraction is to ask individual members of a team how they feel about other members of the team. This is also referred to as a **socio-**

metric measure of cohesion. An example of the indirect approach would be the **sociogram** as illustrated in figure 10.3. In the **direct approach** to measuring attraction, the athlete is merely asked about his or her attraction to the team generally.

In this section I will briefly identify and discuss questionnaires and measurement tools that have been developed since 1971 to measure team cohesion. They

Athlete's Perception of Team

	Group Integration	Individual Attraction
Social	Bonding to the team as a whole to satisfy social needs	Attraction to team and team members to satisfy social needs
Task	Bonding to the team as a whole to satisfy task completion needs	Attraction to team and team members to satisfy task completion needs

(Group Orientation)

Figure 10.2 Widmeyer, Brawley, and Carron's conceptual model of team cohesion. From W. N. Widmeyer, L. R. Brawley, and A. V. Carron, *The measurement of cohesion in sport teams: The group environment questionnaire.* Copyright © 1985, Spodym Publishers. Used with permission of the publisher.

"With which member of the team do you enjoy the greatest friendship?"

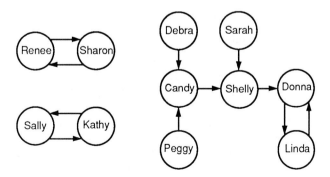

Figure 10.3 Use of the sociogram to ascertain friendships among members of a women's basketball team.

will be presented chronologically, beginning with the very popular Sports Co-hesiveness Questionnaire (SCQ) and ending with the conceptually sound and rig-orously tested Group Environment Questionnaire (GEQ).

Sports Cohesiveness Questionnaire

Based on Cartwright's general guidelines, Martens and Peterson (1971) devel-oped the **Sports Cohesiveness Questionnaire** (SCQ). Despite the fact that the reliability and validity of the SCQ has never been fully tested (Gill, 1978), it has been the most popular sport-related test of team cohesion used by researchers. While not available in published form, a copy of the questionnaire may be ob-tained from the author of the questionnaire.

The Sports Cohesiveness Questionnaire is composed of seven questions. The first two questions are of the indirect variety and ask team members to assess other members of the team relative to feelings of friendship and team influence. The remaining five questions are direct and ask team members to assess team cohesion directly. Three of the direct questions ask the athlete to assess his or her relationship to the team in terms of a sense of belonging, value of membership, and enjoyment. The remaining two direct questions ask the athlete to evaluate the team as a whole in terms of teamwork and closeness (Martens & Peterson, 1971).

All of the items on the SCQ, except those dealing with the group as a whole, measure attraction to either the team or to individuals. For this reason, Carron (1980) argued that the SCQ is primarily a test of interpersonal attraction or social cohesion. Only the items dealing with teamwork closeness seem to address the important concept of task cohesion.

Team Cohesion Questionnaire

The **Team Cohesion Questionnaire** (TCQ) as developed by Gruber and Gray (1981, 1982) is composed of thirteen items that measure six direct measures of team cohesion. The six dimensions of team cohesion include team performance satisfaction, self-performance satisfaction, value of membership, leadership, task cohesion, desire for recognition, and affiliation cohesion. The dimensions of team performance satisfaction, self-performance satisfaction, and task cohesion can be roughly categorized as *task cohesion dimensions*. The dimensions of affiliation, desire for recognition, and value of membership can be categorized as *social cohesion dimensions*. In administering the questionnaire, individual team mem-bers are asked to indicate their intensity of feeling about each item using a 9-point Likert-type scale.

Sport Cohesion Instrument

The **Sport Cohesion Instrument** (SCI) was developed and tested by Yukelson, Weinberg and Jackson (1983, 1984). The Sport Cohesion Instrument is composed of twenty-two items that measure four dimensions of team cohesion. They are attraction to the group, sense of purpose, quality of teamwork, and valued roles. Most of the questions in the SCI relate either to task cohesion (quality of teamwork) or social cohesion (attraction to the group). While the Sport Cohesion Instrument was designed for basketball teams, its versatility allows it to be used with other team sports (Yukelson et al., 1984). In responding to each of the twenty-two items on the SCI, the athlete is asked to rate each statement on an 11-point Likert-type scale.

Group Environment Questionnaire

The **Group Environment Questionnaire** (GEQ) is a team cohesion questionnaire that is soundly grounded in theory. Developed and tested by Carron, Widmeyer, and Brawley (1985) and Brawley, Carron, and Widmeyer (1987), the GEQ is based on the conceptual framework presented in figure 10.2. The GEQ is an eighteen-item questionnaire that reliably and *directly* measures four team cohesion dimensions or scales (Widmeyer, Brawley & Carron, 1985). The four dimensions of team cohesion measured by the GEQ include individual attraction/

task (four items), individual attraction/social (five items), group integration/ task (five items), and group integration/social (four items). For source information, the reader is referred to Anshel (1987). The usefulness of the GEQ was recently demonstrated in two studies designed to study exercise adherence (Carron, Widmeyer & Brawley, 1988) and group resistance to disruption (Brawley, Carron & Widmeyer, 1988).

---

2. **Principle** A team-cohesion questionnaire should be carefully selected to be consistent with the dimensions of interest to the coach and athlete.

    Application Select a cohesion questionnaire after consultation with a sport social-psychologist. Incorrect use and interpretation of test results may lead to faulty and misleading conclusions.

Determinants of Team Cohesion

In this section I will introduce some of the sport-related forces that *determine* team cohesion. In figure 10.1 I introduced a simplified version of Cartwright's model of cohesiveness along with Carron's (1982) definition of *team cohesion*. In figure 10.4, this model is expanded to include the important team-cohesion *determinants* of cooperation, stability, homogeneity, and size.

Cooperation and Competition

When teammates cooperate in the satisfactory achievement of a goal, we have a perfect example of task cohesion. Cooperation then becomes a synonym or a determinant of team cohesion. Cooperation is linked in this section with competition. This is due primarily to the direction that research on this subject has taken; cooperation and competition are viewed by theorists such as Deutsch as being mutually exclusive. Thus, as defined by Deutsch (1968), a **cooperative social situation** is one in which the goals of the individuals are so linked together that there is a positive correlation between their attainments; that is, individuals can attain their goals if, and only if, the other participants can attain theirs. Thus, in volleyball, a spiker can only hope for a good set to hit if the setter is successful, and the setter can only be successful if the receiver is successful. On the other hand, Deutsch defined a **competitive social situation** as one in which the goals of

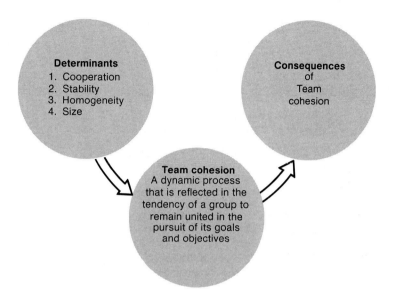

Figure 10.4 Cartwright's basic determinants and consequences model of cohesion, showing the inclusion of Carron's definition of team cohesion. The model is from *Group Dynamics: Research and Theory,* third edition, by Darwin Cartwright and Alvin Zander. Copyright © 1953, 1960 by Harper and Row, Publishers, Inc. Copyright © 1968 by Darwin Cartwright and Alvin Zander. Reprinted by permission of Harper & Row Publishers, Inc. Definition is from Cohesion in sport groups: Interpretations and considerations. *Journal of Sport Psychology, 4,* 123–138, 1982. Quoted by permission of Human Kinetics Publishers, Inc.

the separate participants are so linked that there is a negative correlation between their attainments: Individuals can attain their goals if, and only if, the other participants cannot attain theirs. Thus, in soccer, if your only objective is to score a goal yourself, then you may pass up a sure chance of a team goal by refusing to pass the ball to a teammate.

The dichotomy between cooperation and competition as proposed by Deutsch is useful for testing hypotheses. However, it may at times be incongruent with the athletic situation. For example, competition among athletes for rewards and starting positions can benefit all members of the team. More goals (points) are scored, athletes work harder, and the end result is that the team benefits. With this minor clarification, let us continue with the line of discussion.

Closely linked to the notions of cooperation and competition is the concept of **individualistic behavior.** According to Deutsch, an individualistic social situation is one in which there is no correlation between the goal attainments of the participants. Whether an individual accomplishes his or her goal has no influence on whether others achieve their goals. Thus, a person seeks an outcome that is personally beneficial without regard for the goal achievement efforts of other participants. In bowling, for example, if one player gets three strikes in a row, this in no way reduces the possibility of a teammate accomplishing the same feat, or even doing better. However, it is difficult to imagine a situation in a team sport such as football in which individual task accomplishment does not in some way affect teammates.

Sherif and Sherif (1953) conducted one of the first in-depth investigations of cooperation and competition. The subjects in this research were twenty-four boys

involved in an eighteen-day summer camp session. The researchers studied intragroup cooperation and intergroup competition by forming the boys into two rival camps. During the latter stages of the experiment, competition between the "Red Devils" and the "Bull Dogs" became so fierce that it was necessary to terminate the experiment and generate opportunities for cooperation between the two groups. Some of the cooperative enterprises that the boys engaged in to break down intergroup hostility were getting a stalled Mack truck fixed and helping to repair a broken water line. As a result of studies with boys' camps, researchers concluded that competitive intergroup relations solidify group cohesiveness and that intergroup competition can be broken down through a process of intergroup cooperation (Fisher, 1976; Sherif, 1976).

Perhaps more germane to our study of sport is the relative effect that cooperation and competition have on performance. Since 1920, reports and reviews have concluded both that cooperation was more effective and that competition was more effective in promoting superior performance (Michaels, 1977; Sharan, 1980). These contradictory conclusions have created major controversies. However, Johnson, Maruyama, Johnson, Nelson, and Skon (1981) conducted an indepth **meta-analysis** (a statistical comparison and summary of independent samples) on 122 studies that yielded 286 findings beginning in the 1920s. The results are summarized as follows:

1. Intragroup cooperation is superior to intragroup competition and/or individualistic behavior.
2. Intragroup cooperation without intergroup competition is superior to intragroup cooperation with intergroup competition in terms of productivity and performance.
3. There is no difference between interpersonal competition and individualistic goal behavior in terms of productivity.

In addition to these findings several moderating results were noted that tend to clarify the basic relationships. First, it was concluded that the smaller the group, the greater the superiority of cooperation over competition. Members of small groups are better able to cooperate with each other than members of large groups. The greater cooperation translates into better performance.

The second finding was that the superiority of cooperation over competition is somewhat dependent on the nature of the task. Specifically, the more interaction that is required between members of a team, the greater the positive impact of cooperative behavior. Research by Miller and Hamblin (1963) and Goldman, Stockbauer, and McAuliffe (1977) have clearly demonstrated this point. High athlete interaction tasks such as football and basketball require cooperation, while low interaction tasks such as golf and bowling do not. Running an offensive play in football is clearly an interactive task requiring player cooperation while a sport such as team archery may not. Numerous interactive acts such as blocking, passing, and handing off are required in football. Members of football teams simply must cooperate with each other if they hope to be successful.

Not withstanding the importance of cooperation in interactive team sports, relatively recent evidence points out the importance of cooperative behavior in noninteractive sports such as golf. Johnson, Bjorkland, and Krotee (1984) reported a study in which male and female college students were randomly divided into cooperative, competitive, and individualistic groups. Controlling for skill, the three groups were taught the golf skill of putting while practicing cooperative, competitive, or individualistic behaviors. The results of the study indicate that cooperative interaction among members of a group tends to promote putting skill and more positive attitudes toward the instructor and members of the group. A team that learns to cooperate to achieve worthwhile goals will tend to be a cohesive team, especially in task cohesion. However, the emphasis upon cooperation should not lead the reader to the erroneous conclusion that healthy competition within groups and between groups is not of value. A study by Myers (1969) using ROTC riflery teams in competitive and noncompetitive situations highlights this point. First, self-esteem was reported to be an important by-product of successful teams generally, and competitive teams specifically. Second, low-success competitive teams manifested better self-adjustment to failure than low-success noncompetitive teams. Finally, during adversity, members of competitive teams responded in a more tolerant and adaptive manner than did members of noncompetitive teams.

In summary, it appears that both cooperation and competition are important. Competition taken to its extreme at the exclusion of cooperation can be counterproductive. The notion that intergroup competition enhances the effectiveness of intrateam cooperation is not supported by the literature. The important relationship between cooperation and competition seems to be captured by the cartoon of the three mice in figure 10.5. Cooperation between members of the same team can lead to mutual benefits, increased performance, and team cohesion.

---

3. **Principle** Cooperation among athletes is closely linked to task cohesion and should be actively promoted.

   Application Interactive team games such as volleyball and soccer require cooperation among team members. Cooperation can be taught through drills and lead-up games. Coaches should design game situation drills that underscore the importance of cooperation in achieving team and individual goals.

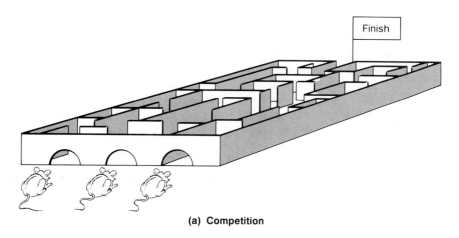

(a) Competition

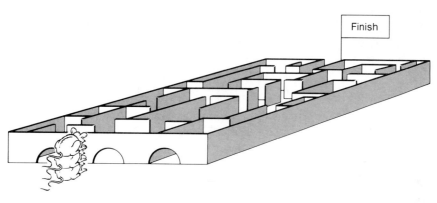

(b) Cooperation

Figure 10.5 Cooperation between team members often improves performance.

Team Stability, Homogeneity, and Size

Many factors can contribute to team cohesion and performance and can thus mediate the relationship between the two. For example, stability or constancy of a team roster, the psychological and cultural makeup of team members, and the size of a team are all factors that can contribute to and determine team cohesion and performance.

The concept of **team stability** as used here relates to team cohesion in terms of the number of years that a group of athletes remain together. This is also referred to as team constancy. We would expect teams that remain relatively constant across a certain period of time to be more stable, cohesive, and ultimately more successful. Evidence from research by Essing (1970), Loy (1970), and Donnelly (1975) seems to support this conclusion. Essing (1970) studied eighteen German Federation Soccer teams across a single season (1966–1967) and reported that teams that changed their line-ups the least were more successful and that teams that played their standard or starting players more and newcomers less tended to be winning teams. Similarly, Loy (1970) studied personnel turnover in major league baseball teams and found an inverse relationship between the number of new players and the win-loss percentage of the team. That is, teams with fewer player changes during a given year had a greater percentage of wins.

Donnelly (1975), as reported by Donnelly, Carron, and Chelladurai (1978), proposed that there is an optimal length of time to keep a group of players together in order to take the greatest advantage of the relationship between team cohesion and success. Data were collected from six major league baseball teams for the years 1901 to 1965. The half-life of a team was considered to be the time it took for a starting roster to be reduced to half of its original size. For example, if the New York Yankees had fourteen regular starters in 1930, these players were traced for successive years until only seven of the fourteen remained. The number of years it took for this to occur was the half-life. By tracing six teams for approximately sixty-five years, 390 cases were studied. Each new season was considered to be a new team, and longer half-lives were presumed to be indicative of more stable teams. To measure success, the researchers used the number of victories each team trailed the leading team by at the conclusion of each season. The results indicated that a half-life of five years was optimal for success. Teams with a half-life of five years concluded their season an average of eleven games behind. Teams with a longer or shorter half-life were less successful. This study suggests that teams need a certain amount of time to develop an optimal level of cohesion for task performance. The amount of time would likely vary from team to team and from sport to sport.

Intuitively, the notion that it takes a professional baseball team approximately five years to mature and learn to play together is very appealing. In retrospect, the World Champion Oakland Athletics of the early 1970s would seem to fit this model. They remained World Champions for three years and then faded as key players either aged, opted for free agency, or were traded.

4. **Principle** Team stability is an important force that leads to team cohesion and possibly team success.

   Application A coach cannot control graduation of seniors in high school or even college, but efforts should be made to avoid the impression that a different team takes the court at the beginning of each game or match. A certain amount of stability is necessary in order for athletes to learn to play well together.

Team Homogeneity

A second factor believed to be related to team cohesion and success is the homogeneity of the team. **Team homogeneity** has to do with how similar teammates are on such factors as cultural background, ethnic background, socioeconomic status, and religion. The basic premise is that more homogeneous teams are likely to resist clique formation, to be higher in team cohesion, and to ultimately enjoy greater success. While this hypothesis is intuitively appealing, there is not a great deal of evidence to support or refute it. One study reported by Eitzen (1973) provides empirical support for the premise. In this study, Eitzen tested and found support for two hypotheses. The first was that fewer cliques would be formed in teams that exhibited greater internal homogeneity. The second was that teams with greater homogeneity would enjoy greater success. Eitzen's sample involved 366 boys on Kansas high school basketball teams. Variables sampled in this study were occupation of father, family prestige, place of residence, and religion. Eitzen concluded that heterogeneity fosters clique formation, and that the presence of cliques reduces a team's chances of winning.

The following true story is provided to illustrate the importance of homogeneity in fostering team cohesion. In 1970 the Seasiders of the Church College of Hawaii enjoyed the distinction of being rated one of the top four college rugby teams in the Nation. For a college of approximately twelve hundred students, this was pretty impressive. However, in 1966 when John Lowell assumed the role as head coach, this did not seem even remotely possible. The team was composed of three or four different cultural groups that tended to band together as cliques both on and off the athletic field. Two of the groups that especially disliked playing together were the Tongans and the Samoans. On several occasions, the team lost scoring opportunities when a member of one group refused to lateral the ball to a member of the other group. Somehow, Coach Lowell was able to get the athletes to rise above their cultural differences and become a homogeneous team in terms of purpose and aspiration.

---

5. **Principle** Extreme cultural, ethnic, and socioeconomic differences among members of a team can foster cliques that can counter attempts to develop team cohesion.

   Application Cultural and racial differences are actually very superficial. Members of sport teams have a great deal in common regardless of cultural or other differences. The coach must find ways to help team members focus on things that help them become more homogeneous and ignore unimportant differences such as race and ethnic background.

Team Size

Finally, in terms of group size, it can be expected that as a team or group increases in size, cohesion and productivity may decline. This is partially due to decreased communication and depersonalization. Also, as a group increases in size, it can be expected that group homogeneity and stability will decline, thus encouraging the development of cliques. Perhaps it is for this reason that it is important to develop team cohesion and pride in sub-units of large teams such as those of football and track and field (Davis, 1969). Thus, it appears that team stability, size, and homogeneity are all factors that can be determinants of, or mediators for, team cohesion and performance.

---

6. **Principle** It is easier to develop team cohesion in small groups than large groups.

   Application Coaches of large teams such as football must take this fact into consideration. They should try to develop team cohesion among members of sub-units of the whole team. It is more realistic to develop cohesion among members of sub-units (kick-off, punt-return, offense, defense) than among members of the whole team.

Consequences of Team Cohesion

According to Cartwright (1968) maintenance of group membership, loyalty to group, and personal security are some of the natural consequences of team or group cohesion. In this section I will discuss three other important consequences of team cohesion that are critically important in sport and athletics: team success, performance, and satisfaction. Perhaps the most important potential consequence of team cohesion is success. Coaches generally believe that a cohesive team is a winning team. Certainly, if team cohesion leads to team success, then team cohesion is an important goal to strive for. Figure 10.6 shows Cartwright's basic model of cohesion expanded to include team success, performance, and satisfaction as consequences of team cohesion. However, *you will note that team success and performance also appear in the model as determinants of team cohesion.* The reason for this will become apparent later on in this section.

Team Performance

In discussing the relationship between team cohesion and team performance it is necessary to consider (1) type of measurements used to measure team cohesion, (2) the nature of the sport involved, and (3) the direction of causality. However, before I do this, it is important to note that a subtle distinction can be made

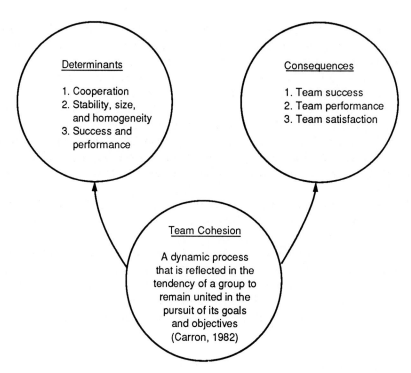

Figure 10.6 Cartwright's basic determinants and consequences model of cohesion, showing the inclusion of Carron's definition of team cohesion. The model is from *Group Dynamics: Research and Theory,* third edition, by Darwin Cartwright and Alvin Zander. Copyright © 1953, 1960 by Harper and Row, Publishers, Inc. Copyright © 1968 by Darwin Cartwright and Alvin Zander. Reprinted by permission of Harper & Row Publishers, Inc. Definition is from Cohesion in sport groups: Interpretations and considerations. *Journal of Sport Psychology, 4,* 123–138, 1982. Quoted by permission of Human Kinetics Publishers, Inc.

between performance and success. Performance relates to quality of effort, while success usually refers to outcome. For example, a team can play very well yet suffer a defeat at the hands of a superior opponent. It is also possible for a team to perform poorly but win because of biased officiating, crowd effect, or inferior opposition. Nevertheless, for the purposes of our discussion these two terms will be considered to be synonymous. This is reasonable, since performance is often measured in terms of team success. In clarifying the relationship between the team's performance and success, it is also important to note that *failure,* or the lack of success, may also be a consequence of the lack of team cohesion.

   At least six literature reviews have appeared that deal with the performance-cohesion relationship in sport (Carron, 1980; Carron, 1982; Donnelly, Carron &

Chelladurai, 1978; Gill, 1978; Gill, 1980a; Nixon, 1977). Each of these reviews cited the contradictory nature of the results from the numerous studies presented. The review by Gill (1978) was of particular significance, as it provided clarity and understanding of the conflicting results. To a large extent, the categorization of studies illustrated in figure 10.7 is based on Diane Gill's excellent review.

As can be observed in figure 10.7, both interactive and coactive sports have been the subject of research. **Interactive sports** are those team sports such as volleyball, basketball, and football that require members of the team to interact with each other. **Coactive sports** are those activities such as bowling, archery, and riflery that do not require members of the team to interact with each other for team success.

The results of the numerous studies presented in figure 10.7 have yielded both positive and negative results. Positive results suggest that high team cohesion is significantly related to high team performance or success. Negative results would suggest that an inverse relationship exists between performance and team cohesion—high team cohesion would be associated with poor team performance. A careful analysis of figure 10.7 will allow us to make at least two important conclusions about the relationship between team cohesion and team performance. These two conclusions relate to the type of measurement used to measure cohesion and the type of sport involved.

Type of Measurement

Figure 10.7 is divided into studies that revealed either a positive or negative relationship between team performance and cohesion. Associated with this basic division is the type of measurement used (direct or indirect) and the type of sport studied (team or individual). Recall from an earlier section on measurement that indirect measures of team cohesion are sociometric in nature and are primarily indicators of social cohesion or *interpersonal attraction*. Direct measures of team cohesion tend to be measures of teamwork or how well the members of the team interact with each other relative to achieving goals. In this respect teamwork is synonomous to what was previously labeled task cohesion.

It is apparent from figure 10.7 that when team cohesion is measured using direct methods of assessment that the relationship between cohesion and performance is positive. Ten studies are cited in which a direct method of assessment yielded a positive relationship between performance and cohesion. In only two cases was a positive relationship observed between cohesion and performance when an indirect method of assessment was used (Bird, 1977a; Klein & Christensen, 1969). Consequently, it is rather apparent that indirect (interpersonal attraction among members) measures of team cohesion rarely result in a positive relationship to team cohesion.

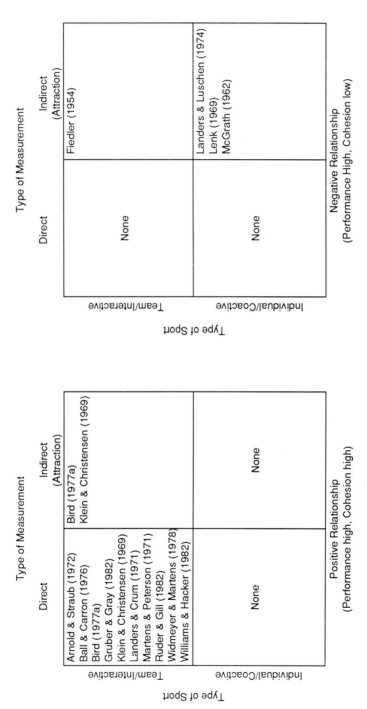

Figure 10.7 Overview of sport related studies in which either a positive or negative relationship was observed between team cohesion and team performance.

7. **Principle** In terms of performance, interpersonal attraction among team members is an important but not necessary goal.

   Application Friendship and attraction among team members is a desirable quality to develop in a group of athletes. However, compared to teamwork and task cohesion, it has little bearing on athletic success. Coaches need not be inordinately concerned about interpersonal attraction among teammates.

8. **Principle** Direct measures of team cohesion are better than indirect measures.

   Application Coaches who are interested in measuring team cohesion should select a measurement tool such as the Group Environment Questionnaire. This test ascertains team cohesion directly and recognizes the multidimensional nature of team cohesion.

Nature of the Sport

A second factor that mediates the relationship between performance and cohesion is the type of sport. As illustrated in figure 10.7, every study that resulted in a positive relationship between performance and team cohesion involved a team or interactive sport. Interactive sports require team members to work together to achieve success and team goals. Sports that do not require member interaction for success are called coactive sports.

Studies that showed a negative relationship between performance and cohesion dealt with teams that were primarily coactive in nature. The prime exception to this conclusion was Fiedler's (1954) study in which the interpersonal attraction among basketball team members was assessed. There are, of course, degrees of coaction and interaction. Rowing, for example, would be partly coactive and partly interactive.

Figure 10.8 presents a system for classifying the predicted relationship between performance and cohesion. The classification system in figure 10.8 is based on proposed systems by Steiner (1972) and Cratty (1983).

Tasks that are coactive and require little interaction among team members for success exemplify **low means interdependence** (Goldman, Stockbauer & McAuliffe, 1977). Tasks that are interactive and require considerable interaction among team members for success exemplify **high means interdependence.** The

| | Mixed | |
Coacting teams	Coacting-interacting	Interacting teams
Low means-interdependent tasks	Moderate means-interdependent tasks	High means-interdependent tasks
Archery	American football	Basketball
Bowling	Baseball/Softball	Field hockey
Field events (track)	Figure skating	Ice hockey
Golf	Rowing	Rugby
Riflery	Track events	Soccer
Skiing	Tug-of-war	Team handball
Ski jumping	Swimming	Volleyball
Wrestling		

Degree of task cohesion required

Low   Moderate   High

Figure 10.8 The relationship of required task cohesion to the nature of the sport and player interaction. From *Psychology in contemporary sport: Guidelines for coaches and athletes,* by Bryant J. Cratty, Copyright © 1983, p. 285. Adapted by permission of Prentice-Hall, Inc., Englewood Cliffs, NJ.

amount of interdependence required between team members is the critical factor. If athletes must depend on each other for success (as in volleyball, soccer, or ice hockey), then interdependence is high. If the athletes perform relatively independent of each other, then interdependence is low.

Along with the method of assessment, the nature of the sport is the critical factor in predicting the importance of task cohesion. If athletes are not required to interact with each other—as in the case in riflery, archery, or bowling—then task cohesion is not very important. Bowling provides a perfect example of this, since the performance of team members is unrelated to how well they interact.

If athletes are required to interact with each other, then success is closely related to task cohesion and teamwork. Volleyball provides a good illustration of this, since success depends on both team and individual performance. For example, successful spiking is related to the quality of the set delivered by the setter. The setter's performance is related to the accuracy of the "bump" made by the athlete receiving the serve. Therefore, whether team cohesion, and specifically task cohesion, is important to performance depends on the nature of the task.

---

9. **Principle** Team cohesion is most effective at facilitating high performance when an interactive as opposed to a coactive sport is involved.

   Application Coaches in sports such as basketball, volleyball, baseball, soccer, and football need to be more concerned with team cohesion than coaches of golf, archery, or bowling teams.

From our previous discussion of performance and cohesion we determined that for certain sports, a positive relationship exists between athletic performance and team cohesion. However, what does this conclusion tell us about the direction of the relationship? Does team cohesion cause improved performance, or does successful performance cause cohesion? The motto of the 1979 Pittsburgh Pirates baseball team was "We are Family," but was this feeling of closeness caused by their phenomenal success, or was their success caused by their togetherness? This is a very good question, and one that we hope to answer in this section.

Studies by Martens and Peterson (1971) and Peterson and Martens (1972) were the first to highlight the question of causality. Before then it was simply assumed that task cohesion improved team performance. However, at about this same time, two other studies also questioned the direction of causality (Arnold & Straub, 1972; Landers & Crum, 1971).

The two studies by Martens and Peterson were both part of the same investigation. They measured team cohesion among twelve hundred male intramural basketball players with the Sports Cohesiveness Questionnaire. The test was administered twice, once two days before each team's first game and once two days after each team's last game. Team performance success was determined by the number of games won. In the original report, Martens and Peterson (1971) measured team cohesion prior to the first game. The results of this comparison revealed that team performance was related to team cohesion as measured by teamwork, closeness, and value of membership—all direct measures of cohesion. Since team cohesion was measured prior to the first game, these results suggested that high cohesion caused high team success.

In the second report (Peterson & Martens, 1972), team cohesion was measured at the end of the season, and was adjusted for by preseason cohesion. In this case, the relationship between team cohesion and team performance was even higher than in the first report. Since they measured team cohesion after the end of the season, they believed the direction of the relationship ran from performance to cohesion. Thus, while a reliable relationship was observed in both cases, it was stronger in terms of performance leading to team cohesion.

Even though the Martens and Peterson studies seemed to suggest that causality in the performance-cohesion relationship flowed from success to perceived team cohesion, it was not until Bakeman and Helmreich (1975) adopted a cross-lagged correlational analysis that the question of causality was specifically studied. The **cross-lagged panel design** is illustrated in figure 10.9; it takes into consideration the time factors involved in the measurement of performance and team cohesion.

As can be observed in figure 10.9, the cross-lagged panel design requires that there be two measures of team cohesion and two measures of team performance. The first measure of team cohesion and performance are taken at time frame one

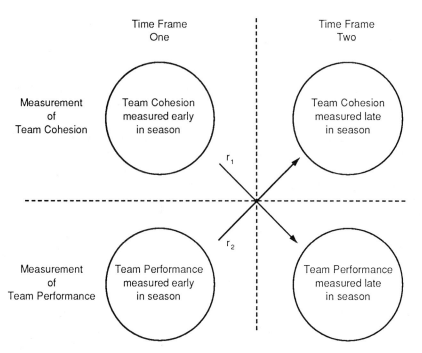

Figure 10.9 Simple illustration of a cross-lagged panel design used to determine the direction of causality between performance and cohesion. From R. Bakeman and R. Helmreich, Cohesiveness and performance: Covariation and causality in an undersea environment. *Journal of Experimental Social Psychology, 11,* 478–487, 1975. Adapted by permission of Academic Press.

(early in season), while the second measure of each are taken at time frame two (late in season). The correlation coefficient (strength of relationship) between early team cohesion and late team performance (r_1) is compared with the correlation obtained between early team performance and late team cohesion (r_2). If r_1 is significantly larger (closer to 1.00) than r_2, then team cohesion causes or leads to team performance. However, if r_2 is significantly larger than r_1, then team performance causes or leads to team cohesion.

I will now summarize each of three sport-related studies that have used the cross-lagged panel design. Each subsequent study tended to improve on the design of the previous research, so that in the final analysis the conclusions are fairly firm. Bakeman and Helmreich (1975) studied forty scientists and eight engineers in an underwater environment. The environment consisted of a four-room habitat placed fifty feet underwater and six hundred feet offshore. For 182 days, each aquanaut's physical activity, location, and conversation were recorded every six minutes. Performance was measured as the percentage of time each aquanaut was seen working compared to the total number of times observed. Cohesiveness was measured as the percentage of time each possible pair in a group of five was observed in leisure time conversation compared to those times when such conversation was possible. Cohesiveness and performance were assessed and split into two parallel segments of time as illustrated in figure 10.9. The cross-lagged correlation for r_1 was $-.144$, while the correlation for r_2 was a robust .861, suggesting that team performance clearly causes team cohesion and not the other way around.

While the results of the Bakeman and Helmreich research were convincing, Carron and Ball (1977) pointed out that they were of questionable value to sport, since the underwater environment and the operational definitions of group cohesion and group performance were so foreign to the athletic environment. So Carron and Ball used members of fifteen intercollegiate male ice hockey teams as subjects in their experiment. They ascertained team cohesion three times using the Sports Cohesiveness Questionnaire: early season, midseason, and postseason. Team performance was ascertained at mid- and postseason, and was operationally defined as the win-loss ratio at those points. Results of the cross-lagged analysis revealed that consistent with Bakeman and Helmreich (1975), team performance causes or leads to team cohesion.

The third study involving the cross-lagged panel design was reported by Williams and Hacker (1982). Subjects in this study were 132 female field hockey players from nine intercollegiate teams. Team cohesion was ascertained with the Sports Cohesiveness Questionnaire at early, mid-, and postseason. Midseason and postseason perfomance scores were assessed at the same time that the mid- and postseason cohesion tests were administered. Performance was assessed as percentage of games won. The results of the partial correlation differential analysis revealed that the direction of causality flowed from performance to cohesion when considering the factors of teamwork and closeness. Considering only the composite score for the Sports Cohesiveness Questionnaire, the correlation (r_1) between early cohesion and late performance was .21, while the correlation (r_2) between early performance and late cohesion was .61. The large difference between these two correlations suggests that the direction of causality flows from performance to cohesion.

In summary, it appears that the bulk of the evidence supports the proposition that causality flows primarily from performance to cohesion. This means that successful teams are much more likely to exhibit feelings of togetherness, team spirit, team unity, teamwork, and closeness than teams that experience failure. This is not to say that high team cohesion is not a desirable quality; it simply means that its value in terms of causing success is probably overrated.

A recent study by Ruder and Gill (1982) in which the cross-lagged panel design was not used provides additional support for our conclusion. Using female volleyball players from ten intramural and eight intercollegiate teams, they measured team cohesion before and after matches. Their findings indicated that while winners had higher prematch team cohesion scores than losers, these differences increased significantly during a postmatch assessment of cohesion. That is, winners became increasingly more cohesive, while losers became increasingly less cohesive. In conclusion, the literature suggests that performance leads to greater cohesion, but provides little support for the more popular notion that cohesive teams are more successful.

---

10. **Principle** Strong feelings of friendship and attraction among members of winning teams are primarily caused by the "glow" of success.

   Application The direction of causality in team cohesion flows primarily from performance to cohesion. This is especially true in the case of friendship and attraction among members. Coaches should recognize this fact and help their athletes experience success by pointing out areas of strength. An athletic team may lose the contest, but still be successful in terms of reaching personal and team goals and in other aspects of the game. The final score is not the only viable measure of success.

Team Satisfaction

As part of their 1971 study with intramural basketball teams, Martens and Peterson studied the relationship between team cohesion and team **satisfaction**— how players felt about participation on their teams. The degree of satisfaction was obtained from a questionnaire measured at the end of the season. The questionnaire asked each person to indicate how satisfied he was with playing on his team. The results of the analysis indicated that all but one of the factors measured by the Sports Cohesiveness Questionnaire—interpersonal attraction—were significantly related to member satisfaction. Based on these results, they concluded that a circular relationship exists between team cohesion, team performance, and team satisfaction. This notion of a circular relationship is illustrated in figure 10.10 and is called the Martens/Peterson model. The suggestion here is that team cohesion leads to success, which leads to feelings of satisfaction, which tends to reinforce and strengthen team cohesion. Thus, team satisfaction serves as a mediating variable in the cohesion-performance relationship.

While the notion of a circular relationship between these three variables has been cited and propagated by many authors, it had never been tested until fairly recently. The Martens and Peterson research merely demonstrated that highly cohesive teams were more successful and more satisfied. The only serious attempt

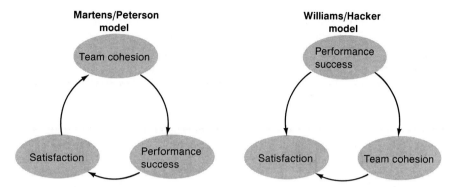

Figure 10.10 Two hypothetical models of the relationship among team cohesion, team performance, and satisfaction.

to test for a causal relationship between cohesion, performance, and satisfaction was conducted by Williams and Hacker (1982) with intercollegiate women field hockey players. Their cross-lagged panel design analysis failed to support the Martens/Peterson model of a circular relationship. Instead, they concluded that performance success and cohesion lead to greater satisfaction, but satisfaction does not lead to anything (see figure 10.10).

One important implication of the Williams and Hacker research on satisfaction and team cohesion is that while coaches may not need to be overly concerned about building cohesion in order to enjoy success, cohesion is still important, since playing on a cohesive team is more satisfying than playing on one that is not.

A comparison of the two models in figure 10.10 reveals two important points. First, the models agree in terms of *existence* of a relationship between cohesion, performance, and satisfaction. These three variables are related. Second, the models disagree in terms of the primary direction of causality. In the Martens/ Peterson model, satisfaction is viewed as a mediator between team cohesion and performance. Thus, the relationship among the three is believed to be circular. In the Williams/Hacker model, performance is the critical variable. High team performance leads to feelings of satisfaction as well as team cohesion. In addition, team cohesion leads to feelings of satisfaction.

What do these conclusions mean to the coach and practitioner? Should the coach abandon all interest in building team cohesion? Certainly not! All of the causality studies reported in this section (with the exception of Bakeman & Helmreich, 1975) used the Sports Cohesiveness Questionnaire to measure team cohesion. As Carron (1980) pointed out, the Sports Cohesiveness Questionnaire primarily measures some form of team or member attraction. According to the Mikalachki (1969) dichotomy, attraction would be closely associated with social cohesion as opposed to task cohesion. The research by Williams and Hacker demonstrates that social cohesion causes member satisfaction, while successful performance causes cohesion and satisfaction. Coaches should continue to develop task cohesion in their athletic teams. However, the development of social cohesion probably does little more than promote satisfaction. Researchers should continue to study the causality question between performance, satisfaction, and team cohesion. However, a measurement tool such as the Group Environment Questionnaire (Carron, Widmeyer & Brawley, 1985) should be adopted for the measurement of team cohesion.

---

11. **Principle** Team cohesion in the form of friendship and interpersonal attraction is a worthwhile goal to strive for because it leads to feelings of satisfaction.

   Application Individual athletes need to feel satisfaction. Satisfaction may not win ball games, but it keeps the athlete interested. A satisfied athlete continues to come to practice, tries hard, and contributes to team goals and aspirations. Coaches should foster feelings of satisfaction among team members. To feel satisfaction is to feel good about yourself and your sport involvement.

Developing Team Cohesion

A sport team can be viewed as having both *social* or interpersonal group activities and group *task*-related activities. As teams develop social and task cohesion, they proceed through four basic stages (Tuckman, 1965). These stages are referred to by Tuckman as *forming, storming, norming,* and *performing.* Thus, it is only in the final stage of the development of team cohesion that it would be possible to discriminate between two groups in terms of task performance. If teams have not worked together long enough to develop team cohesion, then it is unlikely that cohesion would be a factor in helping a team to accomplish its goals. During the forming and storming stages, team members are getting acquainted with each other. Measurements taken of team cohesion during these two stages would tend to be unreliable and unstable. During the norming and performing stages, team members begin to establish relationships and develop an awareness of each other's strengths and weaknesses. It is during these two latter stages that the measurement of team cohesion would be most meaningful.

Therefore, the practice of measuring team cohesion early in the season or before the season starts might not result in a reliable measure of cohesion. It would be better to wait until midseason, after team members have passed through the forming and storming stages of developing team cohesion. However, if the stability of the team remains basically unchanged from season to season, this might not be a serious problem. Professional sports teams tend to remain relatively stable across one or two seasons, whereas high school teams might change significantly from one year to the next.

The following general principles are suggested for helping team cohesion to develop. These guidelines are based upon similar ideas suggested by Lott and Lott (1965), Tutko and Richards (1971), and Cratty (1981).

1. *Acquaint each player with the responsibilities of other players.* This can be done by allowing players to play other positions during practices. This will give them an appreciation for the importance of other players on the team. For example, a spiker in volleyball who complains of poor setting should be given the chance to set once in a while.

2. *As a coach or teacher, take the time to learn something personal about each athlete on the team.* People will come to appreciate and cooperate with those who know little things about them, such as a girlfriend's name, a birthday, or a special hobby.

3. *Develop pride within the sub-units of large teams.* For example, in football the various special teams need to feel important to the team and to have pride in their accomplishments. For smaller units such as basketball teams this may not be so critical. However, the team as a whole should develop pride in its accomplishments.

4. *Develop a feeling of "ownership" among the players.* Individual players need to feel that the team is *their* team and not the coach's team. This is accomplished by helping players become involved in decisions that affect the team and them personally. Individual players need to feel that their voices will be heard.

5. *Set team goals and take pride in their accomplishments.* Individuals and teams as a whole must have a sense of direction. Challenging but obtainable goals should be set throughout the season. When these goals are reached, players should collectively be encouraged to take pride in their accomplishments and then set more goals.

6. *Each player on the team must learn his or her role and come to believe it is important.* In basketball, only five players can be on the floor at one time. The process of keeping the other seven players happy and believing that they too are important is one of the great challenges of teaching and coaching.

Each player on the team has a unique role. If players do not feel this, then they will not feel they are part of the team, and this will detract from team unity.

7. *Do not demand or even expect complete social tranquility.* While it is not conducive to team cohesion to allow interpersonal conflicts to disrupt team unity, it is equally unrealistic to expect interpersonal conflicts to be completely absent. Any time a group of individuals are brought together, there is a potential for conflict. The complete elimination of any friction may actually suggest a complete lack of interest in group goals.

8. *Since cliques characteristically work in opposition to the task goals of a team, their formation must be avoided.* Cliques often form as a result of (1) constant losing, (2) players' needs not being met, (3) players not getting adequate opportunities to play, and (4) coaches who promote the development of cliques through the use of "scapegoats" or personal prejudice.

9. *Develop team drills and lead-up games that encourage member cooperation.* Many drills are designed solely for the purpose of skill development. Many other drills must be developed that teach athletes the importance of reliance upon teammates. For example, in basketball, drills that emphasize the importance of teammate assists could be emphasized.

10. *Highlight areas of team success, even when the team loses a game or match.* Since we know from the literature that performance affects feelings of satisfaction and cohesion, the coach must capitalize on this. If a volleyball team played good team defense in a losing effort, point this out to them.

Summary

Team cohesion is a dynamic process that is reflected in the tendency of a team to stick together and remain united in the pursuit of its goals and objectives. Team cohesion is multidimensional in nature, and may be broken down into social and task cohesion.

Forces such as cooperation, team stability, homogeneity, and size all interact to determine the quality of team cohesion. Team members who learn to cooperate with each other and develop compatible coach-athlete relationships are more likely to experience success.

The relationship between team cohesion and team performance depends to a large degree on the nature of the sport and on the method of measurement. Measurement tools that primarily measure friendship and attraction through sociometric techniques rarely show a positive relationship between cohesion and performance. Interactive sports such as basketball and volleyball require higher levels of task cohesion than do coactive sports such as riflery and bowling.

While the cause-and-effect relationship between performance and cohesion is not completely understood, it does seem clear that the primary direction of causality is from performance to cohesion. Regardless of the direction of causality, one product of team cohesion and success is member satisfaction. Team satisfaction is a worthwhile outcome because it ensures continued participation.

Review Questions

1. Describe the team cohesion model. Explain some of the determinants and consequences of the model.
2. What is the difference between task and social cohesion? How does each influence athletic performance?
3. What is the difference between direct and indirect measures of group cohesion? How does this dichotomy relate to the various tests designed to measure cohesion?
4. Discuss cooperation and competition as they affect team performance. How is cooperation similar to cohesion?
5. How do team constancy and homogeneity affect the cohesion-performance? relationship?
6. How does team size influence team cohesion? What can be done to develop cohesion in large teams?
7. How do the factors of measurement and type of sport influence the relationship between performance and cohesion?
8. Explain the differences between interactive and coactive sports. Give examples of each.
9. What is the relationship between team cohesion and performance?
10. In terms of causality, what is the relationship between performance, cohesion, and satisfaction?
11. Discuss methods for developing cohesion in athletic teams generally.

Glossary

coactive sports Sports in which athletes perform side by side with little interaction.

competitive social situation Situation in which the goals of the separate participants are so linked that there is a negative correlation between their goal attainments.

conceptual model of team cohesion Conceptually based model of team cohesion proposed by Carron, Widmeyer, and Brawley (1985).

consequences With regard to team cohesion, consequences are outcomes derived from cohesion.

cooperative social situation Situation in which the goals of the separate individuals are so linked that there is a positive correlation between their goal attainments.

cross-lagged panel design Correlational design that takes into consideration the time factors involved in the measurement of performance and cohesion.

determinants Factors that lead to the development of team cohesion.

direct measure A measurement of team cohesion in which team members are asked direct questions about cohesion on the team.

group cohesion The "glue" that keeps a group together.

Group Environment Questionnaire Multidimensional cohesiveness questionnaire developed by Carron, Widmeyer, and Brawley (1985).

group integration Integration and functioning of a team as a whole.

high means interdependence Exhibited by interactive sports that require teammates to depend upon each other to achieve team goals.

indirect measure A measurement of team cohesion in which team members are asked questions about other team members, not specifically about cohesion.

individual attraction Factors attracting an individual to a group, team, or individual.

interactive sports Sports in which teammates must interact with each other for success.

low means interdependence Exhibited by coactive sports that do not require teammate interaction for success.

meta-analysis A statistical summary and comparison of independent samples.

multidimensional approach An approach that recognizes that cohesion is composed of several independent factors.

satisfaction A measurement of how good a team or team member feels about participation.

social cohesion The degree to which the members of a team like each other and enjoy each other's company.

sociogram Graphic representation of how individual team members relate to each other.

sociometric measure An indirect measure that primarily indicates social cohesion or interpersonal attraction.

Sport Cohesion Instrument Multidimensional cohesiveness questionnaire developed by Yukelson, Weinberg, and Jackson (1984).

Sports Cohesiveness Questionnaire Cohesiveness questionnaire developed by Martens and Peterson (1971).

task cohesion The degree to which members of a group work together to achieve a specific and identifiable goal.

team cohesion A dynamic process that is reflected in the tendency of a group to stick together and remain united in the pursuit of its goals and objectives.

Team Cohesion Questionnaire Cohesiveness questionnaire developed by Gruber and Gray (1981, 1982) that measures six dimensions of team cohesion.

team homogeneity Teammate similarity in terms of such things as culture and socioeconomic status.

team stability Degree to which a team or group remains the same in terms of players or members.

unidimensional approach The notion that group cohesion is a single construct.

Recommended Readings

Bird, A. M. (1977a). Development of a model for predicting team performance. *Research Quarterly, 48,* 24–32.

Carron, A. V. (1982). Cohesiveness in sport groups: Interpretations and considerations. *Journal of Sport Psychology, 4,* 123–138.

Carron, A. V., & Chelladurai, P. (1981). The dynamics of group cohesion in sport. *Journal of Sport Psychology, 3,* 123–139.

Carron, A. V., Widmeyer, W. N., & Brawley, L. R. (1985). The development of an instrument to assess cohesion in sport teams: The group environment questionnaire. *Journal of Sport Psychology, 7,* 244–266.

Cartwright, D. (1968). The nature of group cohesiveness. In D. Cartwright & A. Zander (eds.). *Group dynamics: Research and theory* (3d ed.). New York: Harper & Row.

Gill, D. L. (1978). Cohesiveness and performance in sport groups. In R. S. Hutton (ed.). *Exercise and Sport Science Reviews, 5,* 131–155.

Johnson D. W., Maruyama, G., Johnson, R. T., Nelson, D., & Skon, L. (1981). Effects of cooperative, competitive, and individualistic goal structures on achievement: A meta-analysis. *Psychological Bulletin, 89,* 47–62.

Mikalachki, A. (1969). *Group cohesion reconsidered.* London, Ontario: School of Business Administration, University of Western Ontario.

Sherif, M., & Sherif, C. W. (1953). *Groups in harmony and tension.* New York: Harper & Row.

Williams, J. M., & Hacker, C. M. (1982). Causal relationships among cohesion, satisfaction, and performance in women's intercollegiate field hockey teams. *Journal of Sport Psychology, 4,* 324–337.

Yukelson, D., Weinberg, R. & Jackson, A. (1984). A multidimensional group cohesion instrument for intercollegiate basketball teams. *Journal of Sport Psychology, 6,* 103–117.

11   Leadership in Sport

Key Terms

autocratic leadership
CBAS
centrality
coach-athlete
   compatibility
consideration
democratic leadership
Employee Enrichment
   Model
Fiedler's contingency
   theory
functional model
influence system
initiating structure
LBDQ
life cycle theory
LPC

LSS
Managerial Grid
McGregor's Theory X
   and Theory Y
Michigan studies
multidimensional model
Ohio State studies
path-goal theory
power system
propinquity
relationship motivation
scientific management
situational behaviors
situational traits
task dependence
task motivation
universal behaviors
universal traits

It is a lot easier to point to examples of great leadership than it is to explain what great leadership is. For example, in sport, it would be hard to find greater examples of leadership than in the lives of such coaches as Knute Rockne, Vince Lombardi, and John Wooden. For examples of great player leadership, one can point to Johnny Unitas, Roger Staubach, and Bill Russell. What was there about these men that made them such great leaders and sports legends?

Each of these men had an unquenchable desire to succeed, to excel, and to win. As Lombardi put it, "Winning is not everything, it is the only thing!" (Kramer, 1970). Roger Staubach was such a great field general that his teammates never gave up as long as he was in charge. As Billy Joe DuPree said of Staubach, "He never knew when it was over. At the end of a game, even if we're down by 20 points, he'll be standing there by himself trying to figure a way we can win it" (Luksa, 1980). John Wooden, the most successful coach in college basketball history, won ten NCAA national championships. Seven of those wins were in a row, beginning in 1967 and ending in 1973. What made Coach Wooden such a great leader? We may never know the precise answer to a question like this, but we can study it and try to understand the many possibilities.

In some ways, the complexity of the concept of leadership is overwhelming. It is like a puzzle that makes little sense until each piece is put in its place. In an attempt to master this puzzle, this chapter has been organized into four sections. The first section defines leadership and provides some basic guidelines. The second section is the heart of the chapter and deals with the major theories of leadership that have evolved. The third section deals with the nature of the coach-athlete interaction. The fourth section discusses geographical location and leadership opportunity. Finally, section five discusses ways in which a coach can best motivate athletes.

Defining Leadership

Fiedler (1967) listed ten different definitions of leadership and noted that there may be as many definitions and theories of leadership as there are psychologists studying the subject. One of the definitions in his list seems to be particularly germane. According to Stogdill (1950), the minimal social conditions necessary for the existence of leadership are the following: (1) a group of two or more persons; (2) a common task; and (3) differentiation of responsibility. With these three conditions in mind, Stogdill (1950) wrote that *leadership is the process of influencing the activities of an organized group in its efforts toward goal setting and goal achievement.*

Carron (1980) has identified two basic systems for looking at or conceptualizing the leadership process. The first is the **influence system** that is identified in Stogdill's definition. According to this approach, the leader (coach), the athlete, and the situation influence each other in terms of accomplishing goals. Coaches are not an entity unto themselves; they are influenced by the members of the team and by the specific situation that they are in. Most successful coaches recognize the importance of interaction between themselves, the team, and the environment.

Coaches who attempt to isolate themselves from their athletes believe in the **power system** of leadership. This system differs from the influence system in that influence and power flow primarily in one direction: from the leader (coach) to the subordinates (athletes). Athletes are not encouraged to express their feelings or opinions to the leader in this system. This approach to leadership is somewhat antiquated, but nevertheless can be observed in some dictatorial environments. The source of the power in such systems includes such things as coercion, reward, authority, expertise, and affection (French & Raven, 1959).

Another important concept in the understanding of leadership has to do with the difference between an appointed leader and an emerging leader. It would seem that in most cases involving organized athletic teams, leaders and coaches are appointed by a higher authority. For example, in most high schools, the head basketball coach is officially appointed by the principal of the school. The appointed leader who is not the popular choice of the athletes will, over time, become the accepted leader due to the official nature of the appointment. However, in less structured situations, team leaders will tend to emerge rather than be appointed. For example, team leaders of sport clubs and intramural teams will often emerge from the group.

Often, an emergent leader will tend to be a more effective leader than one who is appointed. An excellent example of the difference between these two types of leaders is given by Cratty and Sage (1964). They conducted a study in which a fraternity pledge class (led by the pledge class president) competed against a loosely organized group of students who did not know each other. The task consisted of going through a maze while blindfolded. The a priori hypothesis was that the pledge class would do better because of their well-established lines of communication and leadership. In fact, the group having no previous association with each other outperformed the pledge class. The reason for this finding was due to the quality of the leadership. The pledge group tended to rely on the pledge president, who had no specific experience with such things as navigating a maze blindfolded. However, from among the independent group, a leader quickly *emerged* who had obvious skills at navigating the maze. The members of this group turned to him for instructions and tips that allowed them to outperform their competitors. They were not hampered by an *appointed* leader who had no useful skills for this task.

Somewhat related to the notion of an appointed versus an emerging leader is the dichotomy between power and authority in a leadership situation. The appointed head of an organization such as an athletic team is the person with the authority. The person's power in the organization may not be so clear. It is possible that a leader who has the authority to lead can lack the power to do so effectively. Authority may be conferred on someone, but power is a non-preexisting thing that cannot be handed out. As explained by Gross (1964), the distinction between power and authority can be best explained by focusing on two extreme examples.

At one extreme is the organizational figurehead who enjoys considerable authority but lacks the power or influence to make anything happen. This could be the person who has the title of coach or manager but for some reason has little influence or power in the organization. In professional baseball, for example, some owners have wielded the power, while their appointed managers have been mere figureheads. Such powerful owners may be exemplified by Charlie Finley of the Oakland A's and George Steinbrenner of the New York Yankees. The managers of these two teams rarely exhibited any real influence or power, yet each were appointed and given the authority to lead their teams.

At the other extreme is the individual who is very influential and powerful, yet has no official authority. This person is the "wire-puller" who makes the real decisions on a team. This sort of situation can be very damaging to an organization if the goals of the appointed leader and those of an influential associate contradict each other. An example of this may have existed at the University of Kentucky for a few years when Adolph Rupp resigned as head basketball coach and Joe B. Hall was hired. Coach Hall had to lead his team to a national championship to establish himself as the man in charge.

To be an effective leader, the person with the authority to lead must also have a fair share of the power and influence in the organization. While authority to lead can be conferred on a person, power and influence often must be earned over a period of time.

Theories of Leadership

Early interest in leadership centered on the traits or abilities of great leaders. It was believed that great leaders were born and not made. Since these early beginnings leadership research has evolved from an interest in the behavior of leaders to the notion of situation-specific leadership. Williams and Wassenaar (1975) and Straub (1980) have suggested a sort of evolution from simple beginnings to our current situational approach to leadership. The notion of an evolution in leadership thought is useful, but it suggests that the early researchers were somehow

naive and behind the times. A careful analysis of the early writings of some of the great researchers reveals that they were as aware of our "modern" concerns for situation-specific leadership as we are today. For example, Metcalf and Urwick (1963, p. 277) quoted Mary Parker Follett as saying, "different situations require different kinds of knowledge, and the man possessing the knowledge demanded by a certain situation tends in the best managed business . . . to become the leader of the moment." Stogdill expressed similar sentiment in 1948 when he suggested that a successful leader in one situation may not necessarily be successful in other situations.

Perhaps the most significant contribution to understanding the various approaches to categorizing leadership theory has come from Behling and Schriesheim (1976). They developed a typology of leadership theory that is illustrated in figure 11.1. Their typology categorizes the four major approaches to studying leadership according to whether the theory deals with leadership traits or leadership behaviors and whether the traits or behaviors are universal or situational in nature.

Leadership traits are relatively stable personality dispositions such as intelligence, aggressiveness, and independence. Leadership behaviors have to do with the observed behavior of leaders and have little to do with their personalities. Traits found in *all* successful leaders are referred to as **universal traits** as opposed to situational traits. **Situational traits** and **situational behaviors** are those traits and behaviors that may help make a leader successful in one situation but are of

Characteristics of leaders

		Traits	Behaviors
Generality of situation	**More universal**	Trait or "great man" theory	Michigan and Ohio State studies
	More specific	Fiedler's contingency theory	Situation-specific theories

Figure 11.1 A classification scheme for four types of leadership theories. From O. Behling and C. Schriesheim, *Organizational behavior: Theory, research, and application,* Copyright © 1976 Allyn and Bacon, Inc. Used with permission.

little value in another. Consider, for example, the Cratty and Sage (1964) research. Knowing how to navigate a maze blindfolded may be very useful to a leader in one situation, but useless in another. Thus, within the context of the Behling and Schriesheim typology, we have four different classes of leadership theories. Each of these classes will now be discussed in greater detail.

Trait Theories of Leadership

Trait theory has as its origin in the "great man" theory of leadership, which suggests that certain great leaders have personality traits and personality characteristics that make them ideally suited for leadership. The heyday of trait leadership theory began with the development of objective personality tests in the 1920s and lasted until the end of World War II. Proponents of trait theory believe that successful leaders have certain personality characteristics or leadership traits that make it possible for them to be successful leaders in *any* situation. Since these personality traits are relatively stable, it should be possible to identify potential leaders simply by administering a personality inventory. This approach had a great deal of support from social scientists prior to and during World War II, but support waned rapidly after the war.

Perhaps the beginning of the decline occurred shortly after the publication of Stogdill's (1948) review of 124 studies on the trait theory of leadership. In this review, Stogdill noted that five factors or traits seemed to be associated with successful leadership. These factors were intelligence, achievement motivation, responsibility, participation, and status. Stogdill's review and general conclusions made it clear that the relationship between personality traits and leadership performance was very weak. He concluded that persons who are successful leaders in one situation may not be successful in another, regardless of their personality traits. It would seem that such personality traits as intelligence and the motive to achieve would be valuable assets to a leader, but no guarantee of successful leadership. In addition to the Stogdill review, research by Carter and Nixon (1949) and by Mann (1959) severely discredited trait leadership theory. Mann reported that intelligence, which would be expected to correlate highly with task success, had a very low relationship to performance.

While it no longer seems logical that universal leadership traits can be identified, this should not be interpreted to mean that the trait approach itself is dead. The evidence does suggest that certain traits may lead to effective leadership in certain situations. Perhaps we need more research on the relationship between traits and specific situations.

While a serious interest in trait history waned among social scientists after World War II, the same was not necessarily true among sport psychologists. Hendry (1972), for example, has written that athletic coaches are perceived as being dominant, aggressive, and authoritarian. Additionally, Ogilvie and Tutko (1966) reported that sixty-four successful coaches from basketball, track, football, and baseball could be readily distinguished from the average on a number of personality characteristics. They listed twelve positive personality traits and also identified two personality traits that were negative in terms of handling young athletes. The two negative traits were lack of interest in the dependency of others and inflexibility. The researchers noted that the successful coach's personality profile was very similar to that of the superior athlete. Perhaps this was due to the notion that athletes often adopt the leadership style of former coaches (Mechikoff & Kozar, 1983).

In addition to the reported research by Hendry (1972) and Ogilvie and Tutko (1966); Andrud (1970), and Gagen (1971) suggested that coaches were high in need achievement, enthusiasm, and energy. Furthermore, Longmuir (1972), Hendry (1968), and Sage (1972) observed that coaches do not differ from other populations in dogmatism, emotional detachment, interpersonal relations, and other measured personality traits.

Stogdill's review of the trait research in 1948 led social scientists to discredit the universal trait theory of leadership. A comparable review of the sport literature by Sage (1975) had a similar effect among sport psychologists. Sage concluded from his review that the evidence for trait theory was meager, and that many of the studies suffered from design errors such as small and unrepresentative sampling.

Since 1972 there has been a sharp decline in the number of sport studies investigating trait leadership theory. In some ways this is appropriate, since there does not seem to be a *universal* set of personality traits that would set the successful leader or coach apart from less successful colleagues. However, in some respects this is also unfortunate. While there may not be a universal set of traits associated with successful leadership, this is not to say that certain combinations of traits might not be beneficial in specific situations. Such an approach is evident in Fiedler's contingency model and in some of the situational theories that will be discussed later. In these theories, personality traits, and/or characteristic behaviors are studied in light of the situation. Personality traits and behaviors that lead to successful leadership in one situation are observed to be of little value in another.

1. **Principle** There is no such thing as a universal set of personality traits common to all successful leaders.

   Application Prospective coaches should not be discouraged if they do not share common personality traits with some of the famous leaders and coaches in sport.

Michigan and Ohio State Studies

Shortly after World War II the focus in leadership research turned from universal traits to **universal behaviors** of successful leaders. It was believed that successful leaders had certain universal behaviors. Once these universal behaviors were identified, they could be taught to potential leaders everywhere. This approach to leadership was very optimistic, since anyone could learn to be a successful leader simply by learning certain predetermined behavioral characteristics. If these universal behaviors could be mastered, then anyone could be a successful leader. Unlike trait theory, the belief was that *leaders are made, not born.* The driving force behind this approach to leadership came from two different sources, but at approximately the same time. These two sources were Ohio State University and the University of Michigan.

2. **Principle** Leadership behaviors can be learned, while personality traits cannot.

   Application The distinct advantage of the behavioral approach to effective leadership as opposed to the personality trait approach is that leader behaviors can be learned. Coaches who lack the necessary skills to be effective leaders can learn these skills by learning how effective coaches behave in specific situations.

Table 11.1 Leadership Factors from the Ohio State Studies. Copyright © 1957 by The Ohio State University. Used by permission.

Factor	Description
Consideration	Leadership behaviors indicative of friendship, mutual trust, respect, and warmth.
Initiating Structure	Leadership behaviors that establish well-defined patterns of organization, channels of communication, and ways of getting things done.
Production	Leadership behaviors calculated to motivate subordinates to greater activity.
Sensitivity	Leadership behaviors that show a sensitivity to social interrelationships.

The Ohio State Studies

The **Ohio State studies** began in 1945, shortly after World War II and were designed as a ten-year program of research on leadership problems in military, business, industrial, educational, and civilian government organizations. The program director for the project was Carrol L. Shartle. According to Shartle (Stogdill & Coons, 1957, pp. 1–5), the approach in the Ohio State studies was to examine performance or behavior rather than human traits.

Perhaps the first and most significant step in the Ohio State studies was the development of the **Leader Behavior Description Questionnaire** (LBDQ). A thorough description of the initial development of this research tool is provided by Hemphill and Coons (1957). The LBDQ was developed to describe *how* leaders behave, or how they go about doing whatever it is they do. The original LBDQ began with 1,790 items roughly categorized into nine dimensions of leader behavior. The original 1,790 items were later reduced to 150 items based on logical scrutiny. The 150–item LBDQ described by Hemphill and Coons was further reduced to 130 items by Halpin and Winer (1957) for use in the study of Air Force personnel manning bombardment aircraft. In this investigation, the leader behavior of fifty-two air crew commanders was described by three hundred air crew members. A factor analysis on the selected dimensions resulted in the identification of four factors associated with leader behavior. These four factors are described in table 11.1.

The factors of *consideration* and *initiating structure* accounted for a combined total of 83 percent of the variance. Consequently, since the remaining two factors accounted for only 17 percent of the variance combined, they were dropped from further consideration. Thus, a short form of the LBDQ evolved that had only thirty items measuring consideration and initiating structure. From the original version of the LBDQ, several versions evolved. Some of them are the LBDQ (real, staff) in which group members described leader behavior; the LBDQ (ideal, self) in which leaders describe ideal behavior; and the LBDQ (ideal, staff) in which group members describe the leader's ideal behavior (Halpin, 1966).

Without question, the most significant contribution of the Ohio State studies was the identification of consideration and initiating structure as the two most important factors characterizing the behavior of leaders. **Consideration** refers to leader behavior that is indicative of friendship, mutual trust, respect, and warmth between the leader and subordinates. Conversely, **initiating structure** refers to the leader's behavior in clearly defining the relationship between the leader and subordinates, and in endeavoring to establish well-defined patterns of organization, channels of communication, and methods of procedure.

These two kinds of behavior are considered to be relatively independent but not necessarily incompatible. That is, a leader could be high in both consideration and initiating structure. It is not necessary, according to the construct, to be high in one and low in the other.

---

3. **Principle** Consideration and initiating stucture are the two most important factors characterizing the behavior of leaders.
   Application Coaches and leaders of sport teams should strive to establish well-defined patterns of organization and communication, while at the same time displaying the behaviors of friendship, trust, respect, and warmth.

The Michigan Studies

At the same time that the Ohio State research was in progress, a series of studies in leadership were in progress at the University of Michigan Survey Research Center. Like the Ohio State studies, the **Michigan studies** were an attempt to isolate universal behaviors of successful leaders. In one conceptual scheme, four major factors were believed to be related to employee performance and satisfaction. These four factors were (1) differentiation of the supervisor's role, (2) looseness of supervision, (3) employee orientation, and (4) group relationships (Kahn & Katz, 1960). In a second scheme, two broad dimensions of leadership behavior were identified: the *employee orientation dimension* and the *production orientation dimension*.

The employee orientation dimension is very similar to the consideration dimension of the Ohio State studies and has to do with the human relations aspect of a job. The production orientation dimension is roughly equivalent to the Ohio

Table 11.2 Leadership Styles Equivalent to Consideration and Initiating Structure

Consideration	Initiating Structure
Relationship motivation	Task motivation
Democratic	Autocratic
Equalitarian	Authoritarian
Employee orientation	Production orientation

State construct of initiating structure and has to do with the degree to which a leader's behavior is directed toward task performance, productivity, and the technical aspects of the job. Consequently, it is clear that while a number of differences existed between the Ohio State and Michigan studies, the results of both studies indicated that leaders tend to engage in two basic kinds of behaviors. These two behaviors have to do with the extent to which a leader tends to emphasize structure and performance versus good relationships between employees, and between the leader and employees.

Synthesis and Clarification

The two general dimensions of leadership behavior identified in the Ohio State and Michigan studies have provided a basic framework for many leadership studies. Often the terms *initiating structure* and *consideration* have not been used, but compatible terms have been. Yet the general nature of these two categories has resulted in confusion about the terms used to describe them. Table 11.2 presents some of these terms in relation to the labels that Halpin used. Such leadership styles as authoritarianism, production orientation, and autocratic leadership are roughly equivalent to Halpin's (1966) notion of initiating structure. Leadership styles with such labels as democratic, equalitarian, and employee orientation are similar to Halpin's (1966) notion of consideration. Leadership styles that are basically **autocratic** in nature tend toward behavior that can best be explained in terms of initiating structure or production emphasis. Leadership styles that are basically **democratic** in nature tend toward behavior that can best be explained in terms of consideration and employee orientation (Hersey & Blanchard, 1969).

While the basic dichotomy suggested in table 11.2 may seem simplistic, it does provide the common thread that can give structure and meaning to the dozens of terms that have been used to describe various leadership styles and behaviors.

Table 11.3 McGregor's Theory X and Theory Y. From D. McGregor, *The Human side of enterprise.* Copyright © 1960 by McGraw-Hill Book Company. Adapted with permission.

Theory X	Theory Y
1. People inherently dislike work and will avoid it if they can.	1. The expenditure of physical and mental effort in work is an natural as play or rest.
2. People must be coerced, controlled, directed, and threatened in order to make them work.	2. People can exercise self-direction and self-control in the service of objectives to which they are committed.
3. The average human being perfers to be directed, wishes to avoid responsibility, and has relatively little ambition.	3. The average human being learns under proper conditions, not only to accept but to seek responsibility.

In addition, this dichotomy helps to explain the two directions that universal behavior research and theory took in the 1950s and 1960s. These two directions were identified by Williams and Wassenaar (1975) and by Straub (1980) as formal leadership and human relations theories. Formal leadership theory focuses on the principles of good management—the formal aspects of the organization. Formal leadership functions are considered synonymous with the Ohio State concept of initiating structure. In turn, initiating structure is closely related to Taylor's (1911) notion of **scientific management.** According to Taylor, implementation of efficient management principles would automatically result in increased production.

In contrast, Likert (1961), and specifically McGregor (1960), proposed a leadership style that was employee oriented rather than management oriented. McGregor's Theory Y is consistent with a human relations or consideration approach to leadership. According to McGregor, one must adopt either a Theory X or a Theory Y approach to leadership. In **Theory Y,** the employee is perceived as being self-motivated and responsible, while in **Theory X** the employee is considered lazy and irresponsible. The contrast between these two theories is illustrated in table 11.3. According to McGregor, if one believes Theory Y and rejects Theory X, then it logically follows that a human relations approach to management and leadership is the only viable alternative (Sage, 1973).

The production-orientation and human relations approaches to leadership were considered for many years to be incompatible with each other. However, one of the important findings to come out of the Ohio State and Michigan studies was that initiating structure and consideration were *independent* of each other. That is, a leader could be high in both, low in both, or some other combination.

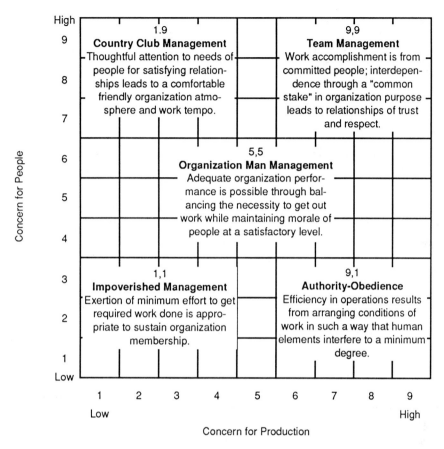

Figure 11.2 The Managerial Grid. From Blake, Robert R., and Mouton, Jane Srygley. *The Managerial Grid III: The Key to Leadership Excellence.* Houston: Gulf Publishing Company, Copyright © 1985, p. 12. Reproduced by permission.

The **Managerial Grid ®2,** as conceptualized by Blake and Mouton (1978, 1985), builds on the observation that attitudinal variables such as *concern for production* and *concern for people* may operate independently of each other. According to the Managerial Grid, there are five main approaches to leadership, and each approach represents some combination of concern for people and concern for production. For example, the 9,9 Managerial Grid style, called team management, integrates high concern for people with high concern for production. Effective integration is possible by involving people and their ideas in determining the strategies of work and achievement. The aim of a 9,9 orientation, then, is to promote participation, involvement, and commitment to teamwork. The Managerial Grid is illustrated in figure 11.2.

Table 11.4 Coaching Behaviors in Sport

Dimension	Description
Competitive training	Behaviors associated with training, performance, and motivation.
Initiation	Behaviors associated with an open approach to solving problems using new methods.
Interpersonal team operation	Behaviors associated with getting members to work together for efficiency.
Social	Behaviors associated with social interaction outside athletics.
Representation	Behaviors concerned with representing the team favorably in contacts with outsiders.
Organized communication	Behaviors associated with a concern for organization or communication with little concern for interpersonal support.
Recognition	Behaviors concerned with feedback and reinforcement as rewards for performance and participation.
General excitement	Behaviors associated with arousal and activation; involves a disorganized approach to team operation.

Adapted from ''Multidimensional scaling and factor analysis of coaching behavior as perceived by high school hockey players'' by R. R. Danielson, P. F. Zelhart, Jr., and C. J. Drake, *Research Quarterly,* 1975, *46,* 323–334. Copyright © 1975 by the American Alliance for Health, Physical Education, Recreation, and Dance. Adapted with permission.

Sports-Related Research

This section introduces a number of important studies that have adopted a universal behavioral approach to sports-related leadership research. These investigations show how sport psychologists have extended the use of behavioral measurement tools into the realm of sport and athletics.

Danielson, Zelhart, and Drake (1975) administered a 140-item coaching behavior questionnaire to junior and senior high school ice hockey players in order to identify the dimensions of leadership behavior in hockey coaches. The Coach Behavior Description Questionnaire (CBDQ) represented a modification of the LBDQ. From twenty commonly perceived coaching behaviors, factor analysis procedures extracted eight general dimensions of coaching behavior. The eight coaching behaviors identified in this study are listed in table 11.4, along with descriptions of the major behavioral characteristics of each. Perhaps the most important finding of the Danielson et al. (1975) research was that measured behaviors of hockey coaches were communicative in nature, as opposed to the commonly perceived emphasis on domination. This contradicts Hendry's (1972) assertion that coaching behavior is characterized by dominance, aggression, and authoritarianism. This conclusion is also consistent with findings of Carron and Bennett (1977), who observed that compatibility between coach and athlete was best determined on the basis of communication as opposed to social affection or control.

Similar to the Danielson et al. (1975) approach, Chelladurai and associates (Chelladurai & Carron, 1981; Chelladurai & Saleh, 1978, 1980) developed the **Leadership Scale for Sports** (LSS). As with the CBDQ, the LSS was developed from items drawn from various versions of the LBDQ. Factor analysis procedures performed upon the LSS resulted in the identification of five coaching behaviors. These behaviors include (1) training behavior, (2) autocratic behavior, (3) democratic behavior, (4) social support, and (5) rewarding behavior. While these five coaching behaviors differ in number from those extracted by Danielson et al., they have definite parallels. For example, the dimensions of training behavior, social support, and rewarding behavior are equivalent to Danielson's dimensions of competitive training, social behavior, and recognition behavior.

Neil and Kirby (1985) used the LSS to identify preferred leadership and coaching styles among competitive rowers. The research revealed that the younger and less skilled athletes had a clear preference for coaches who demonstrated relationship person-oriented behaviors (i.e., consideration behavior). Also using the LSS, Weiss and Friedrichs (1986) showed that leader behavior is related to the win-loss record of the coach and to player satisfaction. Coaches of losing basketball teams score high on the behavior of social support, suggesting that behaviors conducive to the development of social relationships do not necessarily lead to team success. Rewarding behavior was observed to be the best predictor of team satisfaction. Athletes who are verbally and in other ways rewarded for their efforts tend to be more satisfied with their situation than athletes who are not.

While the foregoing research in sport and coaching behavior has provided important information about coaching behaviors, it has all been somewhat subjective, since it is based on athletes' *perceptions* of their coaches, using a pencil-and-paper test. An entirely different and objective approach to identifying coaching behaviors has been developed by sport pyschologists from the University of Washington. Smith, Smoll, and Hunt (1977) documented the development of the **Coaching Behavior Assessment System** (CBAS) used for coding and analyzing the behavior of athletic coaches in naturalistic field settings. The kinds of behaviors observed were reactive and spontaneous coaching behaviors. As can be observed in figure 11.3, eight different kinds of reactive and four kinds of spontaneous behaviors are categorized by CBAS. Reactive behaviors are coach responses or reactions to player or team behaviors. For example, a player makes a mistake and the coach responds by verbally chastising the player. Spontaneous behaviors are initiated by the coach and do not occur in response to a player behavior.

Class I. Reactive behaviors

A. Player performs well

    1. Positive reinforcement (R)

    2. Nonreinforcement (NR)

B. Player makes mistake

    3. Mistake-contingent encouragement (EM)

    4. Mistake-contingent technical instruction (TIM)

    5. Punishment (P)

    6. Punitive TIM (TIM + P)

    7. Ignoring mistakes (IM)

C. Player misbehaves

    8. Keeping control (KC)

Class II. Spontaneous behaviors

A. Game-related

    9. General technical instruction (TIG)

    10. General encouragement (EG)

    11. Organization (O)

B. Game-irrelevant

    12. General communication (GC)

Figure 11.3 Coaching behavior assessment system. From Ronald E. Smith, Frank L. Smoll, and Earl Hunt, 1977. A system for the behavioral assessment of athletic coaches. *Research Quarterly, 48,* 401–407, Reprinted by permission of the publisher, the American Alliance for Health, Physical Education, Recreation and Dance.

In field-testing the Coaching Behavior Assessment System, Smoll, Smith, Curtis, and Hunt (1978) compared CBAS coaching behaviors with player perceptions of coaching behavior and with player attitudes toward coaches. Player perceptions were ascertained through personal interviews using the twelve-categories of the CBAS as a guideline. Subjects for the study were fifty-one Little League baseball coaches observed during a season. The mean number of behaviors coded for each coach was 1,122. Approximately two-thirds of all observed behaviors fell into the categories of *positive reinforcement, general technical instruction,* and *general encouragement.* The behavior of keeping control (maintaining order) was perceived by players to occur much more often than it actually did. Although punitive behaviors (punishment and punitive technical instruction) accounted for only 2.8 percent of the overt behavior, these variables correlated quite high with players' perceptions. Apparently, players are very good at identifying and recognizing punitive behavior in their leaders. Finally, observed behavior of coaches was significantly related to player attitudes toward sport and teammates.

Having established the reliability and utility of the CBAS, Smith, Smoll, and Curtis (1979) designed a study calculated to determine if the CBAS could be used to improve coaching skills through behavioral training programs. Specifically, Little League baseball coaches were exposed to a preseason training program designed to help them relate more effectively to young athletes. Empirically derived coaching behavioral guidelines (do's and don'ts of coaching) were presented to an experimental group of coaches, but not to a control group. Throughout the season, the experimental group received feedback about their actual coaching behaviors through the CBAS. The coaches were encouraged to use the feedback to help them to implement their preseason training on do's and don'ts of coaching. In addition, the players' perceptions of the coach's behavior, players' attitude, and players' self-esteem were ascertained at the end of the season. The results of the Smith et al. (1979) research indicated that the experimental training program was effective. The program has a positive effect on overt coaching behavior, players' perceptions of coaching behavior, and players' attitudes toward sport. In addition, positive changes in player self-esteem were observed in players associated with the coaches in the experimental group. While the win-loss records of the two groups of coaches did not differ as a result of the leadership training program, the players associated with the experimental coaches evaluated their coach and the interpersonal climate of their teams more positively.

Horn (1984) used the CBAS to test the self-fulfilling prophecy theory relative to coach expectations. This theory proposes that teachers and coaches treat students in a manner consistent with the coach's expectations. If a coach's expectations are high, self-fulfilling prophecy theory predicts that the coach's behavior will be more supportive. Coaching behavior was assessed using the CBAS and athletes were classified as being high or low relative to coach's expectations. A comparison of coaching behaviors relative to categorized grouping revealed that coaches did not favor high expectation athletes. Rather, it was the low expectation athlete who received more technical instruction and feedback. Self-fulfilling prophecy theory was not supported.

In summary, sport research dealing with universal coaching behaviors is very promising. Results suggest that desirable coaching behaviors can be identified and conveyed. This finding is very important in terms of coach training programs. Desirable coaching behaviors can be taught to new coaches. This training should result in better coaching and more desirable sport environments for young athletes.

4. **Principle** Well-planned leadership training programs are effective in teaching coaches how to be good leaders.

Application Effective coaching behaviors can be learned. Therefore, coaches should be encouraged to attend training sessions designed to teach effective leadership skills.

Fiedler's Contingency Theory

Fiedler's contingency theory provides an excellent example of a leadership theory that is specific in terms of the situation, but retains the notion of personality traits (see figure 11.1). Fiedler's theory is one of many theories that use the contingency approach. The contingency approach to leadership suggests that leader effectiveness is somehow situation specific, and that leader behaviors that are effective in one situation may not be in another (Hunt & Larson, 1974). In a sense, effective leadership depends on specific environmental situations. However, Fiedler's theory differs from most situational theories, since the emphasis is on relatively stable personality traits as opposed to behaviors. Thus, a particular personality disposition that seems to be effective in one leadership situation may not be effective in another.

The Basic Theory

According to Fiedler (1967), the contingency model of effective leadership posits that the effectiveness of a group is *contingent* on the relationship between leadership style (personality traits) and the degree to which the situation enables the leader to exert influence. The theory holds that the effectiveness of a group depends on two factors: the personality of the leader and the degree to which the situation gives the leader power, control, and influence over the situation.

In terms of the personality, Fiedler believes that leaders are either relationship motivated or task motivated. **Relationship motivation** refers to concern with the interpersonal relationships between leader and followers. Successful performance of the task is of secondary importance to this type of leader. **Task motivation,** on the other hand, refers to the leader's concern with accomplishing the task at hand. The satisfactory completion of the task is important to this type of leader, while establishing and maintaining positive interpersonal relationships is secondary.

To measure these two personality types, Fiedler has developed the **Least Preferred Co-Worker** (LPC) scale, which measures the leader's empathy for his or her least preferred team member. A high score on the LPC would indicate that the leader is able to have positive feelings toward a weak or nonproductive member of the group and thus is relationship motivated. A low score on the LPC would indicate that the leader is unable to rate the least preferred co-worker very high and thus is task motivated. The Least Preferred Co-Worker scale is composed of sixteen to twenty items, depending on the version used. Two typical items used to rate the least preferred co-worker are:

Supportive							Hostile
8	7	6	5	4	3	2	1

Gloomy							Cheerful
1	2	3	4	5	6	7	8

The second major factor in Fiedler's contingency model is situational favorableness This construct indicates the degree to which the situation gives the leader control and influence over the environment. According to Fiedler, situational favorableness depends upon three sub-factors: leader-member relations, task structure, and leader position power.

Leader-member relations refers to quality of the personal relationship between the leader and members of the team. When relationships are good between leader and subordinate, or between coach and athlete, the leader's ability to lead is enhanced. It is relatively easy to lead and control people if they like and trust their leader, but not so easy if they don't. A warm relationship between a leader and members of the group would increase situational favorableness. Leader-member relations can be measured using the Leader-Member Relations Scale (Fiedler, Chemers & Mahar, 1977, p. 39). A high score on this scale suggests good leader-member relations. The scale is filled out by the leader.

Task structure refers to the degree to which the task clearly spells out goals, procedures, and task guidelines. A well-defined task places the leader in a position of power and influence, since there is a step-by-step procedure for performing the task. When the nature of the task is poorly defined, the leader is placed at a disadvantage, since the members of the group may know more about completing the task than the leader does. In most sport situations, the nature of the task is well defined, and the goals and procedures used for accomplishing the task are relatively structured. The task structure of a situation can be measured with the Task Structure Rating Scale (Fiedler et al., 1977, p. 53). A high score on the scale suggests high task structure, while a low score suggests low task structure, and hence less leader influence. But this scale does not appear to be very applicable to sport settings, although perhaps it could be adapted for that purpose.

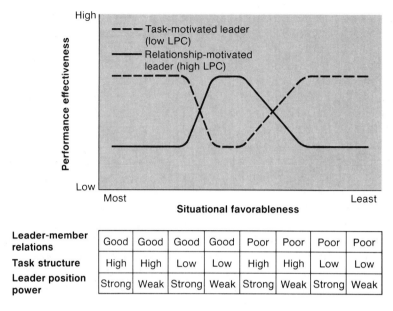

Figure 11.4 Fiedler's contingency model for leadership. From F. E. Fiedler. The contingency model—new directions for leadership utilization. *Journal of Contemporary Business, 4,* 65–79, 1974. Adapted with permission.

Position power refers to the degree to which the leader's position gives the leader authority to reward and punish group members. According to Fiedler, position power is the least important of the three factors contributing to situational favorableness, while leader-member relationships is the most important. Superficially, it may appear that position power would be the most important, but as Fiedler points out, without the support of the group and without a well-defined task, authority in and of itself is of little value to the leader. Position power may be measured with the Position Power Rating Scale (Fiedler et al., 1977, p. 77). A high score on this test suggests that the leader is in a position to make important decisions with power and authority.

The interaction between the leader's personality style and the favorableness of the situation is graphically illustrated in figure 11.4. The horizontal axis indicates the eight cells of the situational favorableness dimension, with the left side of the graph representing the most favorable situation and the right side the least favorable situation. The vertical axis represents performance effectiveness for the relationship-oriented person (high-LPC leader) and the task-oriented person (low-LPC leader). The two curves in figure 11.4 represent Fiedler's basic predictions. Specifically, relationship-oriented leaders perform best in situations of moderate favorableness, while task-oriented leaders perform best in either favorable or unfavorable situations.

There is ample evidence to support the Fiedler model (Fiedler, 1967, 1971, 1974; Fiedler & Chemers, 1974; Fiedler et al., 1977). However, the model is not without its critics (Behling & Schriesheim, 1976). Some authors have criticized Fiedler's research, while others have questioned the conceptualization of his variables. Perhaps the most controversial aspect of the theory is the basic proposition that leadership training programs are of little value. According to Fiedler, leadership training programs only help the leader learn how to enhance power and influence. However, increased power and influence would not benefit the relationship-oriented person who does best in a moderately favorable situation. Therefore, Fiedler proposes that there are only two ways to improve leadership effectiveness. The first involves changing a leader's personality. This is unlikely to happen, since core personality dispositions cannot be easily changed. The second approach involves modifying the degree to which the situation is favorable to a certain type of leader. Fiedler suggests that this could be done by adjusting some aspect of organizational structure, or looking for specific personality types to fill positions consistent with their personalities.

---

5. **Principle** Leaders tend to be endowed with a disposition toward task orientation or relationship orientation.

    Application Coaches should learn to recognize their own personality dispositions and work to compensate for their weaknesses through personal adjustments or through the help of assistant coaches. If the head coach is a task-oriented person, a relationship-oriented assistant coach might be hired to provide the personal touch.

Sports-Related Research

The clear message of Fiedler's contingency theory is that coaches who are successful in one situation are not guaranteed success in a different situation. In sport, there are many cases of highly successful coaches who seem to be successful wherever they go. In football, Lou Holtz was successful at the University of Arkansas and Notre Dame. In basketball, Larry Brown has been successful with UCLA, the New Jersey Nets of the National Basketball Association, and the University of Kansas. However, the situations that these successful coaches go into are often very similar to the ones they left. It could be argued that highly successful coaches are primarily task orientated. Most well-developed athletic programs provide the coach with a very favorable situation. This is because the task is well defined and the coach enjoys great position power. While the Fiedler theory would seem to apply to sport environments, it has a number of serious weaknesses. The greatest of these is that it has failed to receive support from research in the athletic context. While part of the reason for lack of support may be due to a paucity of research (only two studies have been reported), the research that has been done is consistent in rejecting the theory.

A study by Inciong (1974) involved 43 high school basketball teams, 60 coaches, and 535 players. The leadership style of the coaches was assessed with the LPC scale. Coach-athlete relations were measured using Fiedler's (1967) Group Atmosphere Questionnaire. Since leader-member relations is considered to be the most important sub-factor in situational favorableness, no attempt was made to measure task structure or position power. Each team's win-loss record was used as a measure of performance effectiveness. Consistent with Fiedler's model, Inciong hypothesized that the LPC score would be positively correlated with performance effectiveness in moderately favorable situations and negatively correlated in very favorable and unfavorable situations. While the correlations were in the predicted direction, they were not significant. From these results, Inciong concluded that leadership style is unrelated to team success. However, the Inciong study falls short of being a valid test of the Fiedler theory. Situational favorableness was not fully assessed. Only coach-athlete relationships were measured, while the components of task structure and position power were ignored. It is possible that the situational favorableness variable was inaccurate due to incomplete assessment. It would seem that a fair test of the theory would require that all three aspects of situational favorableness be ascertained.

While a study by Danielson (1977) appears to be a more valid test of Fiedler's theory, it, too, failed to fully ascertain all three aspects of situational favorableness. Danielson studied forty youth ice hockey coaches and their teams, a total of 506 players, in testing the theory. The LPC scale was used to measure the leadership motivation of the coaches. In terms of situational favorableness, the Team Atmosphere Scale (Fiedler, 1967) was used to measure coach-athlete relations, while the Goal Direction Scale of the Learning Environment Inventory (Anderson, 1973) was used to measure task structure. Position power was not measured, but was assumed to be high for all coaches. Based on the scores on the two situational favorableness measures, four situations were created. These four situations ranged from favorable to unfavorable. It was hypothesized, consistent with Fiedler's theory, that correlations between coaches' LPC scores and win-loss records would be negative for the favorable and unfavorable situations but positive for the two moderately favorable situations. However, the results showed that in all four conditions, the more relationship oriented the coach was, the greater the chance of team success. Danielson concluded from his study that leadership in hockey situations appears to be more effective when the leader is oriented to personal relationships than task motivation, regardless of the favorableness of the situation. Another possible explanation for this finding is that young athletes made up the sample. A personal relationship approach to coaching may be more effective with this age group (Chelladurai & Carron, 1978).

From these two studies it would appear that Fielder's contingency theory is not applicable to a sport setting. However, it also seems that the theory has not adequately been tested. Both the Inciong and Danielson studies failed to completely ascertain the favorableness of the situation. Danielson alludes to this possibility by stating that he considered his research to be a preliminary exploration of the application of Fiedler's theory in a sport situation, and not a test of the contingency model. Further testing of Fiedler's contingency theory of leadership in the sport setting is needed.

Situation-Specific Theories

There are many contingency theories of leadership, or theories that hypothesize an interaction between the leader and the situation. The basic difference between Fiedler's contingency theory and those that are to be discussed in this section is that Fiedler insisted on looking at relatively stable pesonality traits as opposed to behaviors. The theories in this section tend to view leadership as a function of the interaction between how a leader behaves in a specific situation and the situation itself.

Some of the situation-specific theories are: path-goal theory (House, 1971); life cycle theory (Hersey & Blanchard, 1969); functional theory (Behling & Schriesheim, 1976); adaptive-reactive theory (Osborn & Hunt, 1975); the role-making model (Graen & Cashman, 1975); and the normative model of decision making (Vroom & Yetton, 1973). Unfortunately, space does not allow a thorough review of each of these theories, so only the first three will be considered. These three were selected for consideration because of their potential application to athletics. In addition, Chelladurai's multidimensional model of leadership will be introduced. The Chelladurian model is an example of a leadership theory that evolved from the discipline of sport psychology.

The Path-Goal Theory

Whereas in Fiedler's theory the emphasis was on the personality of the leader and the favorableness of the situation, in **path-goal theory** the emphasis is on the needs and goals of the subordinate or the athlete (Carron, 1980). In other words, the leader is viewed as a *facilitator*. The coach or leader helps athletes to realize their goals. The leader's success is viewed in terms of whether or not the subordinates achieve their goals (House, 1971). Thus, the basic proposition of path-goal theory is that the function of the leader is to provide a "well-lighted path" to assist the follower in achieving goals (House & Mitchell, 1974). This is done by rewarding subordinates for goal attainment, pointing out roadblocks and pitfalls on the path to success, and increasing the opportunities for personal satisfaction. For example, if an athlete's goal is to break a school record in the mile run, it is the coach's job to provide a training program that is rewarding and enables the athlete to accomplish this goal.

A second basic proposition of path-goal theory is that the specific leader behavior that will accomplish goals is determined by the specific characteristics of the situation. Two classes of situational variables identified by House and Dessler (1974) are the personality characteristics of the subordinate and the environmental demands and pressures placed on the subordinate to carry out the task and meet the goals.

Let us consider the first variable. As subordinates work to achieve their goals, path-goal theory posits that they will prefer certain types of behavior from their leaders. That is, subordinates with a high need for social relationships will prefer an interpersonally oriented leader, while subordinates with a high need for achievement will prefer a task-oriented leader. Therefore, as different subordinates proceed toward their personal goals, the types of behaviors, styles of coaching, and reward systems required and desired from the leader can differ markedly. This means that the leader's behavior will need to vary depending on the personality of the follower.

The second variable, environmental demands placed on the subordinate, may be divided into three main categories: (1) the task demands, (2) the formal authority system, and (3) the primary work group. Of these three, the task demands seem to be the most relevant to sport. This is because different tasks require different patterns of behavior from the leader. Ill-defined tasks introduce ambiguity into the path-goal relationship. Reducing ambiguity is one of the leader's responsibilities in facilitating goal attainment.

Path-goal theory has received some research support, but the difficulty encountered by those attempting to test it is caused by its rather sketchy nature (Behling & Schriesheim, 1976). By comparison, Fiedler's theory is much more clearly defined. However, path-goal theory's emphasis on the specific behaviors of leader and follower make it an important theory to consider in the athletic context.

Path-goal theory has not been investigated very much either in or out of sport environments, perhaps due to its lack of clarity. However, one study that looked at the theory from a sport context was reported by Chelladurai and Saleh (1978).

Their research showed partial support for the theory in that individuals who demonstrated a preference for team sports also indicated a preference for leader behavior that was calculated to improve performance through training procedures. Thus, leader behavior correlated with the athlete's preference for an interdependent type of sport. As predicted by the theory, a particular athlete personality consistently preferred a particular leader behavior.

A test of path-goal theory in a sport setting was reported by Vos Strache (1979). In this investigation, the LBDQ was administered to women basketball players at twenty-nine public and private colleges and universities. Results showed that players on losing teams perceived the coach to be high in tolerance, while players on winning teams perceived the coach to be concerned with production emphasis, predictive accuracy, and persuasiveness. These results were taken as support for the theory, since it was expected that effective leaders would provide more goal orientation than less effective leaders.

6. **Principle** The basic proposition of path-goal theory is that the function of the leader is to assist the follower in achieving his or her goals.

   Application To be an effective leader, the coach must assist the athlete in selecting worthwhile goals and by pointing out the "path" to follow in order to reach goals successfully.

Life Cycle Theory

Life cycle theory also places the emphasis in leadership behavior on the subordinates and not on the leader. The appropriate leadership style for any specific situation depends on the maturity of the subordinate (Hersey & Blanchard, 1969, 1977). Two different types of leadership behavior are possible. These two are conceptualized in terms of relationship behavior (consideration) and task behavior (initiating structure). The appropriate combination of task and relationship behavior depends on the maturity of the follower. Maturity is defined by Hersey and Blanchard (1977) in terms of the capacity to set and obtain goals, willingness and ability to assume responsibility, and education and/or experience. According to this model, the need for task structure behavior decreases with increased maturity. However, the need for relationship behavior forms an inverted U relative to maturity. At low and high levels of maturity, relationship behavior should be low, but at the moderate levels of maturity if should be high.

Based on the findings of Danielson (1977) with youth ice hockey players, Chelladurai and Carron (1978) proposed a slightly altered version of the life cycle model. Since Danielson observed that relationship-oriented behavior was related to team effectiveness at all levels of situational favorableness, Chelladurai and Carron proposed that relationship behavior must be important for young athletes. Therefore, they suggested a modification in the Hersey and Blanchard model. According to this model, the need for relationship behavior (not task behavior) decreases with increased maturity, whereas the need for task behavior forms an inverted-U relationship to maturity. At low and high levels of maturity, task behavior should be low, but at the moderate levels of maturity it should be high. In essence, the Hersey and Blanchard model and the proposed Chelladurai and Carron model yield predictions that are essentially opposite of one another.

While neither version of the life cycle theory has been adequately tested, several sport-related studies have addressed the issue. A previously cited study by Vos Strache (1979) also included a test of Hersey and Blanchard's life cycle theory. As you may recall, the LBDQ was administered to female collegiate basketball players. Two hypotheses were tested. The first had to do with path-goal theory, but the second dealt with the life cycle theory. It was predicted that the less mature athletes (freshmen) would prefer high-task/low-relationship leadership, while the seniors would prefer low-task/low-relationship leadership. However, the seniors were higher than the freshmen on desire for both task and relationship behaviors.

The Chelladurai and Carron version of life cycle theory was tested by Case (1980), who administered the LBDQ to forty successful basketball coaches and their athletes. The results were mixed. They supported the proposal that task-oriented behavior should be minimal at the high and low levels of maturity and high during the middle stages. However, the results did not support the Chelladurai and Carron proposal for relationship-oriented behavior, nor did they support the Hersey and Blanchard model.

A relatively recent test of life cycle theory was reported by Chelladurai and Carron (1983). They administered the Leadership Scale for Sports (LSS) to 262 high school and college-age basketball players (Chelladurai & Saleh, 1980). The LSS measures five dimensions of leadership, including task and relationship behavior. The sample represented four levels of age, ability, and maturity: high school midget, high school junior, high school senior, and intercollegiate. The results of the testing showed a linear relationship between maturity and relationship behavior and a quadratic relationship between maturity and task behavior. In both cases, the results were opposite those predicted by the revised version of life cycle theory, and the results did not conform to the Hersey and Blanchard model.

Case (1987) reported an investigation in which the basic tenants of Hersey and Blanchard's life cycle theory were tested in an applied setting. Leadership behaviors of successful head basketball coaches were ascertained using the LBDQ. A total of 399 basketball players completed the LBDQ pertaining to their respective coaches. Athletes were categorized according to the maturity dimensions of junior high, high school, college, and A.A.U. participation. Initiating

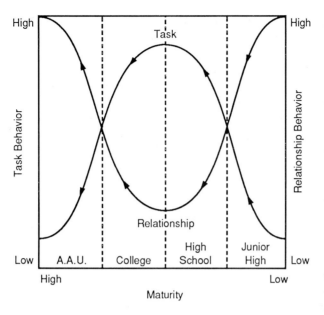

Figure 11.5 Case's modified model of life cycle theory. From B. Case, Leadership behavior in sport: A field test of the situational leadership theory. *International Journal of Sport Psychology, 18*, 256–268. Adapted with permission.

structure (task behavior) and consideration (relationship behavior) leadership scores were calculated for each of forty coaches and then categorized according to maturity (competitive) level. The results revealed a quadratic relationship between maturity and relationship behavior and between maturity and task behavior. Task behavior of successful coaches was low at the junior high and A.A.U. levels of maturity and high for the high school and collegiate levels. Conversely, relationship behavior of successful coaches was high at the junior high and A.A.U. levels of maturity and low for the high school and collegiate levels. These results led Case to propose the Life Cycle Model as illustrated in figure 11.5.

The Case model requires additional testing before it can be used for prediction purposes. Intuitively, the model is appealing because it is somewhat consistent with expectations. Young athletes who lack maturity and highly skilled and mature athletes would not be expected to respond well to a great deal of task structure. Yet, these same athletes might be expected to respond well to an environment in which concern for the athlete was openly expressed. Moderately mature athletes (high school and collegiate level) would require a fair amount of task structure in order to perform well. In this case, relationship behavior might appear to be less pronounced and less important.

7. **Principle** The type of leadership behavior appropriate for any given situation may be mediated by the maturity level of the athlete.

   Application While it is difficult to predict exactly what sort of leader behavior is best for which maturity level, coaches and leaders must be sensitive to the maturity level of the athlete.

Functional Model of Leadership

The **functional model** of leadership as proposed by Behling and Schriesheim (1976) is so new and untested that the originators refer to it as an "unorthodox idea" rather than a theory. Nevertheless, because of its potential applicability to the athletic situation, it deserves to be presented here. Basically the theory states that two basic functions are necessary for a group to survive or operate. These are the expressive or socioemotional function and task orientation or the instrumental function. They parallel very closely the notions of consideration and initiating structure identified in the Ohio State studies. In athletics, the expressive function would deal with the maintenance of interpersonal relations and team cohesion. The instrumental function would deal with successful completion of task goals such as winning basketball games.

Since it is very unlikely that the coach could satisfy both of these functions simultaneously, Behling and Schriesheim suggest that they be satisfied by more than one person. Thus, a task-oriented head volleyball coach should hire a relationship-motivated person as an assistant. In this way, the expressive and instrumental needs of the team can be met at the same time. One coach need not change personality styles to try to meet the various requirements of the situation and different needs of the athletes. Such a utilitarian approach to leadership is very intriguing. In fact, it is not uncommon to observe that the head coach and one or more of the assistants differ markedly in terms of their concern for the expressive and instrumental functions. This theory deserves to be more completely investigated and tested in the sport setting.

8. **Principle** It is very difficult for a single leader or coach to display a high level of task and relationship behavior at the same time.

   Application A head coach might select an assistant coach to compliment his or her strengths and/or weaknesses. If the head coach is very task oriented and a "hard-driver," a "person"-oriented assistant coach might be selected to complement the head coach's strength.

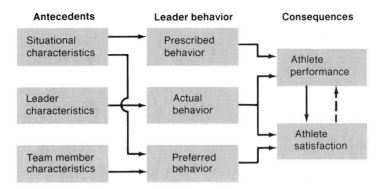

Figure 11.6 Chelladurai's multidimensional model of leadership. From P. Chelladurai and A. V. Carron, *Leadership.* Copyright © 1978 by the Canadian Association for Health, Physical Education and Recreation. Used with permission of the Publisher.

Chelladurai's Multidimensional Model of Leadership

Chelladurai's (1978) **multidimensional model** of leadership, illustrated in figure 11.6, provides an interactional approach to conceptualizing the leadership process. In this model, athlete satisfaction and performance are viewed as the products of the interaction of three components of leadership: prescribed leader behavior, preferred leader behavior, and actual leader behavior. *Prescribed leader behaviors* are those that conform to the established norms of the organization. In the military, for example, officers are expected to behave in a certain manner in the presence of their subordinates. *Preferred leader behaviors* are those behaviors that are preferred by the athletes. For example, members of a rugby team might prefer that the coach party with the team after a game. Finally, *actual leader behaviors* are those behaviors that the leader exhibits irrespective of the norms or preferences of the team.

Based on the model illustrated in figure 11.6, Chelladurai (1978) and Chelladurai and Carron (1978) hypothesized certain consequences of the *congruence* among the three types of leader behavior. As can be observed in table 11.5, when there is congruence between all three types of leader behavior, the outcome should be ideal in terms of performance and satisfaction. A laissez-faire outcome is predicted when all three leader behaviors are incongruent with each other. If actual behavior is incongruent with both prescribed and preferred leader behavior, it is expected that the leader will be removed. If the prescribed and actual behaviors are congruent, but both are incongruent with preferred behavior, then performance may be high, but athletes may be dissatisfied. Finally, if actual and preferred behavior is congruent, but prescribed behavior is incongruent, then athletes may be satisfied, but performance may suffer.

Table 11.5 Leader Behavior Congruence and Outcomes

Leader Behavior			Outcome
Prescribed	*Actual*	*Preferred*	
+	+	+	Ideal
−	−	−	Laissez faire
+	−	+	Removal of leader
+	+	−	Performance
−	+	+	Satisfaction

+ Congruence with other types of behavior
− Lack of congruence with other types of behavior

From P. Chelladurai and A. V. Carron, *Leadership*. Copyright © 1978 by the Canadian Association for Health, Physical Education and Recreation. Used with permission of the publisher.

While the specifics of the Chelladurai model have not yet been adequately tested or verified, several studies have been reported that provide support for the basic model. Chelladurai (1984) examined the discrepancy between preferred and perceived leadership and an athlete's satisfaction. Congruence between preferred and perceived (actual) leadership should result in an increase in an athlete's satisfaction. Leadership behavior was measured with the Leadership Scale for Sports and athlete satisfaction through a prepared questionnaire. Subjects for the research were 196 college basketball players, wrestlers, and track and field athletes. As predicted by the Chelladurai Model, the results showed that if an athlete's perception of a coach's behavior was incongruent with the athlete's preference, satisfaction declined. Furthermore, athlete satisfaction declines rapidly if the discrepancy occurs as a function of training and instruction and/or positive feedback.

In a related investigation, Royal, Whiteside, and McClelan (1985) reported that an athlete's perception of a coach is mediated by a similarity bias. For example, a coach may be viewed as being intelligent by an athlete if the athlete perceives him- or herself to be similar to the coach. Conversely, an athlete would rate the coach as being less intelligent if the athlete perceived dissimilarities between him- or herself and the coach. Finally, Chelladurai and Arnott (1985) placed four leadership decision styles on a continuum and asked athletes to specify their preference across sixteen different evaluative situations. The four decision styles were autocratic, consultive, participatory, and delegative in nature. A total of 144 male and female college varsity basketball players participated in the research. Results revealed that the preferred leadership styles for both men and women were the autocratic (36%) and the participatory styles (41%). Very few athletes preferred the delegative style in any situation. Female athletes preferred the participatory decision style to a much greater degree than did male athletes.

9. **Principle** Discrepancies between an athlete's preferred coaching behavior and actual or prescribed coaching behavior has a measurable effect on an athlete's performance and/or satisfaction.

   Application Athletes enter into the athletic environment with certain predetermined expectations about coaching behavior. Coaches should take this into account as they attempt to motivate athletes to superior performance.

Coach-Athlete Compatibility

An important factor that has been linked with leader effectiveness is **coach-athlete compatibility** (Horne & Carron, 1985). The quality of the relationship between the coach and the athlete is an important determinant of team success and satisfaction.

Coach-athlete compatibility was studied in some detail by Carron and Bennett (1977). The purpose of this investigation was to examine the factors contributing to compatibility between coaches and athletes. This was accomplished by comparing compatible coach-athlete dyads with incompatible dyads. As explained by Carron and Bennett, coach-athlete compatibility exists when the coach's behavior is compatible with that which the athlete desires, and vice versa. Dyads were formed and compared using the Fundamental Interpersonal Relations Orientation-Behavior Questionnaire (FIRO-B) developed by Schutz (1966). This tool measures two aspects of behavior—those expressed to others, and those desired of others—and three dimensions of interpersonal needs—affection, inclusion, and control. According to Schutz's classification system, *affection* refers to close personal emotional feelings between two people. *Control* is related to such terms as power, authority, and dominance. Finally, *inclusion* refers to association among people and is related in a positive sense to such terms as communication and interaction. In a negative sense, inclusion is reflected in the terms *exclusion, isolation,* and *withdrawal.*

The results of the Carron and Bennett research revealed that compatible and incompatible coach-athlete dyads could be mildly differentiated on the basis of control and affection. Highly compatible dyads were characterized by athletes and coaches who were able to initiate both affection and control. However, the prime discriminator between the compatible and incompatible dyads was the social behavior of inclusion. It appears that the relationship within the incompatible dyads was characterized by relatively detached, withdrawn, and isolated behavior on the part of both coach and athlete. Those in the incompatible dyads were simply unable to *communicate* with each other. This finding underscores the importance of quality interaction between coaches and athletes.

Along with the important ability to communicate, another important discriminator between compatible and incompatible coach-athlete dyads is *rewarding behavior.* Compatible coach-athlete dyads are characterized by coaches who consistently reward athletes for effort and performance (Horne & Carron, 1985). Rewarding behavior is also very important for the development of feelings of satisfaction on the part of the athlete (Weiss & Friedrichs, 1986). Some of the differences between compatible and incompatible coach-athlete dyads are illustrated in figure 11.7.

Observing that the leader of a team is often responsible for the climate of the group, Fisher, Mancini, Hirsch, Proulx, and Staurowsky (1982) designed a study to determine the relationship between coach-athlete interaction and perceived satisfaction. Four hundred and seventy-four high school basketball players and their coaches completed a social climate scale and had their practices videotaped for later analysis. The videotape practices were then analyzed using a descriptive analysis procedure that allowed the coding of specific behaviors into verbal and

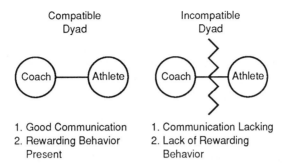

Figure 11.7 Some characteristics of compatible and incompatible dyads.

nonverbal categories. The results of the study provided some interesting insights into coach-player relationships. Athletes who are members of teams high in satisfaction receive more praise and are more likely to initiate coach-athlete communication. Coaches of athletic teams that are high in satisfaction design creative and imaginative practices, and spend very little time dispensing information. Coaches and athletes are responsible to some degree for each other's behavior. Finally, a significant disparity exists between the coaches' and the athletes' perceptions of the difference between the real and the ideal environment. Coaches tend to view the real environment as being ideal, while the athletes often see a great disparity between what is happening and what they think should be happening.

Other researchers have also identified disparity between coach and athlete perceptions. Percival (1971) reported an investigation in which 382 athletes and 66 coaches rated coaches on a scale of 1 to 10 on selected coaching behaviors: personality, techniques, knowledge, and mechanics. The results revealed that for all four areas evaluated, the athletes rated the coaches lower than the coaches rated themselves. In all categories, the coaches gave themselves positive evaluations more often than negative evaluations. The athletes, however, rated the coaches negatively in each category except mechanics. Bird (1977b) reported that women volleyball coaches perceived themselves to be task oriented, while players perceived the coaches to be more socioemotional (relationship oriented). The notion that coaches and athletes often differ on their perception of the coach's behavior was also documented by Horne and Carron (1985).

The research on coach-athlete interaction suggests that the relationship between the athlete and the coach has plenty of room for improvement. In light of the lack of quality interaction between coach and athlete, Miller (1982) suggested assertiveness training for coaches to help them relate to athletes. Assertiveness involves appropriate expression of thoughts and feelings on the part of the coach so that the self-esteem of the athlete is not damaged. Overly assertive coaches may damage interpersonal relationships. Unassertive coaches, on the other hand, allow players to take advantage of them. Miller's assertiveness training module for coaches involves eight essential components and eight associated therapeutic objectives. Actual execution of the model involves following three steps:

1. Describe the situation to the athlete. "Your assignment was to cover the power angle on that spike."
2. Tell how it affects the team. "When you follow through with your assignment, it provides the coverage necessary for an effective defense."
3. Tell what you think should be done. "I'd appreciate it if you would master your assignment and follow the strategy now and in the future."

The three steps in Miller's training program allow the coach to maintain a quality relationship. The athlete receives specific information and is told exactly how to perform. More importantly, athletes are not shamed or embarrassed by attacks on their self-esteem.

---

10. **Principle** The quality of coach-athlete interaction is a critical factor in team success and satisfaction.

   Application Perhaps the most important factor in improving coach-athlete interaction is communication. Coaches must encourage two-way communication between themselves and their athletes. If the athletes feel that the coach values their input, they will feel comfortable in a two-way interaction.

Geographic Location and Leadership Opportunity

Of interest to sport psychologists are situations that seem to promote leadership opportunity. For example, Grusky (1963) designed a study that hypothesized that player position in baseball was related to leadership opportunity. Specifically, Grusky proposed that the *geographical location* of a baseball player was predictive of whether or not the player would later become a major league manager.

Grusky argued that the critical factor in player location was the opportunity for player interaction. He further proposed that the opportunity for high interaction was associated with centrality, communication, and the nature of the task. The term **centrality** refers to the spatial location of the athletes (central versus peripheral), while communication relates to the degree of verbal and visual interaction between players. The nature of the task is closely associated with interaction, since some tasks in baseball require a high degree of communication while others do not. For example, the outfielder's task of catching a line drive is a highly independent task, while the infielder's task of turning a double play is highly interdependent.

In Grusky's design, the infielders and catchers were categorized as being high interactors, while the outfielders and pitchers were considered to be low interactors. Looking at all major league managers from 1921 to 1941 and 1951 to 1958, Grusky determined that 97 percent of them played major league ball. Additionally, 77 percent of the managers were from the high interaction group, while only 23 percent were from the low interaction group. Thus playing position appeared to be highly related to leadership opportunity. Furthermore, former catchers made up 26 percent of the total sample of major league managers, but they made up only 11 percent of the original player sample during the years studied. Apparently, the position of catcher is highly related to player interaction and leadership opportunity.

An important follow-up to the Grusky research was a study by Loy and Sage (1970) in which the relationship between player position in baseball and leadership qualities was again investigated. Using a sample of high school athletes, Loy and Sage hypothesized that player interaction, in terms of position, would be related to the selection of team captains and interpersonal attraction. As predicted, the results indicated that high interactors (catchers and infielders) were selected as the team captains much more often than low interactors (pitchers and outfielders). High interactors were also perceived to be better liked and more valuable to the team than low interactors.

Chelladurai and Carron (1977) proposed a geographical location model based on the dimensions of *propinquity* and *task dependence*. In so doing, they argued against the notion of centrality, since in many sports, being located in the geographical center of the team cannot be deemed crucial to task dependency or interaction. For example, the catcher in baseball and the point guard in basketball are not at the geographical center of the team yet they are the individuals highest in interaction potential.

Chelladurai and Carron's dimension of **propinquity** is associated with the observability and visibility of an athlete by teammates. The catcher in baseball, though not always central to the action, is definitely the most observable and visible. The second dimension of **task dependence** is associated with the level of interaction required to successfully complete a task. For example, a double play in baseball is a highly dependent task requiring coordination between the shortstop and second baseman.

Using the two-dimensional model, Chelladurai and Carron reconsidered the Grusky (1963) and Loy and Sage (1970) baseball data. The results of their analysis are illustrated in figure 11.8. As can be observed in this figure, the baseball position highest in propinquity and task dependence is the catcher. Lowest in

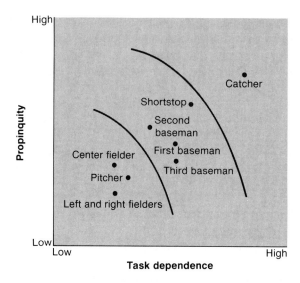

Figure 11.8 Categorization of baseball positions on the basis of propinquity and task dependence. From P. Chelladurai and A. V. Carron. A reanalysis of formal structure in sport. *Canadian Journal of Applied Sport Sciences, 2,* 9–14, 1977. Reproduced by permission of the Publisher.

these two dimensions were the outfielders. Clearly, certain positions on an athletic team enjoy greater propinquity and dependence. These positions are associated with greater leadership potential and opportunity.

More recently, Fabianic (1984) reconsidered the playing position hypothesis and related it to the paucity of minority managers in Major League Baseball. A highly visible characteristic of professional baseball is the relative absence of minorities serving in managerial positions. Traditionally it has been argued that blacks are seldom selected as managers because they did not occupy highly interactive positions as players (Loy & McElvogue, 1970).

Data from 1951 to 1980 and 1980 alone show that the majority of baseball managers continue to be selected from the interactive positions (infield), even though infielders made up fewer players than noninteractive players combined (outfield, pitchers, and designated hitters). Thus according to Fabianic's analyses, managers continue to be selected from highly interactive positions. However, in 1980 minority players (black and Hispanic) made up 29 percent of all players and were distributed in the high and low interactive position groups in the same proportion. Based on expected representation, nine of the total thirty-two managers should have been from minority groups—six from the high interactive group and three from the low interactive group. Yet in 1980 there were only two managers representing minority groups (Maury Wills and Preston Gomez). Clearly race bias is involved in the selection of managers in professional baseball. While geographical location continues to be a salient factor in the selection of white managers, this generalization does not include minorities.

Most of the geographical location research that has dealt with leadership has focused on baseball. However, there is no reason why the Chelladurai and Carron two-dimensional model could not be applied to football (Ball, 1973), basketball, and volleyball. Based on the Grusky (1963), Loy and Sage 1970), and Fabianic (1984) research, we can predict that leadership opportunities in football, basketball, and volleyball would fall primarily to quarterbacks, point guards, and setters, respectively.

---

11. **Principle** The coach can develop leadership skills in young athletes by placing them in team positions requiring observability, visibility, and task dependence.

   Application It is usually the athlete who already has leadership ability who gets to be the quarterback in football or the catcher in baseball. Coaches should use this knowledge to help their players develop leadership skills. Young athletes who lack leadership ability could benefit from playing point guard on the basketball team or quarterback on the football team.

Motivation through Task Enrichment

The main purpose of this chapter has been to explain what leadership is and what makes a leader effective. Having accomplished this, I now turn the reader's attention to a discussion of how a coach or leader can best motivate followers, employees, and/or athletes.

According to Hackman and Oldham's (1975) **Employee Enrichment Model,** employee production and performance is a function of how the employee or follower perceives his or her task or job. The model proposes that positive outcomes (self motivation, satisfaction, and performance) are obtained when three critical *psychological states* are present in the employee. These three psychological states include perceived meaningfulness of task, perceived responsibility, and immediate knowledge of results.

Whether or not the psychological states are present depends on the presence of five "core" *job dimensions*. The five job dimensions include skill variety, task identity, task significance, autonomy, and feedback. In summary, the employee enrichment model proposes that task motivation, performance, and satisfaction

can be enhanced if the five core task dimensions are present. The presence of these five dimensions creates the three psychological states which in turn give rise to greater motivation, satisfaction, and performance.

The basic model, as proposed by Hackman and Oldham, is presented in figure 11.9. The model has been adapted to an athletic or sport situation. In this respect, the employees are athletes, the tasks are the skills involved in sport, and the outcomes are those factors associated with success and/or failure in sport. The Employee Enrichment Model has been a topic of management textbooks (Dessler, 1982; Donnelly, Gibson & Ivancevich, 1984) and has received considerable research support in industry (Brief & Aldag, 1975; Jenkins, Nadler & Lawler, 1975).

The Hackman and Oldham model of employee motivation lends itself well to sport. Athletes are placed in a situation where they repetitively practice skills

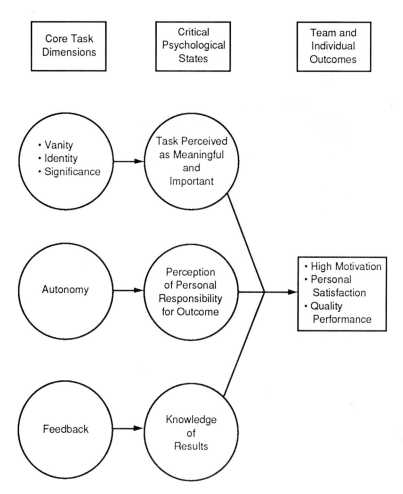

Figure 11.9 Hackman and Oldham's Employee Enrichment Model. From J. R. Hackman and G. R. Oldham, Development of the job diagnostic survey. *Journal of Applied Psychology, 60,* 159–170. Copyright © 1975 by the American Psychological Association. Adapted by permission of the author.

and team situations. Without proper motivation, practices can become boring and nonrewarding. The Employee Enrichment Model identifies specific aspects of an activity or task that can be addressed and improved on in order to facilitate greater athlete motivation.

The theory holds that followers are most responsive and motivated when the three psychological states are present. It is the responsibility of the coaches and assistant coaches to ensure the presence of all three of these factors simultaneously. In order for an athlete or sportsperson to be fully motivated, he or she must feel that his or her task is meaningful. In this respect, there are three ways in which the athlete recognizes meaningfulness. First, the assigned task must be interesting and involve *variety*. A task that is perceived by the athlete as mundane or uninteresting will not be motivating. An individual who requires a great deal of variety should not be assigned a playing position that they find uninteresting. For this reason, some young athletes might find playing in the outfield in baseball or softball to be boring since most of the "action" occurs in the infield.

A second way in which meaningfulness might be manifested is through task *identity*. Athletes need to feel that they are involved from beginning to end in the accomplishment of a task. If they are not involved in the final outcome or do not recognize their own involvement in the completion of a task, they will not identify with it. In sport, it is the job of the coach to help all members of a team feel a part of the successful outcome of a game, tournament, or season. The coach must highlight the importance of substitutes and players who play bit roles in an outcome.

The third way in which meaningfulness is manifested in sport is through task *significance*. Regardless of an athlete's role on a team, he or she must feel that it is important and significant to the goals of the team generally. In basketball some players are identified as the primary scorers, while others may be encouraged to play support roles. If the athlete does not view the support role as being significant, motivation will suffer.

The second psychological state that must be present is *autonomy* or the notion that one feels personal responsibility for an outcome. An athlete feels responsibility for his or her own outcomes when he or she feels personally accountable to success as well as failure. Accountability is associated with the degree to which the athlete is involved in decision making and planning. In football, the quarterback who either calls his own plays or is deeply involved in the game plan will feel more accountability than the quarterback who merely carries out instructions from the sidelines. Human beings generally display greater levels of motivation when they are given significant amounts of freedom and independence, and then held accountable for their actions.

Finally, the psychological state of knowing how one is doing is critical to player motivation. Athletes will be much more responsive and motivated if they receive immediate and continuous *feedback* (knowledge of results) on how well they are playing their position. In conclusion, athletes will be more motivated, more successful, and more satisfied if they perceive that their job is important, they feel responsible, and they receive immediate feedback on their performance.

12. **Principle** An athlete's level of motivation, performance, and feeling
of satisfaction can be enhanced through task enrichment.

    Application The leader or coach must strive to help each athlete
perceive that his or her role is meaningful, that he or she is
personally responsible for outcomes, and that he or she is
constantly aware of his or her own performance (knowledge of
results/feedback).

Summary

Stogdill (1950) defined leadership as the process of influencing the activities of
an organized group in its efforts toward goal setting and goal achievement. This
definition is consistent with Carron's (1980) notion of an influence system as opposed to a power system of leadership. Behling and Schriesheim (1976) proposed
a typology of leadership theory that provides a logical approach to the study of
leadership theory. This typology categorizes various theories in terms of traits
and behaviors and in terms of whether the theory emphasizes universal or situation-specific leader characteristics. According to this system, there are four basic
types of leadership theories.

    The "great man" or trait theory of leadership placed an emphasis on the notion
that great leaders possess a set of universally consistent personality traits or dispositions that facilitate successful leadership. A second important type of leadership theory is based on the notion that successful leaders possess a relatively
universal set of behavioral characteristics that can be identified. This type of
leadership theory was spearheaded by researchers at the University of Michigan
and Ohio State University. An important outcome of this research was the identification of consideration and initiating structure as the two most important leader
behaviors. A third typological approach to the study of leadership was represented by Fiedler's contingency theory. Fiedler emphasized the notion that leader
effectiveness is situation specific and contingent on certain factors associated with
the favorableness of the situation and the personality of the leader. The fourth
broad category of theories discussed in this chapter was referred to as situation-
specific theories. The basic difference between these theories and Fiedler's theory
is that the emphasis is on situation-specific leader behaviors as opposed to stable
personality traits. Leadership theories discussed under this heading included path-
goal theory, life cycle theory, functional theory, and Chelladurai's multidimensional model of leadership.

Coach-athlete interaction was discussed as an important factor influencing leadership. The quality of the relationship between the coach and the athlete is an important determinant of team success and athlete satisfaction. Geographical location is a factor that is related to leadership opportunity. Research shows that the majority of Major League managers are selected from former players who played in positions of high visibility and interaction.

An athlete's motivation, success, and satisfaction are enhanced when the coach helps the athlete to perceive his or her role as meaningful and autonomous. Performance feedback is also important for player success and motivation.

Review Questions

1. According to Behling and Schriesheim (1976), approaches to studying leadership can be categorized according to two dimensions. Describe these dimensions and give the names of the basic theories that fall into the typology.
2. Discuss the trait or "Great Man" theory of leadership. Explain the strengths and shortcomings of this approach to leadership.
3. Outline and describe the universal behavior approach to leadership theory. Include a discussion of the Ohio State and Michigan studies and major contributions they made.
4. Outline and describe Fiedler's contingency theory. How does it compare to trait theory and behavioral theories?
5. Discuss Chelladurai's multidimensional model of leadership. What sort of theory is this? What are its strengths and weakness?
6. Which theory or combination of theories can you best relate to? Explain why.
7. In your judgment, how important is the specific situation in terms of leadership effectiveness? Explain.
8. What are some of the factors that can improve the quality of interaction between the coach and the athlete? What are compatible and incompatible dyads? Explain.
9. What is the relationship between player position and leadership opportunity? Does this relationship apply to minorities in sport? Explain your answer.
10. Describe the Employee Enrichment Model of employee motivation. What are the critical psychological states that are necessary for the athlete to experience high motivation, success, and satisfaction? How can the coach facilitate greater motivation?

Glossary

autocratic leadership A task-structured form of leadership that discourages coach-athlete interaction.

CBAS Abbreviation for the Coaching Behavior Assessment System designed by Smith et al. (1977).

centrality A term that refers to a central geographical location on an athletic team.

coach-athlete compatibility Situation in which the coach's behavior is compatible with that which the athlete desires, and vice versa.

consideration Indicative of friendship, mutual trust, respect, and warmth between the coach and athlete.

democratic leadership A relationship-oriented form of leadership that encourages coach-athlete interaction.

Employee Enrichment Model An athlete or follower's capacity for increased motivation, success, and satisfaction as enhanced through task enrichment.

Fiedler's contingency theory A leadership theory that is situation specific but retains an emphasis on general personality traits.

functional model A leadership theory proposed by Behling and Schriesheim (1976) that proposes that a single leader cannot satisfy the needs of all the athletes.

influence system A system in which influence or interaction between coach and athlete runs both ways.

initiating structure A leadership style in which patterns of organization, channels of communication, and procedures are well established.

LBDQ Abbreviation for the Leader Behavior Description Questionnaire developed in the Ohio State studies.

life cycle theory A situational theory that proposes that preferred leadership style depends upon the maturity of the athlete.

LPC Abbreviation for the Least Preferred Co-Worker scale developed by Fiedler for identifying leadership motivation.

LSS Abbreviation for the Leadership Scale for Sports developed by Chelladurai and Saleh (1978).

Managerial Grid The notion that leadership style is a function of concern for production and concern for people.

McGregor's Theory X Workers are lazy and irresponsible and therefore need motivation and direction.

McGregor's Theory Y Workers are naturally self-motivated and responsible and therefore only need encouragement.

Michigan studies Leader behavior research that took place at the University of Michigan shortly after World War II. Like the Ohio State studies, the Michigan studies identified two main kinds of leader behavior. These were labeled employee orientation and production orientation.

multidimensional model An interaction model of leadership proposed by Chelladurai and Carron (1978).

Ohio State studies Leader behavior research conducted at Ohio State University at the same time, but independent of, the Michigan studies. The Ohio State studies identified consideration and initiating structure as the two most important factors in leader behavior.

path-goal theory Theory of leadership in which the emphasis is on the needs and goals of the athlete.

power system Basic system of leadership in which the influence runs from coach to athlete.

propinquity A term associated with geographical location, used to indicate the visibility and observability of an athlete by teammates.

relationship motivation A leadership orientation consistent with consideration, in which the athlete's needs receive high priority.

scientific management Theory of management developed by Taylor that focused on the efficiency of the management process.

situational behaviors Leadership behaviors that are effective in one situation but not another.

situational traits Leadership traits that are effective in one situation but not another.

task dependence A term associated with geographical location that refers to the amount of interaction required between teammates for a task to be completed.

task motivation A leadership orientation consistent with initiating structure in which the successful completion of the task is the critical factor.

universal behaviors A certain set of leadership behaviors believed to be possessed by all successful leaders.

universal traits A certain set of personality traits believed to be possessed by all successful leaders.

Recommended Readings

Ball, D. W. (1973). Ascription and position: Comparative analysis of stacking in professional football. *Canadian Review of Sociology and Anthropology, 10,* 97–113.

Behling, O., & Schriesheim, C. (1976). *Organizational behavior: Theory, research and application.* Boston: Allyn and Bacon.

Blake, R. R., & Mouton, J. S. (1985). *The managerial grid III: The key to leadership excellence.* Houston: Gulf Publishing Company.

Case, B. (1987). Leadership behavior in sport: A field test of the situational leadership theory. *International Journal of Sport Psychology, 18,* 256–268.

Chelladurai, P., & Carron, A. V. (1977). A reanalysis of formal structure in sport. *Canadian Journal of Applied Sport Sciences 2,* 9–14.

Chelladurai, P., & Carron, A. V. (1978). *Leadership.* Canadian Association for Health, Physical Education and Recreation, Sociology of Sport Monograph Series.

Fabianic, D. (1984). Minority managers in professional baseball. *Sociology of Sport Journal, 1,* 163–171.

Fiedler, F. E. (1974). The contingency model—new directions for leadership utilization. *Contemporary Business, 4,* 65–79.

Fiedler, F. E., Chemmers, M. M., & Mahar, L. (1977). *Improving leadership effectiveness: The leader match concept.* New York: John Wiley and Sons.

Grusky, O. (1963). The effects of formal structure on managerial recruitment: A study of baseball organization. *Sociometry, 26,* 345–353.

Hackman, J. R., & Oldham, G. R. (1975). Development of the job diagnostic survey. *Journal of Applied Psychology, 60,* 159–170.

Halpin. A. W., & Winer, B. J. (1957). A factorial study of the Leader Behavior Description Questionnaire. In R. M. Stogdill & A. E. Coons (eds.), *Leader behavior: Its description and measurement.* Columbus: Ohio State University Press.

Horn, T. S. (1984). Expectancy effects in the interscholastic athletic setting: Methodological considerations. *Journal of Sport Psychology, 6,* 60–76.

Likert, R. (1961). *New patterns of management.* New York: McGraw-Hill.

McGregor, D. (1960). *The human side of enterprise.* New York: McGraw-Hill.

Sage, G. H. (1973). The coach as management: Organizational leadership in American sport. *Quest, 19,* 35–40.

Sage, G. H. (1975). An occupational analysis of the college coach. In D. W. Ball & J. W. Loy (eds.), *Sport and social order.* Reading, MA: Addison-Wesley.

Smith, R. E., Smoll, F. L., & Curtis, B. (1979). Coach effectiveness training: A cognitive-behavioral approach to enhancing relationship skills in youth sport coaches. *Journal of Sport Psychology, 1,* 59–75.

Williams, P. M., & Wassenaar, D. J. (1975). *Leadership.* San Jose, CA: Lansford.

References

Aguglia, E., & Sapienza, S. (1984). Locus of control according to Rotter's S.R.I. in volleyball players. *International Journal of Sport Psychology, 15,* 250–258.

Alberti, R. E. (1977). Comments on differentiating assertion and aggression: Some behavioral guidelines. *Behavioral Therapy, 8,* 353–354.

Albrecht, R. R., & Feltz, D. L. (1987). Generality and specificity of attention related to competitive anxiety and sport performance. *Journal of Sport Psychology, 9,* 231–248.

Allison, J. (1970). Respiration changes during transcendental meditation. *Lancet, 1,* 833–834.

Allport, F. H. (1924). *Social psychology.* Boston: Houghton-Mifflin.

Allport, G. W. (1937). *Personality—a psychological interpretation.* New York: Holt and Company.

Ames, C. (1978). Children's achievement attributions and self-reinforcement: Effects of self-concept and competitive reward structures. *Journal of Educational Psychology, 70,* 345–355.

Anderson, G. L. (1973). *The assessment of learning environments: A manual for the learning environment inventory and the my class inventory.* Halifax, Nova Scotia: Atlantic Institute of Education.

Anderson, M. B., & Williams, J. M. (1987). Gender role and sport competition anxiety: A re-examination. *Research Quarterly for Exercise and Sport, 58,* 52–56.

Andrud, W. E. (1970). "The personality of high school, college, and professional football coaches as measured by the Guilford-Zimmerman temperament survey." Master's thesis, University of North Dakota, Grand Forks.

Anshel, M. A. (1979). Effect of age, sex, and type of feedback on motor performance and locus of control. *Research Quarterly, 50,* 305–317.

Anshel, M. H. (1987). Psychological inventories used in sport psychology research. *The Sport Psychologist, 1,* 331–349.

Ardrey, R. (1966). *The territorial imperative.* New York: Dell.

Arkes, H. R., & Garske, J. P. (1982). *Psychological theories of motivation* (2d ed.). Monterey, CA: Brooks/Cole Publishing Company.

Arms, R. L., Russell, G. W., & Sandilands, M. L. (1980). Effects of viewing aggressive sports on the hostility of spectators. In R. M. Suinn (ed.), *Psychology in sports: Methods and applications.* Minneapolis: Burgess Publishing Company.

Arnold, G. E., & Straub, W. F. (1972). Personality and group cohesiveness as determinants of success among interscholastic basketball teams. In I. D. Williams & L. M. Wankel (eds.), *Proceedings of the Fourth Canadian Psychomotor Learning and Sports Psychology Symposium.* Ottawa, Ontario: Department of National Health and Welfare.

Atkinson, J. W. (1958). *Motives in fantasy, action, and society.* New York: D. Van Nostrand Company.

Atkinson, J. W. (1964). *An introduction to motivation.* New York: D. Van Nostrand Company.

Atkinson, J. W., & Litwin, G. H. (1960). Achievement motivation and test anxiety conceived as motive to approach success and motive to avoid failure. *Journal of Abnormal and Social Psychology, 60,* 52–63.

Atkinson, J. W., & Raphelson, A. C. (1956). Individual differences in motivation and behavior in particular situations. *Journal of Personality, 24,* 349–363.

Bacon, S. J. (1974). Arousal and the range of cue utilization. *Journal of Experimental Psychology, 102,* 81–87.

Baer, L. (1980). Effect of a time-slowing suggestion on performance accuracy on a perceptual motor task. *Perceptual and Motor Skills, 51,* 167–176.

Bagchi, B. K., & Wenger, M. A. (1957). Electrophysiological correlates of some yoga exercises. *Electroencephalography and Clinical Neurophysiology, 7,* 132–149.

Bahrick, H. P., Fitts, P. M., & Rankin, R. E. (1952). Effect of incentives upon reactions to peripheral stimuli. *Journal of Experimental Psychology, 44,* 400–446.

Bahrke, M. S. (1979). Exercise, meditation and anxiety reduction: A review. *American Corrective Therapy Journal, 33,* 41–44.

Bakan, D. (1966). *The duality of human existence.* Chicago: Rand McNally.

Bakeman, R., & Helmreich, R. (1975). Cohesiveness and performance: Covariation and causality in an undersea environment. *Journal of Experimental Social Psychology, 11,* 478–489.

Ball, D. W. (1973). Ascription and position: Comparative analysis of stacking in professional football. *Canadian Review of Sociology and Anthropology, 10,* 97–113.

Ball, J. R., & Carron, A. V. (1976). The influence of team cohesion and participation motivation upon performance success, and intercollegiate ice hockey. *Canadian Journal of Applied Sport Sciences, 1,* 271–275.

Balog, L. F. (1983). The effects of exercise on muscle tension and subsequent muscle relaxation training. *Research Quarterly for Exercise and Sport, 54,* 119–125.

Bandura, A. (1973). *Aggression: A social learning analysis.* Englewood Cliffs, NJ: Prentice-Hall.

Bandura, A. (1977). Self-efficacy: Toward a unifying theory of behavioral change. *Psychological Review, 84,* 191–215.

Bandura, A. (1982). Self-efficacy mechanism in human agency. *American Psychologist, 37,* 122–147.

Bandura, A., Ross, D., & Ross, S. (1961). Transmission of aggression through imitation of aggressive models. *Journal of Abnormal and Social Psychology, 63,* 575–582.

Barber, T. X. (1971). Physiologic effects of hypnosis and suggestion. In T. X. Barber et al. (eds.), *Biofeedback and self-control (1971): An Aldine reader on the regulation of bodily process and consciousness.* New York: Aldine-Atherton.

Barber, T. X., Spanos, N. P., & Chaves, J. F. (1974). *Hypnosis, imagination, and human potentialities.* New York: Pergamon Press.

Barnes, M. W., Sime, W., Dienstbier, R., & Plake, B. (1986). A test of construct validity of the CSAI-2 questionnaire on male elite college swimmers. *International Journal of Sport Psychology, 17,* 364–374.

Baron, R. A. (1971). Exposure to an aggressive model and apparent probability of retaliation from the victim as determinants of adult aggressive behavior. *Journal of Experimental Social Psychology, 7,* 343–355.

Baron, R. A. (1977). *Human aggression.* New York: Plenum Press.

Baron, R. A., & Bell, P. A. (1976). Aggression and heat: The influence of ambient temperature, negative affect, and a cooling drink on physical aggression. *Journal of Personality and Social Psychology, 33,* 245–255.

Baron, R. S., Moore, D., & Sanders, S. (1978). Distraction as a source of drive in social facilitation research. *Journal of Personality and Social Psychology, 36,* 816–824.

Baumeister, R. F., & Steinhilber, A. (1984). Paradoxical effects of supportive audiences on performance under pressure: The home field advantage in sports championships. *Journal of Personality and Psychology, 47,* 85–93.

Beary, J. F., Benson, H., & Klemchuk, H. P. (1974). A simple psychophysiologic technique which elicits the hypometabolic changes of the relaxation response. *Psychosomatic Medicine, 36,* 115–120.

Behling, O., & Schriesheim, C. (1976). *Organizational behavior: Theory, research, and application.* Boston: Allyn and Bacon.

Bem, S. L. (1974). The measurement of psychological androgyny. *Journal of Consulting and Clinical Psychology, 42,* 155–162.

Bem, S. L. (1977). On the utility of alternative procedures for assessing psychological androgyny. *Journal of Consulting and Clinical Psychology, 45,* 196–205.

Bennett, B. K., & Stothart, C. M. (1980). The effects of a relaxation-based cognitive technique on sport performances. In P. Klavora & K. A. W. Wipper (eds.), *Psychological and sociological factors and sport.* Toronto: University of Toronto Press.

Benson, H., Beary, J. F., & Carol, M. P. (1974). The relaxation response. *Psychiatry, 37,* 37–46.

Berger, B. C. (1970). "Effect of three sport environmental factors upon selected personality characteristics of athletes." Unpublished doctoral dissertation, Teachers College, Columbia University, New York.

Bergum, B. O., & Lehr, D. J. (1963). Effects of authoritarianism on vigilance performance. *Journal of Applied Psychology, 47,* 75–77.

Berkowitz, L. (1958). The expression and reduction of hostility. *Psychological Bulletin, 55,* 257–283.

Berkowitz, L. (1962). *Aggression: A social psychological analysis.* New York: McGraw-Hill.

Berkowitz, L. (1964). Aggressive cues in aggressive behavior and hostility catharsis. *Psychological Review, 71,* 104–122.

Berkowitz, L. (1965). The concept of aggressive drive: Some additional considerations. In L. Berkowitz (ed.), *Advances in experimental social psychology* (Vol. 2, 301–329).

Berkowitz, L. (1969a). The frustration-aggression hypothesis revisited. In L. Berkowitz (ed.), *Roots of aggression.* New York: Atherton Press.

Berkowitz, L. (1969b). Simple views of aggression, an essay review. *American Scientist, 57,* 372–383.

Berkowitz, L. (1970). Experimental investigations of hostility catharsis. *Journal of Consulting and Clinical Psychology, 35,* 1–7.

Berkowitz, L. (1972). Sports, competition, and aggression. In I. D. Williams & L. M. Wankel (eds.), *Proceedings of the Fourth Canadian Psychomotor Learning and Sport Psychology Symposium.* Waterloo, Ontario: University of Waterloo.

Berkowitz, L. (1981). On the difference between internal and external reactions to legitimate and illegitimate frustrations: A demonstration. *Aggressive Behavior, 7,* 83–96.

Berkowitz, L., & Alioto, J. T. (1973). The meaning of an observed event as a determinant of its aggressive consequences. *Journal of Personality and Social Psychology, 28,* 206–217.

Berkowitz, L., & LePage, A. (1967). Weapons as aggression-eliciting stimuli. *Journal of Personality and Social Psychology, 7,* 202–207.

Beuter, A., & Duda, J. L. (1985). Analysis of the arousal/motor performance relationship in children using movement kinematics. *Journal of Sport Psychology, 7,* 229–243.

Bird, A. M. (1977a). Development of a model for predicting team performance. *Research Quarterly, 48,* 24–32.

Bird, A. M. (1977b). Leadership and cohesion within successful and unsuccessful teams: Perceptions of coaches and players. In D. M. Landers & R. W. Christina (eds.), *Psychology of motor behavior and sport* (Vol. 2). Champaign, IL: Human Kinetics Publishers.

Bird, A. M., & Williams, J. M. (1980). A developmental-attributional analysis of sex-role stereotypes for sport performance. *Developmental Psychology, 16,* 319–322.

Bird, E. I. (1972). A review and evaluation of the assessment of aggression among women athletes as measured by personality inventories. In I. D. Williams & L. M. Wankel (eds.), *Proceedings of the Fourth Canadian Psychomotor Learning and Sport Psychology Symposium.* Waterloo, Ontario: University of Waterloo.

Blake, R. R., & Mouton, J. S. (1978). *The new managerial grid.* Houston, TX: Gulf Publishing Company.

Blake, R. R., & Mouton, J. S. (1985). The managerial grid III: The key to leadership excellence. Houston, TX: Gulf Publishing Company.

Block, N. (ed.). (1981). *Imagery.* Cambridge, MA: MIT Press.

Boutcher, S. H., & Crews, D. J. (1987). The effect of a preshot attentional routine on a well-learned skill. *International Journal of Sport Psychology, 18,* 30–39.

Boutcher, S. H., & Rotella, R. J. (1987). A psychological skills education program for closed-skill performance enhancement. *The Sport Psychologist, 1,* 127–137.

Bowers, K. S. (1973). Situationalism in psychology: An analysis and a critique. *Psychological Review, 80,* 307–336.

Bradley, G. W. (1978). Self-serving biases in the attribution process: Reexamination of the fact or fiction question. *Journal of Personality and Social Psychology, 36,* 56–71.

Brawley, L. R. (1984). Unintentional egocentric biases in attributions. *Journal of Sport Psychology, 6,* 264–278.

Brawley, L. R., Carron, A. V., & Widmeyer, W. N. (1987). Assessing the cohesion of teams: Validity of the group environment questionnaire. *Journal of Sport Psychology, 9,* 275–294.

Brawley, L. R., Carron, A. V., & Widmeyer, W. N. (1988). Exploring the relationship between cohesion and group resistance to disruption. *Journal of Sport & Exercise Psychology, 10,* 199–213.

Bredemeier, B. J. (1978). The assessment of reactive and instrumental athletic aggression. *Proceedings of the International Symposium on Psychological Assessment.* Neyanya, Israel: Wingate Institute for Physical Education and Sport.

Bredemeier, B. J. (1980). Applications of aggression research. In W. F. Straub (ed.), *Sport psychology: An analysis of athlete behavior* (2d ed.). Ithaca, NY: Mouvement Publications.

Bredemeier, B. J. (1983). Athletic aggression: A moral concern. In J. H. Goldstein (ed.), *Sports Violence.* New York: Springer-Verlag.

Bredemeier, B. J. (1985). Moral reasoning and the perceived legitimacy of intentionally injurious sport acts. *Journal of Sport Psychology, 7,* 110–124.

Bredemeier, B. J., & Shields, D. L. (1984). The utility of moral stage analysis in the investigation of athletic aggression. *Sociology of Sport Journal, 1,* 138–149.

Bredemeier, B. J., & Shields, D. L. (1986). Athletic aggression: An issue of contextual morality. *Sociology of Sport Journal, 3,* 15–28.

Bredemeier, B. J., Weiss, M. R., Shields, D. L., & Cooper, B. A. B. (1986). The relationship of sport involvement with children's moral reasoning and aggression tendencies. *Journal of Sport Psychology, 8,* 304–318.

Bredemeier, B. J., Weiss, M. R., Shields, D. L., & Cooper, B. A. B. (1987). The relationship between children's legitimacy judgements and their moral reasoning, aggression tendencies, and sport involvement. *Sociology of Sport Journal, 4,* 48–60.

Brief, A. P., & Aldag, R. J. (1975). Employee reactions to job characteristics: A constructive replication. *Journal of Applied Psychology, 60,* 182–186.

Broadbent, D. E. (1957). Mechanical model for human attention and immediate memory. *Psychological Review, 64,* 205–215.

Broadbent, D. E. (1958). *Perception and communication.* London: Pergamon Press.

Broadbent, D. E. (1970). Stimulus set and response set: Two kinds of selective attention. In D. I. Mostofsky (ed.), *Attention: Contemporary theory and analysis.* Englewood Cliffs, NJ: Prentice-Hall.

Brody, N. N. (1963). Achievement, test anxiety, and subjective probability of success in risk-taking behavior. *Journal of Abnormal and Social Psychology, 66,* 413–418.

Broen, W. F., Jr., & Storms, L. H. (1961). A reactive potential ceiling and response decrements in complex situations. *Psychological Review, 68,* 405–415.

Brown, B. A. (1977). *Stress and the art of biofeedback.* New York: Harper & Row.

Brustad, R., & Weiss, M. R. (1987). Competence perceptions and sources of worry in high, medium, and low competitive trait-anxious athletes. *Journal of Sport Psychology, 9,* 97–105.

Bryant, J., & Zillman, D. (1983). Sports violence and media. In J. H. Goldstein (ed.), *Sports violence.* New York: Springer-Verlag.

Buck, J. N. (1948, October). The H-T-P technique: A qualitative and quantitative scoring manual. *Journal of Clinical Psychology* (Monog. Suppl. No. 5).

Bursill, A. F. (1958). The restriction of peripheral vision during exposure to hot and humid conditions. *Quarterly Journal of Experimental Psychology, 10,* 113–129.

Burton, D. (1988). Do anxious swimmers swim slower?: Reexamining the elusive anxiety-performance relationship. *Journal of Sport and Exercise Psychology, 10,* 45–61.

Burwitz, L., & Newell, K. M. (1972). The effects of the mere presence of coactors on learning a motor skill. *Journal of Motor Behavior, 4,* 99–102.

Buss, A. H. (1963). Physical aggression in relation to different frustrations. *Journal of Abnormal and Social Psychology, 67,* 1–7.

Buss, A. H. (1971). Aggression pays. In J. E. Singer (ed.), *The control of aggression and violence: Cognitive and physiological factors.* New York: Academic Press.

Buss, A. H., & Durkee, A. (1957). An inventory for assessing different kinds of hostility. *Journal of Consulting Psychology, 21,* 343–348.

Carment, D. W. (1970). Rate of simple motor responding or a function of variation of competition and sex of the participants. *Psychonomic Science, 19,* 342–343.

Carron, A. V. (1975). Personality and athletics: A review. In B. S. Rushall (ed.), *The status of psychomotor learning and sport psychology research.* Dartmouth, Nova Scotia: Sport Science Associates.

Carron, A. V. (1980). *Social psychology of sport.* Ithaca, NY: Mouvement Publications.

Carron, A. V. (1982). Cohesiveness in sport groups: Interpretations and considerations. *Journal of Sport Psychology, 4,* 123–138.

Carron, A. V., & Ball, J. R. (1977). An analysis of the cause-effect characteristics of cohesiveness and participation motivation in intercollegiate hockey. *International Review of Sport Sociology, 12,* 49–60.

Carron, A. V., & Bennett, B. B. (1976). The effects of initial habit strength differences upon performance in a coaction situation. *Journal of Motor Behavior, 8,* 297–304.

Carron, A. V., & Bennett, B. B. (1977). Compatibility in the coach-athlete dyad. *Research Quarterly, 48,* 671–679.

Carron, A. V., & Chelladurai, P. (1981). The dynamics of group cohesion in sport. *Journal of Sport Psychology, 3,* 123–139.

Carron, A. V., Widmeyer, W. N., & Brawley, L. R. (1985). The development of an instrument to assess cohesion in sport teams: The group environment questionnaire. *Journal of Sport Psychology, 7,* 244–266.

Carron, A. V., Widmeyer, W. N., & Brawley, L. R. (1988). Group cohesion and individual adherence to physical activity. *Journal of Sport & Exercise Psychology, 10,* 127–138.

Carter, L. F., & Nixon, M. (1949). An investigation of the relationship between four criteria of leadership ability for three different tasks. *Journal of Psychology, 27,* 245–261.

Cartwright, D. (1968). The nature of group cohesiveness. In D. Cartwright & A. Zander (eds.), *Group dynamics: Research and theory* (3d ed.). New York: Harper & Row.

Cartwright, D., & Zander, A. (eds.). (1968). *Group dynamics: Research and theory* (3d ed.). New York: Harper & Row.

Case, B. (1987). Leadership behavior in sport: A field test of the situational leadership theory. *International Journal of Sport Psychology, 18,* 256–268.

Case, R. W. (1980). "An examination of the leadership behaviors of selected successful basketball coaches at four competitive levels." Unpublished doctoral dissertation, Ohio State University, Columbus, OH.

Castaneda, A., & Lipsitt, L. P. (1950). Relation of stress and differential position habits to performance in motor learning. *Journal of Experimental Psychology, 57,* 25–30.

Cataldi, P., Jr. (1980). Sport and aggression: A safety valve or a pressure cooker? In W. F. Straub (ed.), *Sport psychology: An analysis of athlete behavior* (2d ed.). Ithaca, NY: Mouvement Publications.

Cattell, R. B. (1965). *The scientific analysis of personality.* Baltimore: Penguin.

Cattell, R. B. (1973, July). Personality pinned down. *Psychology Today,* 40–46.

Cattell, R. B., Eber, H. W., & Tatsuoka, M. M. (1980). *Handbook for the Sixteen Personality Factor Questionnaire (16 PF).* Champaign, IL: Institute for Personality and Ability Testing.

Caudill, D., Weinberg, R., & Jackson, A. (1983). Psyching-up and track athletes: A preliminary investigation. *Journal of Sport Psychology, 5,* 231–235.

Chalip, L. (1980). Social learning theory and sport success: Evidence and implications. *Journal of Sport Behavior, 3,* 76–85.

Chapman, A. J. (1973). Social facilitation of laughter in children. *Journal of Experimental Social Psychology, 9,* 528–541.

Chapman, A. J. (1974). An electromyographic study of social facilitation: A test of the "mere presence" hypothesis. *British Journal of Psychology, 65,* 123–128.

Chelladurai, P. (1978). "A multidimensional model of leadership." Unpublished doctoral dissertation, University of Waterloo, Waterloo, Ontario.

Chelladurai, P. (1984). Discrepancy between preferences and perceptions of leadership behavior and satisfaction of athletes in varying sports. *Journal of Sport Psychology, 6,* 27–41.

Chelladurai, P., & Arnott, M. (1985). Decision styles in coaching: Preferences of basketball players. *Research Quarterly for Exercise and Sport, 56,* 15–24.

Chelladurai, P., & Carron, A. V. (1977). A reanalysis of formal structure in sport. *Canadian Journal of Applied Sport Sciences, 2,* 9–14.

Chelladurai, P., & Carron, A. V. (1978). *Leadership.* Canadian Association for Health, Physical Education and Recreation, Sociology of Sport Monograph Series. Ottawa, Ontario: Canadian Association for Health, Physical Education and Recreation.

Chelladurai, P., & Carron, A. V. (1981). Applicability to youth sports of the leadership scale for sports. *Perceptual and Motor Skills, 53,* 361–362.

Chelladurai, P., & Carron, A. V. (1983). Athletic maturity and preferred leadership. *Journal of Sport Psychology, 5,* 371–380.

Chelladurai, P., & Saleh, S. D. (1978). Preferred leadership in sport. *Canadian Journal of Applied Sport Sciences, 3,* 85–97.

Chelladurai, P., & Saleh, S. D. (1980). Dimensions of leader behavior in sports: Development of a leadership scale. *Journal of Sport Psychology, 2,* 34–35.

Cherry, E. C. (1953). Some experiments on the recognition of speech, with one and with two ears. *Journal of the Acoustical Society of America, 25,* 975–979.

Christy, P. R., Gelfand, D. M., & Hartmann, D. P. (1971). Effects of competition-induced frustration on two classes of modeled behavior. *Developmental Psychology, 5,* 104–111.

Church, R. M. (1962). The effects of competition on reaction time and palmar skin conductance. *Journal of Abnormal and Social Psychology, 65,* 32–40.

Clark, L. V. (1960). Effect of mental practice on the development of a certain motor skill. *Research Quarterly, 31,* 560–569.

Clarke, J. C., & Jackson, J. A. (1983). *Hypnosis and behavior therapy: The treatment of anxiety and phobias.* New York: Springer Publishing Company.

Coakley, J. J. (1982). *Sport in society: Issues and controversies.* St. Louis: C. V. Mosby.

Cofer, C. N., & Johnson, W. R. (1960). Personality dynamics in relation to exercise and sports. In W. R. Johnson (ed.), *Science and medicine of exercise and sport.* New York: Harper & Row.

Coleman, T. R. (1976). "A comparative study of certain behavioral, physiological, and phenomenological effects of hypnotic induction and two progressive relaxation procedures." Ph.D. dissertation, Brigham Young University, Provo, UT.

Cooper, L. (1969). Athletics, activity, and personality: A review of the literature. *Research Quarterly, 40,* 17–22.

Corbin, C. B. (1967a). The effects of covert practice on the development of a complex motor skill. *Journal of General Psychology, 76,* 143–150.

Corbin, C. B. (1967b). Effects of mental practice on skill development after controlled practice. *Research Quarterly, 38,* 534–538.

Corbin, C. B. (1977). The reliability and internal consistency of the motivation rating scale and the general trait rating scale. *Medicine and Science in Sports, 9,* 208–211.

Corbin, C. B. (1981). Sex of subject, sex of opponent, and opponent ability as factors affecting self-confidence in a competitive situation. *Journal of Sport Psychology, 3,* 265–270.

Corbin, C. B., & Nix, C. (1979). Sex-typing of physical activities and success predictions of children before and after cross-sex competition. *Journal of Sport Psychology, 1,* 43–52.

Costa, A., Bonaccorsi, M., & Scrimali, T. (1984). Biofeedback and control of anxiety preceding athletic competition. *International Journal of Sport Psychology, 15,* 98–109.

Cottrell, N. B. (1972). Social facilitation. In C. G. McClintock (ed.), *Experimental social psychology.* New York: Holt, Rinehart and Winston, 1972.

Cottrell, N. B., Wack, D. L., Sekerak, G. L., & Rittle, R. H. (1968). Social facilitation of dominant responses by the presence of an audience and the mere presence of others. *Journal of Personality and Social Psychology, 9,* 245–250.

Cox, F. N. (1962). An assessment of the achievement behavior system in children. *Child Development, 33,* 907–916.

Cox, R. H. (1980). *Teaching volleyball.* Minneapolis: Burgess Publishing Company.

Cox, R. H. (1986). Relationship between skill performance in women's volleyball and competitive state anxiety. *International Journal of Sport Psychology, 17,* 183–190.

Cox, R. H. (1987b). An exploratory investigation of a signal discrimination problem in tennis. *Journal of Human Movement Studies, 13,* 197–210.

Cox, R. H. (1987a). "Relationship between psychological variables with player position and experience in women's volleyball." Unpublished manuscript.

Crable, J. M., & Johnson, G. V. (1980). Male and female coaction in a competitive environment. *Journal of Sport Behavior, 3,* 86–94.

Craighead, D. J., Privette, F. V., & Byrkit, D. (1986). Personality characteristics of basketball players, starters, and non-starters. *International Journal of Sport Psychology, 17,* 110–119.

Crandall, V. C. (1963). Achievement. In H. W. Stevenson (ed.), *Child psychology.* Chicago: University of Chicago Press.

Crasilneck, H. B., & Hall, J. A. (1959). Physiological changes associated with hypnosis: A review of the literature since 1948. *International Journal of Clinical and Experimental Hypnosis, 7,* 9–50.

Cratty, B. J. (1981). *Social psychology in athletics.* Englewood Cliffs, NJ: Prentice-Hall.

Cratty, B. J. (1983). *Psychology in contemporary sport: Guidelines for coaches and athletes.* Englewood Cliffs, NJ: Prentice-Hall.

Cratty, B. J., & Sage, J. N. (1964). The effects of primary and secondary group interaction upon improvement in a complex movement task. *Research Quarterly, 35,* 164–175.

Cullen, J. B., & Cullen, F. T. (1975). The structure and contextual conditions of group norm violations: Some implications from the game of ice hockey. *International Review of Sport Sociology, 10,* 69–77.

Dabbs, J. M., Jr., Johnson, J. E., & Leventhal, H. (1968). Palmar sweating: A quick and simple measure. *Journal of Experimental Psychology, 78,* 347–350.

Dahlstrom, W. G., & Walsh, G. W. (1960). *A Minnesota multiphasic personality handbook.* Minneapolis: University of Minnesota Press.

Daniels, F. S., & Landers, D. M. (1981). Biofeedback and shooting performance: A test of disregulation and systems theory. *Journal of Sport Psychology, 3,* 271–282.

Danielson, R. R. (1977). Leadership motivation and coaching classification as related to success in minor league hockey. In D. M. Landers & R. W. Christina (eds.), *Psychology of motor behavior and sport, 1976* (Vol. 2). Champaign, IL: Human Kinetics Publishers.

Danielson, R. R., Zelhart, P. F., & Drake, C. J. (1975). Multidimensional scaling and factor analysis of coaching behavior as perceived by high school hockey players. *Research Quarterly, 46,* 323–334.

Danskin, D. G., & Crow, M. A. (1981). *Biofeedback: An introduction and guide.* Palo Alto, CA: Mayfield Publishing Company.

Dashiell, J. E. (1935). Experimental studies of the influence of social situations on the behavior of individual human adults. In C. Murchison (ed.), *A handbook of social psychology.* Worcester, MA: Clark University Press.

Davis, J. H. (1969). *Group performance.* Reading, MA: Addison-Wesley.

Davis, R. C., & Kantor, J. R. (1935). Skin resistance during hypnotic states. *Journal of General Psychology, 13,* 62–81.

Deabler, H. L., Fidel, E., Dillenkoffer, R. L., & Elder, S. (1973). The use of relaxation and hypnosis in lowering high blood pressure. *American Journal of Clinical Hypnosis, 16,* 75–83.

DeCharms, R. C., & Carpenter, V. (1968). Measuring motivation in culturally disadvantaged school children. *Journal of Experimental Education, 37,* 31–41.

Deci, E. L. (1971). Effects of externally mediated rewards on intrinsic motivation. *Journal of Personality and Social Psychology, 18,* 105–115.

Deci, E. L. (1972). Intrinsic motivation, extrinsic reinforcement. *Journal of Personality and Social Psychology, 22,* 113–120.

Deci, E. L. (1975). *Intrinsic motivation.* New York: Plenum Press.

Deci, E. L. (1978). Intrinsic motivation: Theory and application. In D. M. Landers & R. W. Christina (eds.), *Psychology of motor behavior and sport, 1977.* Champaign, IL: Human Kinetics Publishers.

Deci, E. L. (1980). *The psychology of self-determination.* Lexington, MA: Lexington Books.

Deci, E. L., Cascio, W. F., & Krusell, J. (1975). Cognitive evaluation theory and some comments on the Calder and Straw critique. *Journal of Personality and Social Psychology, 31,* 81–85.

Deluty, R. H. (1979). Children's action tendency scale: A self-report measure of aggressiveness, assertiveness, and submissiveness in children. *Journal of Consulting and Clinical Psychology, 47,* 1061–1071.

Dessler, G. (1982). *Organization & Management.* Reston, Virginia: Reston Publishing Company.

Deutsch, M. (1968). The effects of cooperation and competition upon group processes. In D. Cartwright & A. T. Zander (eds.), *Group dynamics: Research and theory.* New York: Harper & Row.

DeWitt, D. J. (1980). Cognitive and biofeedback training for stress reduction with university athletes. *Journal of Sport Psychology, 2,* 288–294.

DiCara, L. V. (1970). Learning in the autonomic nervous system. *Scientific American, 222,* 30–39.

DiGuiseppe, R. A. (1973). Internal-external control of reinforcement and participation in team, individual, and intramural sports. *Perceptual and Motor Skills, 36,* 33–34.

Dmitrova, S. (1970). Dependence of voluntary effort upon the magnitude of the goal and the way it is set in sportsmen. *International Journal of Sport Psychology, 1,* 29–33.

Dollard, J., Miller, N., Doob, L., Mourer, O. H., & Sears, R. R. (1939). *Frustration and aggression.* New Haven, CT: Yale University Press.

Donnelly, J. H., Jr., Gibson, J. L., & Ivancevich, J. M. (1984). *Fundamentals of management.* Plano, Texas: Business Publications, Inc.

Donnelly, P. (1975). "An analysis of the relationship between organizational half-life and organizational effectiveness." Paper completed for an advanced topics course, Department of Sport Studies, University of Massachusetts, Amherst.

Donnelly, P., Carron, A. V., & Chelladurai, P. (1978). *Group cohesion and sport.* Ottawa, Ontario: Canadian Association for Health, Physical Education and Recreation.

Dowthwaite, P. K., & Armstrong, M. R. (1984). An investigation into the anxiety levels of soccer players. *International Journal of Sport Psychology, 15,* 149–159.

Duda, J. L. (1987). Toward a developmental theory of children's motivation in sport. *Journal of Sport Psychology, 9,* 130–145.

Dudley, D. L., Holmes, T. H., Martin, C. J., & Ripley, H. S. (1963). Changes in respiration associated with hypotically induced emotion, pain, and exercise. *Psychosomatic Medicine, 26,* 46–57.

Duffy, E. (1957). The psychological significance of the concept of arousal or activation. *Psychological Review, 64,* 265–275.

Duffy, E. (1962). *Activation and behavior.* New York: John Wiley and Sons.

Duke, M., Johnson, T. C., & Nowicki, S., Jr. (1977). Effects of sports fitness campus experience on locus of control orientation in children, ages 6 to 14. *Research Quarterly, 48*(2), 280–283.

Dulberg, H. N., & Bennett, F. W. (1980). Psychological changes in early adolescent males induced by systematic exercise. *American Corrective Therapy Journal, 34*(5), 142–146.

Duncan, T., & McAuley, D. (1987). Efficacy expectations and perceptions of causality in motor performance. *Journal of Sport Psychology, 9,* 385–393.

Duquin, M. E. (1978). Attributions made by children in coeducational sport settings. In D. M. Landers & R. W. Christina (eds.), *Psychology of motor behavior and sport, 1977.* Champaign, IL: Human Kinetics Publishers.

Dweck, C. S. (1975). The role of expectations and attributions in the alleviation of learned helplessness. *Journal of Personality and Social Psychology, 31,* 674–685.

Dweck, C. S. (1980). Learned helplessness in sport. In C. H. Nadeau, W. R. Halliwell, K. M. Newell & G. C. Roberts (eds.), *Psychology of motor behavior and sport, 1979*. Champaign, IL: Human Kinetics Publishers.

Dweck, C. S., & Goetz, T. E. (1978). Attributions and learned helplessness. In J. H. Harvey, W. J. Ickes & R. F. Kidd (eds.), *New directions in attribution research* (Vol. 2). Hillsdale, NJ: Erlbaum.

Dweck, C. S., & Reppucci, N. (1973). Learned helplessness and reinforcement responsibility in children. *Journal of Personality and Social Psychology, 25,* 109–116.

Easterbrook, J. A. (1959). The effect of emotion on cue utilization and the organization of behavior. *Psychological Review, 66,* 183–201.

Edmonston, W. E., Jr. (1981). *Hypnosis and relaxation: Modern verification of an old equation.* New York: John Wiley and Sons.

Edwards, A. C. (1959). *Manual, Edwards personal preferences schedule.* New York: The Psychological Corporation.

Edwards, J. (1979). The home field advantage. In J. H. Goldstein (ed.), *Sports, games, and play: Social and psychological viewpoints.* Hillsdale, NJ: Halstead Press.

Eitzen, D. S. (1973). The effect of group structure on the success of athletic teams. *International Review of Sport Sociology, 8,* 7–17.

Ellis, H. C., Goggin, J. P., & Parenté, F. J. (1979). Human memory and learning: The processing of information. In M. E. Meyer (ed.), *Foundations of contemporary psychology.* New York: Oxford University Press.

Endler, N. S., & Hunt, J. M. (1966). Sources of behavioral variance as measured by the S-R inventory of anxiousness. *Psychological Bulletin, 65,* 336–346.

Epstein, M. L. (1980). The relationship of imagery and mental rehearsal to performance of a motor task. *Journal of Sport Psychology, 2,* 211–220.

Epstein, S., & Taylor, S. P. (1967). Instigation to aggression as a function of degree of defeat and perceived aggressive intent of opponent. *Journal of Personality, 35,* 265–270.

Essing, W. (1970). Team line-up and team achievement in European football. In G. S. Kenyon (ed.), *Contemporary psychology of sport.* Chicago: The Athletic Institute.

Estabrooks, G. H. (1930). The psychogalvanic reflex in hypnosis. *Journal of General Psychology, 3,* 150–157.

Etzel, E. F. (1979). Validation of a conceptual model characterizing attention among international rifle shooters. *Journal of Sport Psychology, 1,* 281–290.

Eysenck, H. J. (1972). Primaries of second-order factors: A critical consideration of Cattell's 16 PF battery. *British Journal of Social and Clinical Psychology, 11,* 265–269.

Eysenck, H. J. (1976). *The measurement of personality.* London: MTP Press.

Eysenck, H. J., & Eysenck, S. B. G. (1968a). *Eysenck personality inventory manual.* London: University of London Press.

Eysenck, S. B. G., & Eysenck, H. J. (1968b). The measurement of psychoticism: A study of factor stability and reliability. *British Journal of Social and Clinical Psychology, 7,* 286–294.

Fabianic, D. (1984). Minority managers in professional baseball. *Sociology of Sport Journal, 1,* 163–171.

Feather, N. P. (1961). The relationship of persistence at a task to expectation of success and achievement-related motives. *Journal of Abnormal and Social Psychology, 63,* 552–561.

Feigley, D. A. (1983). Is aggression justifiable? *Journal of Physical Education, Recreation and Dance, 54* (9), 63–64.

Feltz, D. L., & Landers, D. M. (1983). The effects of mental practice on motor skill learning and performance: A meta-analysis. *Journal of Sport Psychology, 5,* 25–57.

Feltz, D. L., Landers, D. M., & Raeder, U. (1979). Enhancing self-efficacy in high-avoidance motor tasks: A comparison of modeling techniques. *Journal of Sport Psychology, 1,* 112–124.

Feltz, D. L., & Mugno, D. A. (1983). A replication of the path analysis of the causal elements in Bandura's theory of self-efficacy and the influence of autonomic perception. *Journal of Sport Psychology, 5,* 263–277.

Fenigstein, A. (1979). Does aggression cause a preference for viewing media violence? *Journal of Personality and Social Psychology, 37,* 2307–2317.

Fenker, R. M., & Lambiotte, J. G. (1987). A performance enhancement program for a college football team: One incredible season. *The Sport Psychologist, 1,* 224–236.

Fenz, W. D. (1975). Coping mechanisms and performance under stress. In D. M. Landers (ed.), *Psychology of sport and motor behavior II*, Penn State HPER Series, No. 10. University Park: Pennsylvania State University Press.

Fenz, W. D. (1988). Learning to anticipate stressful events. *Journal of Sport and Exercise Psychology, 10*, 223–228.

Feshbach, S. (1971). Dynamics and morality of violence and aggression: Some psychological considerations. *American Psychologist, 26*, 281–292.

Festinger, L., Schachter, S., & Back, K. (1950). *Social pressures in informed groups: A study of a housing project*. New York: Harper.

Fiedler, F. E. (1954). Assumed similarity measures as predictors of team effectiveness. *Journal of Abnormal and Social Psychology, 49*, 381–388.

Fiedler, F. E. (1967). *A theory of leadership effectiveness*. New York: McGraw-Hill.

Fiedler, F. E. (1971). *Leadership*. Morristown, NJ: General Learning Press.

Fiedler, F. E. (1974). The contingency model—new directions for leadership utilization. *Journal of Contemporary Business, 4*, 65–79.

Fiedler, F. E., & Chemers, M. M. (1974). *Leadership and effective management*. Glenview, IL: Scott, Foresman and Company.

Fiedler, F. E., Chemers, M. M., & Mahar, L. (1977). *Improving leadership effectiveness—the leader match concept*. New York: John Wiley and Sons.

Fimrite, R. (1985, November 4). K. C. had a blast. *Sports Illustrated*, 22–38.

Fineman, S. (1977). The achievement motive construct and its measurement: Where are we now? *British Journal of Psychology, 68*, 1–22.

Finn, J. A. (1976). Perception of violence among high-hostile and low-hostile women athletes and nonathletes before and after exposure to sport films. In F. Landry & W. A. R. Orban (eds.), *Motor learning, sports psychology, pedagogy, and didactics of physical activity* (Book 7). Miami, FL: Symposia Specialists.

Finn, J. A., & Straub, W. F. (1977). Locus of control among Dutch and American women softball players. *Research Quarterly, 48*, 56–60.

Fisher, A. C. (1976). *Psychology of sport*. Palo Alto, CA: Mayfield Publishing Company.

Fisher, A. C. (1986, April). "Imagery from a sport psychology perspective." Paper presented at the meeting of the American Alliance for Health, Physical Education, Recreation and Dance, Cincinnati, Ohio.

Fisher, A. C., Borowicz, S. K., & Morris, H. H. (1978). Behavioral rigidity across sport situations. In D. M. Landers & R. W. Christina (eds.), *Psychology of motor behavior and sport, 1977*. Champaign, IL: Human Kinetics Publishers.

Fisher, A. C., Mancini, V. H., Hirsch, R. L., Proulx, T. J., & Staurowsky, E. J. (1982). Coach-athlete interactions and team climate. *Journal of Sport Psychology, 4*, 388–404.

Fisher, A. C., & Zwart, E. F. (1982). Psychological analysis of athletes' anxiety responses. *Journal of Sport Psychology, 4*, 139–158.

Fisher, R. J. (1982). *Social psychology of an applied approach*. New York: St. Martin's Press.

Fitts, P. M., & Posner, M. I. (1967). *Human performance*. Belmont, CA: Brooks/Cole.

Fleishman, E. A., Harris, E. F., & Burtt, H. E. (1955). *Leadership and supervision in industry*. Columbus: Ohio State University, Bureau of Educational Research.

Fodero, J. M. (1980). An analysis of achievement motivation and motivational tendencies among men and women collegiate gymnasts. *International Journal of Sport Psychology, 11*, 100–112.

Fontaine, C. (1975). Causal attribution on simulated versus real situations: When are people logical, when are they not? *Journal of Personality and Social Psychology, 32*, 1021–1029.

Fouts, G. T. (1980). Effect of sex of audience on speed of performance of preadolescents. *Perceptual and Motor Skills, 51*, 565–566.

Fredenburgh, F. A. (1971). *The psychology of personality and adjustment*. Menlo Park, CA: Benjamin-Cummings.

Freedson, P. S., Mihevic, P., Loucks, A., & Girandola, R. (1983). Physique, body composition, and psychological characteristics of competitive female bodybuilders. *The Physician and Sports Medicine, 11*, 85–90, 93.

Freischlag, J., & Schmedke, C. (1980). Violence in sports: Its causes and some solutions. In W. F. Straub (ed.), *Sport psychology: An analysis of athlete behavior* (2d ed.). Ithaca, NY: Mouvement Publications.

French, J. R. P., & Raven, B. (1959). The bases of power. In D. Cartwright (ed.), *Studies in social power.* Ann Arbor: University of Michigan, Institute for Social Research.

French, S. N. (1978). Electromyographic biofeedback for tension control during gross motor skill acquisition. *Perceptual and Motor Skills, 47,* 883–889.

Freud, S. (1950). Why war? In J. Strachey (ed.), *Collected papers.* London: Hogarth.

Friedman, M., & Rosenman, R. H. (1974). *Type A behavior and your heart.* New York: Alfred A. Knopf.

Frieze, I. H. (1976). Causal attributions and information seeking to explain success and failure. *Journal of Research in Personality, 10,* 293–305.

Frieze, I. H., & Weiner, B. (1971). Cue utilization and attributional judgements for success and failure. *Journal of Personality, 39,* 591–605.

Furst, D. M., & Gershon, T. (1984). A correlation of body-cathaxis and anxiety in athletes and nonathletes. *International Journal of Sport Psychology, 15,* 160–168.

Gagen, J. J. (1971). "Risk-taking within football situations of selected football coaches." Master's thesis, Kent State University, Kent, OH.

Gammon, C. (1985, June 10). A day of horror and shame. *Sports Illustrated, 62,* 20–35.

Gauron, E. F. (1984). *Mental training for peak performance.* Lansing, New York: Sport Science Associates.

Geen, R. G., & Gange, J. G. (1977). Drive theory of social facilitation: Twelve years of theory and research. *Psychological Bulletin, 84,* 1267–1288.

Geen, R. G., & O'Neal, E. C. (1969). Activation of cue-elicited aggression by general arousal. *Journal of Personality and Social Psychology, 11,* 289–292.

Geron, D., Furst, P., & Rotstein, P. (1986). Personality of athletes participating in various sports. *International Journal of Sport Psychology, 17,* 120–135.

Gershon, T. (1984). A note on the measurement and relationships of physiological and psychological components of anxiety. *International Journal of Sport Psychology, 15,* 88–97.

Gerson, R., & Deshaies, P. (1978). Competitive trait anxiety and performance as predictors of pre-competitive state anxiety. *International Journal of Sport Psychology, 9,* 16–26.

Gilbert, B., & Twyman, L. (1983, January 31). Violence: Out of hand in the stands. *Sports Illustrated,* 62–68.

Gill, D. L. (1978). Cohesiveness and performance in sport groups. In R. S. Hutton (ed.), *Exercise and Sport Science Reviews, 5,* 131–155.

Gill, D. L. (1980a). Cohesiveness and performance in sport teams. In W. F. Straub (ed.), *Sport psychology: An analysis of athlete behavior* (2d ed.). Ithaca, NY: Mouvement Publications.

Gill, D. L. (1980b). Success-failure attributions in competitive groups: An exception to egocentrism. *Journal of Sport Psychology, 2,* 106–114.

Gill, D. L., Gross, J. B., Huddleston, S., & Shifflett, B. (1984). Sex differences in achievement cognitions and performance. *Research Quarterly for Exercise and Sport, 55,* 340–346.

Gill, D. L., Ruder, M. K., & Gross, J. B. (1982). Open-ended attributions in team competition. *Journal of Sport Psychology, 4,* 159–169.

Gill, D. L., & Strom, E. H. (1985). The effect of attentional focus on performance of an endurance task. *International Journal of Sport Psychology, 16,* 217–223.

Gilligan, C. (1977). In a different voice: Women's conceptions of self and morality. *Harvard Education Review, 47,* 481–517.

Gillis, J. H. (1979). Effects of achieving tendency, gender, and outcome on causal attributions following motor performance. *Research Quarterly, 50,* 610–619.

Ginsburg, H., & Opper, S. (1969). *Piaget's theory of intellectual development.* Englewood Cliffs, NJ: Prentice-Hall.

Goldman, M., Stockbauer, J. W., & McAuliffe, T. G. (1977). Intergroup and intragroup competition and cooperation. *Journal of Experimental Social Psychology, 13,* 81–88.

Goldstein, J. H. (1983). *Sports violence.* New York: Springer-Verlag.

Goldstein, J. H., & Arms, R. L. (1971). Effects of observing athletic contests on hostility. *Sociometry, 34,* 83–90.

Goranson, R. E. (1970). Media violence and aggressive behavior: A review of experimental research. In L. Berkowitz (ed.), *Advances in experimental social psychology* (Vol. 5, 1–31). New York: Academic Press.

Gore, W. V., & Taylor, D. A. (1973). The nature of the audience as it affects social inhibition. *Representative Research in Social Psychology, 4,* 18–27.

Gorton, B. E. (1949). The physiology of hypnosis. *Psychiatric Quarterly, 23,* 457–485.

Gough, H. G. (1975). *Manual for the California psychological inventory.* Palo Alto, CA: Consulting Psychological Press.

Gould, D. (1983). Developing psychological skills in young athletes. In N. Wood (ed.), *Coaching science update.* Ottawa, Ontario: Coaching Association of Canada.

Gould, D., Horn, T., & Spreeman, J. (1983a). Competitive anxiety in junior elite wrestlers. *Journal of Sport Psychology, 5,* 58–71.

Gould, D., Horn, T., & Spreeman, J. (1983b). Sources of stress in junior elite wrestlers. *Journal of Sport Psychology, 5,* 159–171.

Gould, D., Petlichkoff, L., Simons, J., & Vevera, M. (1987). Relationship between competitive state anxiety inventory-2 subscales scores and pistol shooting performance. *Journal of Sport Psychology, 9,* 33–42.

Gould, D., Petlichkoff, L., & Weinberg, R. S. (1984). Antecedents of, temporal changes in, and relationships between CSAI-2 subcomponents. *Journal of Sport Psychology, 6,* 289–304.

Gould, D., & Weinberg, R. (1985). Sources of worry in successful and less successful intercollegiate wrestlers. *Journal of Sport Behavior, 8,* 115–127.

Gould, D., Weinberg, R., & Jackson, A. (1980). Mental preparation strategies, cognitions, and strength performance. *Journal of Sport Psychology, 2,* 329–339.

Gould, D., & Weiss, M. (1981). The effects of model similarity and model task on self-efficacy and muscular endurance. *Journal of Sport Psychology, 3,* 17–29.

Gould, D., Weiss, M., & Weinberg, R. (1981). Psychological characteristics of successful and nonsuccessful Big Ten wrestlers. *Journal of Sport Psychology, 3,* 69–81.

Graen, G., & Cashman, J. F. (1975). A rolemaking model of leadership in formal organizations. In J. G. Hunt & L. L. Larson (eds.), *Leadership frontiers.* Kent, OH: Kent State University Press.

Greene, D., & Lepper, M. R. (1974a). Effects of extrinsic rewards on children's subsequent intrinsic interest. *Child Development, 45,* 1141–1145.

Greene, D., & Lepper, M. R. (1974b, September). Intrinsic motivation: How to turn play into work. *Psychology Today,* 49–54.

Greenwell, J., & Dengerink, H. A. (1973). The role of perceived versus actual attack in human physical aggression. *Journal of Personality and Social Psychology, 26,* 66–71.

Greer, D. L. (1983). Spectator booing and the home advantage: A study of social influence in the basketball arena. *Social Psychology Quarterly, 46,* 252–261.

Griffiths, T. J., Steel, D. H., & Vaccaro, P. (1979). Relationship between anxiety and performance in SCUBA diving. *Perceptual and Motor Skills, 48,* 1009–1010.

Griffiths, T. J., Steel, D. H., Vaccaro, P., Allen, R., & Karpman, M. (1985). The effects of relaxation and cognitive rehearsal on the anxiety levels and performance of scuba students. *International Journal of Sport Psychology, 16,* 113–119.

Gross, B. M. (1964). *The managing of organizations* (Vol. 1). New York: The Free Press of Glencoe.

Grove, J. R., & Pargman, D. (1986). Attributions and performance during competition. *Journal of Sport Psychology, 8,* 129–134.

Groves, P., & Scheslinger, K. (1979). *Biological psychology.* Dubuque, IA: Wm. C. Brown Company Publishers.

Gruber, J. J., & Beauchamp, D. (1979). Relevancy of the competitive state anxiety inventory in a sport environment. *Research Quarterly, 50,* 207–214.

Gruber, J. J., & Gray, G. R. (1981). Factor patterns of variables influencing cohesiveness at various levels of basketball competition. *Research Quarterly for Exercise and Sport, 52,* 19–30.

Gruber, J. J., & Gray, G. R. (1982). Responses to forces influencing cohesion as a function of player status and level of male varsity basketball competition. *Research Quarterly for Exercise and Sport, 53,* 27–36.

Grusky, O. (1963). The effects of formal structure on managerial recruitment: A study of baseball organization. *Sociometry, 26,* 345–353.

Guyton, A. C. (1976). *Structure and function of the nervous system.* Philadelphia: W. B. Saunders Company.

Haan, N. (1982). Can research on morality be scientific? *American Psychologist, 37,* 1096–1104.

Haas, J., & Roberts, G. C. (1975). Effects of evaluative others upon learning and performance of a complex motor task. *Journal of Motor Behavior, 7,* 81–90.

Hackman, J. R., & Oldham, G. R. (1975). Development of the job diagnostic survey. *Journal of Applied Psychology, 60,* 159–170.

Hagstrom, W. O., & Selvin, H. C. (1965). The dimensions of cohesiveness in small groups. *Sociometry, 28,* 30–43.

Hale, B. D. (1982). The effects of internal and external imagery on muscular and ocular concomitants. *Journal of Sport Psychology, 4,* 379–387.

Hall, E. G., & Erffmeyer, E. S. (1983). The effect of visuo-motor behavior rehearsal with videotaped modeling of free throw accuracy of intercollegiate female basketball players. *Journal of Sport Psychology, 5,* 343–346.

Hall, H. K., & Byrne, A. T. J. (1988). Goal setting in sport: Clarifying recent anomalies. *Journal of Sport and Exercise Psychology, 10,* 184–198.

Hall, H. K., Weinberg, R. S., & Jackson, A. (1987). Effects of goal specificity, goal difficulty, and information feedback on endurance performance. *Journal of Sport Psychology, 9,* 43–54.

Halliwell, W. R. (1978). A reaction to Deci's paper on intrinsic motivation. In D. M. Landers & R. W. Christina (eds.), *Psychology of motor behavior and sport, 1977.* Champaign, IL: Human Kinetics Publishers.

Halliwell, W. R. (1980). A reaction to Dweck's paper on learned helplessness in sport. In C. H. Nadeau, W. R. Halliwell, K. M. Newell & G. C. Roberts (eds.), *Psychology of motor behavior and sport, 1979.* Champaign, IL: Human Kinetics Publishers.

Halpin, A. W. (1954). The leadership behavior and combat performance of airplane commanders. *Journal of Abnormal and Social Psychology, 49,* 19–22.

Halpin, A. W. (1966). *Theory and research in administration.* London: Macmillan.

Halpin, A. W., & Winer, B. J. (1957). A factorial study of the Leader Behavior Description Questionnaire. In R. M. Stogdill & A. E. Coons (eds.), *Leader behavior: Its description and measurement.* Columbus: Ohio State University Press.

Hamberger, K., & Lohr, J. M. (1980). Relationship of relaxation training to the controllability of imagery. *Perceptual and Motor Skills, 51,* 103–110.

Hardman, K. (1973). A dual approach to the study of personality and performance in sport. In H. T. A. Whiting, K. Hardman, L. B. Hendry, & M. G. Jones (eds.), *Personality and performance in physical education and sport.* London: Kimpton.

Harlow, R. G. (1951). Masculine inadequacy and compensatory development of physique. *Journal of Personality, 19,* 312–323.

Harrell, W. A. (1980). Aggression by high school basketball players: An observational study of the effects of opponents' aggression and frustration-inducing factors. *International Journal of Sport Psychology, 11,* 290–298.

Harris, D. V. (1972). Female aggression and sport involvement. In I. D. Williams & L. M. Wankel (eds.), *Proceedings of the Fourth Canadian Psychomotor Learning and Sport Psychology Symposium.* Waterloo, Ontario: University of Waterloo.

Harris, D. V. (1978). Assessment of motivation in sport and physical education. In W. F. Straub (ed.), *Sport psychology: An analysis of athlete behavior* (2d ed.). Ithaca, NY: Mouvement Publications.

Harris, D. V. (1980). On the brink of catastrophe. In R. M. Suinn (ed.), *Psychology in sports: Methods and applications.* Minneapolis: Burgess Publishing Company.

Harris, D. V., & Harris, B. L. (1984). *The athlete's guide to sports psychology: Mental skills for physical people.* New York: Leisure Press.

Harris, D. V., & Robinson, W. J. (1986). The effects of skill level on EMG activity during internal and external imagery. *Journal of Sport Psychology, 8,* 105–111.

Harris, M. B. (1974). Mediators between frustration and aggression in a field experiment. *Journal of Experimental Social Psychology, 10,* 561–571.

Harrison, J., & MacKinnon, P. C. B. (1966). Physiological role of the adrenal medulla in the palmar anihidrotic response in stress. *Journal of Applied Physiology, 21,* 88–92.

Harrison, R. P., & Feltz, D. L. (1979). The professionalization of sport psychology: Legal considerations. *Journal of Sport Psychology, 1,* 182–190.

Harter, S. (1978). Effectance motivation reconsidered: Towards a developmental model. *Human Development, 21,* 34–64.

Harter, S. (1982). The perceived competence scale for children. *Child Development, 53,* 87–97.

Hathaway, S. R., & McKinley, J. C. (1967). *Minnesota Multiphasic Personality Inventory manual.* New York: Psychological Corporation.

Hayberg, J. M., Mullin, J. P., Bahrke, M., & Limberg, J. (1979). Physiological profiles and selected psychological characteristics of national class American cyclists. *Journal of Sports Medicine and Physical Fitness, 19,* 341–346.

Healey, T. R., & Landers, D. M. (1973). Effect of need achievement and task difficulty on competitive and noncompetitive motor performance. *Journal of Motor Behavior, 5,* 121–128.

Heider, F. (1944). Social perception and phenomenal causality. *Psychological Review, 51,* 358–374.

Heider, F. (1958). *The psychology of interpersonal relations.* New York: John Wiley and Sons.

Hellstedt, J. C. (1987a). Sport psychology at a ski academy: Teaching mental skill to young athletes. *Journal of Sport Psychology, 1,* 56–68.

Hellstedt, J. C. (1987b). The coach/parent/athlete relationship. *The Sport Psychologist, 1,* 151–160.

Helmreich, R., & Spence, J. T. (1977). Sex roles and achievement. In R. W. Christina & D. M. Landers (eds.), *Psychology of motor behavior and sport, 1976* (Vol. 2). Champaign, IL: Human Kinetics Publishers.

Hemphill, J. K., & Coons, A. E. (1957). Development of the leader behavior description questionnaire. In R. M. Stogdill & A. E. Coons (eds.), *Leader behavior: Its description and measurement.* Columbus: Ohio State University Press.

Henchy, T., & Glass, D. C. (1968). Evaluation apprehension and the social facilitation of dominant and subordinate responses. *Journal of Personality and Social Psychology, 4,* 446–454.

Hendry, L. B. (1968). The assessment of personality traits in the coach-swimmer relationship, and a preliminary examination of the "father-figure" stereotype. *Research Quarterly, 39,* 543–551.

Hendry, L. B. (1972). The coaching stereotype. In H. T. A. Whiting (ed.), *Readings in sport psychology.* London: Kimpton.

Henry, F. M. (1941). Personality differences in athletes, physical education, and aviation students. *Psychological Bulletin, 38,* 745.

Hersey, P., & Blanchard, K. H. (1969). Life cycle theory of leadership. *Training and Developmental Journal, 23,* 26–34.

Hersey, P., & Blanchard, K. H. (1977). *Management of organizational behavior.* Englewood Cliffs, NJ: Prentice-Hall.

Hess, R. (1957). *Diencephalon-autonomic and extra-pyramidal functions.* New York: Grune and Stratton.

Heyman, S. R. (1987). Research and intervention in sport psychology: Issues encountered in working with an amateur boxer. *The Sport Psychologist, 1,* 208–223.

Hickman, J. L. (1979). How to elicit supernormal capabilities in athletes. In P. Klavora & J. V. Daniel (eds.), *Coach, athlete, and the sport psychologist.* Champaign, IL: Human Kinetics Publishers.

Highlen, P. S., & Bennett, B. B. (1979). Psychological characteristics of successful and nonsuccessful elite wrestlers: An exploratory study. *Journal of Sport Psychology, 1,* 123–137.

Hill, K. T. (1980). Motivation, evaluation, and educational testing policy. In L. J. Fyans (ed.), *Achievement motivation: Recent trends in theory and research.* New York: Plenum Press.

Hole, J. W., Jr. (1981). *Human anatomy and physiology.* Dubuque, IA: Wm. C. Brown Company Publishers.

Hollander, E. P. (1971). *Principles and methods of social psychology.* New York: Oxford University Press.

Hollandsworth, J. G. (1977). Differentiating assertion and aggression: Some behavioral guidelines. *Behavioral Therapy, 8,* 347–353.

Holsopple, J. Q., & Miale, F. R. (1954). *Sentence completion.* Springfield, IL: Charles C. Thomas.

Horn, T. S. (1984). Expectancy effects in the interscholastic athletic setting: Methodological considerations. *Journal of Sport Psychology, 6,* 60–76.

Horne, T., & Carron, A. V. (1985). Compatibility in coach-athlete relationships. *Journal of Sport Psychology, 7,* 137–149.

Horner, M. S. (1968). "Sex differences in achievement motivation and performance in competitive and noncompetitive situations." Unpublished doctoral dissertation, University of Michigan, Ann Arbor.

Horner, M. S. (1972). Towards an understanding of achievement-related conflicts in women. *Journal of Social Issues, 28*(2), 157–175.

Horsfall, J. S., Fisher, A. C., & Morris, H. H. (1975). Sport personality assessment: A methodological reexamination. In D. M. Landers (ed.), *Psychology of sport and motor behavior II.* University Park: Pennsylvania State University Press.

House, R. J. (1971). A path-goal theory of leader effectiveness. *Administrative Science Quarterly, 16,* 321–338.

House, R. J., & Dessler, C. (1974). The path-goal theory of leadership: Some post hoc and a priori tests. In J. A. Hunt & L. L. Larson (eds.), *Contingency approaches to leadership.* Carbondale: Southern Illinois University Press.

House, R. J., & Mitchell, T. R. (1974, Autumn). Path-goal theory of leadership. *Journal of Contemporary Business,* 81–97.

Huband, E. D., & McKelvie, J. S. (1986). Pre- and post-game state anxiety in team athletes high and low in competitive trait anxiety. *International Journal of Sport Psychology, 17,* 191–198.

Hull, C. L. (1933). *Hypnosis and suggestibility.* New York: Appleton.

Hull, C. L. (1943). *Principles of Behavior.* New York: Appleton-Century-Crofts, Inc.

Hull, C. L. (1951). *Essentials of behavior.* New Haven, CT: Yale University Press.

Humphrey, J. H. (1986). *Profiles in stress.* New York: AMS Press, Inc.

Hunt, J. A., & Larson, L. L. (1974). *Contingency approaches to leadership.* Carbondale: Southern Illinois University Press.

Hunt, P. J., & Hillery, J. M. (1973). Social facilitation in a coaction setting: An examination of the effects over learning trials. *Journal of Experimental Social Psychology, 9,* 563–571.

Husak, W. S., & Hemenway, D. P. (1986). The influence of competition day practice on the activation and performance of collegiate swimmers. *Journal of Sport Behavior, 9,* 95–100.

Hutchinson, B. (1972). "Locus of control and participation in intercollegiate athletics." Doctoral dissertation, Springfield College, Springfield, MA.

Hutchinson, T. P. (1981). A review of some unusual applications of signal detection theory. *Quality and Quantity, 15,* 71–98.

Ickes, W. J., & Layden, M. A. (1978). Attributional styles. In J. H. Harvey, W. J. Ickes & R. F. Kidd (eds.), *New directions in attribution research* (Vol. 2). Hillsdale, NJ: Erlbaum.

Ikai, M., & Steinhaus, A. H. (1961). Some factors modifying the expression of human strength. *Journal of Applied Physiology, 16,* 157–163.

Inciong, P. A. (1974). "Leadership styles and team success." Unpublished doctoral dissertation, University of Utah, Salt Lake City.

Institute for Personality and Ability Testing. (1979). *Eight state questionnaire.* Champaign, Illinois.

Isaacson, R. L. (1964). Relation between achievement test anxiety and curricular choices. *Journal of Abnormal and Social Psychology, 68,* 447–452.

Iso-Ahola, S. E. (1977a). Immediate attributional effects of success and failure in the field: Testing some laboratory hypotheses. *European Journal of Social Psychology, 7,* 275–296.

Iso-Ahola, S. E. (1977b). A test of the attributional theory of success and failure with Little League baseball players. In J. H. Salmela (ed.), *Canadian Symposium for Psychomotor Learning and Sport Psychology, 1975.* Ithaca, NY: Mouvement Publications.

Iso-Ahola, S. E. (1978). Perceiving the causes of objective and subjective outcomes following motor performance. *Research Quarterly, 49*(1), 62–70.

Iso-Ahola, S. E. (1979). Sex-role stereotypes and causal attributions for success and failure in motor performance. *Research Quarterly, 50,* 630–640.

Ito, M. (1979). The differential effects of hypnosis and motivational suggestions on muscular strength. *Japanese Journal of Physical Education, 24,* 93–100.

Jacobson, E. (1929). *Progressive relaxation.* Chicago: University of Chicago Press.

Jacobson, E. (1931). Electrical measurements of neuromuscular states during mental activities. *American Journal of Physiology, 96,* 115–121.

Jacobson, E. (1938). *Progressive relaxation.* Chicago: University of Chicago Press.

Jacobson, E. (1976). *You must relax.* New York: McGraw-Hill.

James, W. (1890). *The principles of psychology* (Vol. 1). New York: Henry Holt and Co.

Janis, I. L., Mahl, G. F., Kagen, J., & Holt, R. R. (1969). *Personality dynamics, development, and assessment.* New York: Harcourt Brace and World.

Jenkins, G. D., Jr., Nadler, D. A., & Lawler, E. E., III. (1975). Standard observations: An approach to measuring the nature of jobs. *Journal of Applied Psychology, 60,* 171–181.

Johnson, D. W., Maruyama, G., Johnson, R. T., Nelson, D., & Skon, L. (1981). Effects of cooperative, competitive, and individualistic goal structures on achievement: A meta-analysis. *Psychological Bulletin, 89,* 47–62.

Johnson, J. E., & Dabbs, J. M., Jr. (1967). Enumeration of active sweat glands: A sample physiological indicator of psychological changes. *Nursing Research, 16,* 273–276.

Johnson, R. T., Bjorkland, R., & Krotee, M. L. (1984). The effects of cooperation, competitive, and individualistic student interaction patterns on the achievement and attitudes of students learning the golf skill of putting. *Research Quarterly for Exercise and Sport, 55,* 129–134.

Johnson, W. R. (1961). Hypnosis and muscular performance. *Journal of Sports Medicine and Physical Fitness, 1,* 71–79.

Jung, C. G. (1971). *Psychological types* (H. G. Baynes, Translation revised by R. G. C. Hull). Volume 6 of Princeton, NJ: Princeton University Press. (Original work published in 1921.)

Kahn, R. L., & Katz, D. (1960). Leadership practices in relation to productivity and morale. In D. Cartwright & A. T. Zander (eds.), *Group dynamics.* Evanston, IL: Row, Peterson and Company.

Kahneman, D. (1970). Remarks on attention control. *Acta Psychologica, 33,* 118–131.

Kahneman, D. (1973). *Attention and effort.* Englewood Cliffs, NJ: Prentice-Hall.

Kane, J. E. (1970). Personality and physical abilities. In G. S. Kenyon (ed.), *Contemporary psychology of sport: Second International Congress of Sports Psychology.* Chicago: The Athletic Institute.

Kane, J. E. (1976). Personality and performance in sport. In J. G. W. Williams & P. N. Sperryn (eds.), *Sports medicine.* Baltimore: The Williams and Wilkins Company.

Kane, J. E. (1980). Personality research: The current controversy and implications for sport studies. In W. F. Straub (ed.), *Sport psychology: An analysis of athlete behavior* (2d ed.). Ithaca, NY: Mouvement Publications.

Karolezak-Biernacka, B. (1986). Anxiety and stress is sport: A tenative theoretical reflection. *International Journal of Sport Psychology, 17,* 398–410.

Karteroliotis, C., & Gill, D. L. (1987). Temporal changes in psychological and physiological components of state anxiety. *Journal of Sport Psychology, 9,* 261–274.

Kaufmann, H. (1970). *Aggression and altruism.* New York: Holt, Rinehart and Winston.

Kavanagh, D., & Hausfeld, S. (1986). Physical performance and self-efficacy under happy and sad moods. *Journal of Sport Psychology, 8,* 112–123.

Kay, J. (1988, June 30). Trouble in river city: Players can't cite reason for Red's poor play. *Muncie Evening Press,* 15.

Keele, S. W. (1973). *Attention and human performance.* Pacific Palisades, CA: Goodyear Publishing Company.

Kelley, H. H. (1972). *Causal schemata and the attribution process.* Morristown, NJ: General Learning Press.

Kimiecik, J. S., & Duda, J. L. (1985). Self-serving attributions among children in a competitive sport setting: Some theoretical and methodological considerations. *Journal of Sport Behavior, 8,* 78–91.

Kirkpatrick, C. (1987, February 2). Fight night. *Sports Illustrated, 66,* 59.

Kirschenbaum, D. S., Wittrock, D. A., Smith, R. J., & Monson, W. (1984). Criticism inoculation training: Concept in search of a strategy. *Journal of Sport Psychology, 6,* 77–93.

Klavora, P. (1977). An attempt to derive inverted-U curves based on the relationship between anxiety and athletic performance. In D. M. Landers & R. W. Christina (eds.), *Psychology of motor behavior and sport.* Champaign, IL: Human Kinetics Publishers.

Klein, M., & Christensen, G. (1969). Group composition, group structure, and group effectiveness of basketball teams. In J. W. Loy & G. S. Kenyon (eds.), *Sport, culture, and society.* London: Macmillan.

Klint, K. A., & Weiss, M. R. (1987). Perceived competence and motives for participating in youth sports: A test of Harter's competence motivation theory. *Journal of Sport Psychology, 9,* 55–65.

Knott, P. D., & Drost, B. A. (1972). Effects of varying intensity of attack and fear arousal on the intensity of counteraggression. *Journal of Personality, 4,* 27–37.

Kohl, R. M., Roenker, D. L., & Turner, P. E. (1985). Clarification of competent imagery as a prerequisite for effective skill imagery. *International Journal of Sport Psychology, 16,* 37–45.

Kohlberg, L. (1969). Stage and sequence: The cognitive-developmental approach to socialization. In D. A. Goslin (ed.), *Handbook of socialization theory and research.* Chicago: Rand McNally.

Kolonay, B. J. (1977). "The effects of visual-motor behavior rehearsal on athletic performance." Unpublished master's thesis, Hunter College, New York.

Korten, D. C. (1962). Situational determinants of leadership structure. *Journal of Conflict Resolution, 6,* 222–235.

Kosslyn, S. M., Pinker, S., Smith, G. E., & Schwartz, S. P. (1981). On the demystification of mental imagery. In N. Block (ed.), *Imagery.* Cambridge, MA: MIT Press.

Kramer, J. (1970). *Lombardi: Winning is the only thing.* New York: The World Publishing Company.

Kroll, W. (1967). Sixteen personality factor profiles of collegiate wrestlers. *Research Quarterly, 38,* 49–57.

Kroll, W. (1970). Current strategies and problems in personality assessment of athletes. In L. E. Smith (ed.), *Psychology of motor learning.* Chicago: The Athletic Institute.

Kroll, W., & Carlson, R. B. (1967). Discriminant function and hierarchical grouping analysis of karate participants' personality profiles. *Research Quarterly, 38,* 405–411.

Kroll, W., & Crenshaw, W. (1970). Multivariate personality profile analysis of four athletic groups. In G. S. Kenyon (ed.), *Contemporary psychology of sport: Second International Congress of Sport Psychology.* Chicago: The Athletic Institute.

Kroll, W., & Lewis, G. (1970). America's first sport psychologist. *Quest, 13,* 1–4.

Kroll, W., & Peterson, K. H. (1965). Personality factor profiles of collegiate football teams. *Research Quarterly, 36,* 433–440.

Krug, S. E. (1978). Further evidence on 16 PF distortion scales. *Journal of Personality Assessment, 42* (5), 513–518.

Kushnir, T., & Duncan, K. D. (1978). An analysis of social facilitation effects in terms of signal detection theory. *Psychological Record, 28,* 535–541.

Lacey, J., & Lacey, B. (1958). Verification and extension of the principle of autonomic response-stereotype. *American Journal of Psychology, 71,* 50–73.

Laird, D. A. (1923). Changes in motor control and individual variations under the influence of "razzing." *Journal of Experimental Psychology, 6,* 236–246.

Lake, D. G., Mites, M. B., & Earle, R. B. (1973). *Measuring human behavior.* New York: Columbia University Press.

Lan, L. Y., & Gill, D. L. (1984). The relationships among self-efficacy, stress responses, and a cognitive feedback manipulation. *Journal of Sport Psychology, 6,* 227–238.

Landers, D. (1988, April). "Cognitive states of elite performers: Psychological studies of attention." Paper presented at the meeting of the American Alliance for Health, Physical Education, Recreation and Dance (Research Consortium Scholar Lecture), Kansas City, Missouri.

Landers, D. M. (1974). Taxonomic considerations in measuring group performances and the analysis of selected group motor performance tasks. In M. G. Wade & R. Martens (eds.), *Psychology of motor behavior and sport*. Champaign, IL: Human Kinetics Publishers.

Landers, D. M. (1975). Social facilitation and human performance: A review of contemporary and past research. In D. M. Landers (ed.), *Psychology of sport and motor behavior II*. University Park: Penn State Press.

Landers, D. M. (1980a). Motivation and performance: The role of arousal and attentional factors. In W. F. Straub (ed.), *Sport psychology: An analysis of athlete behavior* (2d ed.). Ithaca, NY: Mouvement Publications.

Landers, D. M. (1980b). The arousal-performance relationship revisited. *Research Quarterly for Exercise and Sport, 51*, 77–90.

Landers, D. M. (1982). Arousal, attention, and skilled performance: Further considerations. *Quest, 33*, 271–283.

Landers, D. M., Boutcher, S. H., & Wang, M. Q. (1986). A psychobiological study of archery performance. *Research Quarterly for Exercise and Sport, 57*, 236–244.

Landers, D. M., Brawley, L. R., & Hale, B. D. (1978). Habit strength differences in motor behavior: The effects of social facilitation paradigms and subject sex. In D. M. Landers & R. W. Christina (eds.), *Psychology of motor behavior and sport, 1977*. Champaign, IL: Human Kinetics Publishers.

Landers, D. M., & Courtet, P. A. (1979, June). "Peripheral narrowing among experienced and inexperienced rifle shooters under low and high stress conditions." Paper presented at a meeting of the North American Society for Psychology of Sport and Physical Activity, Trois Rivieres, Quebec.

Landers, D. M., & Crum, T. F. (1971). The effect of team success and formal structure on interpersonal relations and cohesiveness of basketball teams. *International Journal of Sport Psychology, 2*, 88–96.

Landers, D. M., Furst, D. M., & Daniels, F. S. (1981, May–June). "Anxiety/attention and shooting ability: Testing the predictive validity of the Test of Attentional and Interpersonal Style (TAIS)." Paper presented at a meeting of the North American Society for Psychology of Sport and Physical Activity, Monterey, CA.

Landers, D. M., & Luschen, G. (1974). Team performance outcome and the cohesiveness of competitive coaching groups. *International Review of Sport Sociology, 9*, 57–71.

Landers, D. M., & McCullagh, P. D. (1976). Social facilitation of motor performance. *Exercise and Sport Sciences Reviews, 4*, 125–162.

Landers, D. M., Qi, W. M., & Courtet, P. (1985). Peripheral narrowing among experienced rifle shooters under low and high stress conditions. *Research Quarterly for Exercise and Sport, 56*, 122–130.

Landers, D. M., Wilkinson, M. O., Hatfield, B. D., & Barber, H. (1982). Causality and the cohesion-performance relationship. *Journal of Sport Psychology, 4*, 170–183.

Lansing, R. W., Schwartz, E., & Lindsley, D. B. (1956). Reaction time and EEG activation. *American Psychologist, 11*, 433.

Layman, E. M. (1980). Meditation and sports performance. In W. F. Straub (ed.), *Sport psychology: An analysis of athlete behavior* (2d ed.). Ithaca, NY: Mouvement Publications.

Lee, C. (1982). Self-efficacy as a predictor of performance in competitive gymnastics. *Journal of Sport Psychology, 4*, 405–409.

Lefebvre, L. M. (1979). Achievement motivation and causal attribution in male and female athletes. *International Journal of Sport Psychology, 10*, 31–41.

Lefebvre, L. M., Leith, L. L., & Bredemeier, B. B. (1980). Modes for aggression assessment and control. *International Journal of Sport Psychology, 11*, 11–21.

Lefebvre, L. M., & Passer, M. W. (1974). The effects of game location and importance on aggression in team sport. *International Journal of Sport Psychology, 5*(2), 102–110.

Leith, L. M. (1977). "An experimental analysis of the effect of direct and vicarious participation in physical activity on subject aggressiveness." Unpublished doctoral dissertation, University of Alberta, Edmonton.

Leith, L. M. (1978). The psychological assessment of aggression in sport: A critique of existing measurement techniques. *Proceedings of the International Symposium on Psychological Assessment.* Neyanya, Israel: Wingate Institute for Physical Education and Sport.

Leith, L. M. (1982). An experimental analysis of the effect of vicarious participation in physical activity on subject aggression. *International Journal of Sport Psychology, 13,* 234–241.

Lenk, H. (1969). Top performance despite internal conflict: An antithesis to a functional proposition. In J. W. Loy & G. S. Kenyon (eds.), *Sport, culture, and society.* New York: Macmillan.

Lenney, E. (1977). Women's self-confidence in achievement situations. *Psychological Bulletin, 84,* 1–13.

Lepper, M. R., & Greene, D. (1975). Turning play into work: Effects of adult surveillance and extrinsic rewards on children's intrinsic motivation. *Journal of Personality and Social Psychology, 31,* 479–486.

Lepper, M. R., & Greene, D. (1976). On understanding overjustification: A reply to Reiss and Sushinsky. *Journal of Personality and Social Psychology, 33,* 25–35.

Lepper, M. R., Greene, D., & Nisbett, R. E. (1973). Undermining children's intrinsic interest with extrinsic rewards: A test of the "overjustification" hypothesis. *Journal of Personality and Social Psychology, 28,* 129–137.

Levitt, E. E. (1967). *The psychology of anxiety.* New York: Bobbs-Merrill.

Levitt, E. E. (1980). *The psychology of anxiety.* Hillsdale, NJ: Erlbaum.

Likert, R. (1961). *New patterns of management.* New York: McGraw-Hill.

Lindsley, D. B., Schreiner, L. H., Knowles, W. B., & Magoun, H. W. (1950). Behavioral and EEG changes following chronic brain stem lesions in the cat. *Electroencephalography and Clinical Neurophysiology, 2,* 483–498.

Lipetz, M. E., & Ossorio, P. G. (1967). Authoritarianism, aggression, and status. *Journal of Personality and Social Psychology, 5*(4), 418–472.

Llewellyn, J. H., & Blucker, J. A. (1982). *Psychology of coaching: Theory and application.* Minneapolis, Minnesota: Burgess Publishing Company.

Locke, E. A. (1968). Toward a theory of task motivation and incentives. *Organizational Behavior and Human Performance, 3,* 157–189.

Locke, E. A., & Latham, G. P. (1985). The application of goal setting to sports. *Journal of Sports Psychology, 7,* 205–222.

Locke, E. A., Shaw, K. M., Saari, L. M., & Latham, G. P. (1981). Goal setting and task performance: 1969–1980. *Psychological Bulletin, 90,* 125–152.

Long, B. S. (1980). Stress management for the athlete: A cognitive behavioral model. In C. H. Nadeau (ed.), *Psychology of motor behavior and sport, 1979.* Champaign, IL: Human Kinetics Publishers.

Longmuir, G. E. (1972). "Perceived and actual dogmatism in high school athletes and coaches: Relationships and some consequences." Unpublished doctoral dissertation, University of New Mexico, Albuquerque.

Lorenz, K. (1966). *On aggression.* New York: Harcourt Brace and World.

Lott, A. J., & Lott, B. E. (1965). Group cohesiveness as interpersonal attraction. A review of relationships with antecedent and consequent variables. *Psychological Bulletin, 64,* 259–309.

Lowe, R. (1973). "Stress, arousal, and task performance of Little League baseball players." Unpublished doctoral dissertation, University of Illinois, Urbana-Champaign.

Loy, J. W. (1970). "Where the action is: A consideration of centrality in sport situations." Paper presented at the meeting of the Second Canadian Psychomotor Learning and Sport Psychology Symposium, Windsor, Ontario.

Loy, J. W., & McElvogue, J. F. (1970). Racial segregation in American sport. *International Review of Sport Sociology, 5,* 5–24.

Loy, J. W., & Sage, J. N. (1970). The effects of formal structure on organizational leadership: An investigation of interscholastic baseball teams. In G. S. Kenyon (ed.), *Contemporary psychology of sport.* Chicago: The Athletic Institute.

Luksa, F. (1980). *Time enough to win: Roger Staubach.* Waco, TX: Word.

Luthe, W. (ed.). (1969). *Autogenic therapy* (Vol. 15). New York: Grune and Stratton.

Lykken, D. (1968). Neuropsychology and psychophysiology in personality research. In E. F. Borgatta & W. W. Lambert (eds.), *Handbook of personality theory and research*. Chicago: Rand McNally.

MacCracken, M. J., & Stadulis, R. E. (1985). Social facilitation of young children's dynamic balance performance. *Journal of Sport Psychology, 7*, 150–165.

Mace, R. D., & Carroll, D. (1985). The control of anxiety in sport: Stress inoculation training prior to abseiling. *International Journal of Sport Psychology, 16*, 165–175.

Magill, R. A. (1985). *Motor learning: Concepts and applications*. Dubuque, IA: Wm. C. Brown Company Publishers.

Magni, G., Rupolo, G., Simini, G., DeLeo, D., & Rampazzo, M. (1985). Aspects of the psychology and personality of high altitude mountain climbers. *International Journal of Sport Psychology, 16*, 12–19.

Mahoney, M. J., & Avener, M. (1977). Psychology of the elite athlete: An exploratory study. *Cognitive Therapy and Research, 1*, 135–141.

Mahoney, M. J., Gabriel, T. J., & Perkins, T. S. (1987). Psychological skills and exceptional athletic performance. *The Sport Psychologist, 1*, 181–199.

Malmo, R. B. (1959). Activation: A neuropsychological dimension. *Psychological Review, 66*, 367–386.

Man, F., & Hondlik, J. (1984). Use of compulsory lessons of physical training for the stimulation of achievement motivation of pupils at an elementary school. *International Journal of Sport Psychology, 15*, 259–270.

Mandler, G., Mandler, J. M., & Urviller, E. T. (1958). Autonomic feedback: The perception of autonomic activity. *Journal of Abnormal and Social Psychology, 56*, 367–373.

Mandler, G., & Sarason, S. B. (1952). A study of anxiety and learning. *Journal of Abnormal Social Psychology, 47*, 166–173.

Mann, L. (1974.) On being a sore loser: How fans react to their team's failure. *Australian Journal of Psychology, 26*, 37–47.

Mann, R. D. (1959). A review of the relationship between personality and performance in small groups. *Psychological Bulletin, 56*, 241–270.

Martens, R. (1969). Effect of an audience on learning and performance of a complex motor skill. *Journal of Personality and Social Psychology, 12*, 252–260.

Martens, R. (1971a). Anxiety and motor behavior: A review. *Journal of Motor Behavior, 3*, 151–179.

Martens, R. (1971b). Internal-external control and social reinforcement. *Research Quarterly, 42*, 307–313.

Martens, R. (1974). Arousal and motor performance. *Exercise and Sport Sciences Reviews, 2*, 155–188.

Martens, R. (1975). *Social psychology and physical activity*. New York: Harper & Row.

Martens, R. (1976). The paradigmatic crises in American sport personology. In A. C. Fisher (ed.), *Psychology of sport*. Palo Alto, CA: Mayfield Publishing Company.

Martens, R. (1978). *Joy and sadness in children's sports*. Champaign, IL: Human Kinetics Publishers.

Martens, R. (1982). *Sport competition anxiety test*. Champaign, IL: Human Kinetics Publishers.

Martens, R. (1987). *Coaches guide to sport psychology*. Champaign, IL: Human Kinetics Publishers, Inc.

Martens, R. (1987). Science, knowledge, and sport psychology. *The Sport Psychologist, 1*, 29–55.

Martens, R., Burton, D., Vealey, R. S., Bump, L. A., & Smith, D. E. (1983). "Competitive state anxiety inventory-2." Unpublished manuscript, University of Illinois at Urbana-Champaign.

Martens, R., Burton, D., Vealey, R. S., Bump, L. A., & Smith, D. E. (1989). The competitive state anxiety inventory-2 (CSAI-2). In D. Burton & R. Vealey (eds.), *Competitive anxiety*. Champaign, IL: Human Kinetics Publishers.

Martens, R., & Gill, D. L. (1976). State anxiety among successful competitors who differ in competitive trait anxiety. *Research Quarterly, 47*, 698–708.

Martens, R., & Landers, D. M. (1969). Coaction effects on a muscular endurance task. *Research Quarterly, 40*, 733–737.

Martens, R., & Landers, D. M. (1970). Motor performance under stress: A test of the inverted-U hypothesis. *Journal of Personality and Social Research, 16*, 29–37.

Martens, R., & Landers, D. M. (1972). Evaluation potential as a determinant of coaction effects. *Journal of Experimental Social Psychology, 8*, 347–359.

Martens, R., & Peterson, J. A. (1971). Group cohesiveness as a determinant of success and member satisfaction in team performance. *International Review of Sport Sociology, 6*, 49–61.

Martens, R., & Simon, J. A. (1976). Comparison of three predictors of state anxiety in competitive situations. *Research Quarterly, 47,* 381–387.

Martin, L. A. (1976). Effects of competition upon the aggressive responses of college basketball players and wrestlers. *Research Quarterly, 47,* 388–393.

McAuley, E. (1985). Modeling and self-efficacy: A test of Bandura's model. *Journal of Sport Psychology, 7,* 283–295.

McAuley, E., & Gross, J. B. (1983). Perceptions of causality in sport: An application of the casual dimension scale. *Journal of Sport Psychology, 5,* 72–76.

McAuley, E., Russell, D., & Gross, J. B. (1983). Affective consequences of winning and losing: An attributional analysis. *Journal of Sport Psychology, 5,* 278–287.

McCallum, J. (1987, June 8). The mystique goes on. *Sports Illustrated, 66,* 30–37.

McCarthy, J. F., & Kelly, B. R. (1978a). Aggression, performance variables, and anger self-report in ice hockey players. *Journal of Psychology, 99,* 97–101.

McCarthy, J. F., & Kelly, B. R. (1978b). Aggressive behavior and its effect on performance over time in ice hockey athletes: An archival study. *International Journal of Sport Psychology, 9,* 90–96.

McClelland, D. C., Atkinson, J. W., Clark, R. W., & Lowell, E. L. (1953). *The achievement motive.* New York: Appleton-Century-Crofts.

McCullagh, P. D., & Landers, D. M. (1976). Size of audience and social facilitation. *Perceptual and Motor Skills, 42,* 1067–1070.

McCutcheon, L. E. (1984). The home advantage in high school athletics. *Journal of Sport Behavior, 7,* 135–138.

McElroy, M. A., & Willis, J. D. (1979). Women and the achievement conflict in sport: A preliminary study. *Journal of Sport Psychology, 1,* 241–247.

McGhie, A., & Chapman, J. (1961). Disorders of attention and perception in early schizophrenia. *British Journal of Medical Psychology, 34,* 103–116.

McGill, J. C., Hall, J. R., Ratliff, W. R., & Moss, R. F. (1986). Personality characteristics of professional rodeo cowboys. *Journal of Sport Behavior, 9,* 143–151.

McGrath, J. E. (1962). The influence of positive interpersonal relations on adjustment and effectiveness in rifle teams. *Journal of Abnormal and Social Psychology, 65,* 365–375.

McGrath, J. E. (1970). A conceptual formulation for research on stress. In J. E. McGrath (ed.), *Social and psychological factors in stress.* New York: Holt, Rinehart and Winston.

McGrath, J. E. (1984). *Groups: Interaction and performance.* Englewood Cliffs, NJ: Prentice-Hall.

McGregor, D. (1960). *The human side of enterprise.* New York: McGraw-Hill.

McNair, D. M., Lorr, M., & Droppleman, L. F. (1971). *Profile of Mood States manual.* San Diego, CA: Educational and Industrial Testing Service.

Mechikoff, R. A., & Kozar, B. (1983). *Sport psychology: The coaches' perspective.* Springfield, IL: Charles C. Thomas.

Mehrabian, A. (1968). Male and female scales of the tendency to achieve. *Educational and Psychological Measurement, 28,* 493–502.

Mehrabian, A., & Bekken, M. L. (1986). Temperament characteristics of individuals who participate in strenuous sports. *Research Quarterly for Exercise and Sport, 57,* 160–166.

Meichenbaum, D. (1977). *Cognitive behavior modification.* New York: Plenum Press.

Metcalf, H.C., & Urwick, L. (eds.). (1963). *Dynamic administration: The collected papers of Mary Parker Follett,* 277. London: Harper & Brothers.

Meyer, M. E. (1979). *Foundations of contemporary psychology.* New York: Oxford University Press.

Meyers, A. (1969). Team competition, success, and the adjustment of group members. In J. W. Loy and G. S. Kenyon (editor), *Sport, Culture, and Society.* London: The Macmillan Company.

Meyers, A. W., Cooke, C. J., Cullen, J., & Liles, L. (1979). Psychological aspects of athletic competitors: A replication across sports. *Cognitive Therapy and Research, 3,* 361–366.

Meyers, I. B., and McCaulley, M. H. (1985). A guide to the development and use of the Meyers-Briggs type indicator. Palo Alto, California: Consulting Psychologists Press.

Michaels, J. (1977). Classroom reward structures and academic performance. *Review of Educational Research, 47,* 87–99.

Mikalachki, A. (1969). Group cohesion reconsidered. London, Ontario: School of Business Administration, University of Western Ontario.

Miller, B. P., & Eddington, G. P. (1984). Psychological distortion in a sporting context. *Journal of Sport Behavior, 7,* 91–94.

Miller, D. T., & Ross, M. (1975). Self-serving biases in the attribution of causality: Fiction or fact? *Psychological Bulletin, 82,* 213–225.

Miller, J. T., & McAuley, E. (1987). Effects of a goalsetting training program on basketball free-throw self-efficacy and performance. *The Sport Psychologist, 1,* 103–113.

Miller, L. K., & Hamblin, R. L. (1963). Interdependence, differential rewarding, and productivity. *American Sociological Review, 28,* 768–777.

Miller, N. E. (1941). The frustration-aggression hypothesis. *Psychological Review, 48,* 337–342.

Miller, T. W. (1982). Assertiveness training for coaches: The issue of healthy communication between coaches and players. *Journal of Sport Psychology, 4,* 107–114.

Milner, P. M. (1970). *Physiological psychology.* New York: Holt, Rinehart and Winston.

Mischel, W. (1986). *Introduction to personality.* New York: Holt, Rinehart and Winston.

Moede, W. (1914). Der Wetteifer, seine Struktur und sein Ausmas. *Zeitschrift für Pädagogische Psychologie und Experimentelle Pädagogik, 15,* 353–368.

Montagu, J. D., & Coles, E. M. (1966). Mechanism and measurement of the galvanic skin response. *Psychological Bulletin, 65,* 261–279.

Monte, C. F. (1977). *Beneath the mask: An introduction to theories of personality.* New York: Praeger.

Morgan, W. P. (1968). Personality characteristics of wrestlers participating in the world championships. *Journal of Sports Medicine and Physical Fitness, 8,* 212–216.

Morgan, W. P. (1972a). Hypnosis and muscular performance. In W. P. Morgan (ed.), *Ergogenic aids in muscular performance.* New York: Academic Press.

Morgan, W. P. (1972b). Sport psychology. In R. N. Singer (ed.), *The psychomotor domain: Movement behaviors.* Philadelphia: Lea and Febiger.

Morgan, W. P. (1974). Selected psychological considerations in sport. *Research Quarterly, 45,* 324–339.

Morgan, W. P. (1978, April). The mind of the marathoner. *Psychology Today,* 38–49.

Morgan, W. P. (1979a). Anxiety reduction following acute physical activity. *Psychiatric Annals, 9,* 141–147.

Morgan, W. P. (1979b). Prediction of performance in athletics. In P. Klavora & J. V. Daniel (eds.), *Coach, athlete, and the sport psychologist.* Champaign, IL: Human Kinetics Publishers.

Morgan, W. P. (1980a). Sport personology: The credulous-skeptical argument in perspective. In W. F. Straub (ed.), *Sport psychology: An analysis of athlete behavior* (2d ed.). Ithaca, NY: Mouvement Publications.

Morgan, W. P. (1980b). The trait psychology controversy. *Research Quarterly for Exercise and Sport, 51,* 50–76.

Morgan, W. P. (1981). Psychophysiology of self-awareness during vigorous physical activity. *Research Quarterly for Exercise and Sport, 52,* 385–427.

Morgan, W. P., & Brown, D. R. (1983). Hypnosis. In M. H. Williams (ed.), *Ergogenic aids in sport.* Champaign, IL: Human Kinetics Publishers.

Morgan, W. P., & Costill, D. L. (1972). Psychological characteristics of the marathon runner. *Journal of Sports Medicine and Physical Fitness, 12,* 42–46.

Morgan, W. P., & Johnson, R. W. (1977). Psychological characterizations of the elite wrestler: A mental health model. *Medicine and Science in Sports, 9*(1), 55–56.

Morgan, W. P., & Johnson, R. W. (1978). Psychological characteristics of successful and unsuccessful oarsmen. *International Journal of Sport Psychology, 11,* 38–49.

Morgan, W. P., & Pollock, M. L. (1977). Psychologic characterization of the elite distance runner. *Annals of the New York Academy of Science, 301,* 382–403.

Morris, D. (1968). *The naked ape.* New York: McGraw-Hill.

Morrow, G. R., & Labrum, A. H. (1978). The relationship between psychological and physiological measures of anxiety. *Psychological Medicine, 8,* 95–101.

Mosher, D. L. (1966). The development and multitrait-multimethod matrix analysis of three measures of three aspects of guilt. *Journal of Consulting Psychology, 30,* 25–29.

Moyer, K. E. (1973, July). The physiology of violence. *Psychology Today,* 35–38.

Murphy, A. (1987, March 30). A bloody mess. *Sports Illustrated, 66,* 24–31.

Murphy, S. M., & Woolfolk, R. L. (1987). The effects of cognitive interventions on competitive anxiety and performance on a fine motor skill accuracy task. *International Journal of Sport Psychology, 18,* 152–166.

Murray, H. A. (1938). *Explorations in personality: A clinical and experimental study of fifty men of college age.* New York: Oxford University Press.

Murray, J. F. (1983). Effects of alone and audience on motor performance for males and females. *International Journal of Sport Psychology, 14,* 92–97.

Myers, A. (1969). Team competition, success, and the adjustment of group members. In J. W. Loy & G. S. Kenyon (eds.), *Sport, culture, and society.* London: Macmillan.

Myers, I. B., & McCaulley, M. H. (1985). *A guide to the development and use of the Myers-Briggs type indicator.* Palo Alto, CA: Consulting Psychologists Press.

Nagle, F. G., Morgan, W. P., Hellickson, R. V., Serfass, P. C., & Alexander, J. F. (1975). Spotting success traits in Olympic contenders. *Physician and Sports Medicine, 3*(12), 31–34.

Neil, G. I., & Kirby, S. L. (1985). Coaching styles and preferred leadership among rowers and paddlers. *Journal of Sport Behavior, 8,* 3–17.

Nelson, J. D., Gelfand, D. M., & Hartmann, D. P. (1969). Children's aggression following competition and exposure to an aggressive model. *Child Development, 40,* 1085–1097.

Nicholls, J. G. (1975). Causal attributions and other achievement-related cognitions: Effects of task outcome, attainment value, and sex. *Journal of Personality and Social Psychology, 31,* 379–389.

Nicholls, J. G. (1984). Conceptions of ability and achievement motivation. In R. Ames & C. Ames (eds.), *Research on motivation in education: Student motivation* (Vol. I). New York: Academic Press.

Nideffer, R. M. (1976a). *The inner athlete: Mind plus muscle for winning.* New York: Thomas Y. Crowell Company.

Nideffer, R. M. (1976b). Test of attentional and interpersonal style. *Journal of Personality and Social Psychology, 34,* 394–404.

Nideffer, R. M. (1978). *Attention control training.* New York: Wyden Books.

Nideffer, R. M. (1980a). Attentional focus—self assessment. In R. M. Suinn (ed.), *Psychology in sports: Methods and applications.* Minneapolis: Burgess Publishing Company.

Nideffer, R. M. (1980b). The relationship of attention and anxiety to performance. In W. F. Straub (ed.), *Sport psychology: An analysis of athlete behavior* (2d ed.). Ithaca, NY: Mouvement Publications.

Nideffer, R. M. (1981). *The ethics and practice of applied sport psychology.* Ithaca, NY: Mouvement Publications.

Nideffer, R. M. (1985). *Athlete's guide to mental training.* Champaign, IL: Human Kinetics Publishers.

Nideffer, R. M. (1986). Concentration and attention control training. In J. M. Williams (ed.), *Applied sport psychology* (pp. 257–269). Palo Alto, CA: Mayfield Publishing Company.

Nideffer, R. M. (1987). Issues in the use of psychological tests in applied settings. *The Sport Psychologist, 1,* 18–28.

Nideffer, R. M., & Deckner, C. W. (1970). A case study of improved athletic performance following use of relaxation procedures. *Perceptual and Motor Skills, 30,* 821–822.

Nideffer, R. M., DuFresne, P., Nesvig, D., & Selder, D. (1980). The future of applied sport psychology. *Journal of Sport Psychology, 2,* 170–174.

Nighswander, J. K., & Mayer, G. R. (1969). Catharsis: A means of reducing elementary school students' aggressive behaviors. *Personnel and Guidance Journal, 47,* 461–466.

Nixon, H. L. (1977). Cohesiveness and team success: A theoretical reformulation. *Review of Sport and Leisure, 2,* 36–57.

Noel, R. C. (1980). The effect of visual-motor behavior rehearsal on tennis performance. *Journal of Sport Psychology, 2,* 221–226.

Norman, D. A. (1968). Toward a theory of memory and attention. *Psychological Review, 75,* 522–536.

Norman, D. A. (1976). *Memory and attention: An introduction to human information processing* (2d ed.). New York: John Wiley and Sons.

North American Society for the Psychology of Sport and Physical Activity. (1982, Fall). *Ethical standards for provision of services by NASPSPA members.* NASPSPA Newsletter, addendum.

Noverr, D. A., & Ziewaez, L. E. (1981). Violence in American sports. In W. J. Baker & J. M. Carroll (eds.), *Sports in modern America.* St. Louis: River City Publishers.

Nowlis, V. (1965). Research with the mood adjective checklist. In S. S. Tompkins & C. Izard (eds.), *Affect, cognition, and personality.* New York: Springer Publishing Company.

Oaklander, H., & Fleishman, E. H. (1964). Patterns of leadership related to organizational stress in hospital settings. *Administrative Science Quarterly, 8,* 520–532.

Ogilvie, B. C. (1968). Psychological consistencies within the personality of high-level competitors. *Journal of the American Medical Association, 205,* 780–786.

Ogilvie, B. C. (1976). Psychological consistencies within the personality of high-level competitors. In A. C. Fisher (ed.), *Psychology of sport.* Palo Alto, CA: Mayfield Publishing Company.

Ogilvie, B. C., Johnsgard, K., & Tutko, T. A. (1971). Personality: Effects of activity. In L. A. Larson (ed.), *Encyclopedia of sport sciences and medicine.* New York: Macmillan.

Ogilvie, B. C., & Tutko, T. A. (1966). *Problem athletes and how to handle them.* London: Palham Books.

Orlick, T. (1986). *Psyching for sport mental training for athletes.* Champaign, Illinois: Leisure Press.

Orlick, T., & Partington, J. (1987). The sport psychology consultant: Analysis of critical components as viewed by Canadian Olympic athletes. *The Sport Psychologist, 1,* 4–17.

Orne, M. T. (1959). The nature of hypnosis: Artifact and essence. *Journal of Abnormal and Social Psychology, 58,* 277–299.

Osborn, R. N., & Hunt, J. G. (1975). An adaptive-reactive theory of leadership: The role of macro variables in leadership research. In J. G. Hunt & L. L. Larson (eds.), *Leadership frontiers.* Kent, OH: Kent State University Press.

Ostrow, A. C. (1976). Goal setting behavior and need achievement in relation to competitive motor activity. *Research Quarterly, 47,* 174–183.

Oxendine, J. B. (1970). Emotional arousal and motor performance. *Quest, 13,* 23–30.

Passer, M. W. (1981). Children in sport: Participation motives and psychological stress. *Quest, 33,* 231–244.

Passer, M. W. (1983). Fear of failure, fear of evaluation, perceived competence, and self-esteem in competitive-trait-anxious children. *Journal of Sport Psychology, 5,* 172–188.

Paulus, P. B., Shannon, J. C., Wilson, D. L., & Boone, T. D. (1972). The effect of spectator presence on gymnastic performance in a field situation. *Psychonomic Science, 29,* 88–90.

Peplau, L. A. (1976). Impact of fear of success and sex-role attitudes on women's competitive achievement. *Journal of Personality and Social Psychology, 34,* 561–568.

Peppler, M. (1977). *Inside volleyball for women.* Chicago: Contemporary Books.

Percival, L. (1971). The coach from the athlete's viewpoint. In J. W. Taylor (ed.), *Proceedings for the First International Symposium on the Art and Science of Coaching* (Vol. 1). Willowdale, Ontario: Fitness Institute Productions.

Pessin, J. (1933). The comparative effects of social and mechanical simulation on memorizing. *American Journal of Psychology, 45,* 263–281.

Peterson, J. A., & Martens, R. (1972). Success and residential affiliation as determinants of team cohesiveness. *Research Quarterly, 43,* 62–76.

Posner, M. I., & Boies, S. J. (1971). Components of attention. *Psychological Review, 78,* 391–408.

Powell, F. M., & Verner, J. P. (1982). Anxiety and performance relationships in first-time parachutists. *Journal of Sport Psychology, 4,* 184–188.

Pressman, M. D. (1980). Psychological techniques for the advancement of sports potential. In R. M. Suinn (ed.), *Psychology in sports: Methods and applications.* Minneapolis: Burgess Publishing Company.

Price, E. E., & Meacci, W. G. (1985). Acquisition and retention of golf putting skill through the relaxation, visualization, and body rehearsal intervention. *Research Quarterly for Exercise and Sport, 56*, 176–179.

Pulos, L. (1979). Athletes and self-hypnosis. In P. Klavora & J. V. Daniel (eds.), *Coach, athlete, and the sport psychologist.* Champaign, IL: Human Kinetics Publishers.

Ranson, S. W. (1939). Somnolence caused by hypothalamic lesions in the monkey. *Archives of Neurological Psychiatry, 41*, 1–23.

Ravizza, K., & Rotella, R. (1982). Cognitive somatic behavioral interventions in gymnastics. In L. D. Zaichkowsky & W. E. Sime (eds.), *Stress management for sport.* Reston, VA: AAHPERD Publications.

Raynor, J. O. (1968). "The relationship between distant future goals and achievement motivation." Unpublished doctoral dissertation, University of Michigan, Ann Arbor.

Raynor, J. O. (1969). Future orientation and motivation of immediate activity: An elaboration of the theory of achievement motivation. *Psychological Review, 76*, 606–610.

Raynor, J. O. (1970). Relationship between achievement-related motives, future orientation, and academic performance. *Journal of Personality and Social Psychology, 15*, 28–33.

Raynor, J. O., & Rubin, I. S. (1971). Effects of achievement and future orientation on level of performance. *Journal of Personality and Social Psychology, 17*, 36–41.

Reddy, J. K., Bai, A. J. L., & Rao, V. R. (1976). The effects of the transcendental meditation program on athletic performance. In D. J. Orme-Johnson & I. Farrow (eds.), *Scientific research on the transcendental meditation program* (Collected papers, Vol. 1). Weggis, Switzerland: MERU Press.

Rejeski, W. J., & Brawley, L. R. (1983). Attribution theory in sport: Current status and new perspectives. *Journal of Sport Psychology, 5*, 77–99.

Richardson, P. A., Jackson, A., & Albury, K. W. (1984). Measurement of fear of failure using the self-deprecation and insecurity scale. *Journal of Sport Behavior, 7*, 115–119.

Richman, C. L., & Heather, R. (1986). The development of self-esteem through the martial arts. *International Journal of Sport Psychology, 17*, 234–239.

Riemer, B. (1975). Influence of causal beliefs on affect and expectancy. *Journal of Personality and Social Psychology, 31*, 1163–1167.

Roberts, G. C. (1972). Effect of achievement motivation and social environment on performance of a motor task. *Journal of Motor Behavior, 4*, 37–46.

Roberts, G. C. (1974). Effect of achievement motivation and social environment on risk taking. *Research Quarterly, 45*, 42–55.

Roberts, G. C. (1977). Win-loss causal attributions of Little League players. In J. Salmela (ed.), *Canadian symposium for psychomotor learning and sport psychology, 1975.* Ithaca, NY: Mouvement Publications.

Roberts, G. C. (1980). Children in competition: A theoretical perspective and recommendation for practice. *Motor Skills: Theory into Practice, 4*, 37–50.

Roberts, G. C. (1982). Achievement motivation in sport. In R. Terjung (ed.), *Exercise and sport science reviews* (Vol. 10). Philadelphia: Franklin Institute Press.

Roberts, G. C., Kleiber, D. A., & Duda, J. L. (1981). An analysis of motivation in children's sport: The role of perceived competence in participation. *Journal of Sport Psychology, 3*, 206–216.

Roberts, G. C., & Pascuzzi, D. (1979). Causal attributions in sport: Some theoretical implications. *Journal of Sport Psychology, 1*, 203–211.

Robinson, D. W. (1985). Stress seeking: Selected behavioral characteristics of elite rock climbers. *Journal of Sport Psychology, 7*, 400–404.

Rosen, B. C., & D'Andrade, R. (1959). The psycho-social origins of achievement motivation. *Sociometry, 22*, 185–218.

Rosenbaum, L. L., & Rosenbaum, W. B. (1971). Morale and productivity consequences of group leadership style, stress, and type of task. *Journal of Applied Psychology, 55*, 343–388.

Ross, L. (1977). The intuitive psychologist and his shortcomings: Distortions in the attribution process. In L. Berkowitz (ed.), *Advances in experimental social psychology* (Vol. 10). New York: Academic Press.

Ross, M. (1976). The self-perception of intrinsic motivation. In J. H. Harvey, W. J. Ickles & R. F. Kidd (eds.), *New directions in attribution research*. Hillsdale, NJ: Erlbaum.

Rotella, R. J., Gansneder, B., Ojala, D., & Billings, J. (1980). Cognitive and coping strategies of elite skiers: An exploratory study of young developing athletes. *Journal of Sport Psychology, 2,* 350–354.

Rotella, R. J., Malone, C., & Ojala, D. (1985). Facilitating athletic performance through the use of mastery and coping tapes. In L. K. Bunker, R. J. Rotella & A. S. Reilly (eds.), *Sport psychology*. University of Virginia: Authors.

Rotter, J. B. (1966). Generalized expectancies for internal versus external control of reinforcement. *Psychological Monographs: General and Applied, 80* (1, Whole No. 609).

Rotter, J. B. (1971, June). External control and internal control. *Psychology Today, 5*(1), 37–42, 58–59.

Royal, E. G., Whiteside, H., & McClelan, P. (1985). Attitude similarity and evaluation of an athletic coach. *International Journal of Sport Psychology, 16,* 307–311.

Ruder, M. K., & Gill, D. L. (1982). Immediate effects of win-loss on perceptions of cohesion in intramural and intercollegiate volleyball teams. *Journal of Sport Psychology, 4,* 227–234.

Ruffer, W. A. (1975). Personality traits of athletes. *The Physical Educator, 32*(1), 105–109.

Ruffer, W. A. (1976a). Personality traits of athletes. *The Physical Educator, 33*(1), 50–55.

Ruffer, W. A. (1976b). Personality traits of athletes. *The Physical Educator, 33*(4), 211–214.

Rupnow, A., & Ludwig, D. A. (1981). Psychometric note on the reliability of the sport competition anxiety test: Form C. *Research Quarterly for Exercise and Sport, 52,* 35–37.

Rushall, B. S. (1970a). An evaluation of the relationship between personality and physical performance categories. In G. S. Kenyon (ed.), *Contemporary psychology of sport: Second International Congress of Sports Psychology*. Chicago: The Athletic Institute.

Rushall, B. S. (1970b). Some practical applications of personality information to athletics. In G. S. Kenyon (ed.), *Contemporary psychology of sport: Second International Congress of Sport Psychology*. Chicago: The Athletic Institute.

Rushall, B. S. (1972). Three studies relating personality variables to football performance. *International Journal of Sport Psychology, 3,* 12–24.

Rushall, B. S. (1973). The status of personality research and application in sports and physical education. *Journal of Sports Medicine and Physical Fitness, 13,* 281–290.

Rushall, B. S. (1974). *Psychological inventories for competitive swimmers*. Dartmouth, Nova Scotia: Sport Science Associates.

Rushall, B. S. (1975). Alternative dependent variables for the study of behavior in sport. In D. M. Landers (ed.), *Psychology of sport and motor behavior II*. University Park: Pennsylvania State University Press.

Russell, D. (1982). The causal dimension scale: A measure of how individuals perceive causes. *Journal of Personality and Social Psychology, 42,* 1137–1145.

Russell, G. W. (1974). Machiavellianism, locus of control, aggression, performance and precautionary behavior in ice hockey. *Human Relations, 27,* 825–837.

Russell, G. W. (1981a). Conservatism, birth order, leadership, and the aggression of Canadian ice hockey players. *Perceptual and Motor Skills, 53,* 3–7.

Russell, G. W. (1981b). Spectator moods at an aggressive sporting event. *Journal of Sport Psychology, 3,* 217–227.

Russell, G. W. (1986). Does sports violence increase box office receipts? *International Journal of Sport Psychology, 17,* 173–183.

Russell, G. W., & Drewery, B. P. (1976). Crowd size and competitive aspects of aggression in ice hockey: An archival study. *Human Relations, 29,* 723–735.

Ryan, E. D. (1961). Motor performance under stress as a function of the amount of practice. *Perceptual and Motor Skills, 13,* 103–106.

Ryan, E. D. (1962). Effects of stress on motor performance and learning. *Research Quarterly, 33,* 111–119.

Ryan, E. D. (1970). The cathartic effect of vigorous motor activity on aggressive behavior. *Research Quarterly, 41,* 542–551.

Ryan, E. D. (1976). The questions we ask and the decisions we make. In A. C. Fisher (ed.), *Psychology of sport*. Palo Alto, CA: Mayfield Publishing Company.

Ryan, E. D. (1980). Attribution, intrinsic motivation and athletics: A replication and extension. In C. H. Nadeau (ed.), *Psychology of motor behavior and sport, 1979.* Champaign, IL: Human Kinetics Publishers.

Ryan, E. D. (1981). Attribution and affect. In G. C. Roberts & D. M. Landers (eds.), *Psychology of motor behavior and sport, 1980.* Champaign, IL: Human Kinetics Publishers.

Ryan, E. D., & Lakie, W. L. (1965). Competitive and noncompetitive performance in relation to achievement motivation and manifest anxiety. *Journal of Personality and Social Psychology, 1,* 344–345.

Ryan, E. D., & Simons, J. (1981). Cognitive demand, imagery, and frequency of mental rehearsal as factors influencing acquisition of motor skills. *Journal of Sport Psychology, 3,* 35–45.

Ryan, F. (1981). *Sports and psychology.* Englewood Cliffs, NJ: Prentice-Hall.

Sage, G. H. (1972). Machiavellianism among college and high school coaches. *Seventy-Fifth Proceedings of the National Collegiate Physical Education Association for Men,* 45–60.

Sage, G. H. (1973). The coach as management: Organizational leadership in American sport. *Quest, 19,* 35–40.

Sage, G. H. (1975). An occupational analysis of the college coach. In D. W. Ball & J. W. Loy (eds.), *Sport and social order.* Reading, MA: Addison-Wesley.

Sage, G. H. (1978). Humanistic psychology and coaching. In W. F. Straub (ed.), *Sport psychology: An analysis of athlete behavior.* Ithaca, NY: Mouvement Publications.

Sage, G. H. (1984a). *Introduction to motor behavior: A neuropsychological approach* (3d ed.). Reading, MA: Addison-Wesley.

Sage, G. H. (1984b). *Motor learning and control: A neuropsychological approach.* Dubuque, IA: Wm. C. Brown Company Publishers.

Salili, F., Maehr, M. L., & Gillmore, G. (1976). Achievement and morality: A cross-cultural analysis of causal attribution and evaluation. *Journal of Personality and Social Psychology, 33,* 327–337.

Salmela, J. H. (1981). *The world sport psychology sourcebook.* Ithaca, NY: Mouvement Publications.

Sanguinetti, C., Lee, A. M., & Nelson, J. (1985). Reliability estimates and age and gender comparisons of expectations of success in sex-typed activities. *Journal of Sport Psychology, 7,* 379–388.

Sarason, I. G., & Smith, R. E. (1971). Personality. *Annual Review of Psychology, 22,* 393–446.

Sarason, S. B. (1954). *The clinical interaction, with special reference to the Rorschach.* New York: Harper.

Sarason, S. B., Davidson, K. S., Lighthall, F. F., Waite, R. R., & Ruebush, B. K. (1960). *Anxiety in elementary school children.* New York: John Wiley and Sons.

Sarason, S. B., Hill, K. T., & Zimbardo, P. G. (1964). A longitudinal study of the relationship of test anxiety to performance on intelligence and achievement tests. *Monographs of the Society for Research in Child Development* (Serial No. 9829, Whole No. 7).

Scanlan, T. K. (1977). The effects of success-failure on the perception of threat in a competitive situation. *Research Quarterly, 48,* 144–153.

Scanlan, T. K. (1978). Perception and responses of high and low competitive trait-anxious males to competition. *Research Quarterly, 49,* 520–527.

Scanlan, T. K. (1982). Motivation and stress in competitive youth sports. *Journal of Physical Education, Recreation and Dance, 53*(3), 27–28.

Scanlan, T. K., & Passer, M. W. (1978). Factors related to competitive stress among male youth sport participants. *Medicine and Science in Sports, 10,* 103–108.

Scanlan, T. K., & Passer, M. W. (1979a). Factors influencing the competitive performance expectancies of young female athletes. *Journal of Sport Psychology, 1,* 212–220.

Scanlan, T. K., & Passer, M. W. (1979b). Sources of competitive stress in young female athletes. *Journal of Sport Psychology, 1,* 151–159.

Scanlan, T. K., & Ragan, J. T. (1978). Achievement motivation and competition: Perceptions and responses. *Medicine and Science in Sports, 10,* 276–281.

Scheer, J. K., & Ansorge, C. J. (1979). Influence due to expectations of judges: A function of internal-external locus of control. *Journal of Sport Psychology, 1,* 53–58.

Schell, B., Hunt, J., & Lloyd, C. (1984). An investigation of future market opportunities for sport psychologists. *Journal of Sport Psychology, 6,* 335–350.

Schmidt, R. A. (1972). The case against learning and forgetting scores. *Journal of Motor Behavior, 4,* 71–88.

Schmidt, R. H. (1987). *Motor control and learning.* Champaign, IL: Human Kinetics Publishers.

Schomer, H. H. (1986). Mental strategies and the perception of effort of marathon runners. *International Journal of Sport Psychology, 18,* 133–151.

Schomer, H. H. (1987). Mental strategy training programme for marathon runners. *International Journal of Sport Psychology, 18,* 133–151.

Schriesheim, C. A., & Murphy, C. J. (1976). Relationship between leader behavior and performance: A test of some situational moderators. *Journal of Applied Psychology, 61,* 634–641.

Schultz, D. D. (1965). *Sensory restriction: Effects on behavior.* New York: Academic Press.

Schultz, J. H., & Luthe, W. (1959). *Autogenic training: A psychophysiological approach to psychotherapy.* New York: Grune and Stratton.

Schurr, K. T., Ashley, M. A., & Joy, K. L. (1977). A multivariate analysis of male athlete characteristics: Sport type and success. *Multivariate Experimental Clinical Research, 3,* 53–68.

Schurr, K. T., Ruble, V. E., & Ellen, A. S. (1985). Myers-Briggs type inventory and demographic characteristics of students attending and not attending a college basketball game. *Journal of Sport Behavior, 8*(4), 181–194.

Schurr, K. T., Ruble, V. E., Nisbet, J., & Wallace, D. (1984). Myers-Briggs type inventory characteristics of more and less successful players on an American football team. *Journal of Sport Behavior, 7,* 47–57.

Schutz, W. C. (1966). *The interpersonal underworld.* Palo Alto, CA: Science and Behavior Books.

Schwartz, B., & Barsky, S. F. (1977). The home advantage. *Social Forces, 55,* 641–661.

Schwartz, G. E., Davidson, R. J., & Goleman, D. J. (1978). Patterning of cognitive and somatic processes in the self-regulation of anxiety: Effects of meditation vs. exercise. *Psychosomatic Medicine, 40,* 321–328.

Schwartz, M. S. (1987). *Biofeedback: A practitioner's guide.* New York: Guilford Press.

Scott, J. P. (1970). Sport and aggression. In G. S. Kenyon (ed.), *Contemporary psychology of sport.* Chicago: The Athletic Institute.

Scott, J. P. (1975). *Aggression.* Chicago: University of Chicago Press.

Seabourne, T. G., Weinberg, R. S., & Jackson, A. (1982). "Effect of visuo-motor behavior rehearsal in enhancing karate performance." Unpublished manuscript, North Texas State University, Denton, TX.

Seabourne, T. G., Weinberg, R. S., & Jackson, A. (1984). The effect of individualized practice and training of visuomotor behavior rehearsal in enhancing karate performance. *Journal of Sport Behavior, 7,* 58–67.

Seabourne, T. G., Weinberg, R. S., Jackson, A., & Suinn, R. M. (1985). Effect of individualized, nonindividualized, and package intervention strategies on karate performance. *Journal of Sport Psychology, 7,* 40–50.

Segal, J. D., & Weinberg, R. S. (1984). Sex, sex role orientation and competitive trait anxiety. *Journal of Sport Behavior, 7,* 153–159.

Seligman, M. E. P. (1975). *Helplessness on depression, development, and death.* San Francisco: W. H. Freeman.

Selye, H. (1975). *Stress without distress.* New York: New American Library.

Sharan, S. (1980). Cooperative learning in teams: Recent methods and effects on achievement, attitudes, and ethnic relations. *Review of Educational Research, 50,* 241–272.

Shelton, T. O., & Mahoney, M. J. (1978). The content and effect of "psyching-up" strategies in weight lifters. *Cognitive Therapy and Research, 2,* 275–284.

Sherif, C. W. (1976). The social context of competition. In D. M. Landers (ed.), *Social problems in athletics: Essays in the sociology of sport.* Champaign, IL: University of Illinois Press.

Sherif, M., & Sherif, C. W. (1953). *Groups in harmony and tension.* New York: Harper & Row.

Siedentop, D., & Ramey, G. (1977). Extrinsic rewards and intrinsic motivation. *Motor Skills: Theory into Practice, 2,* 49–62.

Silva, J. M., III. (1979). Changes in the affective state of guilt as a function of exhibiting proactive assertion on hostile aggression. In G. C. Roberts & K. M. Newell (eds.), *Psychology of motor behavior and sport, 1978.* Champaign, IL: Human Kinetics Publishers.

Silva, J. M., III. (1980a). Assertive and aggressive behavior in sport: A definitional clarification. In C. H. Nadeau (ed.), *Psychology of motor behavior and sport, 1979.* Champaign, IL: Human Kinetics Publishers.

Silva, J. M., III. (1980b). Understanding aggressive behavior and its effects upon athletic performance. In W. F. Straub (ed.), *Sport psychology: An analysis of athlete behavior* (2d ed.). Ithaca, NY: Mouvement Publications.

Silva, J. M., III. (1982). An evaluation of fear of success in female and male athletes and non-athletes. *Journal of Sport Psychology, 4*(1), 92–96.

Silva, J. M., III. (1983). The perceived legitimacy of rule violating behavior in sport. *Journal of Sport Psychology, 5,* 438–448.

Silva, J. M., III. (1984). Personality and sport performance: Controversy and challenge. In J. M. Silva, III & R. S. Weinberg (eds.), *Psychological Foundations of Sport.* Champaign, Illinois: Human Kinetics Publishers.

Silva, J. M., III, & Andrew, J. A. (1987). An analysis of game location and basketball performance in the Atlantic coast conference. *International Journal of Sport Psychology, 18,* 188–204.

Silva, J. M., III, Andrew, J. A., & Richey, S. (1983). "Game location and basketball performance variation." Paper presented at the North American Society for the Psychology of Sport and Physical Activity Annual Convention, Michigan State University, East Lansing, MI.

Silva, J. M., III, & Hardy, C. J. (1986). Discriminating contestants at the United States Olympics marathon trials as a function of precompetitive affect. *International Journal of Sport Psychology, 17,* 100–109.

Silva, J. M., III, Shultz, B. B., Haslam, R. W., Martin, T. P., & Murray, D. F. (1985). Discriminating characteristics of contestants at the United States Olympic wrestling trials. *International Journal of Sport Psychology, 16,* 79–102.

Silva, J. M., III, Shultz, B. B., Haslam, R. W., & Murray, D. (1981). A psychological assessment of elite wrestlers. *Research Quarterly for Exercise and Sport, 52*(3), 348–358.

Silverman, J. (1964). The problem of attention in research and theory in schizophrenia. *Psychological Review, 71,* 352–379.

Simon, J. A., & Martens, R. (1979). Children's anxiety in sport and nonsport evaluative activities. *Journal of Sport Psychology, 1,* 160–169.

Singer, R. N. (1969). Personality differences between and within baseball and tennis players. *Research Quarterly, 40,* 582–587.

Singer, R. N. (1970). Effect of an audience on performance of a motor task. *Journal of Motor Behavior, 2,* 88–95.

Singer, R. N. (1975). *Myths and truths in sports psychology.* New York: Harper & Row.

Singer, R. N. (1984). What sport psychology can do for the athlete and coach. *International Journal of Sport Psychology, 15,* 52–61.

Singer, R. N., Harris, D., Kroll, W., Martens, R., & Sechrest, L. (1977). Psychological testing of athletes. *Journal of Physical Education and Recreation, 48*(5), 30–32.

Skinner, B. F. (1938). *The behavior of organisms: An experimental analysis.* New York: Appleton-Century-Crofts.

Smith, D. (1987). Conditions that facilitate the development of sport imagery training. *The Sport Psychologist, 1,* 237–247.

Smith, E. E. (1968). Choice reaction time: An analysis of the major theoretical positions. *Psychological Bulletin, 69,* 77–110.

Smith, M. D. (1980). Hockey violence: Interring some myths. In W. F. Straub (ed.), *Sport psychology: An analysis of athlete behavior* (2nd ed.). Ithaca, NY: Mouvement Publications.

Smith, R. E. (1980). A cognitive-affective approach to stress management training for athletes. In C. H. Nadeau (ed.), *Psychology of motor behavior and sport, 1979.* Champaign, IL: Human Kinetics Publishers.

Smith, R. E., Smoll, F. L., & Curtis, B. (1979). Coach effectiveness training: A cognitive-behavioral approach to enhancing relationship skills in youth sport coaches. *Journal of Sport Psychology, 1,* 59–75.

Smith, R. E., Smoll, F. L., & Hunt, E. (1977). A system for the behavioral assessment of athletic coaches. *Research Quarterly, 48,* 401–407.

Smoll, F. L., Smith, R. E., Curits, B., & Hunt, E. (1978). Toward a mediational model of coach-player relationships. *Research Quarterly, 49,* 528–541.

Snyder, E. E., & Purdy, D. A. (1985). The home advantage in collegiate basketball. *Sociology of Sport Journal, 2,* 352–356.

Sonstroem, R. J., & Bernardo, P. (1982). Intraindividual pregame state anxiety and basketball performance: A reexamination of the inverted-U curve. *Journal of Sport Psychology, 4,* 235–245.

Spence, J. T. (1971). What can you say about a twenty-year-old theory that won't die? *Journal of Motor Behavior, 3,* 193–203.

Spence, J. T., & Helmreich, R. L. (1978). *Masculinity and femininity.* Austin: University of Texas Press.

Spence, J. T., Helmreich, R. L., & Stapp, J. (1975). Rating of self and peers on sex role attributes and their relationship to self-esteem and comceptions of masculinity and femininity. *Journal of Personality and Social Psychology, 32,* 29–39.

Spence, K. W. (1956). *Behavior theory and conditioning.* New Haven, CT: Yale University Press.

Sperling, G. (1960). The information available in brief visual presentations. *Psychological Monographs, 74*(11), 1–29.

Spielberger, C. D. (1966). Theory and research on anxiety. In C. D. Spielberger (ed.), *Anxiety and behavior.* New York: Academic Press.

Spielberger, C. D. (1971). Trait-state anxiety and motor behavior. *Journal of Motor Behavior, 3,* 265–279.

Spielberger, C. D. (1983). *Manual for the state-trait anxiety inventory* (Form Y). Palo Alto, CA: Consulting Psychologists Press.

Spielberger, C. D., Gorsuch, R. L., & Lushene, R. F. (1970). *Manual for the state-trait anxiety inventory.* Palo Alto, CA: Consulting Psychologists Press.

Spigolon, L., & Annalisa, D. (1985). Autogenic training in frogmen. *International Journal of Sport Psychology, 16,* 312–320.

Spink, K. S. (1978a). Correlation between two methods of assessing causal attribution. *Perceptual and Motor Skills, 46,* 1173–1174.

Spink, K. S. (1978b). Win-loss causal attributions of high school basketball players. *Canadian Journal of Applied Sport Sciences, 3,* 195–201.

Spink, K. S., & Roberts, G. C. (1980). Ambiguity of outcome and causal attributions. *Journal of Sport Psychology, 2,* 237–244.

Steers, D. (1982, November). Trapped in Peru, U. S. women shouted down. *Volleyball Monthly,* 15–21.

Steiner, J. D. (1972). *Group processes and productivity.* New York: Academic Press.

Stennet, R. C. (1957). The relationship of performance level to level of arousal. *Journal of Experimental Psychology, 54,* 54–61.

Stogdill, R. M. (1948). Personal factors associated with leadership: Survey of literature. *Journal of Psychology, 25,* 35–71.

Stogdill, R. M. (1950). Leadership, membership, and organization. *Psychological Bulletin, 47,* 1–14.

Stogdill, R. M., & Coons, A. E. (1957). *Leader behavior: Its description and measurement.* Columbus, OH: Ohio State University Press.

Storr, A. (1968). *Human aggression.* New York: Atheneum.

Straub, W. F. (1980). How to be an effective leader. In W. F. Straub (ed.), *Sport psychology: An analysis of athlete behavior* (2d ed.). Ithaca, NY: Mouvement Publications.

Sugi, Y., & Akutsu, K. (1968). Studies on respiration and energy-metabolism during sitting in Zazen. *Research Journal of Physical Education, 12,* 190–206.

Suinn, R. M. (1972). Removing emotional obstacles to learning and performance by visuo-motor behavior rehearsal. *Behavioral Therapy, 31,* 308–310.

Suinn, R. M. (1976, July). Body thinking: Psychology for Olympic champs. *Psychology Today,* 38–43.

Suinn, R. M. (1980). Body thinking: Psychology for Olympic champs. In R. M. Suinn (ed.), *Psychology in sports: Methods and applications.* Minneapolis: Burgess Publishing Company.

Suinn, R. M. (1983). *The seven steps to peak performance: Mental training manual for athletes.* Fort Collins, Colorado: Rocky Mountain Behavioral Sciences Institute.

Sutarman & Thompson, H. L. (1952). A new technique for enumerating active sweat glands in man. *Journal of Physiology* (London), 117, 51.

Tamaren, A. J., & Carney, R. M. (1985). Assessment of cognitive and somatic anxiety: A preliminary validation study. *Behavioral Assessment, 7*, 197–202.

Tattersfield, C. R. (1971). "Competitive sport and personality development." Unpublished doctoral dissertation, University of Durham, NC.

Taylor, F. W. (1911). *The principles of scientific management.* New York: Harper.

Taylor, J. A. (1951). The relationship of anxiety to the conditioned eyelid response. *Journal of Experimental Psychology, 41*, 81–92.

Taylor, J. A. (1953). A personality scale of manifest anxiety. *Journal of Abnormal and Social Psychology, 48*, 285–290.

Tenenbaum, G., & Furst, D. (1985). The relationship between sport achievement responsibility, attribution, and related situational variables. *International Journal of Sport Psychology, 16*, 254–296.

Thayer, R. E. (1967). Measurement of activation through self report. *Psychological Reports, 20*, 663–678.

Thirer, J., & Greer, D. L. (1981). Personality characteristics associated with beginning, intermediate, and competitive bodybuilders. *Journal of Sport Behavior, 4*, 3–11.

Thune, A. R. (1949). Personality of weight lifters. *Research Quarterly, 20*, 296–306.

Titley, R. W. (1980). The loneliness of a long-distance kicker. In R. M. Suinn (ed.), *Psychology in sports: Methods and applications.* Minneapolis: Burgess Publishing Company.

Tompkins, S. S. (1947). *The Thematic Apperception Test: The theory and technique of interpretation.* New York: Grune and Stratton.

Treisman, A. M. (1965). Our limited attention. *The Advancement of Science, 22*, 600–611.

Tresemer, D. (1974, March). Fear of success: Popular but unproven. *Psychology Today*, 82–85.

Tresemer, D. (1976). The cumulative record of research on "fear of success." *Sex Roles, 2*, 217–236.

Triplett, N. (1987). The dynamogenic factors in pacemaking and competition. *American Journal of Psychology, 9*, 507–553.

Tuckman, B. W. (1965). Developmental sequences in small groups. *Psychological Bulletin, 63*, 384–399.

Tuckman, B. W. (1972). *Conducting educational research.* New York: Harcourt Brace Jovanovich.

Turner, E. J. (1970). The effects of viewing college football, basketball, and wrestling on the elicited aggressive responses of male spectators. In G. S. Kenyon (ed.), *Contemporary psychology of sport.* Chicago: The Athletic Institute.

Tutko, T. A., & Richards, J. W. (1971). *Psychology of coaching.* Boston: Allyn and Bacon.

Tutko, T. A., & Richards, J. W. (1972). *Coaches' practical guide to athletic motivation.* Boston: Allyn and Bacon.

Ulett, G. A., & Peterson, D. B. (1965). *Applied hypnosis and positive suggestion.* St. Louis: C. V. Mosby.

Ulrich, B. D. (1987). Perceptions of physical competence, motor competence and participation in organized sport: Their interrelationships in young children. *Research Quarterly for Exercise and Sport, 58*, 57–67.

Ulrich, R. P. (1973). "The effect of hypnotic and non-hypnotic suggestions on archery performance." Unpublished doctoral dissertation, University of Utah, Salt Lake City.

Valle, V. A., & Frieze, I. H. (1976). The stability of causal attributions as a mediator in changing expectations for success. *Journal of Personality and Social Psychology, 33*, 579–587.

Vallerand, R. J., & Reid, G. (1984). On the causal effects of perceived competence on intrinsic motivation: A test of Cognitive Evaluation Theory. *Journal of Sport Psychology, 6*, 94–102.

Valzelli, L. (1981). *Psychobiology of aggression and violence.* New York: Raven Press.

Vanek, M., & Cratty, B. J. (1970). *Psychology and the superior athlete.* London: Macmillan.

Van Schoyck, S. R., & Grasha, A. F. (1981). Attentional style variations and athletic ability: The advantages of the sports specific test. *Journal of Sport Psychology, 3,* 149–165.

Varca, P. E. (1980). An analysis of home and away game performance of male college basketball teams. *Journal of Sport Psychology, 2,* 245–257.

Vealy, R. (1988). "Competitive trait anxiety: Use and interpretation of the sport competition anxiety test." Paper presented at the annual convention of the North American Society for the Psychology of Sport and Physical Activity. Knoxville, Tennessee.

Vealey, R. S. (1986). Conceptualization of sport-confidence and competitive orientation: Preliminary investigation and instrument development. *Journal of Sport Psychology, 8,* 221–246.

Voelz, C. (1982). *Motivation in coaching a team sport.* Reston, VA: AAHPERD Publications.

Volkamer, N. (1972). Investigations into the aggressiveness in competitive social systems. *Sportwissenschaft, 1,* 33–64.

Vos Strache, C. (1979). Players' perceptions of leadership qualities for coaches. *Research Quarterly, 50,* 679–686.

Vroom, V. H., & Yetton, P. W. (1973). *Leadership and decision making.* Pittsburgh: University of Pittsburgh Press.

Wachtel, P. (1967). Conceptions of broad and narrow attention. *Psychological Bulletin, 68,* 417–429.

Wall, B. R., & Gruber, J. J. (1986). Relevancy of athletic aggression inventory for use in women's intercollegiate basketball: A pilot investigation. *International Journal of Sport Psychology, 17,* 23–33.

Wallace, R. K. (1970). Physiological effects of transcendental meditation. *Science, 167,* 1751–1754.

Wallace, R. K., & Benson, H. (1972). The physiology of meditation. *Scientific American, 226,* 85–90.

Wallace, R. K., Benson, H., & Wilson, A. F. (1971). A wakeful hypometabolic state. *American Journal of Physiology, 221,* 795–799.

Walters, R. H., & Brown, M. (1963). Studies of reinforcement of aggression: III. Transfer of responses to an interpersonal situation. *Child Development, 34,* 563–571.

Wankel, L. M. (1972). An examination of illegal aggression in intercollegiate hockey. In I. D. Williams & L. M. Wankel (eds.), *Proceedings of the Fourth Canadian Psychomotor Learning and Sport Psychology Symposium.* Waterloo, Ontario: University of Waterloo.

Wankel, L. M. (1975). Social facilitation: A review of theory and research pertaining to motor performance. In B. S. Rushall (ed.), *The status of psychomotor learning and sport psychology research.* Dartmouth, Nova Scotia: Sport Science Associates.

Wankel, L. M. (1977). Audience size and trait anxiety effects upon state anxiety and motor performance. *Research Quarterly, 48,* 181–186.

Wankel, L. M. (1980). Social facilitation of motor performance: Perspective and prospective. In C. H. Nadeau (ed.), *Psychology of motor behavior and sport, 1979.* Champaign, IL: Human Kinetics Publishers.

Wankel, L. M., & Kreisel, S. J. P. (1985). Factors underlying enjoyment of youth sports: Sport and age group comparisons. *Journal of Sport Psychology, 7,* 51–64.

Wankel, L. M., & McEwan, R. (1976). The effect of privately and publicly set goals upon athletic performance. In K. F. Landry & W. A. R. Arban (eds.), *Motor learning, sport psychology, pedagogy, and didactics of physical activity.* Miami: Symposia Specialists.

Watson, G. G. (1986). Approach-avoidance behavior in team sports: An application to leading Australian national hockey players. *International Journal of Sport Psychology, 17,* 136–155.

Watzlawick, P. (1978). *The language of change.* New York: Basic Books.

Weber, B. (1978, February 9). Violence in sports: What next? *Senior Scholastic, 28.*

Weinberg, R. S. (1978). The effects of success and failure on the patterning of neuromuscular energy. *Journal of Motor Behavior, 10,* 53–61.

Weinberg, R. S. (1979). Intrinsic motivation in a competitive setting. *Medicine and Science in Sports, 11,* 146–149.

Weinberg, R. S. (1985). Relationship between self-efficacy and cognitive strategies in enhancing endurance performance. *International Journal of Sport Psychology, 17,* 135–155.

Weinberg, R. S., Bruya, L. D., & Jackson, A. (1985). The effects of goal proximity and goal specificity on endurance performance. *Journal of Sport Psychology, 7,* 296–305.

Weinberg, R. S., Bruya, L., Longino, J., & Jackson, A. (1988). Effect of goal proximity and specificity on endurance performance of primary-grade children. *Journal of Sport and Exercise Psychology, 10,* 81–91.

Weinberg, R. S., & Genuchi, M. (1980). Relationship between competitive trait anxiety, state anxiety, and golf performance: A field study. *Journal of Sport Psychology, 2,* 148–154.

Weinberg, R. S., Gould, D., & Jackson, A. (1979). Expectations and performance: An empirical test of Bandura's self-efficacy theory. *Journal of Sport Psychology, 1,* 320–331.

Weinberg, R. S., Gould, D., & Jackson, A. (1980). Cognition and motor performance effect of psyching-up strategies on three motor tasks. *Cognitive Therapy and Research, 1980, 4,* 239–245.

Weinberg, R. S., & Hunt, U. V. (1976). The interrelationship between anxiety, motor performance, and electromyography. *Journal of Motor Behavior, 8,* 219–224.

Weinberg, R. S., & Jackson, A. (1979). Competition and extrinsic rewards: Effect on intrinsic motivation and attribution. *Research Quarterly, 50,* 494–502.

Weinberg, R. S., & Jackson, A. (1985). The effects of specific vs. nonspecific mental preparation strategies on strength and endurance performance. *International Journal of Sport Psychology, 8,* 175–180.

Weinberg, R. S., & Ragan, J. (1979). Effects of competition, success/failure, and sex on intrinsic motivation. *Research Quarterly, 50*(3), 503–510.

Weinberg, R. S., Seabourne, T. G., & Jackson, A. (1981). Effects of visuomotor behavior rehearsal, relaxation, and imagery on karate performance. *Journal of Sport Psychology, 3,* 228–238.

Weinberg, R. S., Yukelson, D., & Jackson, A. V. (1980). Effect of public and private efficacy expectations on competitive performance. *Journal of Sport Psychology, 2,* 340–349.

Weinberg, W. T. (1977). Future orientation and competence motivation: New perspectives in achievement motivation research. In R. W. Christina & D. M. Landers (eds.), *Psychology of motor behavior and sport, 1976* (Vol. 2), Champaign, IL: Human Kinetics Publishers.

Weiner, B. (1972). *Theories of motivation: From mechanism to cognition.* Chicago: Rand McNally.

Weiner, B. (1979). A theory of motivation for some classroom experiences. *Journal of Educational Psychology, 71,* 3–25.

Weiner, B. (1981). The role of affect in sports psychology. In G. C. Roberts & D. M. Landers (eds.), *Psychology of motor behavior and sport, 1980.* Champaign, IL: Human Kinetics Publishers.

Weiner, B. (1985). An attributional theory of achievement motivation and emotion. *Psychological Review, 92,* 548–573.

Weiner, B., Heckhausen, H., Meyer, U. U., & Cook, R. E. (1972). Causal ascriptions and achievement motivation: A conceptual analysis of effort and reanalysis of locus of control. *Journal of Personality and Social Psychology, 21,* 239–248.

Weiner, B., & Kukla, A. (1970). An attributional analysis of achievement motivation. *Journal of Personality and Social Psychology, 15,* 1–20.

Weiner, B., Russell, D., & Lerman, D. (1979). The cognition-emotion process in achievement-related contexts. *Journal of Personality and Social Psychology, 37,* 1211–1220.

Weiss, M. R., Bredemeier, B. J., & Shewchuk, R. M. (1985). An intrinsic/ extrinsic motivation scale for the youth sport setting: A confirmatory factor analysis. *Journal of Sport Psychology, 7,* 75–91.

Weiss, M. R., & Friedrichs, W. D. (1986). The influence of leader behaviors, coach attributes, and institutional variables on performance and satisfaction of collegiate basketball teams. *Journal of Sport Psychology, 8,* 332–346.

Weitzenhoffer, A. M. (1963). *Hypnotism: An objective study in suggestibility.* New York: John Wiley and Sons.

Welford, A. T. (1959). Evidence of a single channel decision mechanism limiting performance in a serial reaction task. *Quarterly Journal of Experimental Psychology, 11,* 193–210.

Welford, A. T. (1962). Arousal, channel-capacity and decision. *Nature, 194,* 365–366.

Welford, A. T. (1965). Stress and achievement. *Australian Journal of Psychology, 17,* 1–9.

Welford, A. T. (1973). Stress and performance. *Ergonomics, 16,* 567–580.

Weltman, G., & Egstrom, G. H. (1966). Perceptual narrowing in novice divers. *Human Factors, 8,* 499–505.

Weltman, G., Smith, J. E., & Egstrom, G. H. (1971). Perceptual narrowing during simulated pressure-chamber exposure. *Human Factors, 13,* 99–107.

Wenz, B. J., & Strong, D. J. (1980). An application of biofeedback and self-regulation procedures with superior athletes: The fine tuning effect. In R. M. Suinn (ed.), *Psychology in sports: Methods and applications.* Minneapolis: Burgess Publishing Company.

Wheeler, L. (1970). *Interpersonal influence.* Boston: Allyn and Bacon.

White, R. (1959). Motivation reconsidered. The concept of competence. *Psychological Review, 66,* 297–323.

Whiting, H. T. A., Hardman, K., Hendry, L. B., & Jones, M. G. (1973). *Personality and performance in physical education and sport.* London: Kimpton.

Widmeyer, W. N., Brawley, L. R., & Carron, A. V. (1985). *The measurement of cohesion in sport teams: The group environment questionnaire.* London, Ontario: Sports Dynamics.

Widmeyer, W. N., & Martens, R. (1978). When cohesion predicts performance outcome in sport. *Research Quarterly, 49,* 372–380.

Wiggins, D. K. (1984). The history of sport psychology in North America. In J. M. Silva & R. S. Weinberg (eds.), *Psychological foundations of sport.* Champaign, IL: Human Kinetics Publishers.

Wilkes, R. L., & Summers, J. J. (1984). Cognitions, mediating variables, and strength performance. *Journal of Sport Psychology, 6,* 351–359.

Williams, J. M. (1980). Personality characteristics of the successful female athlete. In W. F. Straub (ed.), *Sport psychology: An analysis of athlete behavior* (2d ed.). Ithaca, NY: Mouvement Publications.

Williams, J. M., & Hacker, C. M. (1982). Causal relationships among cohesion, satisfaction, and performance in women's intercollegiate field hockey teams. *Journal of Sport Psychology, 4,* 324–337.

Williams, J. M., & Straub, W. F. (1986). Sport psychology: Past, present, future. In J. M. Williams (ed.), *Applied sport psychology,* 1–13. Palo Alto, CA: Mayfield Publishing Company.

Williams, L. R. T. (1978). Transcendental meditation and mirror tracing. *Perceptual and Motor Skills, 46,* 371–378.

Williams, L. R. T., & Herbert, P. G. (1976). Transcendental meditation and fine perceptual motor skill. *Perceptual and Motor Skills, 43,* 303–309.

Williams, L. R. T., Lodge, B., & Reddish, P. S. (1977). Effects of transcendental meditation on rotary pursuit skill. *Research Quarterly, 48,* 196–201.

Williams, L. R. T., & Parkin, W. A. (1980). Personality profiles of three hockey groups. *International Journal of Sport Psychology, 11,* 113–120.

Williams, L. R. T., & Vickerman, B. L. (1976). Effects of transcendental meditation on fine motor skill. *Perceptual and Motor Skills, 43,* 607–613.

Williams, M. H. (1983). *Ergogenic aids in sport.* Champaign, IL: Human Kinetics Publishers.

Williams, P. M., & Wassenaar, D. J. (1975). *Leadership.* San Jose, CA: Lansford.

Winter, B. (1982, May). Relax and win. *Sports and Athlete,* 72–78.

Winterbottom, M. R. (1953). "The relation of childhood training in independence to achievement motivation." Unpublished doctoral dissertation, University of Michigan, Ann Arbor, MI.

Wittig, A. F., Duncan, S. L., & Schurr, K. T. (1987). The relationship of gender, gender-role endorsement, and perceived physical self-efficacy to sport competition anxiety. *Journal of Sport Behavior, 11,* 192–199.

Wolpe, J. (1958). *Psychotherapy by reciprocal inhibition.* Stanford, CA: Stanford University Press.

Woodworth, R. S., & Schlosberg, H. (1954). *Experimental psychology* (rev. ed.). New York: Holt, Rinehart and Winston.

Woolfolk, R. L., Murphy, S. M., Gottesfeld, D., & Aitken, D. (1985). Effects of mental rehearsal of task motor activity and mental depiction of task outcome on motor skill performance. *Journal of Sport Psychology, 7,* 191–197.

Wrisberg, C. A., & Shea, C. H. (1978). Shifts in attention demands and motor program utilization during motor learning. *Journal of Motor Behavior, 10,* 149–158.

Wulf, S. (1987, November 2). World Series. *Sports Illustrated,* 28–41.

Yanada, H., & Hirata, H. (1970). Personality traits of students who dropped out of athletic clubs. *Proceedings of the College of Physical Education,* (No. 5), University of Tokyo.

Yeager, R. C. (1977, July). Savagery on the playing fields. *Readers Digest,* 23–24.

Yeager, R. C. (1979). *Seasons of shame: The new violence in sports.* New York: McGraw-Hill.

Yerkes, R. M., & Dodson, J. D. (1908). The relationship of strength of stimulus to rapidity of habit formation. *Journal of Comparative Neurology and Psychology, 18,* 459–482.

Yukelson, D., Weinberg, R., & Jackson, A. (1983). "Group cohesion in sport: A multidimensional approach." Paper presented at the North American Society for the Psychology of Sport and Physical Activity National Convention, Michigan State University, East Lansing, MI.

Yukelson, D., Weinberg, R., & Jackson, A. (1984). A multidimensional group cohesion instrument for intercollegiate basketball teams. *Journal of Sport Psychology, 6*(1), 103–117.

Zaichkowsky, L. D., & Sime, W. E. (1982). *Stress management for sport.* Reston, VA: AAHPERD Publications.

Zajonc, R. B. (1965). Social facilitation. *Science, 149,* 269–274.

Zajonc, R. B. (1972). "Compresence." Paper presented at the Midwestern Psychological Association meeting, Chicago, IL.

Zander, A. (1982). *Making groups effective.* San Francisco: Jossey-Bass.

Zelin, M. L., Adler, G., & Myerson, P. (1972). The anger self-report: An objective questionnaire for the measurement of expression. *Journal of Consulting Psychology, 39,* 340.

Ziegler, S. G. (1980). An overview of anxiety management strategies in sport. In W. F. Straub (ed.), *Sport psychology: An analysis of athlete behavior* (2d ed.). Ithaca, NY: Mouvement Publications.

Ziegler, S. G., Klinzing, J., & Williamson, K. (1982). The effects of two stress management training programs on cardiorespiratory efficiency. *Journal of Sport Psychology, 4,* 280–289.

Zillman, D., Katcher, A. H., & Milarsky, B. (1972). Excitation transfer from physical exercise to subsequent aggressive behavior. *Journal of Experimental Social Psychology, 8,* 247–259.

Zuckerman, M. (1960). The development of an affect adjective checklist for the measurement of anxiety. *Journal of Consulting Psychology, 24,* 457–462.

Zuckerman, M., & Allison, S. N. (1976). An objective measure of fear of success: Construction and validation. *Journal of Personality Assessment, 40,* 422–430.

Author Index

Durkee, A., 272
Dweck, C. S., 241–44, 248

Earle, R. B., 16
Easterbrook, J. A., 65, 101, 319
Eber, H. W., 9
Edmonston, W. E., 164, 166
Edwards, J., 324
Egstrom, G. H., 103
Eitzen, D. S., 351
Elder, S., 148
Ellis, H. C., 52
Endler, N. S., 10
Epstein, M. L., 160
Epstein, S., 290
Erffmeyer, E. S., 176, 177
Essing, W., 350
Estabrooks, G. H., 148
Etzel, E. F., 73
Eysenck, H. J., 9, 19
Eysenck, S. B. G., 9, 19

Fabianic, D., 406, 407
Feather, N. P., 407
Feigley, D. A., 287
Feltz, D. L., xix, 74, 161, 205, 207
Fenigstein, A., 283
Fenker, R. M., 159
Fenz, W. D., 132
Feshback, S., 266
Festinger, L., 337
Fidel, E., 148
Fiedler, F. E., 357, 372, 388, 389–92
Fiedler, F. L., 356
Fimrite, R., 50
Fineman, S., 195
Finn, J. A., 235
Fisher, A. C., 10, 123, 131, 155, 159, 265, 269, 347, 402
Fisher, R. J., 336
Fitts, P. M., 55, 77, 102
Fodero, J. M., 199
Fontaine, C., 246
Fouts, G. T., 329
Fredenburgh, F. A., 13, 15
Freedson, P. S., 37
Freischlag, J., 266, 295, 296
French, J. R. P., 373
French, S. N., 156
Freud, S., 275
Friedrichs, W. D., 385, 402
Frieze, I. H., 230, 238, 239, 241
Furst, D., 245
Furst, D. M., 72, 134
Furst, P., 30

Gabriel, T. J., 145
Gagen, J. J., 377
Gammon, C., 265
Gange, J. C., 319
Gansneder, B., 160
Garske, J. P., 195, 196, 197, 204, 227, 233, 238, 242

Gauron, E. F., 145
Geen, R. G., 285, 319
Gelfand, D. M., 281
Genuchi, M., 125
Geron, D., 30
Gershon, T., 92, 127, 134
Gerson, R., 125
Gibson, J. L., 408
Gilbert, B., 264
Gill, D. L., 76, 125, 127, 128, 205, 210, 245, 247, 342, 355, 356, 361
Gilligan, C., 289
Gillis, J. H., 238, 243
Gillmore, G., 233
Ginsmore, H., 286
Girandola, R., 37
Glass, D. C., 327
Goetz, T. E., 244
Goggin, J. P., 52
Goldman, M., 347, 357
Goldstein, J. H., 268, 283
Goleman, D. J., 125
Goranson, R. E., 283, 284
Gore, W. V., 327
Gorsuch, R. L., 124
Gorton, B. E., 168
Gottesfeld, D., 162
Gough, H. G., 16
Gould, D., 37, 81, 101, 110, 131–34, 136, 137, 171, 181, 182, 205
Graen, G., 393
Grasha, A. F., 73
Gray, G. R., 342, 356
Greene, D., 250, 251
Greenwell, J., 290
Greer, D. L., 33, 326
Griffiths, T. J., 111, 150
Gross, B. M., 374
Gross, J. B., 210, 236, 245
Grove, J. R., 241
Gruber, J. J., 128, 272, 342, 356
Grusky, O., 404, 405, 407
Guyton, A. C., 90, 92

Haan, N., 286
Haas, J., 315, 316
Hacker, C. M., 356, 361, 363
Hackman, J. R., 407, 409
Hagstrom, W. O., 339
Hale, B. D., 160, 312, 313, 314
Hall, E. G., 176, 177
Hall, H. K., 173
Hall, J. A., 148
Hall, J. R., 31
Halliwell, W. R., 233, 252
Halpin, A. W., 379, 380, 381
Hamblin, R. L., 347
Hardman, K., 12, 28, 29, 30
Hardy, C. J., 20, 28, 37
Harlow, R. G., 33
Harrell, W. A., 274, 291
Harris, B. L., 78, 126, 145, 151

Subject Index

achievement motivation, 193–222, 238, 242,
    249
  achievement situation, 194
  Bandura's theory of self-efficacy, 205
  competition, 194
  development of, 216–18
  Harter's competence motivation theory,
        206–7
  McClelland-Atkinson model, 195–204
  models of self-confidence, 204–9
  motive to avoid failure, 195
  principles for developing, 217
  test-anxiety approach, 194
  Vealey's sport specific model of sport
        confidence, 207–9
  women and sex roles, 209–16
achievement situation, 194, 220
affective state, 20
aggression in sport, 264–300
  alcohol and, 296
  angry aggression, 267
  Berkowitz's reformulation, 299
  Bobo doll, 281
  bracketed morality, 287
  brain mechanisms, 277
  catharsis hypothesis, 282–84
  circular effect, 281, 299
  cognitive development approach, 286
  completion tendency, 280
  curtailing in athletes, 294–96
  curtailing in spectators, 296–97
  defining aggression, 266–70
  examples of, 264–65
  fear of retaliation, 291
  female, 289
  functional aggressive behavior, 323
  hostile aggression, 266–67
  innate mechanism, 279
  instrumental aggression, 266–67
  intent to harm, 266
  league standings, 292
  legitimate, 280, 288
  measurement of, 270–75
  media and, 296
  modeling, 281

outcome, 292
  perception of victim's intent, 290–91
  performance and, 293
  periods of play, 292
  physiology of, 277
  playing at home or away, 292
  point differential, 291
  predisposition towards, 280
  psychological constructs, 285–89
  punishment, 294, 297
  reactive aggression, 267
  readying mechanism, 285, 300
  reducing violence, 294
  situational factors, 290–94
  structure of game, 291–92
  theories of, 275–82
aggression inventory, 272
aggression theories, 275–82
  Berkowitz's reformulation, 279–80
  frustration-aggression hypothesis, 278–80
  instinct theory, 275
  social learning theory, 280–82
androgyny, 213–14, 220
anger self-report test, 272
anxiety, 110, 119–40
  behavioral checklist, 126
  behavioral measure of, 125
  cognitive, 137
  cognitive state, 128
  competitive, 130
  correlations among, 127
  defined, 121
  distress, 122
  effects of competition on, 133
  eustress and, 136
  females and, 134
  inverted-V pattern, 132
  measuring, 124–28
  multidimensional nature, 131, 136
  nonsport activities and, 135
  perceived, 131
  performance and, 135–38
  precompetitive, 132–33
  self-confidence and, 128
  somatic, 137

progressive relaxation, 149, 175, 188
projective procedures, 13, 44
projective techniques, 270
propinquity, 414
psyching-up, 181, 188
psyching-up strategies, 181–86
    bulletin board, 183
    fan support, 184
    goal setting, 182
    parent involvement, 185
    pep talks, 183
    precompetition workout, 185
    publicity and new coverage, 184
    self-activation, 185
psychodynamic theories, 7
psychological constructs related to sport
        aggression, 285–89
    arousal, 285
    gender, 289
    guilt, 287
    moral reasoning, 286
    personality and aggression, 288
psychological core, 6, 44
psychological ergogenic aid, 145
psychological presence, 316–17, 332
psychological profile, 37
psychological skills
    education program, 179
    inventory for sports, 145
publicity and news coverage, 184

rating scales, 12
reaction potential, 114
reaction time probe, 64
readying mechanism, 285
reducing violence, 297
refocusing, 81, 84
reinforcement, 254, 258
relationship motivation, 381, 388, 414
relationship procedures, 149–57
    autogenic training, 151
    biofeedback, 154–57
    progressive relaxation, 149
    transcendental meditation, 152–53
relaxation response, 147, 149, 153, 188
relaxation training, 163
Research Sport Psychologist, xviii
response criterion, 105
response delay, 58, 84
response distortion, 26
retaliation hypothesis, 291, 300
reticular formation, 90–91, 114
retrieval, 84
risk-taking behavior, 221
role-related behavior, 6
Rorschach test, 13, 44, 270

sampling procedures, 24
satisfaction, 362–64, 368
scientific management, 382, 414
second-order traits, 26, 44

selective attention, 59–62, 84
    attenuation, 60
    bottleneck, 61
    Broadbent model, 61
    cocktail party phenomenon, 60
    filter, 61
    gate out, 59
    pertinence model, 61
    shadowing, 61
    Triesman model, 61
selective filter, 84
self-activation, 185
self-attention, 328, 332
self-confidence, 204, 221
self-efficacy, 205
self-serving hypothesis, 258
sensory register, 84
sentence completion test, 13
sex differences in attribution, 243–44
sex-typed, 209, 215, 221
shadowing, 61, 84
shock box, 273, 300
short-term memory, 53
signal detection theory, 104–7, 114, 320
signal plus noise, 104, 114
situational approach, 10, 44
situational behaviors, 375, 414
situational traits, 375, 414
skin temperature, 154
skydiving, 132
social cohesion, 339, 368
social comparison, 221
social facilitation, 304–21, 332
    alternatives to Zajonc's model, 319–20
    arousal and, 309–11
    audience, 305
    coactive audience, 305
    coactors, 305
    critique of, 308
    definition, 306
    dominant response, 312
    evaluation apprehension, 315–16
    evidence for, 312–14
    historical perspective, 305
    mere presence, 306
    nondominant response, 312
    noninteractive audience, 304
    psychological presence, 316–17
    signal detection theory and, 320
    Zajonc's model, 306–8
social learning theory, 8, 300
social reinforcement, 9
societies
    Association for the Advancement of
        Applied Sport Psychology, xviii
    Canadian Society for Psychomotor
        Learning and Sport Psychology, xvii
    International Society of Sport Psychology,
        xvii
    North American Society for the
        Psychology of Sport and Physical
        Activity, xvii

sociogram, 341, 368
sociometric measure, 368
somatic state anxiety, 137, 140
source traits, 17
Spielberger state anxiety inventory, 128, 140
Spielberger trait anxiety inventory, 124
sport analysis, 179
sport cohesion instrument, 343, 368
sport competition anxiety test, 124, 140
sport confidence, 207, 221
sport psychology
    academic, xviii
    applied, xvii, xviii
    definition, xvi
    ethical standards, xx
    ethics, xix
    father of, xvi
    history of, xvi
    licensing, xix
sports cohesiveness questionnaire, 342, 368
stability, 229, 258
state aggression, 300
state anxiety, 122, 140
    predicting, 130
state measure of aggression, 273–75
stimulus-response, 51
stress, 122–23, 140
stress coping skills, 179
stress innoculation training, 177–78, 188
stress management, 145, 188
stress management training, 178–79, 188
stress process, 123, 140
structural rating scale, 258
structured questionnaires, 14
subjective competitive situation, 129, 140
subliminal muscle activity, 160
surface traits, 17
sympathetic nervous system, 91, 114, 121

task characteristics, 312
task cohesion, 339, 369
task dependence, 414
task difficulty, 111
task motivation, 381, 414
task-oriented suggestion, 80
task structure, 389
task structure rating scale, 389
Taylor manifest anxiety inventory, 140
Taylor manifest anxiety scale, 124
team cohesion, 336–69
    Cartwright model, 338–39
    competition and, 344–48
    conceptual model, 340
    consequences, 338–39, 353–64
    cooperation and, 344–48
    defining, 337–40
    determinants, 338–39
    determinants of, 344–52
    development of, 364
    direction of causality and performance,
        359–62
    homogeneity and, 349, 351–52

measurement, 340–44
    multidimensional, 339
    nature of the sport, 357–58
    performance and, 353–61
    satisfaction and, 362–64
    size and, 349, 352
    social, 339
    stability and, 349–50
    task, 339
    type of measurement and, 355–57
team cohesion questionnaire, 342, 369
team homogeneity, 351–52, 369
team satisfaction, 362–64
team size, 352
team stability, 369
tension, 121, 145
test anxiety, 194
test-anxiety approach, 194, 221
test of attentional and interpersonal style,
    67–73
    reliability, 72
    sport specific tests, 73–74
    validity, 72
thematic apperception test, 7, 13–14, 44, 270
theories of motivation, 191–259
thought stopping, 80, 84, 162
thought stopping and centering, 80–81
trait aggression, 270, 300
trait anxiety, 123
trait anxiety inventory, 140
trait psychology, 9
trait theory, 8
trait theory of leadership, 376–77
transcendental meditation, 152, 163, 188
Triesman model, 84
typical responses, 6, 44

unidimensional variable, 337
universal behaviors, 375, 414
universal traits, 375, 414
unstructured projective procedures, 13

variables
    dependent, 24
    independent, 23
violence, 266, 300
visualization, 159
visual-motor behavior rehearsal, 163, 174,
    188

waking hypnosis, 188
women and sex roles, 209–16
    androgyny, 213
    Bem sex-role inventory, 214
    classification scale, 213
    cross sex-typed, 215
    femininity, 212
    gender role and competitive trait anxiety,
        214–16
    masculinity, 212
    multifaceted approach, 211–14
    personal attributes questionnaire, 211